CW01180314

The
Iran–United States
Claims Tribunal
The first ten years
1981–1991

The Melland Schill Monographs
in International Law

General editor Gillian M. White

I. M. Sinclair
The Vienna Convention on the Law of Treaties

R. B. Lillich
The human rights of aliens in contemporary international law

E. R. Cohen
Human rights in the Israeli-occupied territories

A. Carty
The decay of international law?

N. D. White
The United Nations and the maintenance of
international peace and security

J. G. Merrills
The development of international law by
the European Court of Human Rights

J. G. Merrills
Human rights in Europe

The Iran–United States Claims Tribunal

The first ten years
1981–1991

An assessment of the Tribunal's jurisprudence and its contribution to international arbitration

WAYNE MAPP

Senior Lecturer in Commercial Law
University of Auckland

Manchester University Press
Manchester and New York
Distributed exclusively in the USA and Canada by St. Martin's Press

Copyright © Wayne Mapp 1993

Published by Manchester University Press
Oxford Road, Manchester M13 9PL, UK
and Room 400, 175 Fifth Avenue, New York, NY 10010, USA

Distributed exclusively in the USA and Canada
by St. Martin's Press, Inc., 175 Fifth Avenue, New York,
NY 10010, USA

British Library Cataloguing-in-Publication Data
A catalogue record for this book is available from the British Library

Library of Congress Cataloging-in-Publication Data
Mapp, Wayne Daniel, 1952–
    The Iran–United States Claims Tribunal: the first ten years: an assessment of the tribunal's jurisprudence and its contribution to international arbitration/Wayne Daniel Mapp.
        p.   cm. — (The Melland Schill monographs in international law)
   Includes bibliographical references.
   ISBN 0-7190-3790-5 (hardback)
    1. United States—Claims vs. Iran. 2. Iran—Claims vs. United States. 3. Iran–United States Claims Tribunal—History.
4. Arbitration. International—History. I. Title. II. Series.
JX238.I7M36   1993
341.7′51—dc20   92-40259

ISBN 0-7190-3790-5 *hardback*

Typeset in Hong Kong
by Best-set Typesetter Ltd.

Printed in Great Britain
by Biddles Ltd, Guildford and Kings Lynn

CONTENTS

Foreword *Gillian White*		*page* xi
Preface		xiii
List of abbreviations		xvi
Acknowledgement		xviii
PART ONE	The establishment of the Tribunal	
Chapter one	The hostage crisis and the Algiers Declarations	3
	The hostage crisis	3
	The Iranian revolution	3
	The United States' litigation prior to the hostage crisis	4
	The seizure of the hostages	5
	The Iranian assets freeze	6
	Protection of United States claimants	6
	The International Court of Justice	7
	The rescue mission	10
	The negotiations to release the hostages and the Algiers Declarations	11
	The Algiers Declarations	13
	Introduction	13
	The General Declaration	14
	The Claims Settlement Declaration	17
	The supporting agreements	20
	The role of the Iran–United States Claims Tribunal in the settlement of United States claims against Iran	21
	The constitutional requirements	21
	The Tribunal as a substitute forum for United States courts and its role as an international claims tribunal	22

	International arbitration as a means of settling international claims	25
Chapter two	*Introduction to the Tribunal*	29
	The structure and administration of the Tribunal	29
	Settlement of claims	32
	Submission and filing of claims before the Tribunal	35
Chapter three	*Appointment, challenges and resignation of members of the Tribunal*	39
	Introduction	39
	The Claims Settlement Declaration and the UNCITRAL rules	39
	Background to the UNCITRAL rules	42
	The initial appointments	43
	Challenges to arbitrators	44
	Resignation of arbitrators	50
	The crisis of 1984	53
	Conclusion	54
PART TWO	*The substantive jurisdiction of the Tribunal*	
Chapter four	*Nationality of claimants before the Tribunal*	59
	The provisions of the Claims Settlement Declaration	59
	Introduction	59
	The Claims Settlement Declaration	59
	Natural persons and dual nationality	61
	International law relating to the espousal of claims of dual nationals	62
	Awards and decisions of the Tribunal	69
	The application of the dual nationality decision	77
	Conclusion	80
	Continuous ownership of claims	81
	Introduction	81
	The Claims Settlement Declaration	83
	Awards of the Tribunal	83
Chapter five	*Claimants in relation to corporate claims*	86
	Introduction	86
	The development of international law in relation to corporate claims	87
	The Claims Settlement Declaration	91

	Shareholder claims in respect of corporations not incorporated in the claimant state: the nature of "control"	92
	Partnership claims	97
	Conclusion	101
Chapter six	The governing law of the claims	103
	The provisions of the Claims Settlement Declaration	103
	The law governing the claims	105
	The application of Article V of the Claims Settlement Declaration by the Tribunal	110
Chapter seven	Claims arising from debts and contracts	114
	State responsibility and debts and contracts	114
	Debts	117
	Introduction	117
	Awards and decisions of the Tribunal	118
	Contracts	120
	Introduction	120
	Applicable law of the contract	121
	Formation of contract	127
	Validity or legality of the contract	129
	Breach and termination of contract	130
	Force majeure, frustration and "changed circumstances"	133
	Commentary on the debt and contract claims	143
Chapter eight	Claims arising from expropriation	145
	Introduction	145
	Governing law of expropriation	145
	The Treaty of Amity	147
	The main issues of expropriation	150
	What constitutes a taking	151
	International law	151
	Awards and decisions of the Tribunal	156
	The legality of expropriation	163
	International law	163
	Awards and decisions of the Tribunal	171
	Conclusion on the legality of expropriation	175
Chapter nine	Entitlement to compensation for expropriation	176
	The standard of compensation	176
	International law	176
	Awards and decisions of the Tribunal	182

	Valuation of property and quantum of compensation	191
	International law	191
	Awards and decisions of the Tribunal	193
	Conclusion on valuation	205
Chapter ten	*Other measures affecting property rights*	207
	Introduction	207
	Delictual or tortious responsibility	208
	Unjust enrichment	210
Chapter eleven	*Exclusions from the jurisdiction of the Tribunal: the hostage crisis and the revolution*	217
	Introduction	217
	Exclusions arising from the hostage crisis	218
	Popular movements in the course of the Islamic revolution	220
	The Algiers Declarations	220
	International law relating to revolutionary movements and the interpretation of the Algiers Declarations	221
	The awards of the Tribunal	228
	Commentary on the scope of the exclusions	233
Chapter twelve	*Exclusions from the jurisdiction of the Tribunal: contracts providing for disputes to be settled in competent Iranian courts*	235
	Introduction	235
	The forum selection exclusion decisions	235
	Application of the forum selection decisions by the Tribunal	249
	Application of non-contractual remedies as a basis for jurisdiction	250
	The meaning of "in response to the Majlis position"	251
PART THREE	*The procedure of the Tribunal and enforcement of awards*	
Chapter thirteen	*The procedure of the Tribunal*	257
	The rules governing the Tribunal	257
	The Claims Settlement Declaration	257
	The Tribunal's Rules of Procedure	259
	Particular procedural issues	261
	Presentation of claims	261
	Evidence	265

Contents

	Interim measures of protection	280
	Interest on awards	285
	Appeals and reviews of awards and decisions of the Tribunal	291
Chapter fourteen	*Satisfaction, recognition and enforcement of the awards and decisions of the Tribunal*	293
	Provisions of the Algiers Declarations	293
	Introduction	293
	The Security Account	293
	Enforcement of awards in the courts of any country	294
	Satisfaction of awards in favour of United States nationals	295
	Satisfaction of awards of international arbitral tribunals	295
	Satisfaction of awards of the Iran–United States Claims Tribunal from the Security Account	296
	Satisfaction of awards in favour of Iran and Iranian nationals	298
	Introduction	298
	Awards and decisions of the Tribunal	299
	Recognition and enforcement of arbitral awards	301
	Nature of international arbitral awards	301
	Convention on the Recognition and Enforcement of Foreign Arbitral Awards	311
	Recognition and enforcement of arbitral awards not governed by the New York Convention	315
	Recognition and enforcement of the awards of the Iran–United States Claims Tribunal in municipal courts	317
	Introduction	317
	Iranian challenges to the awards of the Tribunal	319
	The Dutch law of arbitration	320
	Recognition of the Tribunal and its awards in the courts of third states	326
	Conclusion on the recognition and enforcement of awards of the Iran–United States Claims Tribunal	331

PART FOUR Conclusion

Chapter fifteen An assessment of the contribution of the
Tribunal to international arbitration 339
    Introduction 339
    The development of international law by
      the Tribunal 341
    The relationship of the Tribunal to
      municipal law 347
    Prospects for international arbitration 349

Appendix I The Algiers Declarations 351
Appendix II List of members 362
    Bibliography 367
    Table of cases 368
    Index 385

FOREWORD

By her will the late Olive B. Schill established the Melland Schill Fund, in memory of her brother, who was killed in the First World War. This series of Melland Schill Monographs in International Law replaces the earlier series of Melland Schill Lectures, published by Manchester University Press. Miss Schill's generous bequest was motivated by her wish to contribute to scholarship and learning in international law and relations. No doubt she hoped that the role and rule of law in the relations of states and peoples might increase, and that the likelihood of further devastating armed conflicts might lessen.

Certainly the present work by Dr Wayne Mapp concerns a major modern instance of two states, in a situation of intense and bitter dispute, coming to a negotiated agreement to resolve many of the issues dividing them, and in so doing establishing a legal forum for the application of law and legal procedures to the settlement of numerous individual claims. The saga of the seizure of the United States embassy in Tehran in 1979 and the holding of fifty-two United States nationals hostage there for 444 days has faded into history. The agreements, brokered by Algeria, which brought an end to that crisis included provision for the creation of the Iran–United States Claims Tribunal, comprising Iranian, United States and neutral members. Its main task, as yet unfinished, was to hear and determine the claims of United States nationals against Iran arising from the events of the Iranian revolution, including expropriations of property, breaches of contract and debt claims, but excluding any claims by either state or its nationals arising from the hostage crisis itself.

This tribunal is unique in the annals of modern international law. Since the Second World War states have tended to settle the property claims of their nationals by accepting lump sum payments from the expropriating foreign state rather than resorting to an international judicial tribunal to determine individual claims. The Tribunal's jurisprudence offers a rich mine of argument and authority for commercial and contract lawyers as well as for international lawyers. Dr Mapp has immersed himself in the jurisprudence of the Tribunal's first ten years. His study covers procedural and evidential aspects as well as the Tribunal's awards on substantive legal issues of private commercial law and public international law. The Tribunal's operating experience, in a context of great political sensitivity, especially in the early years, offers valuable lessons for future resort to independent arbitration of contested claims and issues between states *inter se* or between states and foreign nationals, in particular foreign investors. The Melland Schill series is an appropriate context for the publication of this useful and important study in the law of state responsibility, international claims and international commercial arbitration.

Gillian White
Emeritus Professor of International Law
University of Manchester
August 1992

PREFACE

The Iran–United States Claims Tribunal is the most significant international arbitral tribunal since the arbitral tribunals following the peace settlements of World War II. The establishment of the Tribunal pursuant to the Algiers Declarations was part of the settlement of the hostage crisis between Iran and the United States and was intended to settle all property claims between the two states and their nationals arising from the Iranian revolution.

Many of the claims of United States claimants had been the subject of litigation in United States courts. The United States could not discharge this litigation under United States constitutional processes without providing an alternative means of resolving the claims. An international arbitral tribunal was the only forum acceptable to both parties for settling such claims. The more usual remedies, such as Iran making a lump sum payment to cover all United States claims, or United States claimants continuing their litigation in either United States courts or Iranian courts, entailed unacceptable political costs to both parties. An international arbitral tribunal controlled by independent arbitrators removed the claims from the political arena, including the domestic legal systems of either party, to the relative neutrality of the international legal arena.

This work will cover two aspects of the Iran–United States Claims Tribunal, particularly in relation to the large claims by nationals of either party against the other party.[1] First, it will examine how the Tribunal has

---

[1] The Tribunal has jurisdiction over three categories of claims. First, claims by nationals of one party against the government of the other party. These are divided into large claims presented by the claimants themselves and small claims for less than $250,000 presented by the government of the claimant. Second, claims by the two governments against one another in respect of contracts for the sale of goods and services. Third, in respect of the interpretation and implementation of the Algiers Declarations.

applied international law to the issues before it. Second, it will consider whether the Tribunal is properly characterised as an international arbitral tribunal, and the influence the characterisation of the Tribunal has had on the application of international law by the Tribunal and the recognition and enforcement of its awards by municipal courts. These two themes will be considered by analysing the meaning and origin of the Claims Settlement Declaration and the decisions of the Tribunal and the response of other states and courts to the Tribunal and its awards. This cannot be done in isolation and the Tribunal and its decisions are compared with other international and quasi-international tribunals and in the light of the exposition of international law by jurists.

Of the two themes the more important is the application of international law by the Tribunal. The awards in respect of claims of expropriation and unjust enrichment are of particular significance. This area of international law is arguably the most important in relations between the Western investing states and the developing host states. The awards are noteworthy in the way they have consolidated Western views on the status of the law. They also illustrate the tensions within the Tribunal and are an important indicator of the potential of the Tribunal to encourage other states to submit such disputes to international arbitration. Accordingly, the work although not neglecting the other heads of jurisdiction gives special emphasis to the decisions in this area.

The second theme of the characterisation of the Tribunal is essentially a theoretical question in the context of the Iran–United States Claims Tribunal.

The provision of the Security Account to satisfy awards in favour of United States nationals ensures that the majority of awards will be honoured. However, the discussion is intended to give an insight into the theory of the governing law of international commercial arbitration. It assumes its greatest importance in the recognition and enforcement of awards of arbitral tribunals and the review of awards by municipal courts.

In order to deal with these issues the work is divided into four parts. The first part deals with the Islamic revolution and the hostage crisis and the establishment of the Tribunal. It is primarily narrative and sets the scene for the substantive part of the work which is contained in Parts Two and Three. These two parts deal with the two essential themes of the work. The final part, concluding the work, examines the nature of the Tribunal and its contribution to international law in the context of the previous discussion. It also considers the prospects for international arbitration in the light of the work of the Tribunal.

This work is not and cannot be a complete dissertation on the work of the Tribunal since it is not possible to cover every issue dealt with by the Tribunal over many hundreds of awards and decisions. As a consequence,

Preface

the book is largely concerned with the awards and decisions on the large claims by nationals of one party against the government of the other party. However, it can be expected that these awards and decisions will be the Tribunal's greatest contribution to international law. The awards and decisions are sufficiently well reasoned and deal with issues of state responsibility and international commercial law that they will be a significant contribution to the international law of state responsibility for economic and property loss to aliens.

The book primarily covers awards and decisions of the Tribunal up to December 31, 1990, although some awards from 1991 are also included.

The work is based on a Ph.D. dissertation completed at the University of Cambridge in 1988. My thanks go to my supervisors, Mr E. Lauterpacht, Q.C., and Professor Sir Kenneth Keith, and to Denese Henare for their unfailing support, encouragement and assistance in its completion, and to Professor Gillian White for her assistance in revising it for publication.

W.M.

ABBREVIATIONS

Principal abbreviations of law reports, journals and international agencies quoted in the text.

Am. J. of Comp. Law	American Journal of Comparative Law
A.J.I.L.	American Journal of International Law
Am. Soc. of I.L.	American Society of International Law
B.Y.I.L.	British Yearbook of International Law
C.L.J.	Cambridge Law Journal
Col. L.R.	Columbia Law Review
F.C.S.C.	Foreign Claims Settlement Commission (United States)
Harv. I.L.J.	Harvard International Law Journal
I.A.L.R.	Iranian Assets Litigation Reporter
I.C.J. Rep.	Reports of Judgments, Advisory Opinions and Orders of the International Court of Justice
I.C.L.Q.	International and Comparative Law Quarterly
I.C.S.I.D.	International Centre for Settlement of Investment Disputes
I.L.C.	International Law Commission
I.L.M.	International Legal Materials
I.L.R.	International Law Reports (continuation of the Annual Digest)
IRAN–U.S.C.T.R.	Iran–United States Claims Tribunal Reports
J. Int. Arb.	Journal of International Arbitration
L.N.T.S.	League of Nations Treaty Series
Mealy's L.R.: Iranian Claims	Mealy's Litigation Reports: Iranian Claims
Mich. L.R.	Michigan Law Review

List of abbreviations

P.C.I.J.	Publications of the Permanent Court of International Justice
R.I.A.A.	United Nations Reports of International Arbitral Awards
T.A.M.	Mixed Arbitral Tribunal Reports
Tex. I.L.J.	Texas International Law Journal
UNCITRAL	United Nations Commission of International Trade Law
U.N.T.S.	United Nations Treaty Series
Va. J.I.L.	Virginia Journal of International Law
U.S.	United States or United States Supreme Court Reports

ACKNOWLEDGEMENT

Extracts from the Iran–US Claims Tribunal Reports reproduced with the permission of Grotius Publications Limited.

PART ONE
The establishment of the Tribunal

CHAPTER ONE

The hostage crisis and the Algiers Declarations

The hostage crisis

The Iranian revolution

The departure of Shah Reza Pahlavi from Tehran in January 1979 and the success of the Islamic revolution was the greatest reversal for United States political and commercial interests in the Middle East this century. For a quarter of a century the United States had assiduously cultivated commercial and military relations with the Imperial government. By 1978 there were 45,000 American military advisers, engineers and advisory personnel and their families living in Iran. There was no other developing nation with which the United States had established such extensive governmental and commercial contacts in such a short space of time.[1]

As a consequence of the relationship between the Imperial government and the United States the Islamic revolutionaries directed much of their rage against the United States. By January 1979, as a result of the hostility directed against them, the number of Americans in Iran had fallen to 2,000. Many of the departing Americans were compelled by Revolutionary Guards to abandon substantial property in Iran.

The success of the Islamic revolution in February 1979 was only the beginning of a transformation of Iranian society. The new government quickly cancelled many of the large defence contracts with United States corporations and purchases from the United States were sharply curtailed.

---

[1] From 1970 to 1978 trade between the two countries had increased from $400 million to $6.5 billion, Tonelson, *Hostage Aftermath* (1986) 257 The Atlantic 22, from Toope *Mixed International Arbitration*, 264, Footnote 3 (1990).

However, major reorganisation of the economy did not begin until June 1979. Banks and insurance companies were the first to be nationalised. In July the principal manufacturing industries were nationalised. The new Constitution, which was approved by national referendum in December 1979, confirmed the leading role of the state in the economy. Article 44 provided:[2]

The economic structure of the Islamic Republic of Iran is composed of three sectors—governmental, co-operative and private—which shall be stabilized by systematic and sound planning.

The governmental sector shall consist of all major industries; foreign trade; large mines; banking; insurance; production of power; dams and large irrigation systems; radio and television; postal, telephone and telegram systems; transportation by air, land and sea; railroads; and the like which shall be publicly owned and administered by the Government.

The restructuring of the economy affected Iranian and foreign-owned enterprises alike. A number of firms which were partially or wholly owned by United States nationals were taken over by state-owned entities. In addition to these formal nationalisations the Iranian government appointed managers and directors to various companies. The government appointees were responsible to the government, and the legal owners had no control over the management of their property. Furthermore, the companies which were subject to the nationalisation decrees or alternatively government control of management had previously entered into a wide variety of contracts with United States companies. Once these companies were brought under government ownership or control their contracts with the United States companies were repudiated by the new management.

The reaction of the United States companies affected by nationalisation or repudiation of contracts was, in many cases, to commence litigation in United States courts against Iran and Iranian governmental entities for breach of contract, particularly after the seizure of the United States diplomats. The actions of the Iranian government and the Revolutionary Guards were also to form the basis of many of the claims by United States individuals and corporations before the Iran–United States Claims Tribunal.

The United States' litigation prior to the hostage crisis[3]

Although many individuals and corporations had valid causes of action against Iran there was an initial reluctance to commence litigation against

[2] From VII *Constitutions of the World* (1980); English translation by Dr C. Vafai.
[3] This section is largely derived from Hertz, *The Hostage Crisis and Domestic Litigation: An Overview*, in Lillich (ed.), *The Iran–United States Claims Tribunal 1981–1983* (1984).

Iran. It was considered that the revolutionary fervour would diminish and the previous commercial relationship between United States nationals and Iran could be restored. In some instances, however, actions were commenced in United States courts by United States nationals.[4]

In two of the cases the court held that it could make pre-judgment attachments against Iranian property.[5] In the third case the court considered that the principle of sovereign immunity barred such attachments.[6]

None of these cases had been concluded when the Algiers Declarations were signed. However, the property rights of the claimants against Iranian assets which were subject to the jurisdiction of United States courts in these cases, and the cases filed after the seizure of the hostages, meant it was essential under United States constitutional law that a substitute means of settling claims should be established if the claims were to be removed from the jurisdiction of United States municipal courts. When the hostage crisis was settled, the court actions were suspended as a result of Executive Order No. 12294. This order had been made in fulfilment of a requirement of the Algiers Declarations that the United States should terminate all legal proceedings in respect of claims of United States persons and institutions against Iran and its state enterprises. Each of the claimants subsequently lodged claims with the Iran–United States Claims Tribunal, which had been established, at least in part, as a substitute forum for United States municipal courts.

The seizure of the hostages[7]

On November 4, 1979 Iranian militants stormed the United States embassy in Tehran, taking prisoner sixty-one United States diplomatic personnel. In addition the senior United States official in Iran, the Chargé d'Affaires, and two other diplomats were detained in the Iranian Ministry of Foreign Affairs. On November 5, 1979 the actions of the militants were endorsed by Ayatollah Khomeini, the dominant figure of the Iranian revolution, an act unheralded in the behaviour of modern nations. The consequences were to be far-reaching both in the political and in the legal spheres.

---

[4] The principal cases were *Electronic Data Systems* v *Social Security Organisation of Iran* 651 F. 2d, 1007 (5th Cir.) (1981); *Behring International Inc.* v *Imperial Iranian Air Force* 475 F. Supp., 383 (D.C.N.J.) (1979); *Reading & Bates Corporation* v *National Iranian Oil Company* 478 F. Supp., 724 (D.C.N.Y.) (1979).

[5] *Electronic Data Systems* v *Social Security Organisation of Iran* 651 F. 2d, 1007 (5th Cir.) (1981) and *Behring International Inc.* v *Imperial Iranian Air Force* 475 F. Supp., 383 (D.C.N.J.) (1979).

[6] *Reading & Bates Corporation* v *National Iranian Oil Company* 478 F. Supp., 724 (D.C.N.Y.) (1979).

[7] General works on the hostage crisis include: Assersohn, *The Biggest Deal* (1981); Heikal, *The Return of the Ayatollah* (1980); Salinger, *America Held Hostage: The Secret Negotiations* (1981); Zahih, *Iran since the Revolution* (1981).

It quickly became apparent to the United States government that it would take some time to resolve the crisis and that the full range of diplomatic, economic, judical and military measures would have to be employed against Iran.

The Iranian assets freeze

It soon became clear that diplomatic pressure would not secure the return of the hostages and the release of the embassy property. On November 12, 1979 the United States President ordered the cessation of all oil purchases from Iran. As a consequence, Iran gave notice that it would take further action to damage the interests of the United States. Mr Bani-Sadr, the acting Foreign Minister, indicated that Iran was going to withdraw all its assets held in United States banks. The response of the United States was perhaps the most significant action undertaken by the United States in the course of the crisis, and eventually provided much of the necessary leverage to secure the release of the hostages.

On November 14, 1979 the President executed an order blocking all dealings in any property and any interests in property of Iran and Iranian governmental entities which were subject to, or within the possession or control of, persons subject to the jurisdiction of the United States.[8] As a result all Iranian bank accounts in United States banks, irrespective of the country in which the funds were located, were frozen. Some $12 billion was affected by this action.

As the crisis deepened the regulatory effort against Iran intensified. In April 1980 the President executed orders blocking all commerce and travel between the United States and Iran, with the exception of food and medical supplies and news people.[9] Thus by April 1980 there was in force a complete freeze on Iranian assets and a comprehensive trade ban against Iran. The frozen assets were ultimately used to provide the necessary leverage for Iran to settle the hostage crisis.

Protection of United States claimants

In addition to the freeze of Iranian assets the United States government was concerned to ensure that United States nationals with claims against Iran were properly protected. Although the revolution had led to the termination of certain contracts and the expropriation of property owned by United States nationals during the period prior to the seizure of the

[8] Executive Order 12170 of November 14, 1979.
[9] These orders were Executive Order 12205 of April 7, 1980 and Executive Order 12211 of April 17, 1980. In all cases the orders were made under the authority of the International Economic Powers Act, 1977.

hostages, there was an almost complete severance of commercial relationships after the hostage crisis. A number of United States nationals whose property had been expropriated and whose contracts had been cancelled prior to the hostage crisis had already commenced proceedings against Iran in United States courts. The hostage crisis brought a new wave of litigants to the United States courts seeking compensation from Iran. By 1980 more than 400 actions against Iran had been filed in United States courts.[10]

The only assets to attach in respect of this litigation were the financial assets belonging to the government of Iran and its various entities. These assets were, in many cases, protected from effective attachment by the doctrine of sovereign immunity, unless the assets belonged directly to the Iranian entity that was the subject of the litigation.

The executive order of November 14, 1979 had prohibited the transfer or removal of all property of the government of Iran, its entities, and of Bank Markazi.[11] On November 26, 1979 the Treasury, acting under delegated authority, granted a general licence authorising judicial proceedings against Iran. A clarifying regulation was issued on December 19, 1979 permitting judicial proceedings, including pre-judgment attachments, against Iranian assets.[12] These authorisations strengthened the court actions against Iran and its various entities, since many of the actions were able to support pre-judgment attachments against Iranian assets. Thus the claimants who had commenced litigation in United States courts had some assurance that their claims would be satisfied from Iranian assets, even if the assets attached had no direct relationship to the subject of the litigation.

Iran therefore faced the prospect of its frozen assets being used to satisfy United States claims. It was a further incentive to Iran to resolve the hostage crisis to the satisfaction of both states. It also meant that any settlement would have to provide an alternative forum for United States claimants.

The International Court of Justice[13]

The major international legal action pursued by the United States to resolve the hostage crisis was the proceedings in the International Court

[10] Eskridge, *The Iranian Nationalization Cases: Towards a General Theory of Jurisdiction over Foreign States*, 22 Harv. J.I.L., 525, 526 (1981). See also Hertz, *The Hostage Crisis and Domestic Litigation: An Overview*, in Lillich (ed.), *The Iran–United States Claims Tribunal 1981–1983* (1984), for a full discussion on the post-hostage seizure litigation in United States courts.
[11] Order No. 12170, 44 Fed. Reg., 65279 (1979).
[12] 31 C.F.R., 535.418 (1980).
[13] The full title of the case is *Case Concerning United States Diplomatic and Consular Staff in Tehran (United States v Iran)* I.C.J. Rep., 7 (1979) *Interim Measures*; I.C.J. Rep., 3

of Justice, the findings of which have been cited numerous times by the Iran–United States Claims Tribunal.

In November 1979 the United States applied to the Court for a ruling that the seizure and detention of the hostages violated international law and for an order that Iran should release the hostages and restore the embassy to the United States. The United States alleged that Iran had violated the Vienna Convention on Diplomatic Relations, 1961, the Vienna Convention on Consular Relations, 1963, the Convention on the Prevention and Punishment of Crimes against Internationally Protected Persons, 1973, and the Treaty of Amity, Economic Relations and Consular Rights, 1955, between Iran and the United States as well as the United Nations Charter and customary international law. The United States also sought an indication of provisional measures in accordance with Article 41 of the Statute of the Court as a matter of urgency to secure the release of the hostages.

Iran did not enter an appearance before the Court. However, it sent a letter to the Court stating that the seizure of the hostages was of marginal and secondary importance in the relationship between Iran and the United States and that in any event the hostage dispute was essentially and directly within the national sovereignty of Iran.

In December 1979 the Court handed down a unanimous judgment giving an indication of the provisional measures that it was prepared to grant. It held, first, that "while no state is under any obligation to maintain diplomatic or consular relations with another, yet it cannot fail to recognise the imperative obligations inherent therein, now codified in the Vienna Conventions of 1961 and 1963 to which both Iran and United States are parties".[14] Secondly, it recognised that the continuation of the situation "exposes the human beings concerned to privation, hardship, anguish and even danger to life and health and thus to a serious possibility of irreparable harm".[15] The Court therefore found that the circumstances required it to indicate the provisional measures as requested by the United States to preserve the rights claimed.[16] The measures were essentially release of the hostages and return of property belonging to the United States.

Iran did not comply with the provisional measures and accordingly the case proceeded to final hearing.

The Court handed down its decision on the merits in May 1980.[17] On

---

(1980) Merits. In the present context it is only necessary to give a relatively brief review of the case and the hostage rescue attempt. The case and its aftermath have been fully considered by a number of writers, including Stein, *Contempt, Crisis and the Court: The World Court and the Hostage Rescue Attempt*, 76 A.J.I.L., 499 (1982).

[14] I.C.J. Rep., 7 (1979).
[15] *Ibid.*, 17.
[16] *Ibid.*, 21–2.
[17] I.C.J. Rep., 3 (1980).

the preliminary question of jurisdiction the Court found that the Optional Protocols to the Vienna Conventions provided for compulsory jurisdiction. In respect of the two non-diplomatic personnel the Court considered that the Treaty of Amity, Economic Relations and Consular Rights between Iran and the United States gave it jurisdiction. The Court's decision that the Treaty of Amity remained in force following the Islamic revolution and the hostage crisis has been an important precedent for the Iran–United States Claims Tribunal in respect of the expropriation claims.[18]

In respect of the substantive questions the Court found that Iran had failed to protect the embassy from seizure. It had also endorsed the actions of the militants. The Court noted that on November 5, 1979 the Foreign Minister of Iran had stated that the militants "enjoy the endorsement and support of the government".[19] Over the next few days Ayatollah Khomeini voiced his approval of the militants' actions, culminating in his decree of November 17, 1979 commending the militants and stating, "the noble Iranian nation will not give permission for the release of the rest of [the hostages]".[20]

The Court therefore considered the seizure and detention of the hostages by the Islamic militants had been adopted by the Iranian government. The Court was in no doubt that these actions constituted a breach of international law relating to diplomats as embodied in the Vienna Conventions of 1961 and 1963 and general international law. In respect to the two non-diplomatic persons being detained the Court held that Iran was in breach of the Treaty of Amity of 1955. The Court took note of the Iranian government's communications which referred to the circumstances justifying Iran's actions. The Court considered that the circumstances, including the alleged United States involvement in the *coup d'état* which restored the Shah to his throne in 1953, did not justify the actions of Iran or constitute a defence to United States claims. Diplomatic law provided a proper remedy: to declare persons *persona non grata* or in more serious cases "to break off diplomatic relations with a sending state and to call for the immediate closure of the offending mission".[21]

Iran had chosen to act unilaterally outside international law governing diplomatic and consular relations, a body of law "of which the traditions of Islam made a substantial contribution".[22] The Court felt compelled to indicate the seriousness of Iran's actions and stated:[23]

The frequency with which at the present time the principles of international law governing diplomatic and consular relations are set at naught by individuals or

---

[18] See Chapters Eight and Nine for awards and decisions of the Iran–United States Claims Tribunal on the status of the Treaty of Amity in respect of the expropriation claims.
[19] *Ibid.*, 33.
[20] *Ibid.*, 34.
[21] *Ibid.*, 40.
[22] *Ibid.*, 40.
[23] *Ibid.*, 42–3.

groups of individuals is already deplorable. But this case is unique and of very particular gravity because here it is not only private individuals or groups of individuals that have disregarded and set at naught the inviolability of a foreign embassy, but the government of the receiving State itself. Therefore in recalling yet again the extreme importance of the principles of law which it is called upon to apply in the present case, the Court considers it to be its duty to draw the attention of the entire international community, of which Iran itself has been a member since time immemorial, to the irreparable harm that may be caused by events of the kind now before the Court.

The Court made a number of determinations. On the immediate point of the detention of the hostages it held unanimously that Iran must release the hostages and return the embassy to the Protecting Power.[24] The Court, by a majority, decided that the conduct of Iran was in violation of international conventions as well as long established rules of general international law and Iran thereby incurred a responsibility to the United States. Although Judges Morozov and Tarazi dissented from this part of the judgment they both recognised that Iran was in breach of its obligations towards diplomats, as contained in the Vienna Conventions of 1961 and 1963, and thus joined in the unamimous finding that Iran should release the hostages. The Court, by a majority, also decided that Iran was under an obligation to make reparations to the United States.[25]

The rescue mission[26]

The United States, from the earliest days, had prepared contingency plans for a military solution to the crisis. In April 1980, after concluding that diplomacy would not secure the release of the hostages, the United States resorted to military means to solve the crisis. The mission, involving over 100 men and several aircraft and helicopters, was commenced on April 24, 1980. It had to be aborted at the first staging point within Iranian territory on April 25, 1980, owing to equipment failure.

Although the United States characterised the military operation as a rescue mission and thus not an infringement of the "territorial integrity or political independence" of Iran, it was clearly a military violation of Iranian territory.[27] Furthermore had the mission been successful there

[24] *Ibid.*, 44.
[25] It was noteworthy that Judges Morozov from the USSR and Tarazi from Syria were the principal dissenting judges.
[26] The rescue mission has been the subject of proceedings before the Iran–United States Claims Tribunal; cf. *Haji-Bagherpour* v *United States* 2 IRAN–U.S.C.T.R., 38 (1983). Refer to Chapter Seven for a discussion of this case.
[27] For discussion of the legality of the rescue mission, see Jeffery, *The American Hostages in Tehran: The I.C.J. and the Legality of Rescue Missions*, 30 I.C.L.Q., 717 (1981); Stein, *Contempt, Crisis and the Court: The World Court and the Hostage Rescue Attempt*, 76 A.J.I.L., 499 (1982). On the right of self-defence and protection of nationals generally, see

The Algiers Declarations

was the likelihood of substantial Iranian casualties and damage to Iranian property out of proportion to the imminent danger, if any, to the lives of the hostages. Thus the mission must be seen as a violation of Articles 2(4) and 33 of the United Nations Charter. The justification of self-defence under Article 51 was not applicable as there had not been an "armed attack" against the United States, apart from its embassy and consulates in Iran.

Moreover, under the customary right of protection of nationals or humanitarian intervention it is necessary to show imminent danger to the lives of the nationals, apart from their detention, before mounting an armed rescue mission.

The International Court of Justice referred to the United States' actions in its decision on the merits.[28] It stated:

Nevertheless, in the circumstances of the present proceedings, the Court cannot fail to express its concern in regard to the United States' incursion into Iran.

Judges Morozov and Tarazi, in separate opinions, stated that the "military invasion"[29] precluded the United States from receiving compensation.

The negotiations to release the hostages and the Algiers Declarations

For some time after the rescue attempt there was little progress toward resolving the crisis. In addition the political situation in Iran had not settled sufficiently for clear authority to be established. It was not until August 1980 that the Iranian Parliament could nominate a Speaker and approve the appointment of the Prime Minister and Cabinet. The Ayatollah Khomeini had given the Iranian Parliament the authority to negotiate with the United States in respect of the hostages.

The death of the Shah on July 27, 1980, although removing a central cause of the crisis, did not promote the resolution of the crisis. He had already become irrelevant in the dispute between the two nations. The invasion of Iran by Iraq in late September 1980 was of greater significance. It demonstrated how isolated Iran had become. This, and other factors, including the economic damage caused by the freeze of assets and the economic sanctions and the forthcoming United States presidential elections, caused the Iranian government to re-evaluate its position and move toward settling the crisis.

Bowett, *Self-defence in International Law* (1958); Brownlie, *International Law and the Use of Force by States*, 289–98 (1963); Schachter, *The Right of States to Use Armed Force*, 82 Mich. L.R., 1620, and especially 1628–33 (1984).

[28] *Ibid.*, 43.

[29] *Ibid.*, 52; Dissenting opinion of Judge Morozov. See also dissenting opinion of Judge Tarazi at 64.

In September 1980 Ayatollah Khomeini indicated that the hostages could be released, subject to various conditions. In response to Ayatollah Khomeini's statement the Iranian Parliament established a commission to recommend the conditions for the release of the hostages. Despite the preoccupation with the war with Iraq the commission reported to the Iranian Parliament in the last week of October 1980. On November 2, 1980 the Iranian Parliament adopted the commission's recommendations for the release of the hostages. The resolution, known as the Majlis resolution, demanded that the United States should fulfil four conditions to secure the release of the hostages. The conditions were:

1 A pledge not to interfere in the affairs of Iran.
2 That the freeze on Iranian assets should be lifted.
3 The cancellation of all economic sanctions against Iran, and the cancellation of all claims against Iran and the assumption of financial responsibility for claims against Iran.
4 The return to Iran of the assets of the Shah and his close relatives.

Once these conditions had been fulfilled Iran would release the hostages. If the United States did not accept the demands the hostages would be tried as spies. The United States indicated that the Majlis resolution was a significant development and a positive basis on which to resolve the crisis.

Following the Majlis resolution the Islamic militants agreed to transfer control of the hostages to the government. The Prime Minister of Iran also stipulated that Algeria should act as intermediary between Iran and the United States. The United States immediately dispatched the Deputy Secretary of State, Mr Christopher, to Algeria with full details of the United States response. He indicated to the Algerian representatives that the United States accepted the principles of the Majlis resolution as a basis for ending the crisis.

Although the United States had stated that the Majlis resolution was acceptable in principle, this was more a recognition that Iran was in a position to seriously negotiate the resolution of the crisis than an acceptance of the demands. In particular the United States was not prepared to assume financial responsibility for the claims against Iran, or to return the assets of the former Shah to Iran. Instead it required the establishment of an international claims tribunal to hear the claims of United States nationals against Iran, backed by financial guarantees. With regard to the Shah's assets it could do no more than facilitate litigation by the government of Iran in United States courts for the recovery of such assets.

During the months of November and December 1980 considerable negotiation took place via the Algerian intermediaries. The Iranian government accepted the requirement to modify the demands of the Majlis resolution and moved steadily toward the United States position.

In early January 1981 the major issues had been resolved and it was a matter of formulating the arrangements as a Declaration of the government of Algeria to which Iran and the United States would adhere. At the same time bankers from the four participating central banks were formulating the technical agreements to give effect to the financial agreements. However, it was necessary for the Iranian Majlis to approve the arrangements. This was done by a resolution passed on January 14, 1981. This resolution, which effectively modified the four principles expressed in the Majlis resolution of November 2, 1980, approved the agreements as negotiated, with the proviso that all contracts providing for the exclusive jurisdiction of Iranian courts should be excluded from the jurisdiction of the Claims Settlement Tribunal. This proviso was accepted by the United States, and embodied in Article III(2) of the Claims Settlement Declaration.[30]

By January 19, 1981 all the necessary documents of the settlement had been completed, including a number of Presidential Orders executed by President Carter to implement the settlement.[31] The hostage crisis between Iran and the United States had been resolved after 444 days by the completion of the agreements constituting the settlement, which have become known as the Algiers Declarations.

The focus of the aggrieved United States claimants would now shift from the United States municipal courts to the implementation of the Algiers Declarations and in particular the international arbitral tribunal established to settle claims.

The Algiers Declarations[32]

Introduction

The settlement primarily consists of two declarations of the government of Algeria known as the Algiers Declarations. The Declarations were also executed by the governments of the United States and Iran. Both Declarations entered into force on January 19, 1981. In addition there are three Supplementary Agreements to further the implementation of the Declara-

---

[30] See Chapter Twelve for decisions of the Iran–United States Claims Tribunal on this exclusion.

[31] There were final delays which prevented the departure of the hostages until January 20, 1981 at about 12.30 p.m.; half an hour after President Reagan had assumed the office of the presidency.

[32] The General Declaration, the Claims Settlement Declaration and the Undertakings are reproduced in Appendix I.

tions. First, there is an Undertaking of the governments of Iran and the United States with respect to the Declarations of the government of Algeria. Secondly, an Escrow Agreement was executed by the Government of the United States, the Federal Reserve Bank of New York as fiscal agent for the United States, the Bank Markazi Iran, and the Banque Centrale d'Algérie. Finally, there is the Technical Agreement between the Banque Centrale d'Algérie as escrow agent, the Bank of England, and the Federal Reserve Bank of New York as fiscal agent of the United States.

The Declarations are the heart of the arrangement between Iran and the United States to conclude the hostage crisis. The first Declaration, the General Declaration, seeks to restore the situation, as far as possible, to what it was on November 4, 1979 prior to the seizure of the hostages, with Iran receiving its blocked assets, and the United States, its nationals. The second Declaration, the Claims Settlement Declaration, establishes the Iran–United States Claims Settlement Tribunal.

The Tribunal's role was to determine all claims and counterclaims existing on January 19, 1981 between nationals of either country against the government of the other state, and all contractual disputes between the two governments that existed on January 19, 1981.

Thus not only did the Declarations conclude the hostage crisis, they were also intended, by means of the Claims Settlement Tribunal, to resolve all major legal difficulties arising from disputes concerning contractual and property rights between the United States and Iran and their nationals arising from the Islamic revolution.

The General Declaration

The General Declaration is the primary document from which all the other documents are derived. The preamble recognises the inability of the governments of the United States and Iran to deal directly with one another. Although it states the resolution of the crisis is made within the framework of the four points stated in the Majlis Resolution of November 2, 1980 of the Islamic Consultative Assembly of Iran it is clear that the General Declaration differs substantially from the Majlis Resolution and reflects United States imperatives as much as it does Iranian requirements.[33]

The General Principles are based on two of the basic objectives of the parties; first, the restoration of Iran's financial position to what it was prior to the presidential orders freezing Iranian assets in November 1979,[34] and second, the termination of all litigation in United States

[33] See *supra* on the negotiating history of the Agreements.
[34] General Principle A of the General Declaration.

courts commenced by United States nationals against Iran, and the resolution of such claims by international arbitration.[35] Lying behind these two basic objectives, however, was the political ojective of the United States of achieving the release of the fifty-two hostages. The balance of the agreement is set out in the form of four points reflecting the four points of the Majlis resolution of the Islamic Consultative Assembly.

The first point, contained in paragraph 1, is a pledge by the United States that it is and will be the policy of the United States not to intervene directly or indirectly, politically or militarily, in Iran's internal affairs. It had originally been the desire of the Iranian government to have the non-intervention pledge phrased in prospective terms, that is, "from now on will be", to imply that the United States had previously intervened in Iran's internal affairs.[36] This was resisted by the United States, and the United States undertook to do no more than it was required to do under Article 2 of the United Nations Charter.

Points II and III are placed together in the Declaration and cover paragraphs 2 to 11 of the Declaration. These paragraphs concern the return of Iranian assets and the settlement of United States claims. Thus they are primarily concerned with the financial aspects of the Iran–United States dispute.

Paragraph 2 provides for an independent central bank, acting under the instructions of the government of Algeria and the Banque Centrale d'Algérie, to deal with the Iranian assets. This paragraph also establishes the validity of the supporting agreements. The Bank of England was agreed upon as the independent central bank.

Paragraph 3 is perhaps the most fundamental of all the provisions of the Agreement. It ties the transfer of the Iranian assets to the safe departure of the fifty-two hostages from Iran. This paragraph also provided for the obligations of either of the two parties to be terminated at seventy-two hours' notice. In the event of the United States giving such notice but Iran nevertheless having released the hostages within the seventy-two-hour period, the assets would still be transferred. However, the wording of the Agreement is such that all other undertakings of the Declaration would appear to have been negated in the event of such notice by the United States. If the United States had terminated its commitments under the Agreement once the hostages had been released, only monies and assets held in escrow with the central bank would have been transferred.[37] The United States could have retained the balance of Iranian assets to satisfy claimants.

---

[35] General Principle B of the General Declaration.
[36] Warren Christopher, Deputy Secretary of State, *The Iran Agreements*, Hearings of the Committee on Foreign Relations: United States Senate, 35 (1981).
[37] See "The Supporting Agreements", *infra*.

Paragraphs 4 to 9 concern the transfer of the various assets of Iran. Paragraph 4 covers the gold bullion and the assets in the Federal Reserve Bank of New York which were to be transferred to the central bank to be held in escrow. Similarly, paragraph 5, concerning the deposits and securities held in foreign branches of the United States banks, required the transfer of these assets, together with interest to December 31, 1980, to the central bank to be held on escrow. It was the aggregate of the sums held in the Federal Reserve Bank, and the foreign branches of the United States banks, that constituted the Iranian assets exchanged in return for the safe departure of the hostages from Iran.[38]

Paragraphs 6 to 9 cover all the assets of the Iranian government held by United States institutions. Paragraphs 6 and 7 cover assets in United States branches of United States banks. The United States had six months to transfer all Iranian deposits and securities in United States banking institutions in the United States to the central bank. Upon receipt of such funds by the central bank, the Banque Centrale d'Algérie was to direct the central bank to transfer half the funds to Iran, and the other half to a special interest-bearing Security Account, until the balance reached $1 billion. Thereafter all additional funds would be transferred direct to Iran. The special interest-bearing Security Account was to be used solely for payment of awards of the Iran–United States Claims Tribunal against Iran in accordance with the Claims Settlement Agreement. A minimum of $500 million had to be maintained by Iran in the Security Account until all claims were satisfied in accordance with the Claims Settlement Agreement.

Paragraphs 8 and 9 concern other Iranian assets in the United States and abroad. Paragraph 8 provided that all Iranian financial assets, being funds or securities not held in banking institutions, were to be transferred to the central bank and dealt with in the same manner as the assets in United States branches of United States banks. There was no time limit on these transfers. Paragraph 9 provided that the United States would arrange for the transfer to Iran of all Iranian properties located within the United States, subject to the provisions of United States law applicable prior to November 14, 1979. This paragraph covered all non-financial properties.

Paragraphs 10 and 11 related to the trade sanctions against Iran and various United States claims against Iran. Paragraph 10 required the United States to revoke all trade sanctions directed against Iran from November 4, 1979 to the date of agreement. The United States did not regard this as requiring it to supply Iran with military equipment,[39] since

---

[38] These deposits and securities amounted to $7.955 billion and the gold was valued at $0.9397 billion.

[39] See *supra* on the negotiating history of the Agreements.

The Algiers Declarations   17

Iran still had to comply with the Arms Control Act, which it has been unable to do.

Under paragraph 11 the United States agreed to withdraw all claims before the International Court of Justice, and to bar and preclude any claim by either the United States or its nationals arising from:

1 The seizure of the fifty-two hostages
2 Their subsequent detention
3 Injury to United States property or its nationals within the United States embassy in Tehran
4 Injury to the United States and its nationals or their property as a result of popular movements in the course of the Islamic revolution in Iran which were not an act of the government of Iran.[40]

In addition the United States agreed to preclude any litigation brought by aliens in United States courts. It was noteworthy that this article did not definitively preclude any claims by the thirteen hostages seized on November 4, 1979, but released within three weeks of their seizure.[41]

The fourth point referred to in the Majlis Resolution concerned the return of the assets of the family of the former Shah. Paragraphs 12 to 16 set out certain rules pertaining to the return of such assets. The United States, however, did not agree to return the assets of the former Shah or his family. It merely agreed to assist and facilitate any Iranian efforts to recover the property through United States courts.

Paragraph 14 removed the principle of sovereign immunity from any such Iranian claims. Under paragraph 15 the United States guaranteed the enforcement of any judgment against any such assets within the United States. Of note is paragraph 16, providing that any disputes between the United States and Iran concerning the fulfilment of the above obligations by the United States would be resolved by the Claims Settlement Tribunal.

The final paragraph of the Declaration is the arbitration provision holding that all disputes arising from the interpretation or performance of any of the provisions of the Declaration shall be resolved by the Claims Settlement Tribunal.

The Claims Settlement Declaration

The second and complementary Declaration established the Iran–United States Claims Tribunal and set out its jurisdiction and procedure.

---

[40] These exclusions have been considered by the Tribunal in several cases. See Chapter Twelve.

[41] Claims have been made by some of the hostages in the United States courts. Thus far the courts have held that they do not have jurisdiction.

Article II is the most important article, providing for the establishment of the Tribunal and its jurisdiction. Although Article II establishes the Tribunal and sets out its jurisdiction, Article I requires the United States and Iran to promote the settlement of any claims within the jurisdictional scope of Article II. If the claims were not settled within six months they would then be subject to arbitration in the Tribunal.[42]

Article II is divided into three paragraphs establishing three categories of jurisdiction. The first category is claims of nationals of the United States against Iran and claims of nationals of Iran against the United States outstanding at the time of the agreement. The subject matter of the claims is limited to debts, contracts, including transactions subject to letters of credit or bank guarantees, expropriations and other measures affecting property rights. There is an exclusion of matters arising directly from the hostage taking or revolutionary actions by popular movements as defined in paragraph 11 of the General Declaration, or the United States' response to the above conduct. The major exclusion, however, is of claims arising from contracts providing for the sole jurisdiction of the competent Iranian courts.[43]

The second category of claims are the official claims of the United States and Iran against one another arising from contractual arrangements between them for the purchase and sale of goods and services.

The third category is concerned with the interpretation and performance of the General Declaration, which is also covered by paragraphs 16 and 17 of the General Declaration.

Article III provides for the appointment of the members of the Tribunal, the conduct of the business of the Tribunal, and the prosecution of claims. Paragraph 1 provides for nine members to be appointed, or such larger multiples of three as the parties agree. The United States wished to have the numbers increased, but eventually was satisfied with a nine-member Tribunal.[44] Of the nine members, three were to be appointed by the United States and three by Iran. These six would appoint three further members, with one of the three members to be appointed President of the Tribunal. The Tribunal could sit either in panels of three, selected as above, or as a full tribunal.

The second paragraph of Article III provides that the appointment of members and the conduct of the business of the Tribunal shall be in accordance with the arbitration rules of the United Nations Commission on international trade law.

---

[42] This was extended by three months until October 19, 1981. See Chapter Two for a full discussion of the filing of claims.

[43] See Chapter Twelve.

[44] E. Lauterpacht, *The Iran–United States Claims Settlement Agreement: International Law Problems*, 18 (1981) (Monograph).

The third paragraph provides that claims of nationals of either state shall be presented by the claimants themselves, or in the case of claims of less than $250,000 by the government of such nationals.

The final paragraph provided a one-year limitation period after the entry into force of the agreement for the presentation of claims. Thus the claims had to be filed by January 19, 1982. By that date some 3,340 claims had been presented by the United States or its nationals and approximately 407 claims had been presented by Iran and its nationals.[45]

Article VI contains further procedural provisions. Paragraph 1 states that the seat of the Tribunal shall be at The Hague. Paragraph 2 provides that each government shall appoint an agent at the seat of the Tribunal to represent it, and to accept service of notices and other communications. Paragraph 3 provides that the costs of the Tribunal shall be shared equally by the two governments. Paragraph 4, however, is of a substantive nature and states any question concerning the interpretation or application of the Agreement shall be decided by the Tribunal at the request of either Iran or the United States.

Article V sets out the law that shall be applied by the Tribunal for the determination of claims. This article gives wide discretion to the Tribunal in determining the law applicable to each claim. Thus it states:

The Tribunal shall decide all cases on the basis of respect for law, applying such choice of law rules and principles of commercial and international law as the Tribunal determines to be applicable, taking into account relevant usages of the trade, contract provisions and changed circumstances.

Article IV states that all decisions of the Tribunal are final and binding, there being no appeal from them. They may be enforced against either government in the courts of any nation in accordance with the laws of that nation.

Article VII contains a number of definitions, particularly in relation to those who may submit claims to the tribunal. Thus "national" and "claims of nationals" are specifically defined to clarify this important issue.

Once a claim has been lodged with the Tribunal it is excluded from the jurisdiction of the courts of the United States, Iran, or any other court. This reinforces the provisions of the General Principles of the General Declaration that the Tribunal shall act as a substitute forum for the legal proceedings commenced by United States nationals in United States courts against Iran and its state enterprises. This provision is also noteworthy by being extended to the courts of all nations.[46]

---

[45] See Chapter Two.

[46] It was not perceived in this light by Mr Muskie, the Secretary of State at the time of the negotiations: *The Iran Agreements*, Hearings of Senate Committee on Foreign Relations: United States Senate, 47 (1981).

"Iran" and "United States" have identical definitions and mean the government of either party, and any political subdivision thereof.

The final provision, Article VIII, provides that the Agreement shall enter into force when the government of Algeria has received a notification of adherence to the Agreement from both parties. The Agreement became effective on January 19, 1981.

The supporting agreements

The Undertakings, the Escrow Agreement and the Technical Arrangement were concluded to enable various financial undertakings of the Algiers Declarations to be implemented. The financial arrangements enabled the departure of the hostages and the establishment of the $1 billion Security Account to satisfy awards of the Iran–United States Claims Tribunal against Iran.

The first of the supplemental documents, the Undertakings of the United States and Iran, provided that the fifty-two hostages would depart Iran when the Banque Centrale d'Algérie received confirmation that Iranian gold, and $7.955 billion in cash and securities had been transferred to the central bank, all of which constituted Iranian assets frozen by the presidential order of November 14, 1979.[47] The Bank of England was appointed as the central bank to receive these deposits, securities and bullion.

The Escrow Agreement, executed by the various central banks, enabled the actual transfer of the funds referred to in the General Declaration and the Undertakings. First, all Iranian deposits and securities in United States banking institutions, whether in the United States or abroad, would be transferred to the Federal Reserve Bank of New York.[48] In the case of United States government securities these would be converted to cash. Once all deposits and securities were held by the Federal Reserve Bank of New York, they would be transferred to the Bank of England for credit to the account of the Banque Centrale d'Algérie as escrow agent.[49] Once the hostages had left Iran the funds would be dealt with in the manner contemplated by the Declarations and Undertakings.[50]

The Technical Arrangement entered into between the three banks provided the detailed instructions on how the banks should deal with the deposits, securities and bullion. In the present context the most important

---

[47] Article 1 of the Undertakings. These were the funds in the Federal Reserve Bank of New York and deposits and securities in foreign branches of United States banks. There were further Iranian assets which did not require to be transferred prior to the release of the hostages.
[48] Article 1.
[49] Paragraph 2.
[50] Paragraph 4.

accounts were those established to receive funds and securities to form the Security Account of $1 billion to help satisfy awards of the Iran–United States Claims Tribunal against Iran. These funds would largely come from the United States branches of the United States banks and other financial institutions. The $1 billion to form the Security Account would be transferred to such bank as the Banque Centrale d'Algérie directed. Instructions were received to transfer the security account to the central bank of the Netherlands. Further Agreements were executed by the various banks some time later in connection with operation of the Security Account.[51]

The role of the Iran–United States Claims Tribunal in the settlement of United States claims against Iran

The constitutional requirements

One of the most important aspects of the Agreement between Iran and the United States was the establishment of an international claims tribunal to settle the claims of United States nationals against Iran. Although the principle of equality of states required that there should be equal access to the Tribunal for nationals of either party to make claims against the government of the other party, there is no doubt that the Tribunal was primarily established for the settlement of the claims of United States nationals.[52]

A notable feature of the Iranian revolution and hostage crisis was that many of the United States nationals who had been affected by Iranian nationalisation laws, or who had had contracts terminated by the Iranian government, commenced proceedings in United States courts against Iran and Iranian governmental entities. Moreover many of these claimants had obtained pre-judgment attachment orders against Iranian assets, although in many cases the assets subject to the attachment orders had no connection with the subject matter of the original litigation. Thus under United States constitutional theory the claimants had acquired property rights in the United States in respect of their claims against Iran.

The Constitution of the United States does not permit the President to deprive persons subject to United States law of their property rights

[51] There was an exchange of notes between Bank Markazi, the Federal Reserve Bank of New York and the Banque Centrale d'Algérie. These were dated July 10, 1981. There were also two technical agreements between these three banks and the two Netherlands banks, both dated August 17, 1981. These documents will be considered in Chapter Fourteen.

[52] This is confirmed by General Principle B of the General Declaration, which requires the United States to terminate all legal proceedings in the United States, and to provide for the termination of such claims through binding arbitration.

without providing compensation. Accordingly the United States was not prepared to assume financial responsibility for the claims against Iran or to return the assets of the Imperial family to Iran. However, the President has wide discretion in dealing with foreign claims, even where those claims have given rise to property rights within the United States. International arbitral tribunals have been a traditional means for the United States to deal with such claims. The United States Supreme Court in its decision on the validity of the United States accession to the Algiers Declarations in *Dames & Moore* v *Regan*[53] referred to the powers of the United States government to settle claims of United States nationals through claims settlement agreements.

Thus for both foreign policy and constitutional reasons the United States insisted on the establishment of an international claims tribunal to settle the claims of United States nationals against Iran. In addition the United States also insisted on Iran providing an internationally controlled fund to satisfy such claims.

The Tribunal as a substitute forum for United States courts and its role as an international claims tribunal[54]

There is considerable evidence in the Algiers Declarations that the Iran–United States Claims Tribunal was established, at least in part, as a substitute forum for United States municipal courts for the resolution of claims that had been filed or could have been filed with United States courts. Under the Algiers Declarations the United States agreed to terminate all legal proceedings in its courts involving claims of United States nationals against Iran and its entities, and to resolve the claims by international arbitration.[55] The claims filed in the Tribunal by nationals of the United States are essentially the same as those previously presented before United States courts. The issue that is raised is the extent to which the Tribunal can properly be characterised as an internationl claims tribunal governed by public international law in the same way as previous international claims commissions.

It is the view of Lloyd-Jones, in his thoughtful analysis of the nature of the Tribunal, that the Tribunal is seized of jurisdiction in disputes that are

---

[53] 101 S. Ct., 2972 (1981).

[54] This issue is more completely dealt with, especially in relation to the nature of the Tribunal, in Chapter Fourteen.

[55] General Principle B of the General Declaration. However, the President only "suspended" claims before United States courts; Executive Order 12294, February 24, 1981. Iran filed a claim with the Tribunal alleging the United States to be in breach of its obligations to terminate claims; *Iran* v *United states (Case A/15)*. Refer to Chapter Thirteen on the decisions of the Tribunal requesting a termination of proceedings in the municipal courts of Iran and the United States and a comparison of these decisions with Executive Order 12294.

private law disputes transferred to a transnational arbitral tribunal.[56] The provisions of Article II(1) lend further support to this view. Lloyd-Jones refers to five aspects of Article II(1) that indicate that it is primarily designed for the solution of private law disputes.[57] First, the reference to "claims of nationals of the United States" envisages private law claims. The language of state responsibility would more appropriately refer to claims of Iran and the United States in respect of injuries to their nationals. Second, the reference to "claims outstanding on the date of the agreement" implies that the nationals had a valid cause of action prior to the Claims Settlement Declaration coming into force and that the claim could have been prosecuted in municipal courts, whether or not the claimant had in fact filed a claim in United States municipal courts. The Tribunal is thus considering claims of the same character as those that would be heard by United States municipal courts, as opposed to claims under public international law. Third, the words "whether or not filed with any court" indicate that the claims, or at least some of them, were claims capable of being decided by municipal courts, but which had been transferred to the Tribunal for resolution. Fourth, the reference to counter-claims by respondent states against individual claimants cannot be readily reconciled with the principles of state responsibility. Finally Lloyd-Jones refers to the transactions capable of supporting claims, and in particular claims arising from "debts, contracts (including transactions which are the subject of letters of credit or bank guarantees) . . .", and suggests that the function of the Tribunal is to decide private law claims.

Toope is of the view that the Tribunal is essentially an "international" tribunal, although this does mean that it is divorced from municipal law. He concludes:[58]

It would seem that the majority of the plenary Tribunal was comfortable with the view that the nature of the Tribunal is "mixed". And yet in other contexts, the Tribunal has held subsequently that "the Tribunal is an international tribunal which, as such, is concerned with the rights and duties of States in public international law". [*Mobil Oil Iran Inc.* v *Iran* 16 IRAN–U.S.C.T.R. 3, 34 (1987)]. It would appear that the nature of the Tribunal depends on the nature of the case.

It should also be noted that the only claims permitted between the two governments pursuant to Article II(2) are claims "arising out of contractual arrangements between them for the purchase and sale of goods and services". Such claims could normally be determined by municipal courts.

---

[56] Lloyd-Jones, *The Iran–United States Claims Tribunal: Private Rights and State Responsibility*, in Lillich (ed.), *The Iran–United States Claims Tribunal 1981–83*, (1984). See also Toope, *Mixed International Arbitration*, Dep. at 265–92 (1990).
[57] *Ibid*. The following discussion in this paragraph on the five aspects is drawn largely from Lloyd-Jones's paper.
[58] Toope, *supra*, 274.

In addition to the provisions of Article II(1) there are also the provisions of Article IV(3) of the Claims Settlement Declaration and paragraph 17 of the General Declaration which provide that awards rendered against either government by the Tribunal shall be enforceable against such government in the courts of any nation in accordance with its laws. It is submitted that such enforcement places the awards on the same plane as any judgment of a municipal court which could be enforced by the courts of other nations.[59] Although this provision is confined to awards, which by and large can be rendered only in respect of claims by individual claimants, awards can be made in respect of damages for breach of either of the Algiers Declarations by the states parties. Such awards raise issues of state responsibility that would never be entertained by municipal courts.[60]

In contrast to these indicators that the Tribunal is acting, at least in part, as a substitute forum for United States municipal courts are the provisions of Article V of the Claims Settlement Declarations. Unlike a municipal court the Tribunal has wide discretion in determining the applicable law of the claim. It may apply "such choice of law rules and principles of commercial and international law as the Tribunal determines to be applicable . . ." However, unlike an arbitral tribunal resolving state claims the Tribunal is not limited to applying public international law to the claims and may apply principles of municipal law should they be appropriate for resolution of the claims. The difference between the Tribunal and a municipal court lies in the fact that the application of municipal law by the Tribunal is discretionary whereas a municipal court would be required, under choice of law principles, to apply a particular system of municipal law to a private law claim.

Although it is reasonable to infer that the Iran–United States Tribunal is acting, in part, as a substitute forum for United States courts it is not bound to resolve the claims on the same basis as a United States court. Thus, while it may apply the same choice of law principles as would a United States court for a particular claim, it is not required to do so.

Moreover the jurisdiction of the Tribunal is more extensive than is usual in municipal courts.[61] The Tribunal has jurisdiction over claims

---

[59] See Chapter Fourteen for a full discussion of this issue.

[60] "*Decisions* are rendered by the Tribunal in cases arising directly between the government of Iran and the United States. *Awards* are rendered in respect of claims by individual claimants, as are *Interlocutory Awards* and *Awards on Agreed Terms*." Editorial note to the IRAN–U.S.C.T.R. (all volumes). It should be noted, however, that awards can also be made in respect of claims between the two governments made pursuant to Article II(2) of the Claims Settlement Declaration and in respect of breaches of either of the Algiers Declarations by the two states parties.

[61] As a rule municipal courts do not decide international disputes by applying the principles of public international law in the absence of a treaty permitting the court to do so. This principle was applied by the United States Supreme Court in *Banco National de Cuba* v

arising from "expropriations or other measures affecting property rights". As noted by Lloyd-Jones, these are traditionally regarded as coming within the context of international responsibility.[62] In addition it has jurisdiction over the implementation and interpretation of the Algiers Declarations, many of the obligations of which involve issues of high state policy which would never be within the jurisdiction of a municipal court.

The implications of the Tribunal being in part a substitute forum for municipal courts and the significance of this to the characterisation of the Tribunal will be more fully considered in Part II of this work on the substantive jurisdiction of the Tribunal and Part III on the recognition and enforcement of awards of the Tribunal.

International arbitration as a means of settling international claims

The use of international arbitration to settle claims of nationals against respondent states has a long history in international law, particularly concerning disputes between Western developed nations and the developing states of the Third World.

Probably the greatest use of tribunals to settle claims has been in respect of European and United States claims against Latin American states in the nineteenth and early twentieth centuries.[63] Typically the European nations and the United States had been able to impose tribunals upon the weaker respondent states through the exercise of economic and military power. The frequent use of arbitral tribunals to settle claims led to some reservations concerning arbitration as a means of resolving claims. The Calvo doctrine, first enunciated by the Argentinian jurist Calvo, was a response to what was perceived as excessively high standards of international law in assessing liability for injuries to aliens in underdeveloped countries still lacking the administrative and judicial machinery to ensure the protection of the rights of both citizens and aliens.

The imposition of arbitral tribunals upon Latin American countries had its parallels in the establishment of the Mixed Arbitral Tribunals as part of the peace settlement of 1919. The defeated respondent states similarly

---

Sabbatino 376 U.S. 398 (1964), where the court held that it did not have competence to hear a claim arising from the Cuban nationalisation measures. Subsequently the United States Congress passed legislation allowing United States courts to hear such claims. As a result there have been a number of decisions where United States courts have examined the principles of public international law relating to state nationalisation measures. See in particular *Banco National de Cuba* v *Chase Manhattan Bank* 658 F. 2d, 875 (1981). Refer also to Chapters Eight and Nine on the application of the principles of public international law to cases of expropriation.

[62] Lloyd-Jones, *supra.*, note 36.

[63] See Feller, *The Mexican Claims Commissions 1923–1934* (1935); Wetter, *The International Arbitral Process* (1976).

had to accept the arbitral tribunals to settle claims of nationals of the Allied states.

The last major use of arbitral tribunals to settle claims was the various claims commissions established by the peace treaties of World War II. As with the Mixed Arbitral Tribunals the commissions were established to settle claims arising from injuries to nationals of the victorious Allies. The establishment of the commissions may be seen as a sign of weakness on the part of the respondent states.

As a consequence, settlement of international claims in respect of injuries to aliens by recourse to international arbitration has not received widespread acceptance, particularly since World War II and the post-colonial era. It has invariably been imposed upon the respondent state through economic or military power. Although the tribunals have applied international law in determining liability, such law has been seen by the respondent states as unduly favouring traditional Western precepts of international conduct. Therefore, respondent states, particularly revolutionary socialist states which transformed their economies by nationalising foreign property and severing economic links with Western states, have resolved Western claims at the political level. Instead of establishing international arbitral tribunals applying international law to the claims the revolutionary states settled the claims by lump sum agreements directly negotiated between the parties.[64] Typically the settlements were only a percentage of the actual losses.[65] The disbursement of the lump sum was in the hands of the national claims commission of the claimant state.[66]

The establishment of the Iran–United States Claims Tribunal is therefore a significant departure from the prevailing practice of lump sum agreements. It reflects the unique political and economic balance between the two states at the time of the settlement. First, it was part of the bargain struck between the two states, essentially the release of Iranian financial assets and the establishment of a claims tribunal with a security account for the settlement of United States claims in return for the release of the United States nationals. Second, it removed United States claims from the political arena to a comparatively neutral legal forum, which was essential in view of the charged atmosphere between the two states. A lump sum settlement of 100 per cent of United States claims would have been unacceptable to Iran and equally a lump sum settlement of less than 100 per cent would have been unacceptable to the United States. The establishment of a international arbitral forum solved this political dilemma.

[64] Lillich and Weston, *International Claims: Their Settlement by Lump Sum Agreements* (1975).
[65] *Ibid*.
[66] See Lillich, *International Claims: Their Adjudication by National Commissions* (1965).

Moreover, lump sum settlements tend to have been negotiated when the two parties have had the flexibility of time and where the resolution of claims has not been central to the political and economic relationship of the parties. Typically the value of assets possessed by the claimant state has been far less than the $12 billion worth of Iranian financial assets frozen in United States financial institutions by the United States government. Iran could not afford to wait several years to settle United States claims except by having them referred to an independent arbitral tribunal. This agreement enabled Iran to obtain the release of its assets, although it had to agree to the establishment of a security account to satisfy awards of the Tribunal as a condition of referring the claims to arbitration.

The attractiveness to Iran of an international arbitral tribunal determining claims by reference, at least in part, to international law was perhaps greater than arbitration had been to the Latin American countries in the early part of the twentieth century. Iran could have reasonably expected that the development of international law particularly since World War II and especially in relation to claims arising from expropriation would reflect the imperatives of the developing nations as much as the perspectives of the Western nations. Thus it could expect that the net result of the determinations of the Tribunal would effectively be only partial compensation in respect of the United States claims in much the same proportions as the majority of lump sum settlements.[67]

The recourse to arbitration by Iran and the United States in the particular circumstances of the hostage crisis therefore raises two issues of major interest in this examination of the Tribunal.

The first and the most important issue is the application and development of international law by the Tribunal. Article V of the Claims Settlement Declaration, however, does not limit the Tribunal to applying only international law to disputes. The Tribunal may also apply principles of commercial law, choice of law rules and contract provisions in determining claims. The application of these different sources of law to the various issues and claims before the Tribunal will provide a significant indication of the boundaries of public international law as it applies to property claims by nationals against foreign states.

The second issue is the relationship of the Tribunal and its awards and decisions to the municipal law of its seat, the Netherlands, and in the countries where the awards could potentially be enforced pursuant to Article IV(3) of the Claims Settlement Declaration.[68] The reference to principles of commercial law and choice of law rules in Article V, as well as the ability to enforce awards in courts of third states in accordance with

---

[67] See Chapters Eight and Nine on Expropriation on the actual standard applied by the Tribunal in the expropriation claims.

[68] This treatment of this issue is largely contained in Chapter Fourteen.

their law, are a clear indication that the Iran–United States Claims Tribunal is not a traditional international arbitral tribunal concerned with inter-state claims to be resolved solely by recourse to international law. The question is raised as to whether the Tribunal should be characterised as a true "international arbitral tribunal" as stated in the Claims Settlement Declaration[69] or as a quasi-international arbitral tribunal which is linked to the municipal law of one or more nations.

The following chapters of this work examine the work of the Tribunal, primarily in the light of the two issues of the application and development of international law by the Tribunal. However, the characterisation of the Tribunal is also of significance, particularly in relation to the enforceability of the awards in municipal courts of third states.

[69] Article II(1).

CHAPTER TWO
Introduction to the Tribunal

The structure and administration of the Tribunal

Introduction

The establishment of a nine-member international arbitral tribunal to hear nearly 4,000 claims required a different approach from that usual in an international arbitration. It necessitated a tribunal with "many of the outward appearances of a fully fledged court system" in contrast to an *ad hoc* tribunal hearing a single claim.[1] This was envisaged in the Claims Settlement Declaration, which had established a tribunal with nine members, able to sit in panels of three to expedite the progress of the hearings. However, apart from the very limited indications in the Claims Settlement Declaration, and a direction that the UNCITRAL rules would apply, the Tribunal has had to determine its own administrative structures to facilitate the work of the Tribunal.

Accordingly the Tribunal has a comprehensive registry and a sophisticated system for filing and distributing documents. To cope with the volume of claims, most aspects of the claims are presented in writing, including much of the evidence and legal argument. The oral hearings are relatively brief, typically taking only one or two days for a multi-million-dollar claim.

This chapter describes the structure of the Tribunal in order to give an appreciation of how the Tribunal has dealt with a large number of claims involving complex issues of municipal law and international law in a reasonably expeditious manner.

---

[1] Bockstiegel, *Applying the UNCITRAL Rules: The Experience of the Iran–United States Claims Tribunal*, 4 Int. Tax and Bus. Lawyer, 266 (1984). Bockstiegel was the President of the Tribunal from December 1984 to 1988.

The organisation of the Tribunal as a full Tribunal and Chambers
Article 1 of the Claims Settlement Declaration provides for a nine-member Tribunal, able to sit as a full Tribunal or in panels of three.

One of the first actions of the Tribunal was the selection of Judge Lagergren as President of the Tribunal. His appointment was made by the six Iranian and United States arbitrators. President Lagergren's first official action was to determine the composition of the Chambers.[2] The allocation was by lot during the tribunal's eighth administrative session.[3] Each Chamber has one Iranian, one United States and one neutral arbitrator, with the neutral arbitrator serving as Chairman of the Chamber. The Tribunal decided at its tenth administrative session that all the claims would be allocated to the Chambers by lot,[4] it being the intention that the majority of the claims would be decided by the Chambers. There are rules governing the reallocation of claims among the Chambers and from the Chambers to the full Tribunal.[5]

The practice has been to refer only issues of general significance to the full Tribunal,[6] and for very large claims to be dealt with by the full Tribunal. All other aspects of the claims are dealt with by the Chambers.

Although the Chambers act independently of one another, it is understood that the Chairmen of the Chambers consult one another on common issues to ensure that the decisions of each of the Chambers are consistent. With the increase in the body of jurisprudence of the Tribunal there has been an increasing tendency for the Chambers to cite one another's decisions to ensure consistency. This practice has meant that issues referred to the full Tribunal which have already been dealt with in the Chambers, as in the dual nationality cases, tend to be decided by the full Tribunal in the same way as in the Chambers.[7]

Following the assault on Judge Mangard by two of the Iranian arbitrators in September 1984, the President suspended the proceedings of the Tribunal, which suspension continued until December 1984.[8] During this period a special Chamber was established to deal with requests for termination of proceedings and requests for awards on agreed terms.[9]

The special Chamber continued in operation until January 1985, after which time the Tribunal was able to resume normal business.

[2] Presidential Order No. 1 (19 October 1981), from 1 IRAN–U.S.C.T.R., 95 (1982).
[3] Annual Report of the Tribunal, No. 1 (1981–83).
[4] Annual Report of the Tribunal, No. 1 (1981–83).
[5] Presidential Order No. 1, as amended by Presidential Orders Nos. 8 and 9.
[6] An example of this was the forum selection clause issues, where each of the Chambers referred a number of claims which raised the issues to the full Tribunal. The full Tribunal made its decision on these issues and referred the claims back to the Chambers for decisions on the merits. See Chapter Twelve for a full discussion of the forum selection decisions.
[7] See Chapter Four on the dual nationality cases.
[8] Presidential Order No. 27. See Chapter Three on the crisis of 1984.
[9] Presidential Order No. 29.

Introduction to the Tribunal 31

The full Tribunal, as already noted, deals with issues of general significance to individual claims and certain very large claims. It also hears all claims in respect of the implementation and interpretation of the Algiers Declarations. However, it does not have review powers over decisions of the panels and does not act as an appeal authority from them. The full Tribunal is also the principal administrative organ of the Tribunal, deciding such issues as the procedure of the Tribunal,[10] and administrative and financial matters.[11]

The Secretariat

The volume of claims to be determined by the Tribunal meant that it was essential for the Tribunal to have a fully developed Secretariat. The Secretariat consists of legal assistants for members of the Tribunal, a Registry, a language service and an administrative section. The chief administrative officer is the Secretary General, who has overall responsibility for the Secretariat. A prominent Sri Lankan jurist, Mr M. C. W. Pinto, was appointed as the Secretary General.

The Registry is responsible for the receipt and distribution of all the documentation, including statements of claim and defence, orders, submissions and briefs of evidence in respect of the claims. The Co-Registrars have the power to refuse claims if the claimants do not have the nationality of the claimant state.

Such refusals can be challenged by the claimant before the Tribunal, and a number of cases have been heard on this issue.[12] The Co-Registrars are also responsible for depositing the Tribunal's awards with the Registrar's office of the District Court of The Hague.[13] The Registry also maintains the statistics of claims filed and claims disposed of by the Tribunal.[14]

The language service ensures that the oral and written proceedings of the Tribunal are translated into the two languages of the parties, English and Farsi, as required by Article 17 of the Tribunal rules. The language service provides translations into both languages of all the written documents generated by the Tribunal itself. The claimants and respondents, however, are required to file all documents in both languages.

The administration of the Tribunal

The Tribunal is administered through three agencies: first, the full Tribunal sitting in administrative session, second, the office of the President and, third, the Secretariat.

[10] See Chapter Thirteen on the Tribunal's Rules of Procedure.
[11] Annual Report of the Tribunal, No. 2 (1983–84).
[12] These cases will be covered in Amendment and Substitution of Claims, *infra*.
[13] The significance of the depositing of awards in Dutch courts will be considered in Chapter Fourteen.
[14] The details of these statistics will be set out in Filing of Claims, *infra*.

The full Tribunal has a dual role, meeting in both judicial and administrative sessions. In the judicial sessions it is fulfilling its function as an arbitral tribunal determining the claims of Iranian and United States nationals.

The Tribunal deals with non-judicial matters, or matters which are not issues in a particular case or cases in administrative session.[15]

When meeting in administrative session the full Tribunal is the paramount administrative organ of the Tribunal. The most significant matter dealt with in administrative session has been the adoption of the Tribunal's rules of procedure. As mandated by Article III(2) of the Claims Settlement Declaration these rules are the UNCITRAL arbitration rules except to the extent modified by the Tribunal. The Tribunal has also decided on the annual budget, the Internal Guidelines, the Staff Rules and the Financial Regulations.[16] The Tribunal has also established a Committee on Administrative and Financial Questions to deal with subsidiary issues.[17]

The second agency concerned with the "orderly performance of Tribunal functions"[18] is the President of the Tribunal. The President acts through "Presidential Orders". The Presidential Orders may implement decisions of the Tribunal sitting in administrative session as in the composition of Chambers[19] or may be in respect of decisions made by the President acting alone. The range of matters dealt with by Presidential Order includes *ad hoc* substitution of one Chamber's Chairman by another, directing claims to particular Chambers, suspension of proceedings during the crisis of 1984, and the constitution of the special Chamber arising from the crisis to deal with certain judicial requirements such as approval of settlements.[20]

The final administrative agency of the Tribunal is the Secretariat, dealing with the matters referred to in the previous section. It ensures that the administrative decisions of the Tribunal and the President can be carried out. It also enables the day-to-day functioning of the Tribunal to proceed in an orderly manner.

Settlement of claims

Negotiations prior to filing of claims in the Tribunal

The Claims Settlement Declaration envisaged two steps to resolve the claims between Iran and the United States. These were, first, direct settlement of claims between the parties, and, second, in the event the

---

[15] Annual Report of the Tribunal, No. 2, p. 5 (1983–84).
[16] *Ibid.*
[17] *Ibid.*
[18] Annual Report of the Tribunal, No. 1 (1981–83).
[19] *Ibid.*
[20] Annual Report of the Tribunal, No. 4 (1985–86).

parties were unable to reach settlement, binding arbitration in the Iran–United States Claims Tribunal.

Article I of the Claims Settlement Declaration required Iran and the United States to promote the settlement of claims by direct negotiations between the parties. However, these direct negotiations under the auspices of the Claims Settlement Declaration were limited to the range of claims within the jurisdiction of the Tribunal as stipulated by Article II.[21]

A period of six months, with an extension of a further three months, allowed the sponsored negotiations between the parties to take place.[22] The two governments agreed to extend the period during which settlements might be promoted by three months until October 19, 1981.[23]

It has been argued that this "negotiating" period was compulsory and that the Tribunal would be unable to hear claims where the parties had not made any attempts to settle the claims.[24] A number of negotiations to settle claims did take place pursuant to Article I of the Claims Settlement Declaration.

The Iranian government notified the United States Department of State that it wished to begin negotiations to settle claims for $250,000 or more.[25] It was suggested by the Iranian government that the United States claimants should inform both the Iranian parties concerned and the Iranian International Legal and Financial Claims Committee located in Bank Markazi Iran of the nature and quantum of the claims, supported by appropriate evidence. It was anticipated that the negotiations would take place in London, and the Iranian parties or the Committee would notify the United States claimants of the time and programme of the negotiations. Various negotiations took place in London, with particular emphasis on the judicial claims involving United States banking institutions.

However, no binding settlements were able to be concluded during the nine-month period envisaged by Article I of the Claims Settlement Declaration. The negotiations were, however, the genesis of a number of settlements subsequently ratified by the Tribunal and satisfied from the Security Account.

Pursuant to Article III(3) of the Claims Settlement Declaration, claims of nationals of less than $250,000 are to be prosecuted by the government

---

[21] Article I of the Claims Settlement Declaration.
[22] *Ibid.*
[23] Iran–United States Claims Tribunal Administrative Directive No. 1, July 4, 1981, paragraph 2.
[24] Suy, *Settling U.S. Claims against Iran by Negotiation*, 29 Am. J. of Comp. Law, 523, 524 (1981).
[25] United States Department of State, Public Notice 753; U.S. Federal Register, Vol. 46, No. 85, pp. 25026–7 (May 4, 1981).

of such nationals on their behalf. The United States claimants with claims in this category were required to register their claims with the Department of State by May 7, 1981.[26] The details of these claims were to be transmitted to Iran to lay the foundations for negotiations for the settlement of such claims by a single lump sum payment. It was the intention of the United States government that the lump sum settlement would be distributed to the claimants through the auspices of the United States Court of Claims. Extensive negotiations took place between the two governments to settle the claims but the United States remained inflexible in its objective of achieving a lump sum settlement. Iran preferred to consider each claim separately, and as a consequence the small claims were not settled during the nine-month period which expired on October 19, 1981. Further settlement discussions took place but did not lead to a lump sum settlement prior to the final date for filing claims. Once the period of compulsory negotiation passed it was necessary for the United States government to file the claims individually before the Iran–United States Claims Tribunal. The Tribunal dealt with a number of small claims either by settlement award or by a fully argued award or by termination. The small claims outstanding in 1990 were finally settled by a single lump sum payment of $105 million.[27]

Settlement of claims filed with the Tribunal
The closing date of January 19, 1982 was three months longer than the period for the promotion of directly negotiated settlements between the parties provided under Article I of the Declaration. Once the attempt at settlement envisaged by Article I had failed there was a three-month period from October 19, 1981 to January 19, 1982 to prepare the claims for filing in the Tribunal.[28] During this time, and prior to the actual filing of the claims, direct settlement between the parties could not readily take place. If settlement was achieved during this period the proper course was to file the claims in the Tribunal, and for the Tribunal to approve and ratify the settlement by an Award on Agreed Terms which could be satisfied from the Security Account. Failure to file a claim, even though settled before filing, but after the lapse of time envisaged in Article I, meant the claimant would be unable to enforce the settlement by payment from the Security Account. By January 19, 1982, the date by which all claims had to be filed, there had not been any settlements concluded between United States claimants and Iran, since only the Tribunal could

[26] United States Department of State, Public Notice 789.
[27] IRAN–U.S.C.T.R., 327 (1990).
[28] It is the view of Erik Suy that the period for filing claims was July 19, 1981 to January 19, 1982; Suy, *Settling U.S. Claims against Iran by Negotiation*, 29 Am. J. of Comp. Law, 523 (1981).

make a settlement award which could be satisfied from the Security Account.[29] However, settlements were among the first of the Tribunal's awards, and these were paid from the Security Account.

A large number of the claims filed with the Tribunal were settled by the parties. In some cases the parties were able to settle the claims without any preliminary hearings or decisions by the Tribunal. In such cases, the Tribunal simply had to conclude that it had jurisdiction over the claim before approving the settlement. In other cases there had been a number of preliminary hearings dealing with a variety of issues before the parties were able to agree on a settlement. Some of these settlements were very large, including a total settlement of $500 million to the Amoco company to be satisfied from the Security Account.[30]

The very large number of small claims were particularly amenable to settlement, if only to reduce the case load of the Tribunal. Discussions on a settlement of all the small claims proceeded over a number of years. In the meantime the Tribunal dealt with a number of the small claims, providing valuable precedents, particularly in the area of responsibility for the actions of revolutionaries. Finally in 1990 the two governments were able to settle the outstanding claims with a payment of $105 million by Iran to the United States, to be satisfied from the Security Account.[31]

Submission and filing of claims before the Tribunal

The requirement to submit claims to the Tribunal

If the parties could not settle the claim within the nine months' compulsory negotiating period, the next step was to submit the claim to binding third-party arbitration. The "binding third-party arbitration" envisaged by Article I of the Claims Settlement Declaration would take place in the "Iran–United States Claims Tribunal" as established by Article II of the Claims Settlement Declaration.

The use of the word "shall" in Article I of the Claims Settlement Declaration indicated that once parties had embarked upon the compulsory negotiated settlement process envisaged by this article, if such negotiations were unsuccessful then arbitration became compulsory. Claims could be withdrawn only with the consent of the Tribunal. However,

---

[29] See Chapter Fourteen on settlement awards and their satisfaction from the Security Account. See in particular *Case A1* 1 IRAN–U.S.C.T.R., 144 (1981–82) on the requirements to be met in order for an Award on Agreed Terms to be satisfied from the Security Account.

[30] *Amoco Iran Oil Company* v *Iran* 25 IRAN–U.S.C.T.R., 301 (1990) and *Amoco International Finance* v *Iran* 25 IRAN–U.S.C.T.R., 314 (1990). The Tribunal had dealt with the principles of compensation for expropiated oil concessions in an Interlocutory Award in 15 IRAN–U.S.C.T.R., 189 (1987).

[31] 25 IRAN–U.S.C.T.R., 327 (1990).

claims were not automatically filed once the period for negotiated settlement had passed. Unless the claim was filed within twelve months of the entry into force of the Claims Settlement Declaration it lapsed. Thus the use of the word "shall" signifies that the only forum that could hear the claims was the Tribunal, being the "binding third-party arbitration in accordance with the terms of the agreement",[32] rather than that the claimant was compulsorily required to file the claim.

Filing of claims in the Tribunal

Article III(4) of the Declaration provided that claims had to be filed with the Tribunal not more than one year after the entry into force of the Declaration, or six months after the date of appointment of the President of the Tribunal, whichever date was the later.

The President of the Tribunal was appointed on June 9, 1981,[33] and thus the closing date for filing claims was January 19, 1982, one year after the Declaration entered into force. This date, however, does not apply to disputes between Iran and the United States concerning the performance of the obligations of the General Declaration. Such claims can be filed at any time.[34]

By January 19, 1982, the last day for filing of claims, a total of 3,816 claims had been filed. In respect of claims by nationals 965 were claims of greater than $250,000 which could be directly presented by the claimant to the Tribunal. The balance of 2,782 claims were all under $250,000 and had to be presented to the Tribunal by the government of the claimant. The figure of 3,816 claims did not include claims arising from the interpretation and implementation of the Algiers Declarations, which could be filed by either of the two states parties at any time.[35] Some twenty-two of these claims had been filed by the two states by June 1986. By June 1990, some twenty-five of these claims had been filed (see *Annual Report (1989–90)*).

The Tribunal was established primarily to resolve claims of United States claimants and this is borne out by a comparison of the number of claims filed by nationals of each country and the awards made by the Tribunal. Of the 965 large claims, 558 were filed by United States nationals and 407 were filed by Iranian claimants.

Amendment and substitution of claimants after January 19, 1982

It was important that claims were filed before January 19, 1982. This was of particular significance in respect of claims filed on behalf of subsidiaries

---

[32] Article I of the Claims Settlement Declaration.
[33] I.L.M., 1002 (1981).
[34] Articles 16 and 17 of the General Declaration.
[35] These statistics are taken from the *Annual Report of the Tribunal*, No. 3 (1985–86).

of Iranian or United States corporations which were incorporated outside Iran or the United States. These claims had to be properly formulated when originally filed before January 19, 1982. The Tribunal has not permitted amendment or substitution by claimants after January 19, 1982 of claims made by foreign subsidiaries when they should have been made by the United States parent corporations.

In *Raymond International (UK) Ltd* v *Shahpur Chemical Company*[36] the claim was dismissed by a majority decision of the Tribunal since the claimant, a corporation incorporated in the United Kingdom, was not a United States national. The parent corporation, Raymond International Buildings Inc. of Texas, applied to substitute itself as the claimant. The Tribunal stated:[37]

> Article 20 of the provisionally adopted Tribunal rules provides that a party during the course of the arbitral proceedings (including the refusal proceedings) may amend or supplement his claim unless the Tribunal considers it inappropriate to allow such amendment, having regard to the delay in making it or prejudice to the other party or any other circumstances. However, to substitute a new Claimant for the original one is tantamount to the filing of a new claim and cannot be regarded simply as an amendment to the existing claim timely received by the registry.

Any new claims had to be filed by January 19, 1982, being within the one-year period for filing claims.

Mr Holtzmann filed a dissenting opinion in which the other two United States arbitrators joined. He stated that the Tribunal had taken "an unnecessarily narrow and technical approach to the pleadings in this case" which led to a denial of justice. Mr Holtzmann considered that international law supported this view and he cited Judge Lauterpacht's statement that in "international cases the importance of the interests at stake precludes excessive or decisive reliance upon formal and technical rules".[38]

The careful distinction between clarification of a claim and substitution of claimants is illustrated by *AMF Overseas Corporation* v *Government of Iran*.[39] The claim was originally filed as "AMF Overseas Corporation (Swiss Company) (wholly owned subsidiary of AMF Inc.)". The Co-Registrar refused to file the claim on the grounds that it had not been presented by a United States national. Subsequently AMF Inc., a United States corporation, sought to reverse the decision of the Co-Registrar and

---

[36] 1 IRAN–U.S.C.T.R., 394 (1981–82).
[37] *Ibid.*, 395.
[38] *Ibid.*, 402; from Lauterpacht, *The Development of International Law by the International Court*, 336 (1958).
[39] 1 IRAN–U.S.C.T.R., 392 (1982).

to authorise the Tribunal to accept claims of AMF Inc. submitted on its behalf by AMF Overseas Corporation.

The Tribunal, by a majority decision, characterised this request as a "clarification of who is the proper claimant, and not an amendment whereby a new claimant is named"; notwithstanding the original statement of claim was in respect of a claim of a Swiss company it indicated that the Swiss company was a wholly owned subsidiary of a United States corporation. The three Iranian arbitrators and the President dissented from the decision.

These two decisions demonstrated to the parties that the Tribunal was not immune from taking a formalistic approach in determining whether or not a claim was properly filed on behalf of corporations incorporated in countries other than Iran or the United States. To properly found a claim, the claimants had to correctly comply with the explicit terms of the Claim Settlement Declaration.

CHAPTER THREE

Appointment, challenges and resignation of members of the Tribunal

Introduction

The trilateral nature of the membership of the Tribunal and the actions of individual members of the Tribunal have demonstrated the tensions inherent in a tribunal dealing with disputes between nations harbouring considerable continuing distrust and hostility toward one another. The divergence of attitude between the Iranian arbitrators and the United States and neutral arbitrators who have been schooled in Western legal thought and tradition caused substantial difficulty to the smooth operation of the Tribunal, particularly in the early years. It also serves to show the limitations of international arbitration in resolving acute differences between conflicting states. Even though the Tribunal's jurisdiction is limited to property claims, and does not extend to the continuing political disputes between the two parties, these political tensions have overflowed into the Tribunal, particularly in 1984.

In relation to the membership of the Tribunal these tensions have been most evident in the following issues to be discussed in this chapter: (a) the appointment of members, (b) challenges to members, and (c) resignations and replacement of members.

The Claims Settlement Declaration and the UNCITRAL rules

Article III(1) of the Claims Settlement Declaration provides that the Tribunal shall consist of nine members, or such larger multiples of three as Iran and the United States may agree are necessary to ensure that the Tribunal can conduct its business expeditiously. Article III(1) also required each government to appoint its respective one-third of the members of the Tribunal within ninety days of the Declaration coming into force. The government-appointed members are required to appoint the remaining one-third neutral members, and appoint one of the neutral members as President of the Tribunal.

Article III(2) of the Claims Settlement Declaration further provides that the members of the Tribunal shall be appointed in accordance with the arbitration rules of UNCITRAL, except to the extent that the rules are modified by the parties. The UNCITRAL rules for appointing members of three-member tribunals shall apply *mutatis mutandis* to the appointment of members to the Tribunal.

Section II of the UNCITRAL rules governs the "Composition of the Arbitration Tribunal". Within this section there are separate rules for the number of members, appointment of members, challenge of members and the repetition of hearings in the event of replacement or substitution of a member.

Since the Claims Settlement Declaration made provision for a number of matters referred to in the UNCITRAL rules it was necessary for the Tribunal to modify the UNCITRAL rules to suit the requirements of the Tribunal.

Accordingly Article 5 was replaced with an article providing that the President of the Tribunal has power to make Orders for the appointment of members to Chambers, to assign cases to Chambers, to transfer cases to Chambers and for Chambers to relinquish cases to the full Tribunal.

Articles 6 to 8 on the appointment of members remained unchanged. Although Article 6 relates to the appointment of a sole arbitrator it has extensive provision for the designation of an appointing authority, who has the power of appointment in the event of a failure by the parties to appoint the arbitrator. Article 7 of the UNCITRAL rules governs the appointment of members to three-member tribunals. Pursuant to Article III(2) of the Claims Settlement Declaration, Article 7 applies *mutatis mutandis* to the appointment of members to the Iran–United States Claims Tribunal. Article 7(4) incorporates the rules of Article 6 concerning the powers of the appointing authority. Article 8 sets out the information that should be sent to the appointing authority by the party which has requested the appointing authority to act.

Articles 9 to 12 govern the procedure for challenges to members of the Tribunal. Article 9 requires any arbitrator prior to his appointment and afterwards to inform the parties of any circumstances that might give rise to justifiable doubts as to his impartiality or independence. The Tribunal made an addition to Article 9 requiring arbitrators to declare to the President any circumstances that might give rise to doubts in respect of any particular case before the Tribunal.[1] In explanatory notes added by

---

[1] This issue arose in the challenge by the claimant R. Carlson to the Iranian arbitrator A. Noori. The relevant materials on this challenge are found in 24 IRAN–U.S.C.T.R., 309 (1990).

the Tribunal only the two governments may make challenges on general grounds such as would disqualify a member from the Tribunal *per se*. Claimants can make challenges if doubts arise as to a member's impartiality in a particular case.

Should the challenge be upheld the member will be disqualified only from that particular case, and the President will order the transfer of the case to another Chamber. Article 10 allows challenges to arbitrators if circumstances exist which give rise to justifiable doubts as to the arbitrator's impartiality or independence. However, challenges by the party who appointed the arbitrator can be made on those grounds only if they came to the notice of the party after the appointment had been made. Articles 11 and 12 set out the criteria for dealing with challenges made under Article 10. Article 11(1) requires the challenge to be made within fifteen days of the circumstances leading to the challenge becoming known to the party making the challenge. The challenge must be notified to the other party, to the arbitrator being challenged and to the other arbitrators. Under Article 11(3) the other party may agree to the challenge or the arbitrator may withdraw. In either case the replacement arbitrator must be appointed in accordance with the provisions of Article 6 or 7. In the event of the other party not agreeing to the challenge, or the arbitrator failing to withdraw, the challenge will be determined by the appointing authority, who may if necessary be designated in accordance with the procedure set out in Article 6. If the challenge is sustained a substitute arbitrator will be appointed as provided by Articles 6 to 9.

Article 13 deals with replacement of members in the event of their death or resignation, or the failure of an arbitrator to act. In the former situation a substitute arbitrator shall be appointed in accordance with the provisions of Articles 6 to 9. In the latter case the challenge procedure will apply. If an arbitrator is unable to act owing to temporary circumstances he is not to be replaced, but a substitute arbitrator shall act in his stead.

Substitute members will continue to serve for any particular case notwithstanding that the member for which they are substitute is again available. In the notes to Article 13 it was noted that Iran and the United States could appoint in advance up to three persons who could act as substitutes in the event that arbitrators appointed respectively by them were unable to act for a temporary period.

The final article on the composition of the Tribunal concerned repetition of hearings in the event of replacement or substitution of a member. Article 14, which was modified by the Tribunal, gave power to the Tribunal to determine at its discretion whether part, all or none of any previous hearing ought to be repeated. In the event of a temporary absence of the President the next senior neutral arbitrator shall act as President.

Background to the UNCITRAL rules

The UNCITRAL rules had been adopted by the General Assembly at the end of 1976 after several years of deliberation by the United Nations Commission on International Trade Law.[2] They were the culmination of thirty years of effort by the United Nations to produce an internationally acceptable set of arbitral rules. The use of the UNCITRAL rules is voluntary, and they must be adopted by the parties to a particular arbitration before they are applicable.[3] Moreover they are intended to apply only to international commercial arbitrations.[4]

The first major effort of the United Nations to formulate a universal set of arbitral rules was made by the International Law Commission. Arbitral procedure had been selected by the ILC in its first session as a priority for codification. In 1951 the Commission submitted a draft set of rules to the General Assembly.[5]

One of the most important issues was the appointment of arbitrators, particularly where one of the parties to the arbitration fails to appoint its national members.[6] This had occurred with the commissions set up pursuant to the peace treaties between the Allies and Bulgaria, Hungary and Romania. The International Court of Justice found on analysis of the disputes clause of the treaties that the appointment of the "third member" was dependent on the parties appointing their respective members.[7] If one party failed to make its appointment, there was no provision for the Secretary General of the United Nations to make the appointment.[8] Similarly, the arbitration between Iran and the Anglo-Iranian Oil Company did not proceed, since Iran did not appoint its arbitrator, and the *compromis* did not have a provision for a third party to make the appointment in the event of such a failure.[9]

The ILC Draft Convention provided for the constitution of the arbitral tribunal, irrespective of whether or not one of the parties failed to

---

[2] Resolution 31/98 of the General Assembly of the U.N. of 15 December 1976. For a full discussion on the UNCITRAL rules and their adoption by the Iran–United States Claims Tribunal refer to Chapter Thirteen.

[3] Article 1.

[4] Resolution 31/98.

[5] *Memorandum prepared by Secretariat*, Yearbook of I.L.C., 157 (1957). The draft rules had been prepared by Schelle (Special Rapporteur), Yearbook of I.L.C., 148–51, (1957).

[6] *Memorandum Prepared by Secretariat*, Yearbook of I.L.C., 161–2 (1957).

[7] *Interpretation of Peace Treaties with Bulgaria, Hungary, Romania (Second Phase)* I.C.J. Rep., 220 (1950).

[8] *Ibid.*, 227.

[9] Subsequently the United Kingdom was also unsuccessful in its attempt to have the substantive dispute heard by the International Court of Justice; *Anglo-Iranian Oil Co. case (United Kingdom v Iran)* I.C.J. Rep., 93 (1952). Iran successfully disputed jurisdiction on the basis that the agreement between Iran and Anglo-Persian Oil Company was not a treaty between Iran and the United Kingdom (*ibid.*, 112).

Members of the Tribunal 43

appoint its members.[10] The ILC Draft Convention was not accepted by the General Assembly and thus a convention did not eventuate. However, the work did identify the key difficulties in constituting arbitral tribunals, particularly where one of the parties does not take part in the proceedings. It is noteworthy that the arbitration provisions in the concession agreements with Libya enabled the Libyan arbitrations to proceed even though Libya did not appoint its arbitrators or appear before the tribunals.[11]

The provisions of the UNCITRAL rules, based on these experiences, ensure that neither party can jeopardise the functioning of the Iran–United States Claims Tribunal by failing to appoint arbitrators or by withdrawing its arbitrators from the Tribunal. In both cases the Tribunal can be constituted and it will be able to determine the claims set before it.

The initial appointments[12]

At the end of April 1981 the United States nominated Judge Malcolm Wilkey of the United States Court of Appeals, District of Columbia Circuit, and private attorneys Howard M. Holtzmann of New York and Richard M. Mosk of California as members of the Tribunal.[13] Judge Wilkey was unable to take up his appointment owing to the work load of the Court of Appeals.[14] The United States government appointed George M. Aldrich as his replacement. Mr Aldrich was a private attorney in Washington who had acted on behalf of the Department of State and other government departments. He had previously been employed in the Department of State and had been a member of the International Law Commission. Mr Holtzmann and Mr Aldrich are unique in that they have served as arbitrators from initial appointment for the first decade and it is anticipated they will serve until the conclusion of the business of the Tribunal.

Iran nominated ten arbitrators, envisaging a Tribunal of thirty members, able to sit in ten panels. These ten nominations were not made public, since the Iranian Foreign Minister wished to ascertain whether the nominations were acceptable.[15]

---

[10] Article 4 of the Draft Convention annexed to *Report on Arbitral Procedure*, Schelle (Special Rapporteur), Yearbook of I.L.C., 1, 12 (1957).
[11] The three Libyan arbitrations are *Liamco* v *Libya* 20 I.L.M., 1 (1981), *Topco* v *Libya* 53 I.L.R., 389 (1979), and *BP* v *Libya* 53 I.L.R., 297 (1979). These arbitrations are extensively considered in Chapters Eight, Nine and Fourteen of this work.
[12] A list of all the Tribunal members is found in Appendix II.
[13] I.A.L.R., 2875 (1981); Carter, *The Iran–United States Claims Tribunal: Observations on the First Year*, 29 U.C.L.A. Law Review, 1093 (1982).
[14] I.A.L.R., 2950 (1981).
[15] I.A.L.R., 2975 (1981).

The United States government, after holding discussions with the claimants, decided to appoint seven additional members, but was unable to reach agreement with Iran on the size of the Tribunal.[16] Iran subsequently notified the United States that it wished to nominate only three members, referring to the costs and the complexity of enlarging the basic nine-member Tribunal. The three arbitrators named were Mahomoud M. Kashani, Seyyed Hossein Enayat and Shafie Shafeiei, all of whom were professors of law and practising lawyers in Tehran.[17]

The six members appointed by Iran and the United States met at The Hague from May 8, 1981 to appoint the remaining three members. On June 9, 1981 they announced their agreement to appoint Judge Gunnar Lagergren of Sweden, Judge Pierre Bellet of France and Judge Nils Mangard of Sweden as the remaining three members of the Tribunal. All three neutral members had extensive involvement in international arbitrations and were jurists of high standing. Judge Lagergren had been the President of the Court of Appeal of Western Sweden, Judge Bellet was a former Chief Justice of the French Supreme Court and Judge Mangard was a Judge of the Court of Appeal of Stockholm.

Judge Lagergren was appointed the President of the Tribunal by the six members appointed by Iran and the United States. Each of the three neutral members became Chairmen of the three Chambers of the Tribunal.

Once the nine members of the Tribunal were appointed the Tribunal was in a position to establish its procedure and adjudicate upon claims.

Challenges to arbitrators

Judge Mangard

Within six months of the appointment of the neutral arbitrators Iran alleged that Judge Mangard was disqualified from acting as a neutral arbitrator, thus setting in motion the challenge procedure of Articles 9 to 12 of the UNCITRAL rules. The challenge procedure led to one of the first decisions of the Tribunal.

The agent for Iran initially wrote direct to Judge Mangard on January 1, 1982 stating:[18]

... that the Islamic Republic of Iran hereby disqualifies your Honour as a "neutral" arbitrator to the Iran–United States Claims Tribunal and Chairman of its Chamber No. 3 and opposes your participation in deciding huge numbers of highly controversial and politically sensitive disputes between the Islamic Republic of Iran and the United States of America.

---

[16] I.A.L.R., 2874 (1981).
[17] I.A.L.R., 3119 (1981).
[18] 1 IRAN–U.S.C.T.R., 509, 515 (1981–82).

The reasons for the "disqualification" were set out in an attached enclosure noting that Judge Mangard had "... unfortunately taken a position accusing the Islamic Republic of Iran of condemning executions" [sic].[19] Iran considered Judge Mangard was "... morally and legally disqualifie[d] ... from rendering any fair judgement in connection with acts attributed to the Islamic Republic before this Tribunal..."[20] and thus Iran requested that he resign from the Tribunal. Judge Mangard did not resign.

The agent of the United States responded to the President of the Tribunal, disagreeing with the Iranian view. The agent for the United States also wrote to the Secretary General of the Permanent Court of Arbitration stating that the United States did not accept the challenge and requesting the Secretary General to designate an appointing authority in accordance with the UNCITRAL rules. On January 11, 1982 the agent for Iran sent to the President of the Tribunal a copy of a note addressed to the United States which stated that the previous letter of Iran should be considered as "the official challenge" to Judge Mangard.[21] The Tribunal heard argument from both parties, and owing to the urgency of the matter reached its decision on January 13, 1982.

The Tribunal, by a majority, noted as a general principle that any right of a state party to remove an arbitrator from office by unilateral decision would seriously impair the integrity of the arbitration process.[22] On the question of the terms of the agreement between Iran and the United States the Tribunal stated:[23]

... [I]t is an element of absolutely fundamental importance in international law that sovereign States must respect the international agreements to which they have become parties. Neither the Claims Settlement Declaration nor any of the other instruments relating to the settlement of disputes between Iran and the United States contains anything that can be interpreted as indicating that alternative means for removing an arbitrator exist.

Thus Article III, Paragraph 2, of the Claims Settlement Declaration makes it abundantly clear that the only method by which an arbitrator may be removed from office is through challenge by a party and decision by the Appointing Authority pursuant to Articles 11 and 12 of the UNCITRAL Rules.

Thus the Tribunal treated the letter of January 1, 1982 as a challenge to Judge Mangard pursuant to Article 11 of the UNCITRAL rules. Two Iranian arbitrators filed a separate dissenting opinion.[24] They considered

---

[19] *Ibid.*
[20] *Ibid.*
[21] *Re Judge Mangard*, 1 IRAN–U.S.C.T.R., 111 (1981–82).
[22] *Ibid.*, 114.
[23] *Ibid.*
[24] Messrs Kashani and Shafeiei filed the separate dissenting opinions; 1 IRAN–U.S.C.T.R., 111, 115 (1981–82).

that since the two governments had appointed Judge Mangard by consent, the withdrawal of such consent by Iran amounted to the disqualification of Judge Mangard as an appointed arbitrator.[25] Since the grounds for the "disqualification" were political the Iranian arbitrators considered that the challenge procedure of the UNCITRAL rules was irrelevant "since a political decision is not subject to judicial scrutiny".[26]

Following the ruling of the Tribunal the Secretary General of the Permanent Court of Arbitration, in accordance with UNCITRAL rules, appointed Dr Moons, the President of the Supreme Court of the Netherlands, as the appointing authority in January 1982. Dr Moons's decision, handed down in March 1982, dealt with two separate points. The first point concerned his competence as appointing authority to hear the challenge; the second point concerned the merits of the challenge.

In considering the first point Dr Moons referred to the provisions of Article III(2) of the Claims Settlement Declaration, incorporating the UNCITRAL rules as modified by the parties or the Tribunal, and to the relevant articles of the UNCITRAL rules, being Articles 6, 10, 11 and 12. These articles had not been modified by either the parties or the Tribunal. Articles 10 to 12 cover the challenge procedure, whilst Article 6 is concerned with the designation of the appointing authority, who must adjudicate upon the challenge. Under Article 6(2) of the rules, either party may request the Secretary General of the Permanent Court of Arbitration to designate an appointing authority.

The letter of the agent of the United States of January 8, 1982 to the Secretary General of the Permanent Court of Arbitration requesting that he designate an appointing authority was in accordance with Article 6. Dr Moons's decision never specifically stated that he had been appointed pursuant to the letter from the agent for the United States. He did, however, reject the contention of Iran that he had not been properly appointed, noting that the power of the Secretary General of the Permanent Court of Arbitration to designate an appointing authority was not dependant upon a decision of the Iran–United States Claims Tribunal.[27] He also rejected the view that the Secretary General of the Permanent Court of Arbitration was unable to designate an appointing authority until the parties had been unable to reach agreement.[28]

Since Dr Moons had been designated by the Secretary General of the Permanent Court of Arbitration in response to a request by the United States he concluded:[29]

[25] *Ibid.*, 116.
[26] *Ibid.*, 116.
[27] *Ibid.*, 513.
[28] *Ibid.*, 514.
[29] *Ibid.*, 514.

Since we do not consider that there are any other grounds either which could prevent Us from having authority to take cognizance of the case instituted before Us, We declare that We are entitled to hear the matter.

Dr Moons went on to consider the merits of the challenge. However, in doing so he was as much concerned with the form of the challenge as with the actual merits.

He first noted that the only means to remove an arbitrator from office was the challenge procedure of Articles 10 to 12 of the UNCITRAL rules, thus rejecting Iran's contention that it had the right to disqualify arbitrators in whom it had lost confidence. Thus Dr Moons stated:[30]

The consequence of the above considerations is that the objections lodged by a High Contracting Party to a duly appointed arbitrator will be admissible only if they satisfy *inter alia* the following conditions:

(a) The High Contracting Party must intend to use the legal remedy of a challenge as provided for in the UNCITRAL Rules;
(b) The regulations contained in Article 11 of the Rules must be observed.

Dr Moons found that Iran had not satisfied either condition. Firstly, Iran had stated in submissions that it could "see no relevance to Article 11 of the UNCITRAL Rules".[31] Accordingly Dr Moons did not consider that Iran intended to make a legal challenge. Secondly, Iran had not specified the particulars of its challenge in accordance with Article 11:[32]

These documents contain neither a sufficiently clear description of the circumstances giving rise to the accusation levelled against Judge Mangard of a "lack of neutrality", nor any indication of the dates on which the actual event on which the disqualification is based took place and on which this event came to the knowledge of the party alleging disqualification. This notification cannot therefore be said to state "the reason for the challenge" within the meaning of Article 11 of the UNCITRAL Rules.

Dr Moons rejected the challenge without considering whether or not Judge Mangard had made any statements condemning executions by Iran, and whether or not such statements would affect his neutrality. Through failing to comply with the procedures of the UNCITRAL rules, Iran's challenge never received full consideration.

The two decisions, being among the first judicial pronouncements arising from the establishment of the Tribunal, served the purpose, particularly for Iran, of demonstrating that the Tribunal was a judicial and not a political body. It was necessary to present arguments in a form familiar to Western jurists, especially since the three neutral arbitrators and

[30] *Ibid.*, 517.
[31] *Ibid.*, 517.
[32] *Ibid.*, 518.

President Briner

In July 1989 Iran filed a Notice of Challenge in the form of a letter to the appointing authority, Dr Moons. In doing so Iran followed the required procedure set down in the Tribunal rules, and referred specifically to Articles 9 to 12 of the rules.

The grounds for the challenge set out in the Notice of Challenge were "Mr Briner's totally improper course of conduct in the proceedings of Case No. 39, *Phillips Petroleum Company Iran* v *The Islamic Republic of Iran and National Iranian Oil Company*".[33]

The basis of the challenge was the account of the proceedings set out by the Iranian arbitrator, Judge Khalilian, in his "Supplemental to the Statement" in connection with the *Phillips* case filed in June 1989.[34] Judge Khalilan alleged that Mr Briner and Mr Aldrich, the third member of the Chamber, had had access to a memorandum prepared by Chase Econometrics which was used as the basis of the discounted cash flow calculations forming the basis of the amount of damages awarded to the claimant.[35] This memorandum was not made available to Judge Khalilian. It was also alleged that the memorandum had been used as the basis of a report by Morgan Stanley on the valuation of the contractual right to extract oil from the Phillips concession. Mr Briner was a director of Morgan Stanley S.A. and this relationship had served as a basis for a challenge and subsequent withdrawal by Mr Briner from *Case No. 55*. Accordingly Iran argued that Mr Briner should have also withdrawn from the *Phillips* case. In addition Judge Khalilian also stated that the award contained various computational errors which were not satisfactorily rectified but instead were the subject of negotiations during the deliberations by the Tribunal on the size of the award.

The Notice Of Challenge included an attached memorandum setting out Judge Khalilian's allegations in detail and elaborating on the basis of the challenge.[36] In many respects the memorandum constituted an appeal against the *Phillips* decision, setting out mistakes of law and inconsistencies with other Tribunal decisions, in particular the *Amoco International*

---

[33] 21 IRAN–U.S.C.T.R., 309, 318 (1989).

[34] *Phillips Petroleum Co.* v *Iran* 21 IRAN–U.S.C.T.R., 79, 245 (1989). Judge Khalilian had made an initial statement in June 1989 indicating why it would have been premature to sign the award. This statement was an extensive recitation of the history of the case, setting out Judge Khalilian's views of the errors, of both substance and procedure, that had been committed by the two other members of the Chamber, Messers Briner and Aldrich.

[35] The discounted cash flow calculations are dealt with at length in Chapter Nine.

[36] 21 IRAN–U.S.C.T.R., 322 (1989).

Finance[37] case, which also dealt with the valuation of expropriated oil concessions.[38]

Mr Briner had previously made a strong rebuttal of the statement that had been made by Judge Khalilian in June 1989, considering it necessary to make it "for the sake of the record".[39] He set out the process of consultation that had occurred between the arbitrators since the hearing of the *Phillips* case had been completed. He stated that there had been extensive consultations between all three arbitrators but that they had been unable to agree on an appropriate award. Accordingly a majority, consisting of Mr Briner and Mr Aldrich, signed the award.

Dr Moons, the appointing authority, dealt with the challenge in September 1989.[40] He essentially rejected the factual allegations made by Judge Khalilian, in particular the allegation that Mr Aldrich had communicated a memorandum to Judge Briner, although he noted that Mr Aldrich's legal assistant had made DCF calculations and passed these to Mr Briner. Based on his investigation, he determined that these calculations were not instrumental in the award, noting that the award stated that "the Tribunal has decided to refrain from performing an alternative DCF calculation".[41] Significantly, the appointing authority would not consider the deliberations of the Tribunal *in camera*, since the proper functioning of the Tribunal depends on an arbitrator being able to "put forward his opinions and arguments in camera in full freedom, without fear of being called upon by the parties to account for them".[42]

Mr Noori

In February 1990 the claimant in the case of *Carlson v Iran and Melli Industrial Group*[43] lodged a challenge to the Iranian arbitrator in Chamber One, Mr Assadollah Noori, on the grounds that from 1980 to 1982 he had been the General Counsel of the Organisation of Nationalised Industries of Iran (NIOI), which controlled the respondent, Melli Industrial Group (MIG). Carlson argued that this gave "rise to justifiable doubts as to his impartiality or independence in deciding cases to which NIOI is an interested party and, accordingly, he should not be permitted to serve as an arbitrator in this case".[44]

The challenge was heard by the appointing authority, Dr Moons, and his decision was handed down in August 1990. Dr Moons noted that

---

[37] 15 IRAN–U.S.C.T.R., 189 (1987).
[38] See Chapter Nine.
[39] 21 IRAN–U.S.C.T.R., 240–1 (1989).
[40] 21 *Ibid.*, 384.
[41] *Ibid.*, 390.
[42] *Ibid.*, 387 and 394.
[43] *Documents Relating to the Challenge*, 24 IRAN–U.S.C.T.R., 309 (1990)
[44] *Ibid.*, 309.

when Mr Noori was appointed to the Tribunal he had disclosed to the President the cases in which he had been involved as a legal adviser at The Hague branch of the Bureau for International Legal Services for Iran. He did not disclose his role as General Counsel of NIOI. However, Dr Moons was not convinced "that Mr Noori as Head of the NIOI Legal Office or as a member of the NIOI Council or in any other capacity has actually been involved in the management of NIOI or in the control of that management by NIOI".[45] In the conclusion to his decision Dr Moons noted that MIG was one of many companies under the purview of NIOI. As a result Mr Noori "had in no way been involved in Case No. 248, especially not as Head of the NIOI Legal Office or as counsellor or adviser to any of the respondents in this case".[46] Accordingly "Mr Noori has wrongly been accused of having infringed article 9 of the Tribunal Rules"[47] and the challenge was dismissed.

Resignation of arbitrators

The UNCITRAL rules governing the procedure of the Tribunal also provide for the resignation and replacement of arbitrators.[48] Since the Tribunal was originally constituted there has been a considerable change in the arbitral personnel through resignation. At the end of the first decade of the Tribunal's business the only two remaining original appointees were Messrs Aldrich and Holtzmann, both of whom had been appointed by the United States at the outset. The initial resignations set the procedure to be followed for the future, particularly in relation to the neutral arbitrators.

The first arbitrator to resign was one of three neutral arbitrators, Mr Bellet, Chairman of Chamber Three of the Tribunal. He resigned from the Tribunal in December 1982.[49] His letter to President Lagergren cited as reasons delays in proceedings, health, and family considerations.[50] The Chamber chaired by Mr Bellet was notable for the relatively large volume of cases it dealt with, in comparison with the two other Chambers. Similarly the Chamber did not lightly grant extensions of time for filing documents or hearing interlocutory applications.

Mr Bellet's resignation was not immediately effective, and he agreed to remain in office until a replacement arbitrator could be named, although he indicated he would be leaving on August 1, 1983 if no replacement had

---

[45] *Ibid.*, 323.
[46] *Ibid.*, 324.
[47] *Ibid.*
[48] Article 13 of the UNCITRAL rules governs resignations of arbitrators.
[49] I.A.L.R., 5168 (1983).
[50] *Ibid.*

been appointed. The process of replacing Mr Bellet set the procedure for subsequent replacements of the neutral arbitrators.

Initially Iran and the United States wished to agree on a replacement arbitrator, and a number of meetings were held between the two parties in an attempt to reach such an agreement. Iran reportedly wished a Moslem to be appointed. The United States was reportedly more concerned with the competence than with the nationality or religion of the successor.

The two parties did agree in January 1983 that if they could not agree on Mr Bellet's successor either party could request the appointing authority to make the choice in accordance with Article 13 of the rules.[51] On March 1, 1983 the United States agent wrote to the appointing authority, Dr Moons, requesting that he name a successor to Mr Bellet.[52]

Dr Moons initially submitted a list of six potential candidates to Iran and the United States. The two parties were unable to agree upon any of the six candidates, and Dr Moons was required to select the replacement arbitrator. His choice was Professor Riphagen of the University of Rotterdam, legal adviser to the Dutch Foreign Ministry. Professor Riphagen was a member of the International Law Commission and was the Special Rapporteur on State Responsibility. Professor Riphagen took up the appointment in August 1983 and remained a member of the Tribunal until his resignation toward the end of 1984.[53]

The Iranian arbitrators have been subject to a much higher turnover than the United States or neutral arbitrators. The first such resignation raised some procedural problems.

In August 1983 the Iranian government notified the Tribunal that Judge Sani, who replaced Professor Enayat, had resigned from the Tribunal, effective August 10, 1983.[54] The United States protested, stating that a resignation was not effective until accepted by the Tribunal, and that Chamber Three should continue its business until the resignation was effective.[55] On September 5 the Tribunal voted to accept Judge Sani's resignation, to be effective when his replacement was able to assume his duties.[56] Chamber Three made a number of awards after August 10 and prior to Judge Sani's successor taking up his appointment.[57] In each of

---

[51] I.A.L.R., 6124 (1983).
[52] *Ibid.*
[53] I.A.L.R., 6849 (1983).
[54] I.A.L.R., 7037 (1983).
[55] *Ibid.* Judge Sani was a member of Chamber Three.
[56] I.A.L.R., 7154 (1983).
[57] *Chas T. Main International Inc.* v *Mahb Consulting Engineers Inc.* 3 IRAN–U.S.C.T.R., 270 (1983); *Craig* v *Ministry of Energy of Iran* 3 IRAN–U.S.C.T.R., 280 (1983); *Blout Bros Corp.* v *Ministry of Housing and Development* 3 IRAN–U.S.C.T.R., 225 (1983); *Warnecke and Associates* v *Bank Mellat* 3 IRAN–U.S.C.T.R., 256 (1983); *Woodward-Clyde Consultants* v *Iran* 3 IRAN–U.S.C.T.R., 239 (1983). In all cases the Chamber

these awards the Tribunal appended an explanation for the failure of Judge Sani to sign the awards.[58]

The Tribunal noted that the letter of the Iranian government did not provide any reasons for the purported resignation.[59] In a meeting of the full Tribunal, convened following receipt of the letter, the President stated that the Tribunal had not received valid reasons for Judge Sani's absence, and that the Tribunal had not authorised the absence.[60]

The President also stated that the Tribunal would prefer Chamber Three to determine the legal consequence of that absence in the cases pending before it.[61] The Chairman of Chamber Three, Judge Mangard, informed Judge Sani that the awards were to be finalised and signed prior to his resignation becoming effective.[62] Judge Sani replied stating that he considered his resignation to Iran to be effective, and therefore he was no longer authorised to participate in the issuance of awards, except for the preparation and drafting of awards that had already been announced.[63] Chamber Three noted that this reply did not indicate that it would be physically impossible for him to take part in deliberations and thus proceeded to sign the awards in his absence pursuant to Article 32(4) of the Tribunal rules.[64]

Mr Mosk's additional comments concerning the reasons for the absence of the signature in *Craig v Ministry of Energy of Iran*[65] made extensive reference to international law and the municipal laws of Iran and the United States concerning the right of arbitral tribunals to proceed with their work after the resignation or absence of an arbitrator. He concluded that there was ample authority for the Tribunal to proceed with its work despite the circumstances concerning Judge Sani's absence.[66]

In early September Iran nominated Dr Ansari, a judge in Iran, to replace Judge Sani.[67] Dr Ansari assumed his office in October 1983.[68]

The resignations of Mr Bellet and Mr Sani raised the problem of

had heard the parties and had held meetings deliberating upon the awards prior to the purported resignation of Judge Sani on August 10, 1983.

[58] This statement was identical in all cases, with the exception of *Craig v Ministry of Energy in Iran*, in which Mr Mosk made additional comments concerning the reasons for the absence of Judge Sani's signature.
[59] From *Craig v Ministry of Energy* 3 IRAN–U.S.C.T.R., 280, 292 (1983).
[60] *Ibid.*, 292.
[61] *Ibid.*, 292.
[62] *Ibid.*, 292.
[63] *Ibid.*, 292.
[64] *Ibid.*, 923; Article 32(4) states: "An award shall be signed by the arbitrators and it shall contain the date on which and the place where the award was made. Where there are three arbitrators and one of them fails to sign, the awards shall state the reason for the absence of the signature."
[65] 3 IRAN–U.S.C.T.R., 280, 294–6 (1983).
[66] *Ibid.*, 294.
[67] I.A.L.R., 7155 (1983).
[68] *Ibid.*

Members of the Tribunal 53

dealing with claims which have been part heard by the arbitration who is resigning. The resignation of one of the United States-appointed arbitrators, Mr Mosk in January 1984, provided an appropriate solution. Mr Mosk remained in office for the purpose of completing proceedings in respect of claims which were part heard.[69]

The crisis of 1984[70]

On September 3, 1984 an event unprecedented in the history of arbitration occurred at the Tribunal. Judge Mangard, one of the third-country arbitrators, was assaulted by two of the Iranian arbitrators, Messrs Kashani and Shafeiei, as he entered the Tribunal building.

The President of the Tribunal immediately suspended all Tribunal proceedings in order to resolve the situation.[71] He did, however, form a special Chamber to enable awards to be made on agreed terms and for parties to terminate proceedings.[72] So far as the United States was concerned the only possible resolution of the crisis was the removal of the offending Iranian arbitrators. Moreover, the Iranian government indicated that the behaviour of the two arbitrators was unacceptable.

The United States requested by way of the challenge procedure that the two Iranian arbitrators be disqualified.[73] Under Article 12 of the Tribunal rules such challenges could only be determined by Dr Moons, the appointing authority. Dr Moons, however, requested the Secretary General of the Permanent Court of Arbitration, who had appointed him, to relieve him of the responsibility for determining challenges.

The government of Iran forestalled the challenge procedure by appointing two new arbitrators at the end of November 1984 to replace Messrs Kashani and Shafeiei. The two new arbitrators were Messrs Bahrami, who had been the chief legal adviser at the Iranian government's Bureau of International Legal Services at The Hague, and Mostafavi, who had been the director of the Ministry of Justice. There had been some delay before they were appointed, and they were not available to assume their duties until January 1985, four months after the incident which led to the crisis. Some commentators believe that this delay arose from the desire of

---

[69] This practice became known as the "Mosk rule" whereby retiring arbitrators would remain in office for the purpose of completing decisions on claims which were part heard.

[70] All the relevant documents relating to the crisis are contained in 7 IRAN–U.S.C.T.R., 281–316 (1984).

[71] Presidential Order No. 27, from 7 IRAN–U.S.C.T.R., 281 (1984). The suspension was later extended indefinitely by Presidential Order No. 29.

[72] Presidential Order No. 29, from 7 IRAN–U.S.C.T.R., 301 (1984).

[73] The full text of the United States challenge is set out in 7 IRAN–U.S.C.T.R., 289–301 (1984).

Iran to pressure Messrs Mangard and Riphagen into resigning from the Tribunal.

As soon as the new Iranian arbitrators had been announced the newly appointed President of the Tribunal, Professor Bockstiegal, ordered the resumption of the proceedings of the Tribunal from December 6, 1984.[74] The Chambers could not be reconvened until the new Iranian arbitrators took up their appointments, and thus the President ordered the continuation of the special Chamber established by President Lagergren until such time as the Chambers were reconvened. In January 1985 with the arrival of the new Iranian arbitrators the Tribunal assumed normal business.

The resolution of the crisis allowed a new era of co-operation at the Tribunal. When the neutral arbitrators, Messrs Riphagen and Mangard, resigned in late 1984 and early 1985 respectively, the Iranian and United States agents were able to agree upon two replacement arbitrators without recourse to the appointing authority.

This new spirit of reasoned discussion between the arbitrators augured well for the proceedings of the Tribunal after the crisis of 1984. The Iranian and United States arbitrators continued to hold widely diverging views on a number of key issues, particularly where the development of international law, as reflected in the expropriation and unjust enrichment claims, had led to a dichotomy between the developed and developing nations. However, the business of the Tribunal was conducted in a more cordial and expeditious manner than during what may be described as the first phase of the Tribunal from June 1981 to October 1984.

Conclusion

The tensions between Iran and the United States have been most starkly presented in the appointment, challenge and resignation of arbitrators. The first case heard by the Tribunal concerned a challenge by Iran to a neutral arbitrator on the grounds of lack of impartiality. Iran's challenge did not comply with the UNCITRAL rules and thus was rejected on this basis by the appointing authority. This decision of the appointing authority and the related decision of the Tribunal were a clear indication to Iran of the legal nature of the proceedings of the Tribunal irrespective of the underlying political tensions between the two states. The very purpose of the Tribunal was to remove the claims from the political arena to the neutrality of the legal arena. However, as noted by De Visscher:[75]

> This separation from politics requires habits and moral traditions which are not shared in equal degree by all peoples, and even less by those which only recently have acquired an independent position in the international sense.

[74] Presidential Order No. 33, from 7 IRAN–U.S.C.T.R., 316 (1984).
[75] De Visscher, *Reflections on the Present Prospects of International Adjudication*, 50 A.J.I.L., 467, 468 (1956).

It took some time for the Iranian arbitrators to place their political objectives within the framework of international law rather than attack the integrity of the arbitral process. This appreciation of the essentially legal nature of the Tribunal was not complete until the replacement of the Iranian arbitrators Kashani and Shafeiei following the incident of September 1984. Their replacement, particularly when coupled with the resignation of the neutral arbitrators, Mangard and Riphagen, meant the arbitrators were better able to articulate in their written judgments the deep differences on the development of international law which exist between Western nations and the developing nations in the awards and decisions of the Tribunal.

The successful operation of the Tribunal, given the depth of the political antagonism between Iran and the United States, has rested heavily on the development of two independent aspects of the international arbitral process. First, the Tribunal is able to render awards and decisions notwithstanding the non-participation by arbitrators chosen by one or other of the states parties. This has encouraged Iran to continue to participate in the Tribunal to influence awards in its favour rather than to abandon the forum to the United States claimants and Western arbitrators. Second, there is the continuing desire of the arbitrators of Iran and the United States to verify the integrity of the arbitral process and to instil confidence in the litigating parties in arbitration as a way to settle disputes. It is undoubted that the success of the Iran–United States Claims Tribunal was essential if the Tribunal was to serve as a model for other states to resolve their differences by arbitration.

PART TWO
The substantive jurisdiction of the Tribunal

CHAPTER FOUR

Nationality of claimants before the Tribunal

The provisions of the Claims Settlement Declaration

Introduction

The Iran–United States Claims Tribunal was established to resolve claims by Iranian and United States nationals against the governments of the United States and Iran respectively. It cannot entertain claims from persons of any other nationality. Thus one of the most important preliminary questions considered by the Tribunal has been the nationality of claimants.

The provisions of the Claims Settlement Declaration governing the nationality of claimants are broadly expressed. Although they provide rules for the determination of the nationality of both natural and juridical persons they do not take into account the various complications of nationality. In particular the issues of dual nationality, claims by shareholders of corporations not entitled to claim, claims by parties who are members of partnerships, and what constitutes control of corporations are not resolved by the provisions of the Claims Settlement Declaration. The Tribunal therefore has had to formulate detailed rules on these issues in its awards and decisions in order to apply the provisions of the Claims Settlement Declaration to particular claimants.

The Claims Settlement Declaration

The purpose of the Tribunal set out in Article II(1) of the Claims Settlement Declaration is to determine "... claims of nationals of the United States against Iran and claims of nationals of Iran against the United

States...".[1] This paramount rule governs both the nationality of claimants and the jurisdiction of the Tribunal. In the first case heard by the Tribunal, *Iran v United States (Case A/2)*,[2] Iran requested the Tribunal to determine whether the Algiers Declarations conferred jurisdiction upon the Tribunal over claims by the government of Iran against nationals of the United States. The Tribunal held that the jurisdiction of the Tribunal was limited to claims by nationals of one party against the government of the other party. The Tribunal stated:[3]

> It can easily be seen that the parties set up very carefully a list of the claims... which could be submitted to the arbitral tribunal. As a matter of fact, they knew very well that such a Tribunal could not have a wider jurisdiction than that which was specifically decided on by mutual agreement.
>
> They mentioned only on that list, aside from requests for interpretation and disputes between governments, *claims which would be made by nationals of one of the two states.*

Thus Article II(1) established the basic principle that claims can only be made by nationals of Iran and the United States and not by their governments. The definition of "national", particularly in relation to corporate claimants, has been progressively evolving, especially in claim settlement agreements. An additional provision, Article VII(1), provides a definition of "national" which accords with recent United States practice, particularly for corporate nationals.[4]

> A "national" of Iran or the United States, as the case may be, means (a) a natural person who is a citizen of Iran or the United States; and (b) a corporation or other legal entity which is organised under the laws of Iran or the United States or any of its states or territories, the District of Columbia or the Commonwealth of Puerto Rico, if, collectively, natural persons who are citizens of such country hold, directly or indirectly, an interest in such corporation or entity equivalent to fifty percent or more of its capital stock.

The Declaration, however, did not leave the matter there. Article VII(2) included a definition of "Claims of Nationals":

> "Claims of Nationals" of Iran or the United States, as the case may be, means claims owned continuously, from the date on which the claim arose to the date on which these agreements enter into force, by nationals of that state, including claims that are owned indirectly by such nationals through ownership of capital stock or other proprietary interests in juridical persons, provided that the ownership interests of such nationals, collectively, were sufficient at the time the claim

---

[1] The two other heads of jurisdiction are government-to-government claims (Article II(2)), and the interpretation and performance of the Algiers Declarations (Article II(3)). In neither case does the nationality of the claimant arise.

[2] 1 IRAN–U.S.C.T.R., 101 (1981–82).

[3] *Ibid.*, 103; emphasis added.

[4] Refer to Chapter Five, *infra*.

arose to control the corporation or the entity, and provided, further, that the corporation or other entity is not itself entitled to bring a claim under the terms of this Agreement.

The two paragraphs of Article VII have been the source of considerable litigation in the Tribunal.

The limitation in Article VII(1) of "nationals" to natural persons who are citizens of either party, without additional clarification, has meant that the Tribunal has had to determine whether persons having citizenship of both Iran and the United States are able to make claims before the Tribunal. Similarly the definition of corporate claimants as entities which are organised under the laws of either party and whose stock is 50 per cent owned by natural persons of such party has meant that the Tribunal has had to establish the evidential rules claimants must comply with in order to satisfy the requirements of Article VII(1).[5]

Article VII(2) sets out two requirements which have been considered by the Tribunal. The first is the requirement for continuous ownership of claims from the date they arose to the date the agreement entered into force by nationals of the claimant state.[6] The second issue relates to the right of shareholders who are nationals of either party to make claims in respect of corporate entities not entitled to make claims provided that the nationals control, directly or indirectly, such corporate entities.[7]

Natural persons and dual nationality

The issue of dual nationality was first considered by the full Tribunal and by Chamber Two of the Tribunal. The full Tribunal was requested by Iran, as an interpretive issue pursuant to Article II(3) of the Claims Settlement Declaration, to determine whether claims filed by citizens of the United States who are also citizens of Iran are inadmissible against Iran.[8] Before the full Tribunal could consider this question, Chamber Two made two awards allowing persons who had citizenship of Iran and the United States to make claims against Iran.[9] Chamber Two, by a majority, applied the rule of real and effective nationality enunciated by the International Court of Justice in *Nottebohm (Liechtenstein v Guatemala)*.[10]

---

[5] This issue concerning evidence before the Tribunal will be addressed in Chapter Thirteen.
[6] This is an accepted requirement of claims settlement tribunals which are empowered to hear claims of one state against another state.
[7] This issue will be considered in Chapter Five.
[8] *Iran v United States (Case A/18)* 5 IRAN-U.S.C.T.R., 251 (1984).
[9] *Esphahanian v Bank Tejarat* 2 IRAN-U.S.C.T.R., 157 (1983) and *Golpira v Iran* 2 IRAN-U.S.C.T.R., 171 (1983).
[10] I.C.J. Rep., 4 (1955).

The full Tribunal handed down its decision over a year later and also accepted the principle of real and effective nationality. However, the Iranian arbitrators filed a lengthy dissent from the Tribunal decision. Subsequently the decision of the full Tribunal has been applied in a large number of claims by persons having dual nationality.

International law relating to the espousal of claims of dual nationals

Dual nationality arises in a number of contexts in international law. In the present case dual nationality is relevant in two of its aspects. First, the validity of the grant of nationality in international law and secondly, the espousal of claims by a state in respect of one of its nationals against a state whose nationality that person also possesses.

It is an established principle of international law that international tribunals may examine a grant of nationality in cases of naturalisation to determine whether there is sufficient connection between the state and its nationals for the state to espouse claims of such nationals against other states.[11] The second aspect arises from the traditional rule of diplomatic protection that a state may not espouse the claim of a national against a state whose nationality that person also possesses.[12] It must therefore be determined the extent to which the Iran–United States Claims Tribunal is an exercise of diplomatic protection and, if it is, whether or not the traditional rule is still applicable.

Recognition of nationality in international law

It is well recognised that every state is competent to determine who are its nationals, this being essentially a question of municipal law. Nevertheless such municipal law must comply with international law as it relates to the granting of nationality if states are to be assured that the grant of nationality will be recognised by other states. The Hague Convention of 1930 "Concerning Certain Questions Relating to the Conflict of Nationality Laws"[13] confirmed existing law of the time, in Article 1:

> It is for each state to determine under its own laws who are its nationals. This law shall be recognised by other states in so far as it is consistent with international conventions, international custom and the principles of law generally recognised with regard to nationality.

---

[11] *Nottebohm Case (Liechtenstein v Guatemala)* I.C.J. Rep., 4 (1955); *Salem (United States v Egypt)* II R.I.A.A., 1163 (1931); *Flegenheimer (United States v Italy)* 25 I.L.R., 91 (1958).

[12] This rule is found in the Hague Convention of 1930, Article 4. It had widespread support among jurists and writers during the early part of the twentieth century. See *Diplomatic Protection of a Dual National against a State whose Nationality the Claimant Possesses*, infra.

[13] 179–80 L.N.T.S. 88. The status of the Convention is considered in *Espousal of Claims of Dual Nationals*, infra.

Nationality of claimants

Thus, for a variety of reasons, an individual may be deemed by the municipal law of two or more states to be a national of both those states.[14] So long as a grant of nationality has been made on proper grounds then other states are bound to recognise such nationality irrespective of any other nationality the person may possess.

The limits of this recognition were considered by the International Court of Justice in the *Nottebohm* case.[15] The facts of the case were that Nottebohm was a German national by birth. For most of his life he had lived in Guatemala and he had extensive business interests there. He did not, however, acquire Guatemalan nationality. In 1939 he travelled to Liechtenstein and acquired, on an accelerated basis, the nationality of Liechtenstein to the exclusion of his German nationality. Nottebohm returned to Guatemala in 1940, travelling on his Liechtenstein passport. In 1943 Nottebohm was arrested by Guatemala as an enemy alien and interned in the United States. His property was confiscated by Guatemala. In 1946 he was denied re-entry to Guatemala and travelled to Liechtenstein, where he lived for the next several years. In 1951 Liechtenstein instituted proceedings in the International Court of Justice, claiming the right of diplomatic protection. The Court considered that although the grant of nationality was a matter of municipal law, the right of diplomatic protection *vis-à-vis* other states was a question of international law:[16]

According to the practice of States, to arbitral and judicial decisions and to the opinion of writers, nationality is a legal bond having as its basis a social fact of attachment, a genuine connection of existence, interests and sentiments, together with the existence of reciprocal rights and duties. It may be said to constitute the juridical expression of the fact that the individual upon whom it is conferred, either directly by law or as a result of an act of the authorities, is in fact more closely connected with the population of the State conferring nationality than with that of any other State. Conferred by a State, it only entitles that State to exercise protection *vis-à-vis* another State, if it constitutes a translation into juridical terms of the individual's connection with the State which has made him its national.

The Court held that although Liechtenstein was entitled to grant nationality to Nottebohm it could not be validly invoked against Guatemala. In so holding the Court noted the "long standing and close connection between [Nottebohm] and Guatemala" compared to his "extremely tenuous" connections with Liechtenstein.[17] Moreover the

---

[14] The concept of dual nationality is sufficiently well recognised not to merit comprehensive examination here of the precedents and literature.
[15] I.C.J. Rep., 4 (1955). See also the *Salem case (United States* v *Egypt)* II R.I.A.A., 1163, 1184 (1931), for application of the principle of real and effective nationality to claims against Egypt made by persons having the nationality of Egypt and the United States.
[16] *Ibid.*, 10.
[17] *Ibid.*, 25–6.

Court also noted that international arbitrators had decided numerous cases of dual nationality on the basis of "real and effective" nationality.[18]

The Court, however, considered the principle of real and effective nationality only in respect of espousal of the claim by Liechtenstein against Guatemala. Guatemala did not argue that Nottebohm was its own national and indeed maintained that he was an enemy alien. Thus the question of whether or not a state could espouse the claim of one of its nationals against a state whose nationality that person also possessed did not arise.

The principle that international tribunals can examine a grant of nationality was also accepted by the Italian–United States Conciliation Commission in the case of *Flegenheimer (United States* v *Italy)*.[19] The Commission stated that "abundant doctrine in international law confirms the power of an international court to investigate the existence of the nationality of the claimant".[20]

Diplomatic protection of a dual national against a state whose nationality the claimant possesses

The espousal of claims by a state of one of its nationals against a state whose nationality the claimant also possesses has two aspects relevant to the Iran–United States Claims Tribunal. Firstly, it must be considered whether a state can afford diplomatic protection in respect of claims of its own nationals against a state whose nationality such persons also possess. Secondly, does the concept of diplomatic protection cover the establishment of an international claims tribunal having the attributes of the Iran–United States Claims Tribunal?

Espousal of claims of dual nationals

The problems of the espousal of the claims of dual nationals against a state whose nationality the person also possesses has received considerable attention from both codifiers of international law and arbitral tribunals during the first half of this century.

The major treaty is the Hague Convention of 1930. Article 4 of the Convention states:

A State may not afford diplomatic protection to one of its nationals against a State whose nationality such person also possesses.

Neither Iran nor the United States is a party to the Convention, and therefore this provision is applicable only if it embodies customary international law established by precedents and commentators.

---

[18] *Ibid.*, 22. It is on the basis of these words, referred to further herein, that the majority applied the principle of real and effective nationality to claims against Iran made by persons having the nationality of Iran and the United States.
[19] 25 I.L.R., 91 (1958). This decision will be referred to later in this chapter.
[20] *Ibid.*, 106.

Nationality of claimants

Prior to the Mixed Claims Tribunals established by the peace treaties following World War I and World War II the usual practice had been to deny claims of persons who had the nationality of the respondent state.

The well known case of *Canevaro (Italy v Peru)*,[21] frequently cited in support of the effective nationality theory, in fact tends to confirm that the principle enshrined in Article 4 of the Convention was applicable at the time of the decision. Canevaro had been born in Peru of an Italian father. He had been a candidate for the Peruvian Senate and conducted his business in Peru. He could properly be regarded as a citizen of Peru. The Permanent Court of Arbitration stated:[22]

> Under these circumstances, whatever Rafael Canevaro's status as a national may be in Italy, the Government of Peru has a right to consider him a Peruvian citizen and to deny his status as an Italian claimant.

The Mixed Arbitral Tribunals established by the Treaty of Versailles did, however, allow claims of dual nationals against states whose nationality they also possessed. The various commissions required only that the claimant had the nationality of an Allied state. Thus in *Hein v Hildesheimer Bank*[23] the Anglo-German Commission considered it sufficient that the claimant was a British national residing in Great Britain on January 10, 1920. It was immaterial that Hein still retained his German nationality.

The French–German Tribunal decided the case *Oskiner v German State*[24] on the same principles. The Tribunal interpreted the Treaty of Versailles as permitting claims of nationals of the Allied powers against Germany, without considering whether or not general principles of international law precluded states from providing protection for their nationals against a state whose nationality such persons also possessed. It is also noteworthy that claimants before the Mixed Arbitral Tribunals were able to present their claims direct to the Tribunals, as can claimants before the Iran–United States Claims Tribunal.

Notwithstanding these decisions, the traditional rule of denying such claims was regarded as having general application. In the Anglo-Mexican Special Claims Commission the British agent conceded in *Re Carlos Ollenburg*[25] and *Frederic Adams and Charles Thomas Blackmore v United Mexican States*[26] that British claimants who were nationals of both Britain and Mexico could not make claims before the Commission.

The International Court of Justice has recognised the general applica-

---

[21] II R.I.A.A., 405 (1912).
[22] *Ibid.*
[23] Annual Digest, Case No. 148, 216 (1919–22).
[24] VI T.A.M., 787.
[25] V R.I.A.A., 216 (1931).
[26] V R.I.A.A., 74 (1929).

bility of the principle of Article 4 of the Hague Convention. In *Reparation For Injuries Suffered in the Service of the United Nations*[27] the Court referred to "the ordinary practice whereby a State does not exercise protection against a State which regards him as its own national...".[28] The Court, however, did not consider that this practice prevented the United Nations from bringing an action against a state in respect of persons who were nationals of that state. The traditional principles relating to dual nationality of claimants were not considered to be applicable to claims made by international organisations.

The commissions established after the Second World War represent a significant departure from the traditional rule as reflected in Article 4 of the Hague Convention. The most significant decision is that of *Mergé (United States v Italy)*[29] made by the Italian–United States Conciliation Commission. The decision was made two months after the decision of the International Court of Justice in *Nottebohm*, and applied the principle of real and effective nationality which had been affirmed by the International Court of Justice. However, the application of the principle was expanded to cover claims on behalf of persons having the nationality of both the plaintiff and respondent states.

The facts of *Mergé* were that Mme Mergé was born in the United States and accordingly was a United States national. She married an Italian diplomat and thereafter resided with her husband except for a brief stay in the United States in 1947. She had accquired Italian nationality by virtue of her marriage. The United States invoked the Treaty of Peace stating that all United Nations nationals were entitled to claim, irrespective of whether they had the nationality of the respondent state. Moreover, since Italy was a defeated state the principle embodied in Article 4 of the Hague Convention of 1930 was not applicable. Italy replied that a defeated state could still rely on the principles of international law in interpreting the Treaty of Peace. Therefore the United States could not afford diplomatic protection to one of its nationals against Italy if the claimant also possessed the nationality of Italy.[30]

The Commission rejected the contentions of the United States. It held that the Treaty of Peace was to be interpreted according to the general principles of international law that apply to sovereign states.[31] Since the treaty did not contain any specific provisions relating to dual nationality the question was to be determined by the general principles of international law.[32]

[27] I.C.J. Rep., 174 (1949).
[28] *Ibid.*, 186.
[29] XIV R.I.A.A., 236 (1955).
[30] *Ibid.*, 238–9.
[31] *Ibid.*, 241.
[32] *Ibid.*, 241.

Nationality of claimants

The Commission noted that the case could be determined either in accordance with the general principles relating to diplomatic protection, or by the principle of dominant and effective nationality. It examined the provisions of the Hague Convention, 1930, and the precedents, particularly the *Nottebohm* decision. The Commission considered that there was no irreconcilable opposition between the two principles and noted the fact that the International Court of Justice had accepted both principles.[33] It stated:[34]

> The principle, based on the sovereign equality of states, which excludes diplomatic protection in the case of dual nationality, must yield before the principle of effective nationality whenever such nationality is that of the claiming state. But it must not yield when such predominance is not proved because the first of these principles is generally recognised and may constitute a criterion of practical application for the elimination of any possible uncertainty.

The Commission considered that Mme Mergé did not have dominant United States nationality and therefore the United States government could not present a claim on her behalf. The Italian–United States Conciliation Commission, however, later questioned the scope of the principle enunciated in the *Nottebohm* decision in the *Flegenheimer* case.[35]

The United States argued that Flegenheimer was a United States national on the basis of his father's naturalisation as a United States national some fifty years previously. Alternatively, Italy had treated Flegenheimer as an enemy alien. Italy denied both claims, in particular arguing that Flegenheimer was not a United States national since there was no effective bond of nationality between Flegenheimer and the United States at the relevant time.

The Commission, in considering whether Italy could raise this argument, in view of the fact that there was no question of Flegenheimer being an Italian national, stated:[36]

> The Commission is of the opinion that it is doubtful that the International Court of Justice intended to establish a rule of general international law in requiring in the *Nottebohm Case* that there must exist an effective link between the person and the State in order that the latter may exercise its right of diplomatic protection on behalf of the former.

The Commission held that Flegenheimer was not at the material time a United States national nor had he been treated as an enemy alien by Italy. Accordingly the United States could not make a claim on his behalf. In reaching this decision the Commission did not have to deter-

---
[33] *Ibid.*, 246.
[34] *Ibid.*, 247.
[35] 25 I.L.R., 91, 148 (1958).
[36] *Ibid.*, 148.

mine the issue of real and effective nationality as it had done in the *Mergé* case. Similarly it did not consider whether a claim could be presented against a state in respect of a dual national possessing the nationality of the respondent state.

The legal literature shows increasing acceptance of the dominant nationality theory even for claims made against a state whose nationality the claimant also possesses. Borchard, writing in 1915, and the most frequently cited jurist of this period, stated that "[a] person having dual nationality cannot make one of the countries to which he owes allegiance a defendant before an international Tribunal".[37] Since the *Nottebohm* decision the majority of writers have taken the view that the test of real and effective nationality is applicable to claims by dual nationals against a state of which the claimant is also a national. The decision in *Mergé* is widely cited as an application of the *dicta* of *Nottebohm*.[38] Brownlie accepted that *Nottebohm* did not concern an espousal of a claim against a state of which the claimant was a national but stated:[39]

> The Court did not base its decision on estoppels against Liechtenstein, but rested on the existence or not of a right of protection, an issue the outcome of which would logically affect states in general and not just the parties.

The concept of diplomatic protection

It is an elementary principle of international law that a state is entitled to protect its subjects when injured by acts contrary to international law committed by another state, from whom they have been unable to obtain satisfaction through ordinary channels. By taking up the case of one of its subjects and by resorting to diplomatic action or judicial proceedings on his behalf, a state is in reality asserting its own rights—its right to ensure, in the person of its subjects, respect for the rules of international law.[40]

This statement of the Permanent Court of International Justice accurately reflected international law as it existed at the time of the decision. The decision in the case of the *Mavrommatis Palestine Concessions* turned on a question of jurisdiction, with the United Kingdom contending that the Court could not entertain a private claim.

After making the above observation, the Court noted that "once a state has taken up a case on behalf of one of its subjects before an international tribunal, in the eyes of the latter the state is the sole

---

[37] Borchard, *Diplomatic Protection of Citizens Abroad*, 588 (1915). Borchard was the Special Rapporteur for the Hague Convention of 1930.

[38] Bar Yaacov, *Dual Nationality*, 225 (1961); Joseph, *Nationality and Diplomatic Protection*, 21, 22 (1969); Greig, *International Law*, 532 (1976).

[39] Brownlie, *Principles of Public International Law*, 410 (1990).

[40] *The Mavrommatis Palestine Concessions (Greece v United Kingdom)* P.C.I.J. A.2, 12 (1924). This view was accepted by the jurists of the time; see especially Borchard, *Diplomatic Protection of Citizens Abroad*, 366 (1915).

Nationality of claimants

claimant".[41] Moreover since the state is asserting its own rights it is able to conduct the claim as it sees fit, and is not governed by the contentions of the subject for whom it is providing protection.

The *Mavrommatis Palestine Concession* decision was made at a time when it was considered that the only subjects of international law were states.[42] Since that time there has been increasing recognition that international law may apply to entities other than states, albeit in limited circumstances.

Nevertheless the International Court of Justice, in the 1970 case *Barcelona Traction (Belgium v Spain)*,[43] restated the traditional view that:[44]

[A] State may exercise diplomatic protection by whatever means and to whatever extent it thinks fit, for it is its own right that the State is asserting. Should the natural or legal persons on whose behalf it is acting consider that their rights are not adequately protected they have no remedy at international law.

The Court also noted that the state had complete freedom of action in presenting the claim.[45] However, if the natural or legal person is able to present the case directly then the state will lose control over the claim. The claimant will be able to raise any arguments he deems appropriate, whether or not such arguments meet with the approval of his state.[46]

Thus once the state has lost control of the claim it is not providing diplomatic protection in the traditional sense, even though the state may have established by treaty the forum to resolve the claims. Claims presented directly by individuals in such a forum therefore need not be restricted by the rules relating to nationality of claims espoused directly by states. Since large claimants present their claims direct to the Iran–United States Claims Tribunal the element of diplomatic protection offered by the claimant's state is minimised, at least in respect of these claims.

Awards and decisions of the Tribunal[47]

Introduction

The issue of dual nationality was one of the first considered by the Tribunal. It was first resolved by Chamber Two of the Tribunal, which

---

[41] *Ibid.*, 12.
[42] *Ibid.*, 12. See also Borchard, *Diplomatic Protection of Citizens Abroad* (1915).
[43] I.C.J. Rep., 3 (1970).
[44] *Ibid.*, 44.
[45] *Ibid.* It was noted by the Court that the exercise of diplomatic protection may be determined by political or other considerations completely unrelated to the particular case; I.C.J. Rep., 44 (1970).
[46] *Ibid.*
[47] The issue of dual nationality has arisen in all three Chambers. Although Chamber Two made two awards in which the question of dual nationality was resolved, Iran had already

made two awards in 1983 on the jurisdictional question of dual nationality. However, Iran had also applied to the full Tribunal for a ruling on the validity of claims made by persons possessing the nationality of both states. The awards of Chamber Two affirmed the reasoning of *Nottebohm* and applied the real and effective nationality test. The full Tribunal, in a more fully reasoned decision, also accepted the principle of real and effective nationality as being applicable to persons having the nationality of both Iran and the United states. In both cases the Iranian arbitrators dissented.

The awards of Chamber Two

The facts of both cases are similar, involving claims against Iran by persons who had been born in Iran, but who had subsequently become naturalised citizens of the United States. In *Esphahanian* v *Bank Tejarat*[48] the claimant had been born in Iran of an Iranian father. At the age of seventeen he was sent to study in the United States. In 1958 he was naturalised as a United States citizen. He married a United States citizen. From 1947 until 1970 he resided continuously in the United States, participating in cultural, civic and business activities. However, from 1970 to 1978 he was employed by a United States firm as Middle East area general manager and spent nine months of every year in Iran. To travel to and from Iran he used an Iranian passport. He used his Iranian identity card to open an account with Bank Tejarat in which he deposited part of his income. In addition he held shares as an Iranian nominee in an Iranian subsidiary of a United States company. Esphahanian alleged that Bank Tejarat failed to honour a cheque drawn against the bank.

There was a similarity of facts in the case of *Golpira* v *Iran*.[49] The claimant had been born in Iran in 1927. His father was an army officer in the Iranian army, ultimately attaining the rank of major-general. Golpira was trained as a doctor in Iran, but completed his internship in the United States, arriving in 1953. Thereafter he resided and worked in the United States, becoming naturalised in 1964. He married an Iranian and both children of the marriage were registered with the Iranian embassy, in the case of the second child, after Golpira had acquired United States

---

petitioned the full Tribunal to make a ruling on the validity of claims by dual nationals. There have been a number of articles on the decisions of the Tribunal in relation to dual nationality; see Leigh, *Judicial Decisions*, 77 A.J.I.L., 624 (1983); Note, *Effect of Dual United States and Iranian Nationality on the Tribunal's Jurisdiction*, 1 J. Int. Arb., 173 (1984); Note, *The Standing of Dual Nationals before the Iran–United States Claims Tribunal*, 24 Va. J.I.L., 695 (1984); Note, *Claims of Dual Nationals in the Modern Era: The Iran–United States Claims Tribunal*, 83 Mich. L.R., 597 (1984).

[48] 2 IRAN–U.S.C.T.R., 157 (1983). The second decision, *Golpira* v *Iran* 2 IRAN–U.S.C.T.R., 171 (1983), applied the reasoning of the *Esphahanian* decision by reference.

[49] 2 IRAN–U.S.C.T.R., 171 (1983).

citizenship. Since 1953 he had made a number of brief visits to Iran, on each occasion using his Iranian passport. In 1970 he purchased stock in an Iranian medical company, with reference being made to his Iranian identity card number. Golpira alleged that the Iranian government had expropriated this stock.

Iran put forward three different arguments before Chamber Two. These arguments were also ultimately put to the full Tribunal. Firstly, in both cases it argued that Article VII(1)(a) of the Claims Settlement Declaration limited the jurisdiction of the Tribunal to claims by persons who are exclusively citizens of either Iran or the United States, thus excluding claims by persons possessing the nationality of both countries. In respect of the claims before Chamber Two, Iran offered a second alternative defence which accepted the principle of real and effective nationality. Iran contended that claimants having the nationality of both states had their closest and most real connections with Iran, particularly in the case of Iranians who had become naturalised United States citizens. However, when Iran presented its case to the full Tribunal it argued only that the principle of Article 4 of the Hague Convention of 1930 was applicable, and that this was reflected in the precedents and the writings of jurists. Finally, Iran contented that the principle of real and effective nationality was not applicable to claims by dual nationals against a state whose nationality such person also possessed.

The United States rejected the contention of Iran that the Claims Settlement Declaration prohibited claims by dual nationals. The United States asserted that the wording of the Declaration was permissive rather than restrictive. The word "citizen", without further definition, did not exclude citizens who had nationality of both states. If the parties had intended to exclude claims by dual nationals the Declaration would have explicitly stated this limitation. Moreover the modern practice of international arbitral tribunals has been to accept claims by dual nationals. In the alternative the United States argued that the principle of real and effective nationality extended to persons who had the nationality of both states and that such persons could make claims against Iran if they had predominant links with the United States.

The principal award is *Esphahanian* v *Bank Tejarat*, in which Chamber Two fully considered the issue of dual nationality. In the first instance the Tribunal rejected the contention of both parties that the Claims Settlement Declaration settled the matter. The Tribunal stated:[50]

In the absence of any specific provision in the Claims Settlement Declaration on this point, the Tribunal must determine the meaning of the text through use of the rules of the Vienna Convention. Paragraph 3(c) of Article 31 directs us to take

[50] 2 IRAN–U.S.C.T.R., 157, 161 (1983).

into account "any relevant rules of international law applicable in the relations between the parties".

There is a considerable body of law, precedents and legal literature, analysed herein, which leads to the conclusion that the applicable rule of international law is that of dominant and effective nationality.

The Tribunal considered each of the categories of law, precedent and legal literature separately. It also examined the role of the Tribunal to determine whether it was established as a classic measure of diplomatic protection.

The appropriate law was that contained in the Hague Convention of 1930. Although Article 4 prevents a state from extending diplomatic protection to a national against a state whose nationality the person also possesses the Tribunal considered that, given the age of the Convention, and the development of the concept of diplomatic protection, Article 4 did not preclude claims made direct by dual nationals.

Thus Article 4 did not cover cases where the dual national presented the claim himself, instead of relying on the state to bring the claim, since this was not diplomatic protection as envisaged by Article 4. Moreover Article 5 of the Convention permitted third states to apply the concept of dominant nationality to dual nationals.

After an examination of its role in determining claims the Tribunal found "itself in a position similar to that of a court of a third State faced with the claim of a dual national against one of the States of his nationality"[51] rather than the usual international arbitral tribunal established as an exercise of diplomatic protection. The Convention therefore allowed the Tribunal to apply the concept of dominant nationality to dual nationals. In considering the precedents the Tribunal first had regard to the decisions of the various claims commissions arbitrating the disputes between Venezuela and certain European states, the *Canevaro* case and the Mixed Claims Commissions established after the First World War.[52] In all these cases the Tribunal considered that the principle of dominant and effective nationality had been applied to determine the nationality of dual nationals. The Tribunal then referred to "the two most important decisions on the subject".[53] These were the *Nottebohm* and *Mergé* cases, which the Tribunal regarded as definitive. The Tribunal noted that the International Court of Justice had stated, "the courts of third States, when they have before them an individual whom two other States hold to be their national, seek to resolve the conflict by having recourse to

[51] *Ibid.*, 162.
[52] *Ibid.*, 162.
[53] *Ibid.*, 163.

international criteria and their prevailing tendency is to prefer the real and effective nationality".[54]

As an additional source of law in support of the principle of real and effective nationality the Tribunal referred to the publicists' acceptance of the "actually dominant theory". The Tribunal stated that the non-responsibility doctrine embodied in Article 4 of the Hague Convention is confined to "diplomatic or consular protection of dual nationals physically present in a State which considers them as its own nationals".[55]

Having determined that international law admitted the principle of real and effective nationality, the Tribunal turned to consider its own capacity to apply this doctrine. The Tribunal examined the background to its establishment and the nature of its jurisdiction. It noted that it had been established as a replacement forum for the courts of Iran and the United States. From this central fact the Tribunal concluded that it is not "unlike the courts of third States" as opposed to an "exercise of diplomatic protection of nationals in which a State, seeking some form of international redress for its nationals, creates a Tribunal to which it, rather than its nationals, is a party".[56] Secondly, since the parties had not established any *lex fori* to determine questions of dual nationality, the Tribunal would "give effect to the real and effective nationality, that which accord(s) with the facts ... based on stronger factual ties between the persons concerned and one of the States whose nationality is involved. *Nottebohm Case* supra at 22".[57]

The Tribunal then applied this principle of real and effective nationality to the facts of the two cases before it.[58]

The Tribunal noted that Iranian law permitted renunciation of Iranian nationality only with the approval of the Council of Ministers and that thereafter such persons could return to Iran only once, to dispose of their property. Thus in respect of the use of the Iranian passport to enter and leave Iran "the laws of Iran in effect forced such use".[59] For all other travel Esphahanian used his United States passport. Secondly, the Tribunal noted that the funds at issue in the claim related primarily to his United States nationality and that with the exception of the use of his passport and the nominal ownership of stock on behalf of his employer his actions could have been performed by a non-Iranian. Moreover the

---

[54] *Ibid.*, 163, from *Nottebohm Case* I.C.J. Rep., 4, 22 (1955).
[55] *Ibid.*, 164.
[56] *Ibid.*, 166.
[57] *Ibid.*, 166.
[58] In *Golpira* v *Iran* 2 IRAN–U.S.C.T.R., 171 (1983), the Tribunal applied the dominant and effective nationality rule without further consideration of the legal issues. A copy of the *Esphahanian Case* was annexed to the *Golpira Case* to show the applicability of the rule.
[59] 2 IRAN–U.S.C.T.R., 157, 167 (1983).

Tribunal noted that the claimant's "contacts with the United States were long and consistent". The Tribunal concluded "that Esphahanian's dominant and effective nationality at all relevant times has been that of the United States".[60] It thus had jurisdiction to determine his claim against Bank Tejarat.[61]

In the case of *Golpira* v *Iran* the Tribunal noted that when Golpira visited Iran he was virtually compelled to use his Iranian passport. In all other respects his life was centred in the United States. The Tribunal concluded that Golpira's dominant and effective nationality was that of the United States and could therefore treat his claim as that of a United States national against Iran.[62]

The decision of the full Tribunal[63]

The majority decision of the full Tribunal followed the reasoning of the awards of *Esphahanian* and *Golpira* closely.

The first issue considered was whether the text of the Claims Settlement Declaration was sufficiently clear to determine the meaning of "national". The two states raised the arguments that had been previously raised. Iran also argued that the Declaration could only be interpreted in light of the "converging will" of the two States.

Since Iran did not regard the term "national" as extending to persons having the nationality of both states, it could not be so interpreted. The Tribunal rejected the arguments of both parties and as directed by Article 31(3)(c) of the Vienna Convention on the Law of Treaties examined the "relevant rules of international law". After such examination the Tribunal concluded that the "applicable rule of international law is that of dominant and effective nationality".[64]

As with Chamber Two the full Tribunal first considered the Hague Convention of 1930, and in particular Article 4 of the Convention. It noted that the Treaty was more than fifty years old and that only twenty states are parties to it.[65]

More significantly it did not consider that the establishment of the Tribunal came within the concept of diplomatic protection, since most of

---

[60] *Ibid.*

[61] In respect of the substance of the claim the Tribunal found that Bank Tejarat was responsible for the dishonour of a bank cheque issued by it. It also decided that interest should be paid on the award, since a "bank cheque usually removes any risk that the cheque will be dishonoured".

[62] In considering the merits of the claim the Tribunal found that Golpira's shares had not been expropriated, even if the majority shareholder's interest had been expropriated. It also found that following the revolution no dividends had been paid. It had only been demonstrated "that a profitable investment has become, at least temporarily, unprofitable".

[63] *Iran* v *United States (Case A/18)* 5 IRAN–U.S.C.T.R., 251 (1984).

[64] *Ibid.*, 260.

[65] Neither Iran nor the United States is a party to the Hague Convention.

Nationality of claimants 75

the disputes before the Tribunal concerned a private party making a claim against a government, or a government-controlled entity. Diplomatic protection was limited to actions between states where one of the states is taking up the claim of one of its nationals.[66] Moreover the majority referred to the fact that the Tribunal was a substitute forum for persons who had commenced litigation in United States courts prior to the Algiers Declarations.

This restrictive view of the rule of non-responsibility was explained by the Tribunal as "consistent with the contemporaneous development of international law to afford legal protection to individuals, even against the State of which they are nationals".[67]

The Tribunal then reviewed the precedents, in particular the *Nottebohm* and *Mergé* cases. Although the Tribunal recognised that *Nottebohm* did not concern a claim against a state of which Nottebohm was a national "the acceptance and approval by the International Court of Justice of the search for the real and effective nationality based on the facts of a case ... have radiated throughout the international law of nationality".[68] The *Mergé* case, which did concern diplomatic espousal of claims of dual nationals against a state whose nationality the claimant possessed, was cited by the Tribunal with approval.[69] The Tribunal also found support for its evaluation of the precedents in the legal literature, particularly that of more recent times.[70]

Thus, the relevant rule of international law which the Tribunal may take into account for purposes of interpretation, as directed by Article 31, paragraph 3(c), of the Vienna Convention, is the rule that flows from the *dictum* of *Nottebohm*, the rule of real and effective nationality, and the search for "stronger factual ties between the person concerned and one of the States whose nationality is involved". In view of this pervasive effect of this rule since the *Nottebohm* decision, the Tribunal concludes that the reference to "national" and "nationals" in the Algiers Declarations must be understood as consistent with the rule unless an exception is clearly stated. As stated above, the Tribunal does not find that the text of the Algiers Declaration provides such a clear exception.

In determining the dominant and effective nationality of claimants having dual nationality the Tribunal would "consider all relevant factors,

---

[66] *Ibid.*, 260.
[67] *Ibid.*, 265.
[68] *Ibid.*, 263.
[69] *Ibid.*, 263.
[70] *Ibid.*, 265. The Tribunal cited, among others, De Visscher, *Cours Général de Droit International Public*, 136 Recueil des Cours, 162 (1962); *Digest of United States Practise in Doctrine of Dominant Nationality*, 53 A.J.I.L., 139 (1959); Donner, *The Regulation of Nationality in International Law*, 399 (1979); Leigh, *Nationality and Diplomatic Protection*, 20 I.C.L.Q., 453 (1971).

including habitual residence, centre of interests, family ties, participation in public life and other evidence of attachments".[71]

In addition to the principal opinion handed down by the majority, concurring opinions were given by Mr Riphagen, one of the neutral arbitrators, and Messrs Holtzmann and Aldrich, two of the United States arbitrators. Mr Riphagen stressed that the Tribunal was not a form of diplomatic protection, pointing to the access by nationals to the Tribunal, the law to be applied by the Tribunal, the enforcement of awards through the Security Account and the exception from jurisdiction of the Tribunal where the parties have chosen an Iranian forum for the resolution of the dispute.[72] He also stated that the question of dual nationality was therefore not merely a jurisdictional issue, since the nationality also went to the merits of claims.[73]

Some months later the Iranian arbitrators filed a voluminous dissenting opinion, in which they agreed with the arguments put forward by Iran. With regard to the interpretation of the Claims Settlement Declaration the Iranian arbitrators noted that it had been largely drafted by the United States and thus "any possible ambiguity in its terms must be interpreted to the disadvantage of the drafting State".[74] The arbitrators noted that the agreement between Egypt and the United States included an annex stating that the United States applied the principle of "dominant and effective nationality of dual nationals" to the definition of "national" in the agreement.[75] Since the Claims Settlement Declaration did not include such an annex the general principles of law relating to espousal of claims of dual nationals must apply.

The Iranian arbitrators pointed to the fact that the Tribunal was established by treaty between two states. Moreover they considered that the Agreement was regarded by both states as a traditional and conventional means of settling international claims.[76] The fact that the claims could be presented by claimants personally, as opposed to the government was merely a "procedural technique".[77]

The Iranian arbitrators then examined the precedents in light of the rule of non-responsibility of states. In a comprehensive review of the decisions they were satisfied with the wide acceptance of the principle

---

[71] 5 IRAN–U.S.C.T.R., 265 (1984).

[72] *Ibid.*, 273–4.

[73] *Ibid.*, 274.

[74] 5 IRAN–U.S.C.T.R., 275, 286 (1984). The *contra proferentum* rule has also been raised by Hakan-Berglin, *Treaty Interpretation and the Impact of Contractual Choice of Forum Cases on the Jurisdiction of International Tribunals: The Iranian Forum Clause Decisions of the Iran–United States Claims Tribunal*, 21 Tex. I.L.J., 39, 64 (1985–86).

[75] *Ibid.*, 283.

[76] *Ibid.*, 294–8.

[77] *Ibid.*, 298. In any event only holders of large claims can directly present their claims. Small claims have to be presented by the government of the national.

that a state could not prosecute a claim of one of its nationals against a state whose nationality the claimant also possessed.[78] Even where the principle of real and effective nationality had been accepted the claim itself was invariably denied.[79] Particular attention was paid to the *Nottebohm* and *Mergé* decisions. The Iranian arbitrators referred to the facts of *Nottebohm* and considered the *obiter* statement concerning real and effective nationality could not be extended to exclude the principle of non-responsibility, particularly since the International Court of Justice had accepted the principle in the *Reparation* case. The *Mergé* case was distinguished by the Iranian arbitrators on the grounds of a misunderstanding by the Commission of the application of Articles 4 and 5 of the Hague Convention of 1930, and the possibility that the Commission was influenced by the fact that it resulted from a peace treaty between the United States and Italy.

The dissenting opinion of the Iranian arbitrators reasserted the paramountcy of state sovereignty *vis-à-vis* the individual in international law. However, their approach restricts the ability of individuals to choose their nationality freely, as in the case of emigrants, and then be able to sustain claims against their former state. Given the relative ease of travel and immigration, the disserting opinion fails to recognise the realities of the modern world.

The application of the dual nationality decision

The decision of the full Tribunal has been applied in a number of claims. The cases fall into a variety of categories, including claims made by persons born in Iran who have emigrated to the United States, persons born to Iranian parents in the United States or elsewhere, persons of Iranian birth who married United States nationals and the contrary category of persons of United States nationality who married Iranian nationals.

The case of *Saghi* v *Iran*[80] is illustrative of the first two categories, since it concerned a claim by a man born in Iran and his two sons. The father claimed United States nationality by virtue of holding a United States passport since 1947, having moved to the United States as a student in 1945. The sons were born in Iran, where the father worked for several years. Their mother was a United States-born citizen.

---

[78] Among the decisions cited were the *Canevaro Case* II R.I.A.A., 405 (1912); *Oldenburg Case* I R.I.A.A., 752; *Adams and Blackmore* III R.I.A.A., 216–17; from 5 IRAN–U.S.C.T.R., 304–10 (1984).
[79] *Canevaro Case* II R.I.A.A., 415 (1912); *Mergé Case* XIV R.I.A.A., 23 (1955); from 5 IRAN–U.S.C.T.R., at 317, 325 (1984).
[80] 14 IRAN–U.S.C.T.R., 3 (1987).

The Tribunal was satisfied that all three claimants were United States nationals. The questions that arose were whether the claimants were also Iranian nationals, and, if so, which of the two nationalities was dominant. In respect of the father and one of the sons the Tribunal held that they were not Iranian nationals. The Tribunal noted:[81]

> The mere potential qualification for nationality, when coupled with official acts of the State concerned which deny the same status, compel the conclusion that neither the State nor the individual concerned considers the potential nationality to have any effect.

The second son had taken some steps to secure his potential Iranian nationality in 1977. However, he retained his United States nationality, travelling only on his United States passport. Since 1975, when he was eighteen, he had lived continuously in the United States apart from limited visits overseas, including Iran in 1977. The Tribunal stated:[82]

> In accordance with the findings that Allan J. Saghi is a national both of the United States and of Iran, and in accordance with the decision in Case No. A18 [5 IRAN–U.S.C.T.R., 251], the Tribunal proceeds to a determination of the dominant and effective nationality of Allan Saghi during the relevant period. In determining his dominant and effective nationality, the Tribunal considers all relevant factors, including habitual residence, centre of interests, family ties, participation in public life, and other evidence of attachment.

The Tribunal concluded that Allan Saghi had the dominant and effective nationality of the United States and thus was an eligible claimant against Iran.

The case of *Michelle Danielpour v Iran*[83] concerns a young woman born in the United States of Iranian parents but who had lived in Iran for the majority of her life. The Tribunal accepted that she was a national of the United States but noted that it was undisputed that she was an Iranian national by virtue of her father's nationality. In determining her dominant and effective nationality the Tribunal primarily had regard to her socialisation in the cultures of both states, rather than her present choice of nationality.

It considered that the eighteen months she had lived in the United States prior to her claim arising "would not have been adequate for the claimant to integrate into American society and to familiarise herself with American culture so as to predominate over her years spent in Iran under the influence of her Iranian family and the society and culture of Iran".[84] Accordingly, her dominant and effective nationality was that of Iran.

---

[81] *Ibid.*, 6.
[82] *Ibid.*, 7.
[83] 22 Iran–U.S.C.T.R., 118 (1989).
[84] *Ibid.*, 121.

A number of other nationality cases also measured the time which the claimant had spent in Iran and the United States. If the balance was in favour of Iran, particularly in recent years, the Tribunal has tended to hold that the dominant nationality was Iranian.[85]

The third category of persons of Iranian birth married to United States nationals, thereby claiming that their United States nationality is dominant, was considered in *Benedix* v *Iran*.[86] Mrs Benedix was of Iranian birth and married a United States national in 1954. They lived in the United States for three years, then lived in Iran for twenty years until 1978. Thereafter the couple lived in the United Kingdom. Mrs Benedix emigrated to the United States in 1957 and was issued several United States passports over a period of years. The Tribunal in considering which of the nationalities was dominant stated:[87]

The Tribunal notes that Mrs Benedix resided in the United States only for a relatively brief period between 1954 and 1957. Following her naturalisation as a United States citizen, she was present in the United States only for sporadic visits. At present she apparently lives in London, England, where she and her husband chose to reside upon leaving Iran in 1978. Evidence provided by the claimant relating to factors such as her habitual residence, centre of interests, family ties, participation in public life and other attachments are insufficient to support a finding that Mrs Benedix's links to the United States were dominant during the relevant period between the time when her claim allegedly arose in 1979 and 12 January 1981.

The opposite situation arises in the case of *Ebrahimi* v *Iran*,[88] whereby a United States-born woman who married an Iranian national asserted that her United States nationality acquired by birth prevailed over her Iranian nationality acquired through her marriage to an Iranian-born national. Mrs Ebrahimi was born in 1948 and lived in the United States from time to time. In 1977 she married an Iranian national in the United States and shifted to Iran in late 1977. She acquired an Iranian passport and an Iranian identity card. She lived in Iran with her husband until mid-1979, when they both left. In considering her dominant nationaity, the Tribunal stated:[89]

---

[85] See especially *Nemazee* v *Iran* 25 IRAN–U.S.C.T.R., 153 (1990), where the claimant, a person of Puerto Rican birth married to an Iranian and who had lived in Iran from 1954 to 1979, was held to be of Iranian nationality. Also *Bakhtiari* v *Iran* 25 IRAN–U.S.C.T.R., 289 (1990), where the claimant, born in Iran in 1918 and residing there from 1957, was held to be Iranian. In both cases, and many similar cases, the dominant nationality was Iranian, even though the claimant also held United States citizenship.
[86] 21 Iran–U.S.C.T.R., 20 (1989).
[87] *Ibid.*, 23.
[88] 22 Iran–U.S.C.T.R., 138 (1989).
[89] *Ibid.*, 144.

The Tribunal notes that Marjorie Ebrahimi's residence in Iran in the years 1977–1979 was not continuous and that she travelled with some frequency outside that country. Although she was married to an Iranian national, her life was that of an American expatriate in Iran. Furthermore if in 1977 Marjorie Ebrahimi had intended to make Iran her home, and despite her participation in an Iranian referendum, her definite departure from Iran to the United States in 1979 suggests that she intended to give up her home in Iran in favour of her native country. Given her extensive Western background and the short time of her residence in Iran, it would not have taken her long to reintegrate into American society. Once she relocated to the United States 1 month prior to the date her claim is alleged to have arisen, her American nationality becomes predominant. Based on these facts, the Tribunal concludes that her dominant and effective nationality during the relevant period is that of the United States.

In each of these cases the various Chambers of the Tribunal have applied the decision of the full Tribunal by examining the stability of the social, cultural and economic ties to the two states of which the claimant was a national at the time the claim arose. The decisions are based not on the person's actions at or immediately prior to the claim arising, but on the weight of the past experience and future intentions of the claimant.

Conclusion

The decision of the majority of the full Tribunal rests on two points. First, that the Tribunal was not established as a result of diplomatic protection as that term is classically understood. Thus Article 4 of the Hague Convention of 1930 is not applicable. Secondly, the principle of real and effective nationality, as defined by the *Nottebohm* case and thence applied by the *Mergé* case to claims by persons having the nationality of both the claimant and the respondent states, is applicable to claims made by persons having the nationality of both Iran and the United States. The decision of the Tribunal, resting so heavily on the *obiter* of the *Nottebohm* case, is a significant extension of the *Nottebohm* principle. Although the decision goes no further than the *Mergé* case it is a substantial consolidation of the *ratio* of that decision. Like the Commission in the *Mergé* case the Tribunal did not consider that the principles of Article 4 of the Hague Convention and the *Nottebohm* decision were irreconcilably opposed. Rather, Article 4 was limited to classical situations of diplomatic protection while the principle of *Nottebohm* was given wider application, as it had been in the *Mergé* case.

The confirmation of the principle of real and effective nationality in respect of claims by dual nationals against a state whose nationality the claimant possesses has been seen by commentators as essential if the Tribunal is to afford a "minimum standard of protection of human rights

Nationality of claimants 81

of individuals", particularly in light of Iran's refusal to allow "voluntary expatriation".[90] The question of the exercise of diplomatic protection precluding the *Nottebohm* principle was not considered by the writer of the note.

The Tribunal, however, chose the superficially easier course of reconciling the two principles rather than rejecting one as outmoded. This approach, which required the Tribunal to hold that it was not established as an exercise of diplomatic protection, does result in a theoretical difficulty. Many awards of the Tribunal raise issues of state responsibility. The principles of international law developed in the area of state responsibility stem from states providing diplomatic protection to their nationals in respect of loss caused by a respondent state.[91] As a result of this attempt to reconcile the two principles, the Tribunal has not been able to clearly indicate where it is acting as a substitute forum for Iranian and United States municipal courts, and where it is a traditional international arbitral tribunal applying the principles of state responsibility.

Continuous ownership of claims

Introduction

The doctrine of nationality of claims has two aspects, first, that a state may only espouse claims of its own nationals, and, secondly, that this link of nationality must be continuously maintained from the time the claim arises until its adjudication.[92] The rule of continuous ownership is that:[93]

[F]rom the time of the occurrence of the injury until the making of the award the claim must continuously and without interruption have belonged to a person or to a series of persons (a) having the nationality of state by whom it is put forward and (b) not having the nationality of the State against whom it is put forward.

---

[90] Note, *Claims of Dual Nationals in the Modern Era: The Iran–United States Claims Tribunal*, 83 Mich. L.R., 597, 624 (1984). The refusal of Iran to allow "voluntary expatriation" was seen as a breach of the principle of law that persons should have the freedom to emigrate. Accordingly international law should not assist Iran by disallowing claims of persons having residual nationality of Iran when their real and effective nationality was that of the United States. The author of the note was also cognisant of the fact that the Tribunal offered the only possible remedy to claimants having the nationality of both Iran and the United States.

[91] See Chapter Six, The Relationship between the Law of State Responsibility and Diplomatic Protection of Aliens, *infra*.

[92] Refer to *Diplomatic Protection* in this chapter. The doctrine is based on the principle that a state providing diplomatic protection is in reality protecting its own rights, since injury to its nationals by another state is injury to itself; *Mavrommatis Palestine Concessions (Greece v United Kingdom)* P.C.I.J., A.2, 12 (1924).

[93] Oppenheim, *International Law*, 347–8 (1955). See also Brownlie, *Principles of Public International Law*, 481 (1990).

The requirement of continuity of nationality ensures that only nationals of a state espousing the claim can benefit from the claim.[94] However, it has been argued that the requirement of continuous nationality is illogical.[95] International practice shows that the full rigour of the rule may be mitigated for certain cases.

The case of *Landreau (United States v Peru)*[96] concerned a claim which arose at the time Landreau was a French citizen. Subsequently he acquired United States nationality by naturalisation and the United States took up his case. The Tribunal stated that since Peru and the United States had entered into an agreement concerning the claim it "cannot enter into the question whether it was proper for the United States government to take up this case".[97] Sinclair refers to the importance that a claim should be national in origin.[98] The British government will, in appropriate cases, provide diplomatic protection for persons who suffer injury at a time when they are British nationals but who subsequently change their nationality.[99]

Post-war United States practice, as embodied in various claims settlement agreements, however, shows acceptance of the principle that the claim must be continuously owned by the United States nationals. The agreement between the United States and Yugoslavia of 1948 required that claimants should have United States nationality at the time of taking.[100] Although the agreement did not specify that the claimants must have United States nationality at the date of the settlement the Foreign Claims Settlement Commission interpreted the agreement as requiring this continuity of nationality.[101]

Similar decisions have been made by the Foreign Claims Settlement Commission in respect of other lump sum agreements. The most recent lump sum agreement was with Czechoslovakia.[102] This agreement provided that claims could be accepted only if they were owned continuously by United States nationals from the date they arose till the date of the agreement.[103]

[94] Sinclair, *Nationality of Claims: British Practice*, 37 B.Y.I.L., 127 (1950). This accords with the view that a state providing diplomatic protection is in reality asserting its own claim. Brownlie, *Principles of Public International Law*, 481 (1990), considers the reason for the requirement of continuous nationality is to prevent claimants choosing a powerful protecting state by changing their nationality.
[95] Jennings, *General Course of International Law*, II Recueil des Cours, 323, 475 (1967). See also O'Connell, *International Law*, 1033–9 (1970).
[96] II R.I.A.A., 347 (1922).
[97] *Ibid.*, 367.
[98] Sinclair, *Natonality of Claims: British Practice*, 37 B.Y.I.L., 127, 128 (1950).
[99] *Ibid.*, 141.
[100] Article 2; 12 U.S. Treaties 1227.
[101] *Bogovich Claim* F.C.S.C. (1957); *Straub Claims* F.C.S.C. (1954); from Whiteman, 8 *Digest of International Law*, 1245–6 (1967).
[102] 21 I.L.M., 371 (1982).
[103] Article 2. The United States legislation implementing the agreement, the Czechoslovakian Claims Settlement Act, 1981, allowed compensation to certain claimants

The Claims Settlement Declaration

Article VII(2) of the Claims Settlement Declaration sets out the requirement that "claims be owned continuously from the date the claim arose to the date on which [the Declaration] enters into force by nationals of that state". The rule reflects existing United States practice in claims settlement agreements. It is of particular relevance in the case of the Iran–United States Claims Tribunal, for it prevents non-United States claimants utilising the Tribunal to receive guaranteed compensation from Iran. The Security Account established by Iran is intended to compensate United States nationals, and the application of the principle of continuous nationality ensures that only persons having United States nationality during the relevant period will benefit from the fund.[104]

Awards of the Tribunal

The claim need only be owned from the date it actually arose, and not from the date upon which the underlying transaction originated. In *Isaiah v Bank Mellat*[105] a bank cheque issued by Bank Mellat for the benefit of a Mr Parkash, an Israeli national, in January 1979 was dishonoured later that month. The cheque was endorsed over to Mr Isaiah, a United States national, by separate instrument in November 1979, some months after the dishonour. The Tribunal considered that a claim could not be based on the dishonour of the cheque since at the time the claim arose it was owned by an Israeli national. However on the alternative claim of unjust enrichment the claim was continuously owned by Isaiah since *vis-à-vis* Isaiah the claims could only arise once Isaiah acquired rights against the Bank in November 1979. From that date to the date of the Algiers Declarations the claim was continuously owned by Isaiah.[106]

The case of *Lianosoff v Iran*[107] illustrates the requirement that the claims must be continuously owned by a national of either party. The facts were that rights to a fishing concession in Iran had been owned by the claimant's father, a stateless person, from 1918 to 1953. The concession was nationalised by Iran in 1953. The claimant's father maintained a claim in respect of the expropriated concession. In 1977 the

who were Czechoslovakian nationals at the time of taking of property by the Czechoslovak government between January 1, 1945 and January 26, 1948, and who had become United States citizens by February 26, 1948. This was not in accordance with the Agreement with Czechoslovakia, but since the United States had the discretion in dispensing the funds paid to it by Czechoslovakia it does not affect the validity of Article 2 of the Agreement.

[104] The Security Account was initially established with $1 billion. It is to be maintained at $500 million by Iran. Iran has made several deposits to maintain the account at $500 million. These deposits have been made from the interest earned on the Security Account. This interest is deposited into a separate account.

[105] 2 IRAN–U.S.C.T.R., 232 (1983).
[106] *Ibid.*, 236.
[107] 5 IRAN–U.S.C.T.R., 90 (1984).

claimant, a naturalised United States citizen, assumed the rights to the claim. The Tribunal held that at the time the claim arose it was not owned by a United States national, and it "failed to fulfil the requirement of continuous ownership embodied in Article VII(2) of the Claims Settlement Declaration".[108]

There is nothing in the Claims Settlement Declaration to prevent the assignment of claims by a national of either Iran or the United States to a national of the same state.[109]

Similarly successors of a deceased claimant may retain the claim provided they possess the same nationality.[110] However, pursuant to Article II(1) of the Declaration, the claim must relate to "property rights". This requirement can alter the nature of the claim as it passes from the party originally suffering the loss to the ultimate claimant.

In the case of *Grimm* v *Iran*[111] the Tribunal held that the widow of a United States oil executive assassinated by Islamic militants did not have a valid claim since her rights in respect of her husband were not property rights. The majority in Chamber One considered that had Mr Grimm survived he would have been ineligible to make a claim since the failure by the Iranian authorities to protect Mr Grimm "just affected the life and safety of Mr Grimm" and not any property rights.[112] The majority did not dispute the right of Mrs Grimm to appear before the Tribunal but since her claim was for "mental anguish, grief and suffering" it was a claim independent of any possible claim by Mr Grimm and was rejected. If Mr Grimm had had a valid claim for breach of property rights then it would seem that the claim could have been sustained by his successors.

The requirement of continuous ownership of claim is of greater significance for corporations, since the nationality of a corporate claimant can change according to the ownership of its stock. If the claim is being made directly by the corporation then it must show that at least 50 per cent of its capital stock has been continuously owned by nationals of the claimant state from the date the claim arose until the date of entry into force of the Claims Settlement Declaration. However, if the claim is being made by a corporation fulfilling the criteria of nationality of one of the parties on behalf of an overseas subsidiary, or on behalf of shareholders of an overseas corporation, or a United States corporation not fulfilling the criteria of United States nationality, the claimant need only show that the "ownership interests of such nationals, collectively, were

---

[108] *Ibid.*, 93.
[109] International law permits such assignments. See also Brownlie, *Principles of Public International Law*, 482 (1990).
[110] *Stevenson Claim* IX R.I.A.A., 385 (1903).
[111] 2 IRAN–U.S.C.T.R., 78 (1983).
[112] *Ibid.*, 79.

sufficient at the time the claim arose to control the corporation or other entity".[113]

In both situations it is a question of providing sufficient evidence of continuous ownership to satisfy the Tribunal.

In the case of *Flexi-Van Leasing Inc.* v *Iran*[114] the Tribunal recognised the "practical impossibility of having evidence of stock ownership on a daily basis".[115] Thus the claimant was required to submit the evidence of ownership of its stock at two points in time: firstly when the claim arose and secondly at the Annual General Meeting closest to January 19, 1981.[116]

The principles established by the *Flexi-Van* decision have been applied many times by the tribunal. Thus the Orders following the *Flexi-Van* decision also required the claimant to submit evidence on the same periodic basis.[117]

Claimants are therefore not obliged to look beyond the documentary evidence that is already in their possession in order to satisfy the Tribunal of the continuous ownership of the claim. Additional evidence may be required if the respondent can produce sufficient evidence rebutting the continuous ownership of the claim by the claimant.

---

[113] Article VII(2). This applies equally to claims by Iranian corporations.
[114] 1 IRAN–U.S.C.T.R., 425 (1981–82). For a full description of this case refer to Chapter Thirteen.
[115] *Ibid.*, 459.
[116] *Ibid.*, 460.
[117] See Chapter Seven on this issue.

CHAPTER FIVE

Claimants in relation to corporate claims

Introduction

The composite nature of corporations with their legal personality contained in the corporate entity and their ownership and control vested in the shareholders leads to special problems for states making international claims on behalf of corporations. There are three possible solutions to problems of corporate nationality:

1 Claims can be made by states on behalf of all corporations incorporated in the claimant state irrespective of the nationality of the shareholders.
2 Claims can be made by states on behalf of corporations incorporated in the claimant state provided a substantial part of the shares are owned by nationals of that state.
3 Claims can be made by states in respect of shareholders who are nationals of the claimant state, irrespective of the nationality of the corporation.

The Claims Settlement Declaration encompasses the second and third solutions. Claims can be made by corporations incorporated in the claimant state if 50 per cent of the stock of the corporation is owned by citizens of the claimant state.[1]

However, if citizens of a claimant state control corporations incorporated elsewhere claims can be made on behalf of such corporations.[2] Finally, shareholders are able to make claims in respect of their shareholder interests, particularly where those interests have been expro-

[1] Article VII(1).
[2] Article VII(2).

Claimants and corporate claims 87

priated.³ In this instance the claim is that of the shareholder, and not of the corporation.

The Claims Settlement Declaration is a significant contribution to state practice in relation to corporate and shareholder claims. It conforms with the present practice of only allowing corporate claims if nationals of the claimant state have a majority interest in the corporation.

The development of international law in relation to corporate claims

International law has vacillated between the place of incorporation and the nationality of the controlling shareholders in determining which nation may make claims on behalf of companies.

Historical practice has tended to favour diplomatic protection based on incorporation, that is, the state where the company is incorporated is the only state able to offer protection to the corporate entity. However, by the end of the nineteenth century British and American practice was to deny protection unless the company was not only incorporated in the claimant state but also predominantly controlled by nationals of the claimant state.⁴ In addition British and American governments were prepared to provide "good offices" for national shareholders in foreign companies but the representations would be taken no further should they prove to be unsuccessful.

By the end of the nineteenth century this practice was beginning to change and claims were being presented on behalf of shareholders, although the claims mostly concerned companies incorporated in the respondent state, with the shares being owned by nationals of the claimant state. The *Delagoa Bay Railway Arbitration*⁵ concerned a claim on behalf of British and United States interests in a Portuguese company, the undertaking of which had been expropriated by Portugal. The arbitration was, however, based on an agreement between the three states submitting the dispute to arbitration. Thus, in principle, it was not a derogation from the principle that diplomatic protection could only be extended to companies incorporated in the protecting state, despite the fact that Great Britain and the United States had gone to some lengths to have the dispute submitted to arbitration.

---

[3] See *Starrett Housing Corporation* v *Iran* 4 IRAN–U.S.C.T.R., 122 (1983), referred to in this chapter *infra*.

[4] See *Enrique Cortes & Co. Case* (1896); *Hong Kong Companies Case* (1898); *Italo-Turkish War Case* (1912); *Bermuda Asphalt Co. Case* (1904); from Parry (ed.) 5 *British Digest of International Law*, 514–21 (1965). For commentary refer Parry (ed.) 5 *British Digest of International Law*, (1976); Schwarzenberger, *International Law*, 392 (1957); Brownlie, *Principles of Public International Law*, 485 (1990); Jones, *Claims on Behalf of Nationals who are Shareholders in Foreign Companies*, 26 B.Y.I.L., 225, 228 (1949).

[5] Moore, 2 *History and Digest of the International Arbitrations to which the United States has been a Party*, 1896 (1899).

Moreover where foreign companies have substantial shareholdings owned by United States or United Kingdom nationals, the practice of the two states has been to provide diplomatic protection only to the extent of the beneficial interests of the American and British investors. Thus in the claim against Panama made by a Panamanian corporation, *Panama Sugar, Fruit and Cattle*,[6] the shares of which were owned by a United States citizen, the Foreign Claims Settlement Commission of the United States held that the corporation did not have a valid claim since it was not incorporated in the United States.[7] The Commission, however, made an award to the United States shareholder to the extent of his interest, noting:[8]

While there is conflict as to whether the claim of stockholders can be espoused under international law, the policy of the United States has been to grant diplomatic intervention where there is a substantial American interest in a foreign corporation (Hackworth, *Digest of International Law*, Vol. V, pp. 840–5). The extent to which such claims are espoused is limited to the extent of the American ownership . . .

In the *Standard Oil Company (United States v Reparations Commission)*[9] case the United States claimed that German oil tankers owned by a German company were beneficially owned by the Standard Oil Company of the United States since that company owned the share capital of the German company.

This was rejected by the Tribunal, which held that shareholders did not have any legal or equitable interest in the assets of a company. Since the company was German the ships had to be delivered to the Reparations Commission in compliance with the Treaty of Versailles. Protection of shareholders of companies incorporated in a respondent state would be permissible only if the actions of the government of such state were "recognised to be wrongful".[10]

Similarly the British government offered diplomatic protection to British shareholders in foreign companies. When Mexico nationalised *Compania Mexicana de Petroleo El Aguila S.A.*,[11] a company incor-

[6] F.C.S.C., 223 (1955). This claim was heard by the F.C.S.C. pursuant to a convention between the United States and Panama of 1950 settling various United States claims by payment of a lump sum; from Whiteman, 8 *Digest of International Law*, 1280–3 (1967). The F.C.S.C. is a national body and tends to apply international law as perceived by the United States.
[7] *Ibid.*
[8] *Ibid.*
[9] II R.I.A.A., 779 (1926).
[10] *Ibid.*, 794.
[11] This claim was made as a result of the nationalisation of the Mexican oil industry. The initial representations were made in 1938. The shareholders were compensated in 1947 pursuant to an agreement between Mexico and the nationalised companies, from Whiteman, 8 *Digest of International Law*, 1273–9 (1967).

porated in Mexico, the British government did not intervene "on behalf of the Mexican Eagle Company but on behalf of the very large majority of shareholders who are of British nationality".[12]

The general principle applied by the United States and Great Britain that diplomatic protection was available only to corporations incorporated in the protecting state has remained a paramount principle of general international law.

The International Court of Justice has affirmed that the right of diplomatic protection for corporations is vested in the state in which the corporation is incorporated.[13] To hold otherwise would mean "in the last analysis that it might be sufficient for one single share to belong to a national of a given state for the latter to be entitled to exercise its diplomatic protection".[14]

Barcelona Traction was concerned with diplomatic protection by Belgium of the majority Belgian shareholder interests in the company, which was incorporated in Canada. The company's undertaking was exclusively located in Spain. Administrative judicial actions by the Spanish authorities transferred control of the undertaking from the company to Spanish interests. Diplomatic protection was initially provided by Canada, on behalf of the company, and by Belgium on behalf of the shareholders. After a period Canada ceased to provide protection and Belgium was left to prosecute the claim of the shareholders by itself.

The Court noted the traditional rule that the state in which the company is incorporated has the right of diplomatic protection.[15] The Court referred to the growth in foreign investment and observed, "it may at first sight appear surprising that the evolution of law has not gone further and that no generally accepted rules in the matter have crystallized on the international plane".[16]

However, since there had been an "intense conflict of systems and interests" it was not possible for such a "body of rules" to develop.[17] The Court therefore stated:[18]

Thus, in the present state of the law, the protection of shareholders requires that recourse be had to treaty stipulations or special agreements directly concluded between the private investor and the State in which the investment is placed. States ever more frequently provide for such protection, in both bilateral and multi-lateral relations, either by means of special instruments or within the

---

[12] Diplomatic Note from Britain to Mexico, 1938; from Whiteman, 8 *Digest of International Law*, 1273 (1967).
[13] *Barcelona Traction (Belguim v Spain) Second Phase*, I.C.J. Rep., 3 (1970).
[14] *Ibid.*, 49.
[15] *Ibid.*, 42, 46.
[16] *Ibid.*, 47.
[17] *Ibid.*, 47.
[18] *Ibid.*, 47.

framework of wider economic arrangements... No such instrument is in force between the parties in the present case.

Although there existed a large body of agreements providing for the protection of shareholder interests the Court did not consider that they established a rule of customary international law. Instead the Court stated:[19]

> Far from evidencing any norm as to the classes of beneficiaries of compensation, such arrangements are *sui generis* and provide no guide in the present case.... To seek to draw from them analogies or conclusions held to be valid in other fields is to ignore their specific character as *lex specialis* and hence to court error.

The only state which could rely on a general principle of international law to present a claim on behalf of Barcelona Traction was Canada, the place of incorporation of the company.

The Court would allow shareholder claims only if the company had ceased to exist, in which case an "independent right of action for [shareholders] and their government could arise".[20] The right to protect shareholders would also arise if the respondent state were the national state of the company.[21]

The *Barcelona Traction* case has been the subject of considerable criticism. In particular, Lillich considered that the Court had not taken proper notice of the very substantial number of claims settlement agreements which provided for compensation of nationalised shareholdings in companies incorporated in third states.[22]

Claims settlement agreements, whether they provide for compensation by a lump sum payment by the respondent state or by espousal of claims before a tribunal constituted under such agreement, have had reference to both the place of incorporation and the nationality of the shareholder as the basis of diplomatic protection.

The United States has had reference to both principles. In the United States–Yugoslav agreement of 1948 corporations could only make claims if they were incorporated in the United States and had 20 per cent of their stock owned by United States citizens.[23] More recently the United States has placed greater emphasis on the ownership of the stock of a corporation. The International Claims Settlement Act of 1949, which

---

[19] *Ibid.*, 40.
[20] *Ibid.*, 40.
[21] *Ibid.*, 48.
[22] Lillich, *The Rigidity of Barcelona*, 65 A.J.I.L., 522, 526–47 (1970). There have been more than eighty lump sum agreements since World War II. See Lillich and Weston, *International Claims: Their Settlement by Lump Sum Agreements* (1975). Generally lump sum agreements provide for compensation of nationalised shareholdings of nationals of the claimant irrespective of the place of incorporation of the nationalised company.
[23] Article 2 of the United States–Yugoslav Agreement.

Claimants and corporate claims

established the Foreign Claims Settlement Commission to disburse the proceeds of lump sum agreements, gave various definitions of United States nationals. In most cases corporations were required to be organised under the laws of the various states of the United States and to have 50 per cent or more of their stock owned by United States nationals.[24] The agreements made since this Act incorporate this definition. Thus in the United States–Hungary agreement a claim could be made by a United States corporation only if 50 per cent of its stock was owned by United States natural persons.[25] Similarly the agreement between the United States and Czechoslovakia permits claims by United States corporations only if 50 per cent or more of their stock is owned by United States nationals.[26] However, where the respondent state has expropriated shareholder interests in corporations which are incorporated in the claimant state there is no minimum shareholding requirement. Provided a national of the claimant state can show ownership of the shareholding, then a claim can be made. In this instance, however, there is no question of the corporation making a claim in respect of its own interests.

The Claims Settlement Declaration

The provisions of the Claims Settlement Declaration on corporate nationality permit claimants to make claims under both principles. Thus corporations may make claims provided they are registered in either Iran or the United States, with a majority of their shareholding owned by Iran or United States citizens. In addition shareholders who are citizens of either Iran or the United States may make claims in respect of corporations incorporated in states other than the two states parties provided they control such corporations. Pursuant to Article VII(1) a corporation has Iranian or United States nationality if it is incorporated in either of the parties and 50 per cent or more of its capital stock is held by citizens of the party in which it is incorporated.

This provision reflects current United States practice. This is not surprising, considering that the United States had the primary role in

---

[24] Section 1641(2), pertaining to claims against Bulgaria, Hungary, Roumania, Italy and the Soviet Union. In some instances claims could be made in respect of ownership interests in corporations incorporated outside the United States for shareholdings of less than 50 per cent. This applies in the case of expropriation of shares in the companies.

[25] Article 3(1); 12 I.L.M., 407 (1973).

[26] Article 2; 21 I.L.M., 371 (1982). These provisions do not prevent shareholder claims. If the assets of a company incorporated in the respondent state have been expropriated, United States nationals who are stockholders in such a company could make a claim to the Foreign Claims Settlement Commission, since the shareholding interests of the United States national will have been affected by the measures of nationalisation, expropriation or other taking (cf. Article 2 of the United States–Hungary Agreement).

drafting the Claims Settlement Declaration. Iran's participation in the preparation of the Declaration was in approving or disapproving the United States drafts. In a new development, however, Article VII(2) of the Declaration provides for the protection of shareholder interests irrespective of the place of incorporation provided the shareholders control the corporation. This effectively means the place of incorporation is not relevant. The key test is whether United States nationals control the corporation which owns the claim.

The application of the provisions of the Claims Settlement Declaration by the Tribunal has given rise to three issues.[27] They are, first, the concept of "control" as set out in Article VII(2), secondly, the basis upon which partnerships may make claims and, thirdly, the requirement that claims must be continuously owned by claimants of the claimant state.

Shareholder claims in respect of corporations not incorporated in the claimant state: the nature of "control"

Introduction

Article VII(1) of the Claims Settlement Declaration defines corporate nationals as those corporations which are incorporated in Iran or the United States with 50 per cent or more of their capital stock owned by Iranian or United States citizens. However, claims need not be directly owned by Iranian or United States nationals. Article VII(2) of the Declaration defines "claims of nationals" as including claims owned indirectly through the ownership of capital stock sufficient to control a juridical person provided that the juridical person could not itself make a claim.

This provision will most frequently apply to foreign corporations owned by United States nationals. These foreign corporations may be incorporated in third countries or in Iran. In the latter case there is ample precedent in international law to permit claims in respect of shareholder interests in corporations incorporated in the respondent state.[28] The International Court of Justice noted the argument that this is an exception to the general principle enunciated in *Barcelona Traction*.[29] Anglo-American practice, particularly as embodied in claims settlement agreements, is to provide diplomatic protection to their nationals in

---

[27] A fourth issue is the evidence required to prove corporate nationality. This issue will be examined in Chapter Thirteen.

[28] Refer to section on "The development of international law, in relation to corporate claims", *infra*. For commentary see Jones, *Claims on Behalf of Nationals who are Shareholders in Foreign Companies*, 26 B.Y.I.L., 225 (1979); Brownlie, *Principles of Public International Law*, 492–3 (1990); O'Connell, *International Law*, 1043 (1970); Whiteman, 8 *Digest of International Law*, 1272–83 (1967).

[29] I.C.J. Rep., 3, 48 (1970).

respect of their shareholdings in corporations incorporated in the respondent state.[30]

Article VII(2) of the Claims Settlement Declaration carries this development a stage further. Thus if United States citizens "control" a corporation incorporated in a third state which has suffered loss in terms of the Claims Settlement Declaration then the United States citizens may make a claim. This "control" may be achieved in a variety of ways. The simplest way is for the United States citizens to directly or indirectly own 50 per cent of the stock of the foreign corporation. However, in the case of foreign subsidiary corporations of United States corporations the ultimate beneficial United States ownership required to "control" the subsidiary may be as low as 25 per cent. A United States corporation is deemed to be a United States national if 50 per cent or more of its stock is owned by United States citizens.[31]

Thus a United States corporation having 50 per cent of its stock owned by United States citizens can have control over a foreign subsidiary by owning 50 per cent of the stock of the subsidiary. The United States citizens would only have a 25 per cent beneficial interest in the foreign subsidiary. Moreover shares in corporations may be subdivided into several classes. Thus if a corporation has "A" and "B" shares with all voting rights being attached to the "A" shares then the owners of the majority of the "A" shares will control the corporation irrespective of the proportion of the beneficial ownership of the corporation such shares represent.

Awards of the Tribunal

The Tribunal has made a number of awards in respect of claims on behalf of corporations incorporated in countries other than Iran and the United States, and in respect of claims on behalf of corporations incorporated in Iran. In both cases the essential jurisdictional issue has been whether the claimant corporation is directly or indirectly controlled by United States citizens. The nature of this control, however, has been fully considered only in the *Alcan* claim,[32] although it has arisen in other claims.

There have been a number of settlements of claims in respect of corporations incorporated in third countries. In the Award *Singer Company v Iran National Airlines Corporation*[33] the claimant, a United

---

[30] Refer note 4, *supra* for references.

[31] Article VII(1) of the Claim Settlement Declaration. This is a standard provision in recent claims settlement agreements entered into by the United States. Refer to "The development of international law in relation to corporate claims", *supra*.

[32] 2 IRAN–U.S.C.T.R., 294 (1983). This case will be considered at the end of this section.

[33] 1 IRAN–U.S.C.T.R., 140 (1981–82).

States corporation, was making a claim on behalf of its wholly owned subsidiary, the Singer Company (UK) Ltd, incorporated in the United Kingdom. The subsidiary had supplied a Boeing 707 flight simulator, and the parent company had supplied a Boeing 727 flight simulator. The sum of $281,056 was owed by Iran Air in respect of both contracts. It was agreed between the parties that Singer would make a claim before the Tribunal for this sum, so that it could be paid from the Security Account. The Tribunal was satisfied that it had jurisdiction within the terms of the Claims Settlement Declaration and the award was satisfied from the Security Account established pursuant to the General Declaration. Similarly the claim by *Honeywell Information Services Inc.* v *Information Systems Iran (Isiran)*[34] was made in respect of a contract between Honeywell Information Systems Italia S.p.A., a wholly owned Italian subsidiary of the claimant, and Isiran. In this case the Memorandum of Undertaking, settling the claim, was between the Italian subsidiary and Isiran. The memorandum stated that, upon ratification by both parties, Isiran and Honeywell Information Services Inc. would request the issuance of an award by the Tribunal, authorising payment of $800,000 from the Security Account. The Tribunal acceded to this request, stating that "it has satisfied itself that it has jurisdiction in this matter within the terms of the Declaration of the Democratic and Popular Republic of Algeria concerning the Settlement of Claims . . .".[35]

The Claims Settlement Declaration makes no differentiation between claims by United States nationals in respect of shareholder interests in companies incorporated in Iran and shareholder interests in companies incorporated in third countries. So long as the United States nationals have control over the foreign company the claim can properly be made. The Tribunal has considered a number of claims made by United States nationals in respect of shareholder interests in Iranian companies. In such instances, however, the issue is not whether the corporation is controlled by United States nationals but whether United States nationals own or control the expropriated shareholder interests.

The case of *Starrett Housing Corporation* v *Iran*[36] concerned claims by Starrett Housing Corporation, a United States corporation, in respect of two subsidiary companies, Shah Goli and Starrett Construction Company Iran, both incorporated in Iran. The case illustrates two points. First, that claims can be made in respect of shareholder interests in companies

---

[34] 1 IRAN–U.S.C.T.R., 181 (1981–82).
[35] *Ibid.*
[36] 4 IRAN–U.S.C.T.R., 122 (1983). Chamber One made an Interlocutory Award in which it held that it had jurisdiction and that the interests of the claimant had been expropriated. An expert was appointed to determine the question of compensation. The Interlocutory Award was made by Judge Lagergren. Mr Holtzmann filed a concurring opinion and Mr Kashani filed a dissenting opinion some months later.

incorporated in Iran, no matter how indirectly they are owned. Second, it shows the nature of the shareholder interests in respect of which the claims can be made.

Shah Goli was 80 per cent owned by Starrett Housing G.m.b.H., a West German company wholly owned by Starrett Housing International Inc. and Starrett Systems Inc., both United States subsidiaries of Starrett Housing Corporation. Starrett Construction Company Iran was wholly owned by Starrett Construction Inc., a United States subsidiary of Starrett Housing Corporation. Starrett Housing created a Swiss subsidiary to enter into an agreement with Bank Iran, owned by the Pahlavi Foundation, to construct apartment buildings.

This agreement was assigned to Shah Goli. Starrett Construction Company was to perform a management function in respect of the project. During and following the revolutionary period it became impossible for the two companies to fulfil their obligations. The government of Iran appointed new managers to the companies. Starrett Housing claimed that its property rights, consisting of loans to Shah Goli and the expectation of profits that would be earned from the project, had been expropriated by Iran, although it accepted that neither the shares of the two Iranian companies nor their assets had been formally nationalised.

In respect of the first issue of the right to make claims, the Tribunal recited the ownership interests that Starrett Housing had in the two Iranian companies, and thereby accepted that Starrett Housing had the right to make the claim through its shareholder interests.[37]

The Tribunal considered that Starrett Housing's rights in respect of its shareholder interests had been infringed, since:[38]

> There can be little doubt that at least by the end of January 1980 the Claimants had been deprived of the effective use control and benefits of the property rights in Shah Goli.

These property rights of shareholders were not clearly identified by the Tribunal but must include the right to receive dividends, the right to appoint directors and, in this particular case, the repayment of the loans to Shah Goli. As a result of the control of the shareholding in Shah Goli by United States nationals through various intermediaries, the Tribunal was able to make an award in favour of the United States nationals for the expropriation of the shareholding in Shah Goli.

A majority interest in the Iranian corporation is not required under Article VII(2) if the claim concerns expropriation of the claimant's interest in the Iranian corporation. However, it must be shown that the shareholder interest that has been expropriated is ultimately subject to the

[37] *Ibid.*, 141–2.
[38] *Ibid.*, 154.

control of United States nationals. The case of *American International Group Inc. v Iran*[39] concerned the expropriation of a 35 per cent shareholding in an insurance company incorporated in Iran. The 35 per cent shareholding was owned by four wholly owned subsidiaries of the claimant, two of which were incorporated in Bermuda and two of which were incorporated in the United States. The Tribunal accepted the evidence of United States nationality of the claimant and of the subsidiaries incorporated in the United States, and that the claimant had control of the subsidiaries incorporated in Bermuda, such evidence conforming to the requirements of the *Flexi-Van* case.[40] There was never any doubt either by the Tribunal or by Iran that the Tribunal had jurisdiction to consider the claim for the expropriation of the 35 per cent of shares in the Iranian insurance company once it could be shown that the claimant directly or indirectly had ownership of the shares.

In the *Alcan* claim[41] the Tribunal specifically considered the nature of "control" in relation to claims being made on behalf of the corporation. The *Alcan* claim was made in respect of a Canadian corporation, the majority of whose shares were alleged to be owned by United States nationals. Since Alcan was unable to make a claim before the Tribunal the claim had to be made by the shareholders, and under Article VII(2) of the Declaration the United States shareholders had to be able "to control" the corporation. On the meaning of the words "to control" the Chamber stated:[42]

That the ownership interests of shareholder-claimants who are United States nationals were, collectively, sufficient to control a corporation at the time the claim arose may be demonstrated in several ways. It may be shown that, at the appropriate time, such shareholders controlled the corporation in fact, regardless of the total proportion of their shares. Although it may be shown that such shareholders had sufficient voting strength or the right to assert control, this would generally require ownership of 50 per cent or more of the shares.

By limiting the definition of stock to voting stock it becomes more probable that the owners of 50 per cent or more of voting stock can in fact control the corporation. In any event the Tribunal noted:[43]

No proof has been presented in supporting the claimants' contention that, even if United States nationals did not hold 50 per cent or more of Alcan's shares, such nationals were in fact in a position to control the company at the time the claim arose.

[39] 4 IRAN-U.S.C.T.R., 96 (1983).
[40] Refer to Chapter Thirteen for a full description of this case.
[41] The full title of the case is *The Management of Alcan Aluminium Limited on behalf of its shareholders who are United States nationals and James P. Monaghan on behalf of himself and other shareholders of Alcan Aluminium Limited who are United States nationals v Ircable Corporation* 2 IRAN-U.S.C.T.R., 294 (1983).
[42] *Ibid.*, 297.
[43] *Ibid.*, 298.

The situation envisaged by the *Alcan* case primarily applies to subsidiary corporations incorporated overseas, and to overseas corporations where the controlling interest is owned by United States nationals. Nevertheless the possibility arises that United States nationals may make a claim by virtue of having a minority, but controlling, shareholding in a corporation incorporated in the United States. Although the corporation could not be classified as a United States national under Article VII(1) the shareholders could make a claim pursuant to Article VII(2) of the Declaration.

Partnership claims[44]

Introduction

The majority of claims before the Tribunal are claims derived from relationships involving only the claimants and respondent. A small number, however, are derived from partnership arrangements where one of the partners is a United States corporation, and the asset of the partnership has been expropriated by Iran or a contract of the partnership has been terminated by Iran.

In Anglo-American law a partnership is not an independent legal person, as is the case with corporations. The interests of the partnership are therefore subdivisible among the partners. The United States government has provided protection to partners having United States nationality to the extent of their interest in the partnership, although the partnership may be constituted in the defendant country. In the case of *P. W. Shufeldt (United States* v *Guatemala)*[45] the arbitrator held:[46]

... [I]t makes no difference which [of two partnerships] was in existence as it is not the rights of the partnership that are in question but the personal interest of Shufeldt in the partnership.

Similarly in *Davis (United States* v *Mexico)*[47] a claim was permitted by the commission to the extent of the United States interest in the partnership.

The British government has generally permitted claims by partnerships constituted under English law irrespective of the nationality of the partners.[48] In the case of partnerships constituted outside Britain, or in the defendant country, protection would only be provided if a substantial interest of the partnership were owned by British partners, in the same manner as corporations.

[44] The leading commentary on partnership claims before the Tribunal is Fauver, *Partnership Claims before the Iran–United States Claims Tribunal*, 27 Va. J.I.L., 307 (1987).
[45] II R.I.A.A., 1079 (1930).
[46] *Ibid.*
[47] IV R.I.A.A., 517 (1929).
[48] Parry (ed.), 5 *British Digest of International Law*, 481–502; Brownlie, *Principles of Public International Law*, 484 (1990).

The Claims Settlement Declaration

Article II(1) of the Claims Settlement Declaration is not inconsistent with nationals of either party who are members of a partnership making claims in respect of their interest in the partnership. This is particularly so if there has been an expropriation or taking of the assets or undertaking of the partnership. In such cases the claims of the United States nationals would be made in respect of their share of the partnership.[49]

However, Article VII(2) of the Claims Settlement Declaration envisages claims by the partnership, rather than the individual partners. The requirement that ownership interests in juridical persons must be sufficient to control the "corporation or entity" relates to the control of the partnership as a whole. Precedent supports this interpretation. The Treaty of Friendship between the United States and Italy defines corporations and associations as meaning "corporations, companies, partnerships and other associations".[50] The Treaty of Amity between Iran and the United States defines "companies [as] corporations, partnerships, companies and other associations".[51] The practice of the United States in international treaties and in particular the Treaty of Amity with Iran, although at variance with the municipal law position that partnerships are not separate legal persons, has been to treat partnerships as legal persons able to act and to make claims in their own right. Accordingly the words "corporation or entity" in Article VII(2) of the Claims Settlement Declaration should be construed to include partnerships.

Two types of partnership claims may be envisaged. The first is where the United States interest in a partnership organised in Iran or a third country is owned by a juridical person. So long as the United States juridical person is owned 50 per cent or more by United States nationals then a claim may be made in respect of that partnership interest irrespective of whether the partnership is organised in Iran or elsewhere. The second situation is where the partnership making the claim is directly or indirectly controlled by United States interests. In this case the claim may be made in respect of the partnership as a whole.

Decisions of the Tribunal

The first case before the Tribunal concerning a claim of an individual partner interest was *Phillips Petroleum Company, Iran* v *Iran and National Iranian Oil Company*.[52] The claimants raised the question of the nationality of the partnership interest in a preliminary hearing. The facts were

---

[49] Refer to *Starrett Housing Corporation* v *Iran* for a claim by a shareholder in respect of the interest owned by the shareholder in an Iranian corporation expropriated by Iran.
[50] Article II(1) of the Treaty.
[51] Article III(1) of the Treaty, U.N.T.S., 284: 93.
[52] 1 IRAN–U.S.C.T.R., 487 (1981–82).

Claimants and corporate claims

that Phillips Petroleum was a member of a partnership, the other two partners being an Italian corporation and an Indian corporation. The three partners entered into a joint structure agreement with National Iranian Oil Company (NIOC) in 1965. Article 12.2 of the agreement provided that the three parties held their interests as undivided interests. In January 1980 the Revolutionary Council of Iran passed a Single Article Act establishing a Special Commission to examine all oil agreements.

In 1980 the Special Commission purported to nullify the agreement between the partnership and NIOC. Following the establishment of the Claims Settlement Tribunal, Phillips Petroleum filed a claim for compensation for its share of the nullified joint structure agreement.

The respondents, as a preliminary point, requested the Tribunal to consider whether it had jurisdiction. There were two aspects to this question. The first was whether the Single Article Act excluded the jurisdiction of the Tribunal.[53] The second point raised by the respondents was that only the partnership as a whole could make a claim for compensation. Since the partnership was not a United States national the Tribunal could not have jurisdiction.

The respondents contended that the obligations of NIOC were owed to the three members of the partnership jointly and severally. This was indicated by Article 12.2 of the joint structure agreement, stating that the three members held their interests as undivided interests. The municipal law of the United States, England and Germany was cited by the respondents in support of the proposition that members of a partnership cannot claim individually for a partnership loss. Since only the partnership could sustain a claim, it had to show United States nationality, with United States registration, and majority ownership by United States nationals. The *Barcelona Traction* decision was cited in support of the proposition.[54] Since the ownership of the partnership was equally divided between United States, Italian and Indian corporations and the place of registration was Iran, the respondents argued, the Tribunal did not have jurisdiction because the true claimant did not have United States nationality.

The United States claimant argued that it was entitled to bring the claim on its own behalf, since its claim related only to the loss it had sustained, and not the loss sustained by the other two members of the partnership.[55] Furthermore the nullification of the joint structure agree-

---

[53] *Ibid.*, 488. This point is fully covered in Chapter Twelve at The Meaning of "In Response to the Majlis Position".
[54] *Ibid.*
[55] The claim is comparable to claims by corporations in respect of expropriated shareholdings. See *Starrett Housing Corp.* v *Iran* 4 IRAN–U.S.C.T.R., 122 (1983), discussed in this chapter, *supra*.

ment by Iran was a breach of international law, and the Treaty of Amity between Iran and the United States of 1955. Finally, the Claims Settlement Declaration expressly conferred jurisdiction upon the Tribunal in so far as Article II(1) referred to "expropriations or other measures affecting property rights".

The Tribunal was concerned with the issue of nullification at the preliminary hearing; whether or not the Single Article Act of January 1980, or the words of Article II(1) of the Declaration—"claims arising under a binding contract between the parties specifically providing that any disputes thereunder shall be within the sole jurisdiction of the competent Iranian courts, in response to the Majlis position"—excluded the jurisdiction of the Tribunal. Since the question of nationality was not related to the question of nullification the Tribunal determined:[56]

> As to the fourth issue [nationality] raised by NIOC, the Tribunal determines that it must be joined to the merits of the case, since it does not relate to the narrow jurisdictional issue related to the alleged nullification of oil agreements, for which NIOC requested and the Tribunal ordered that the Preliminary Hearing be held.

The first major case in which the partnership issues were decided was *Housing and Urban Services International Inc. v Tehran Redevelopment Corporation*[57] The claimant had been party to a joint venture agreement with a German company for the provision of architectural services to the respondent. The respondent argued that the joint venture parties were a partnership and the claim should properly be made by the partnership and not by the claimant alone. The effect would be to bar the claim under Article VII(2) of the Claims Settlement Declaration, since the partnership was not a United States national.

The Tribunal examined the circumstances of the alleged partnership and decided that, under Iranian law, the municipal law governing the agreement, the claimant and the German company were a partnership, although not a separate juridical entity. The Tribunal noted that Iranian law permitted one partner alone to litigate a claim, provided there was agreement on the part of all partners.[58] However, the Tribunal also referred to international law, relying on Article V of the Claims Settlement Declaration.[59] It stated:[60]

> Nevertheless, the Tribunal is an international forum, established by a treaty that bars parties who are not nationals of either the United States or Iran from

---

[56] *Ibid.*, 489. At the time of writing this issue had not been resolved by the Tribunal in respect of this case.
[57] 9 IRAN–U.S.C.T.R., 313 (1985).
[58] *Ibid.*, 329.
[59] *Ibid.*, 330, note 16.
[60] *Ibid.*, 330.

appearing before it. Thus, while the Tribunal may take municipal law as its "point of departure", it must look as well to international law on this question.

The Tribunal noted that while international law accepts that parties cannot sue in their own name, international tribunals have permitted recovery by individual partners of their *pro rata* share where special circumstances warrant it.[61] The Tribunal referred to the major international precedents, including the *Ziat, Ben Kiran* case *(Great Britain v Spain)*[62] and the *Shufeldt* case.[63]

The special reasons in the present case were that the payments due to the claimant from TRC were readily identifiable and separable from that of its partner. More significantly the claimant would otherwise be prevented from claiming, owing to the nationality of its partner thereby infringing the nationality requirements of the Claims Settlement Declaration.[64] Accordingly the claimant was entitled to make a *pro rata* claim being 85 per cent of the amounts due under the joint venture agreement.[65]

The decision will establish the precedent for similar claims where a United States partner is claiming compensation in respect of its own interests. For expropriation claims the claim will be for the partner's share of the assets of the partnership. For contract claims the claim will be for a *pro rata* share of the partnership's contract, provided the partner's interests in the contract is readily identifiable and separable from that of its partners.

Conclusion

The most significant aspect of the provisions of the Claims Settlement Declaration relating to nationality is the contrast between the rules for individual claimants and those for corporate claimants. Whereas the Tribunal has been compelled to prescribe detailed rules for determining which citizens can make claims by reference to public international law in its awards and decisions, for corporate claimants the detailed rules are fully set out in the Claims Settlement Declaration. The reason, perhaps, is that the parties were satisfied that public international law provided adequate guidance in respect of the nationality of individual claimants. In the case of corporate claimants, state practice, as represented by various claims settlement agreements, has diverged from general international law as expressed in the *Barcelona Traction* case. It was therefore essential

---

[61] *Ibid.*
[62] II R.I.A.A., 729 (1924) at 9 IRAN–U.S.C.T.R., 313, 331 (1985).
[63] II R.I.A.A., 1083 (1930) at 9 IRAN–U.S.C.T.R., 313, 331 (1985).
[64] *Ibid.*, 332.
[65] *Ibid.*, 333.

for the parties to make explicit provisions in respect of corporate nationality. Thus the contribution of awards and decisions of the Tribunal to the body of general public international law has been the further development of the concept of the closest and most real connection in respect of individual claimants making claims against a state whose nationality they also possess.

The Claims Settlement Declaration is a further consolidation of state practice in respect of corporate claimants requiring both incorporation and substantial shareholding before a state will provide diplomatic protection to corporate claimants incorporated in its territory. However, the Claims Settlement Declaration also allows claims in respect of shareholder interests if the corporate claimant is unable to make a claim as a result of its not being incorporated in the claimant state. This is a new development, being fundamentally concerned with the protection of shareholder interests rather than the juridical entity of the corporation. Ultimately the wealth of the corporation rests with its shareholders.

Article VII(2) of the Claims Settlement Declaration permits shareholder claims provided the shareholders control the corporation. Arguably, shareholders should only be able to make claims to the extent of their shareholding. This has been accepted by the Tribunal where the shareholding has been expropriated. In such cases the claim is essentially that of the shareholder rather than of the corporation, thereby preserving the distinction between the shareholder and the corporation. The claims permitted by Article VII(2) are in respect of the corporation. Nevertheless Article VII(2) is a recognition that the corporation is essentially the *alter ego* of the majority shareholders. Article VII(2), effectively provides protection to majority shareholders of corporations incorporated outside their state of nationality to the same extent as majority shareholders of corporations which are incorporated in the claimant state.

CHAPTER SIX

The governing law of the claims

The provisions of the Claims Settlement Declaration

The principal jurisdiction of the Iran–United States Claims Tribunal is set out in Articles II(1) and (2) of the Claims Settlement Declaration.[1] These paragraphs cover the contractual and property claims that can be made by nationals of either party against the government of the other party and the contractual claims by the government of either party against the government of the other party.

Of these two heads of jurisdiction of the Tribunal, the most important is the multiplicity of claims by the nationals of either party against the government or government-controlled entity of the other party. Such claims constitute more that 97 per cent of all claims filed with the Tribunal,[2] although some 74 per cent of these claims are small claims of less than $250,000 which will be presented to the Tribunal by the government of the nationals making the claims.[3]

The jurisdiction of the Tribunal over private claims is established by Article II(1) of the Claims Settlement Declaration, which states:

An international arbitral tribunal [the Iran–United States Claims Tribunal] is hereby established for the purpose of deciding claims of nationals of the United states against Iran and claims of nationals of Iran against the United States, and any counterclaim which arises out of the same contract, transaction or occurrence

---

[1] There is a third head of jurisdiction contained in Article II(2) of the Claims Settlement Declaration relating to disputes over the application and interpretation of the Algiers Declarations, which will not be considered in this chapter.

[2] See Chapter Two for a breakdown of statistics on the Claims filed with the Tribunal.

[3] Article III(3) of the Claims Settlement Declaration divides the private claims into two categories: those in excess of $250,000, which must be presented to the Tribunal by the claimants themselves, and those under $250,000, which must be presented to the Tribunal by the government of nationals which own such claims. The significance of this division between small claims and large claims is considered in Chapter Thirteen.

that constitutes the subject matter of that national's claim, if such claims and counterclaims are outstanding on the date of this Agreement, whether or not filed with any court, and arise out of *debts, contracts (including transactions which are the subject of letters of credit or bank guarantees), expropriations or other measures affecting property rights*, excluding claims described in Paragraph 11 of the Declaration of the Government of Algeria of January 19, 1981, and claims arising out of the actions of the United States in response to the conduct described in such paragraph, and excluding claims arising under a binding contract between the parties specifically providing that any disputes thereunder shall be within the sole jurisdiction of the competent Iranian courts, in response to the Majlis position.[4]

In respect of the contractual claims between the governments of the two parties, Article II(2) of the Declaration states:

The Tribunal shall also have jurisdiction over official claims of the United States and Iran against each other arising out of contractual arrangements between them for the purchase and sale of goods and services.

The Claims Settlement Declaration thus restricts private claims to four categories: debts, contracts, expropriations and other measures affecting property rights, while governmental claims may be made only in respect of contracts for goods and services with the government of the other party. The principal exception to the jurisdiction of the Tribunal in respect of private claims is if the claim arises "under a binding contract between the parties specifically providing that disputes thereunder shall be within the sole jurisdiction of the competent Iranian courts".[5] The significance of this exception along with an exception relating to "popular movements" will be considered in Chapter Eleven.

In determining claims under any of the categories the Tribunal is governed by the principles set out in Article V of the Claims Settlement Declaration, which provides:

The Tribunal shall decide all cases on the basis of respect for law, applying such choice of law rules and principles of commercial and international law as the Tribunal determines to be applicable, taking into account relevant usages of the trade, contract provisions and changed circumstances.

This provision is significantly different from the typical choice of law provisions of treaties establishing international claims tribunals. In most cases such treaties simply require the tribunal to decide claims in accordance with the principles of public international law. In the present case, however, the Tribunal is able to apply international law or municipal law to the claims as it thinks fit.

[4] Emphasis added. The exclusions to the jurisdiction of the Tribunal are considered in Chapter Twelve.
[5] Article II(1) of the Claims Settlement Declaration.

There is no direction to the Tribunal on the particular system of law to be applied in a particular claim. Nevertheless the Tribunal must decide "all cases on the basis of respect for law". This implies the Tribunal should apply the appropriate system of law to each claim. Thus for most contract claims municipal law will be applicable, while for expropriation claims and confiscatory and discriminatory breaches or annulments of contract, giving rise to questions of state responsibility, public international law will be applicable. Whenever the issue of state responsibility arises public international law will be the appropriate system of law, since the claim involves obligations that the respondent state owes to the claimant state. Public international law can, however, result in a particular system of municipal law being applied to the claim.

It is noteworthy that in many cases which would ostensibly be governed by a particular system of municipal law, particularly if it is Iranian or United States municipal law, the arbitrators have canvassed various municipal systems of law to find a general principle of law which conforms to the particular system of municipal law. Such an approach would indicate that the direction in Article V to "decide all cases on the basis of respect for law" is not intended to direct the Tribunal to making the appropriate distinction between particular systems of law, but rather to found its decisions on law and not to decide *ex aequo et bono*.

The law governing the claims

The private claims

The private claims being heard by the Iran–United States Claims Tribunal in respect of the four categories of "debts, contracts, expropriation and other measures affecting property rights" may be divided into two classes, first, those claims which are governed by international law and, secondly, those claims governed largely by municipal law.

The first class covers those claims where the respondent government has incurred international responsibility and thus the principles of international law are applicable to such claims. The claims arising from acts of expropriation clearly fall into this class. However, claims arising from debts and contract may also be governed by public international law, particularly where there has been confiscatory annulment[6] or denial of justice. It is the view of some writers that a breach of a contract by a state

---

[6] Brownlie, *Principles of Public International Law*, 547 (1990); Brownlie, *System of the Law of Nations: State Responsibility*, 80 (1983); Mann, *Studies in International Law*, 302 (1973); Greig, *International Law*, 560 (1976); Domke, *Foreign Nationalizations: Some Aspects of Contemporary International Law*, 55 A.J.I.L., 585, 595 (1961); Wortley, *Expropriation in Public International Law*, 56 (1959).

in respect of a contract which it has made with the national of another state is in itself a confiscation of property.[7] Accordingly international responsibility arises in respect of the confiscation of property. However, it is generally regarded that a simple breach of contract by a state does not lead to state responsibility, until there is a denial of justice.[8] In the present case, however, since the claims have already been removed to an international claims arbitral tribunal the issue of denial of justice does not arise and the Tribunal simply has to determine whether the substance of the claims is governed by international law or by a particular system of municipal law. In the latter case a tribunal may not apply municipal law if such application would itself constitute a denial of justice.

The second class of claims are those governed expressly or impliedly by a system of municipal law had they been heard in a municipal court. The majority of claims arising from debt and contract come within this class. In respect of such claims made by United States claimants, the Tribunal is acting as a substitute forum for the United States municipal courts even though the claims have been removed to the international plane.[9] It could be expected therefore that the Tribunal will determine these claims by reference to the system of municipal law which the parties originally intended should apply, provided such law has not subsequently deviated from principles of law generally recognised by states. The Tribunal, however, is not bound to give effect to the parties' choice of law, or to apply a particular system of municipal law. Article V of the Claims Settlement Declaration allows the Tribunal to apply "such choice of law rules and principles of commercial and international law" as it considers applicable to determine the claim, and this applies whether the Tribunal is acting as a substitute forum for United States municipal courts, or as a forum to resolve matters of state responsibility.

A number of jurists consider that once a claim is removed from a domestic forum to an international forum, the responsibility of the state is incurred in respect of breaches of state contracts and non-payment of state debt made or incurred with nationals of another state.[10] It should be noted, however, that, in subjecting the claim to public international law, there is nothing to prevent an international tribunal determining the substantive issues of the claim in accordance with a particular system of

[7] Feller, *The Mexican Claims Commissions 1923–1934*, 173–4 (1935); O'Connell, *International Law*, 70 (1965).
[8] Brownlie, *Principles of Public International Law*, 547 (1990); Amerasinghe, *State Responsibility for Injuries to Aliens*, 70 (1967); O'Connell, *International Law*, 1067–72 (1965).
[9] See General Principle A of the General Declaration.
[10] Brownlie, *Principles of Public International Law*, 548 (1990); Feller, *The Mexican Claims Commissions 1923–1934*, 176 (1935). It should be noted that the United States–Mexico Tribunal was required to make its decisions "in accordance with the principles of international law", a more restrictive provision than Article V of the Claims Settlement Declaration.

The governing law of the claims 107

municipal law, as may have been originally envisaged by the parties.[11] In contrast to those categories of jurisdiction where a tribunal must apply a particular system of municipal law to the claim, it remains a matter of discretion for a tribunal whether to apply a rule of public international law or a system of municipal law. The discretion of the tribunal is limited to the extent that the municipal law cannot offend against principles of law generally recognised by states.

Article V of the Claims Settlement Declaration gives considerable latitude to the Tribunal in determining the law that will govern any particular claim. Thus the Tribunal could be expected to give effect to the parties' choice of law, or apply a system of municipal law if the parties have not expressly or impliedly made a choice of law. Equally the Tribunal may decide that the claim is governed by international law, and the rules of state responsibility will apply. It would be expected, however, that the Tribunal will apply international law in a manner consistent with the present understanding of the law.

Thus, for all private claims, public international law is applicable for the determination of the preliminary issue of the nationality of the claimant. The substantive issues, however, can be governed by either municipal law or international law.

In claims arising from breach of contract or non-payment of debt the appropriate municipal law would be expected to apply in the absence of confiscatory annulment or denial of justice. If the latter two situations arise then the claim will be governed by international law, even though international law permits the substantive issues of the claim to be resolved by reference to a particular system of municipal law.[12] However, the Tribunal is not bound to act in such a fashion. Article V of the Claims Settlement Declaration gives it sufficient discretion to step outside municipal law if it believes the application of municipal law would give an unjust result.

However, public international law governs the substantive aspects of the expropriation claims, as well as being the applicable law of the claim, and in respect of these claims the Tribunal is acting as a classical international arbitral tribunal deciding issues of state responsibility.

The official claims

The official claims between Iran and the United States arising out of contractual arrangements for the sale and purchase of goods and services

---

[11] This occurred in a number of decisions of the United States–Mexico Tribunal. See in particular *Illinois Railway Co. Claim* IV R.I.A.A., 21 (1926).

[12] This was the case in *Illinois Railway Co. Claim* IV R.I.A.A., 21 (1926); *Serbian loans Case* P.C.I.J., Ser. A, No. 20 (1929); *Brazilian Loans Case* P.C.I.J., Ser. A, No. 20 (1929); *Norwegian Loans Case* I.C.J. Rep., 31 (1957), dissenting judgment of Judge Lauterpacht, 36–8.

are of a different nature from the private claims, since the two states have complete freedom in choosing the applicable law governing the official claims. They can choose to subject their contractual relationship to a specific system of municipal law, to the general principles of law or to public international law. On the principle of equality of states the Tribunal will be required to give effect to the choice of law of the two states and decide the official claims accordingly. Thus if the two states have chosen public international law to govern the contractual relationship the Tribunal must apply the rules of public international law to the claim, whereas a similar private contractual claim would be determined in accordance with a particular system of municipal law.

The relationship between the law of state responsibility and the diplomatic protection of aliens

It is a fundamental principle of international law that a state incurs international responsibility if it causes injury to the person or property of nationals of another state as a result of a breach of duty owed by the respondent state to the state of such nationals.[13] Although it is the nationals of the claimant state who suffered the actual loss, the injury is imputed to the claimant state. Accordingly the duty is owed by the

[13] The literature on state responsibility in relation to aliens is quite extensive. The principal texts, setting out the principles of state responsibility in respect of injuries to aliens generally accepted by states, include: Amerasinghe, *State Responsibility for Injuries to Aliens* (1967); Brownlie, *Principles of Public International Law* (1990); *System of the Law of Nations: State Responsibility* (1983); Borchard, *The Diplomatic Protection of Citizens Abroad* (1928); Dunn, *The Protection of Nationals* (1932); Eagleton, *The Responsibility of States in International Law* (1928); Greig, *International Law* (1976); Lauterpacht *Oppenheim's International Law*, 1, especially 336–70 (1955); O'Connell, *International Law* (1965); Schwarzenberger, *International Law* (1957). The work of the I.L.C. on state responsibility is of particular importance. The work of the I.L.C. has proceeded through two distinct phases. Special Rapporteur Garcia-Amador viewed state responsibility in terms of the rules applicable to the treatment of aliens. Special Rapporteurs Ago and Riphagen have been charged with defining the imputability of the state for breaches of rules of international law, irrespective of their content. See report of the Commission to the General Assembly, *Yearbook of the I.L.C.* (1969) II, 203, 229–33, confirmed by Riphagen in *Yearbook of the I.L.C.* (1980) II, 107, 108–9. For a comprehensive consideration of the principles and arbitral precedents on state responsibility reference should be made to the *Yearbooks of the I.L.C.* and in particular to the extensive reports of Special Rapporteurs Garcia-Amador, *Yearbooks of the I.L.C.* (1956–61); Ago, *Yearbooks of the I.L.C.* (1969–80); Riphagen, *Yearbooks of the I.L.C.* (1980–85). As a result of the work of Special Rapporteurs Ago and Riphagen the I.L.C. has now approved a number of articles for a possible Draft Convention on State Responsibility. These articles are notable for their reference to the theoretical principles of state responsibility. General commentary on the work of the I.L.C. is provided by Briggs, *The International Law Commission* (1964), and Sinclair, *The International Law Commission* (1987). In addition there are a number of earlier private draft conventions on state responsibility for injury to aliens. See *Harvard Draft Convention on the International Responsibility of States for Injuries to Aliens (Final Version 1974)*, from Garcia-Amador, Sohn and Baxter, *Recent Codification of the Law of State Responsibility to Aliens* (1978); Sohn and Baxter, *Draft Convention on Responsibility of States for Injuries to the Economic Interests of Aliens*, 55 A.J.I.L., 545 (1961).

respondent state to the claimant state, and not to the injured nationals of the claimant state.

In normal circumstances, the absence of an existing compulsory forum for the enforcement of the international obligations of the respondent state means that generally the only recourse of the claimant state is diplomatic protection, thus exemplifying the fundamental weakness of the international legal order. De Visscher noted:[14]

In the great majority of cases it is diplomatic protection that brings into play the international responsibility of states.

Since states may choose, in any particular case, whether or not to exercise diplomatic protection, the enforcement of the obligations of the respondent state is largely governed by considerations of political expediency, although the substantive issues of state responsibility are inherently legal.[15]

It has been argued by Iran that the establishment of the Iran-United States Claims Tribunal arose from the exercise of diplomatic protection by the states concerned. It may be noted, however, that the Tribunal held that this was not so, owing to ability of nationals to present their claims direct to the Tribunal.[16] It is submitted by the writer that, although nationals are able to present their own claims to the Tribunal, the formation of the Tribunal by means of the Claims Settlement Declaration is a classic exercise of diplomatic protection by the two states, fundamentally no different from the establishment of earlier claims commissions and Mixed Arbitral Tribunals. This is so even if the Tribunal is, in part, a substitute forum for United States municipal courts.

The principles of state responsibility, however, are essentially separate from the exercise of diplomatic protection, even though the enforcement of the obligations is usually dependent on the exercise of diplomatic protection. Once a suitable forum has been established, the aspect of diplomatic protection recedes, and the arbitral tribunal is able to consider the substantive issues of state responsibility irrespective of whether the state itself or its nationals actually present the claims.

The Iran-United States Claims Tribunal is such a forum and accordingly is able to determine whether state responsibility is incurred in respect of particular claims. Even where the Tribunal is acting as a substitute forum for United States municipal courts, the principles of state responsibility may still be applicable, since the claims have been removed by the two

---

[14] De Visscher, *Theory and Reality in Public International Law*, 269 (1957).
[15] *Ibid.*, 270.
[16] *Iran v United States (Case A/18)* 5 IRAN-U.S.C.T.R., 251 (1984); *Iran v United States (Case A/21)* 14 IRAN-U.S.C.T.R., 324 (1986); see Chapter Thirteen for a discussion of this case and the contentions of the parties.

states to an international forum. Pursuant to Article V of the Claims Settlement Declaration the Tribunal has wide discretion in determining the law applicable to the claim, which may include international law. Accordingly the Tribunal will not apply law in the same manner as municipal courts of the United States even though the claims have been removed from such courts to the Tribunal. The Tribunal is primarily governed by Article V of the Claims Settlement Declaration and will apply the principles of state responsibility where appropriate, in particular for expropriation and confiscatory annulment of contract, and municipal law for simple breach of contract and non-payment of debt.

The application of Article V of the Claims Settlement Declaration by the Tribunal

The role of Article V in the Tribunal determining the governing law of claims is of less apparent significance than its inclusion in the Claims Settlement Declaration might indicate. Thus its provisions are cited in relatively few cases. However, it can be argued that it underpins all decisions of the Tribunal, since it directs the Tribunal to "decide all cases on the basis of respect for law". By applying a system of law to determine a particular claim the Tribunal is complying with the injunction of Article V of the Claims Settlement Declaration.

The earliest cases decided by the Tribunal made only passing reference to Article V. More frequently the provision was referred directly by the United States arbitrators in concurring opinions.

Thus in the *Forum Selection* cases[17] Holtzmann in his concurring and dissenting opinion referred to the two governments requiring the Tribunal to make "its decisions on the basis of respect for law, applying principles of international law and taking into account changed circumstances".[18]

In the *Oil Field of Texas Inc.* v *Iran*,[19] concerning a question of the succession by NIOC to the liabilities of a consortium of companies engaged to manage Iran's oilfields, the full Tribunal was specifically concerned with providing a reason for applying international law. The Tribunal stated:[20]

If a *de facto* succession of rights and obligations in a certain field has taken place without the observance of such rules under the applicable national law, it is even more important to establish a rule under international law that such succession must have as a consequence that the surviving company is under an obligation to pay appropriate compensation taking into account all the circumstances of the case.

[17] 1 IRAN–U.S.C.T.R., 284 (1982–82).
[18] *Ibid.*, 294.
[19] 1 IRAN–U.S.C.T.R., 347 (1981–82).
[20] *Ibid.*, 362.

Mr Mosk, in his concurring opinion, made specific reference to Article V when he stated:[21]

> Thus, holding that NIOC's liability can be based on a *"de facto"* succession is justified under Article V of the Claims Settlement Declaration, which requires that all cases be decided "on the basis of respect for law", and which directs the Tribunal to utilize applicable "principles of commercial and international law".

His opinion appears to state the specific authorities that the majority had in mind when "establish[ing] a rule under international law".

Later practice of the Tribunal has been to specifically state the authority upon which the Tribunal is basing its decisions and awards. Thus the Tribunal has made more direct reference to Article V as underpinning the particular choice of law. This trend is exemplified in *Isaiah* v *Bank Mellat*.[22] The Tribunal referred to the principle of unjust enrichment found in both international law and Iranian law. In relation to Article V the Tribunal noted that it gave the Tribunal "considerable flexibility" and concluded:[23]

> Under this rule [Article V] the Tribunal is free to apply general principles of law in a case such as this, although there is no reason to believe the result would be any different if only Iranian law were applied.

This view of the flexibility provided by Article V is well illustrated in *CMI International Inc.* v *Iran*.[24] The Tribunal considered, by reference to Article V, that it was not bound by the law of the contract. In relation to the scope of Article V it stated:[25]

> It is difficult to conceive of a choice of law provision that would give the Tribunal greater freedom in determining case by case the law relevant to the issues before it. Such freedom is consistent with, and perhaps almost essential to, the scope of the tasks confronting the Tribunal, which involve not only claims of a commercial nature, such as the one involved in the present case, but other claims involving alleged expropriations or other public acts, claims between the two Governments, certain claims between banking institutions, and issues of interpretation and implementation of the Algiers Declarations. Thus, the Tribunal may often find it necessary to interpret and apply treaties, customary international law, general principles of law and national laws, "taking into account relevant usages of the trade, contract provisions and changed circumstances", as Article V directs.
>
> With respect to the assessment of damages, the Tribunal considers its main task to be determining what are the losses suffered by the Claimant and to award compensation therefor. Our search is for justice and equity, even in cases when

---

[21] *Ibid.*, 374.
[22] 2 IRAN-U.S.C.T.R., 232 (1983).
[23] *Ibid.*, 237.
[24] 4 IRAN-U.S.C.T.R., 263 (1983).
[25] *Ibid.*, 267.

arguably relevant national laws might be designed to further other and doubtless quite legitimate goals.

As a result of its view of the scope of Article V the Tribunal "analyse[d] the damage questions in accordance with general principles of law rather than by reference to the Code as incorporated in the statutory law of Idaho".[26]

This approach to the application of Article V has been subsequently referred to in the Tribunal. The dissenting Iranian arbitrators in the Dual Nationality case (*Iran* v *United States, Case No. A/18*)[27] relied on the above quotation to demonstrate that the Tribunal "is thus, by its source and function, a true international tribunal".[28] The Iranian arbitrators went on to consider the establishment of the Tribunal "by means of the classic process of diplomatic protection"[29] and to thereby preclude claims against Iran by persons having the nationality of both states.

In relation to contracts, Article V has been used to justify determinations based on general principles of law. The two contract cases cited above demonstrate this approach by the Tribunal and it is confirmed in *DIC of Delaware Inc.* v *IRC*.[30] The specific issue concerned part performance of an oral contract which the Tribunal apprehended to be "proof of a binding contract under Iranian law".[31] However, the Tribunal ultimately relied on Article V:[32]

Under Article V of the Claims Settlement Declaration the Tribunal must look to "principles of commercial and international law" for guidance. It is widely accepted by municipal systems of law that one can prove the existence of an enforceable oral contract through evidence of part performance.

See II K. Zweigert and M. Kötz, *An Introduction to Comparative Law: The Institutions of Private Law* 40–41, 43–50 (1977). Such a principle must be taken to constitute a general principle [of law].

The use of Article V has thus enabled the application of general principles of law to the contract claims. Such general principles are derived from the municipal law of many nations, and in the cases cited it did not appear that the law of Iran or the United States deviated from the general principles applied by the Tribunal. This reference to general principles is nevertheless an indication of the international character of the Tribunal: although it may have the role of a substitute forum for domestic courts, it is not bound to act as if it were a domestic court.

[26] *Ibid.*, 268.
[27] 5 IRAN–U.S.C.T.R., 251 (1984).
[28] *Ibid.*, 294.
[29] *Ibid.*
[30] 8 IRAN–U.S.C.T.R., 144 (1985).
[31] *Ibid.*, 161.
[32] *Ibid.*

The governing law of the claims

Indeed if it had been required to act as if it were a municipal court there would appear to be little reason for its establishment. Since the majority of claims had been initiated in United States they could have simply proceeded through the courts. While this would have required a different political settlement to the crisis such a settlement would not necessarily have been impossible. One of the purposes of removing the claims to an international tribunal was to establish a more neutral forum. Accordingly, the application of general principles of law to the debt and contract claims is indicative of the international character of the forum. Since Islamic law and the common law of the United States have been major contributors to general principles of law as discerned from the practice of many states, the results reached by the Tribunal are not necessarily different from the results that would have been reached by a municipal court.

In respect of the expropriation claims the Tribunal, relying on Article V, had little hesitation in deciding that they were governed by international law.[33] The reason for so deciding is most succinctly described in a recent major decision, *Phillips Petroleum Company, Iran v Iran*.[34] The majority stated:[35]

As the Tribunal has held in a number of cases, expropriation by or attributable to a State of the property of an alien gives rise under international law to liability for compensation, and this is so whether the expropriation is formal or *de facto* and whether the property is tangible, such as real estate or a factory, or intangible, such as the contract rights involved in the present case.

The Tribunal has not cited Article V of the Claims Settlement Declaration as its authority, deciding that expropriation of alien property is governed by international law. However, the mere fact that Article V does refer to "principles of ... international law" would appear to be sufficient authority without having to directly state such a point of trite law.

Thus, by virtue of Article V and the international nature of the Tribunal, whenever there is an issue of state responsibility such as expropriation or unjust enrichment the governing law is necessarily public international law.

---

[33] The awards and decisions in which the Tribunal and its various Chambers have held this to be the correct position are more fully discussed in Chapter Eight.

[34] 21 Iran–U.S.C.T.R., 79 (1989).

[35] *Ibid.*, 106. The Tribunal cited all the leading expropriation cases it had previously decided. See Chapter Eight, *infra*.

CHAPTER SEVEN

Claims arising from debts and contracts[1]

State responsibility and debts and contracts

The categories of jurisdiction set out in Article II(1) of the Claims Settlement Declaration all relate to property rights. They can, however, be divided into contractual rights and non-contractual rights. Both debts and contractual claims are based on contractual rights, whereas claims stemming from expropriation and "other measures affecting property rights" may arise from the mere ownership of property rights. In both cases the respondent state through its acts or omissions can extinguish or limit the property rights, as in the non-payment of debt, breach of contract or the taking of property. A state can also interfere with property rights arising from contracts between private parties by passing decrees preventing the completion of such contracts. In the context of the Iran–United States Claims Tribunal such an action would permit the state of the affected national to present a claim based on expropriation "or other measures affecting property rights".

The division of property rights into contractual and non-contractual rights is instructive in the application of the principles of state responsibility. Generally state responsibility is incurred in respect of a breach of contractual rights only if there has been a denial of justice.[2]

A state may enter into a variety of contracts with aliens, including loan agreements, contracts for the supply of goods and services, construction

---

[1] These two categories of claims are grouped together since they both stem from contractual relationships.

[2] Refer to arbitral decisions, *Lighthouses arbitration between France and Greece* XII R.I.A.A., 217 (1956); *Shufeldt Claim (United states v Guatemala)* II R.I.A.A., 1079 (1930). Refer also to Brownlie, *System of the Law of Nations: State Responsibility*, 80 (1983); Greig, *International Law*, 560 (1976); O'Connell, *International Law*, 1066–8 (1965).

contracts,[3] and concession agreements. These contracts have been divided into two separate categories by many writers, with concession agreements being subject to a different legal regime from the other contracts.[4] This stems in large measure, first, from the provisions of such contracts frequently providing for arbitration and for disputes to be determined in accordance with international law or general principles of law, and secondly from the concept of acquired rights.[5] Without these features concession agreements would be no different from any other contract. It should be noted that the traditional concession contract which has featured so frequently in the major international commercial arbitrations is essentially a relic of the period of economic colonisation. There are no claims before the Iran–United States Claims Tribunal concerning traditional concession contracts, and any contracts providing certain exclusive rights to foreign nationals, as in the *Amoco* case and the other oil cases,[6] do not come within this category.

As has been noted it is generally accepted that a simple breach of contract by a state does not lead to international responsibility, until there has been a denial of justice. A denial of justice will arise if the alien is unable to gain access to the courts or if the judicial system operates so unfairly as to preclude a legitimate settlement of the claim. It will also apply where a state which has entered into a contract with an alien subsequently annuls or substantially modifies its obligations under the contract by legislative or administrative action without formal termination or breach of the contract itself. Such a confiscatory annulment is analogous to expropriation, and international responsibility is immediately incurred without the necessity of the injured alien having to exhaust local remedies.

Where a forum to hear claims based on contract is created, as with the Iran–United States Claims Tribunal, the requirement of denial of justice is removed, since the claim is immediately removed to the international plane. The question then arises as to whether the principles of state responsibility should be applied by the tribunal or whether the international tribunal should apply municipal law as if there had been no denial of justice. However, in those cases where there has been a con-

---

[3] These contracts are often for the construction of complete industrial facilities, such as steel mills, oil refineries, railways.

[4] Carlston, *Concession Agreements and Nationalization*, 52 A.J.I.L., 260, 267 (1958); Wortley, *Expropriation in Public International Law*, 56 (1959); O'Connell, *International Law*, 1074 (1965); Schwarzenberger, *The Protection of British Property Abroad*, 5 Current Legal Problems (1952).

[5] The concept of "acquired rights" was given approval in *Aramco v Saudi Arabia* 27 I.L.R., 117, 125 (1963). It meant that the rights of the concessionaire acquired under the concession were to be upheld. Essentially it is an application of the principle of *pacta sunt servanda*.

[6] 15 IRAN–U.S.C.T.R., 189 (1987).

fiscatory annulment of the contract by the respondent state, international responsibility may still arise even if the contract is ostensibly governed by domestic law.

A number of jurists consider that once a claim is removed to the international arena state responsibility necessarily arises and the claim will be decided without reference to the municipal law of the respondent state.[7] While there may be a requirement for the tribunal to determine such claims in accordance with the principles of international law, this can still effectively be a reference to municipal law, since international law may require the tribunal to apply the appropriate municipal law unless the *compromis*, or the contract itself otherwise directs. The United States–Mexico Tribunal applied municipal law as required by the principles of international law in a number of decisions, the most notable of which is the *Illinois Railway Company* claim.[8] In determining the applicable law of this claim the tribunal stated:[9]

International claims . . . may belong to any of four types:
. . .
(d) Claims as between a citizen of one country and the government of another country acting in its civil capacity. These claims, too, are international in character and they too must be decided "in accordance with principles of international law", even in cases where international law should merely declare the municipal law of one of the countries involved to be applicable.

Where it is not possible to apply municipal law, owing to its inadequate nature, or to changed circumstances arising from revolution or other fundamental change in the respondent state, international tribunals will apply the principles of international law.[10]

In the case of property rights flowing from contract, or the ownership of assets,[11] the principles of international law, including *pacta sunt servanda*, respect for acquired rights, the prohibition of unjust enrichment and the obligation to provide appropriate compensation, will be applied by international tribunals to determine the responsibility of a respondent state.

---

[7] Feller, *The Mexican Claims Commissions 1923–1934* (1935); O'Connell, *International Law*, 1068 (1965).

[8] IV R.I.A.A., 21 (1926). It should be noted that the United States–Mexico Tribunal was required to make its decisions "in accordance with the principles of international law" (Article 1 of the United States–Mexican General Claims Commission), a significantly more restrictive provision than Article V of the Claims Settlement Declaration establishing the Iran–United States Arbitral Tribunal.

[9] IV R.I.A.A., 21, 23–4 (1926).

[10] The issue of "changed circumstances" arises in Article V of the Claims Settlement Declaration.

[11] The four heads of jurisdiction of the Iran–United States Claims Tribunal set out in Article II(1) of the Claims Settlement Declaration are all property rights arising from contracts and ownership of assets. The assets may be physical assets or contractual rights.

Debts

Introduction

The first category of jurisdiction for private claims is claims arising out of debts owed by either of the states parties to nationals of the other party which had not been honoured by January 19, 1981.[12]

The non-payment of debts by a state to nationals of another state is a breach of contract, and as a general rule breach of contract does not lead to state responsibility.[13] Non-payment of a debt, however, is a confiscatory breach of contract, since the debtor effectively expropriates the property of the creditor by the non-payment of the debt. Thus the non-payment by a state of a debt which is owed to nationals of another state gives rise to international responsibility on the part of the debtor state. This has been recognised, at least impliedly, by the Permanent Court of International Justice and the International Court of Justice.

The *Serbian loans* case[14] concerned the interpretation of a gold clause in loan agreements between French bondholders and the Serbian government. The French bondholders did not pursue their remedies in the Serbian courts but appealed to the French government to intervene. By way of special agreement between the two governments the dispute was submitted to the Permanent Court of International Justice. Although the Court noted that the relations between the borrowing state and private persons are within the domain of municipal law, once a state intervenes to protect its nationals the dispute becomes one between governments and thus within the domain of the Court's jurisdiction.[15] However, in the absence of a denial of justice by the debtor state, the Court applied municipal law to the substance of the dispute, since its decision was based on the "relations existing between the borrowing State and the bondholders".[16]

The *Norwegian loans* case[17] was based on similar facts, with various instrumentalities of the Norwegian government being indebted to French nationals. As with the *Serbian loans* case the substantive issue was whether

---

[12] Article II(1).

[13] Brownlie, *Principles of Public International Law*, 547–8 (1990); Greig, *International Law*, 560 (1976); O'Connell, *International Law*, 1066–8 (1965).

[14] P.C.I.J., Ser. A, No. 20 (1929).

[15] *Ibid.*, 18–20.

[16] *Ibid.*, 20. In this case, the dispute was whether the coupon payments on the bonds should be in gold francs or paper francs. Serbia was paying the coupons in the depreciated paper form. As such the question of denial of justice did not arise, as it would have if the Serbian government had simply failed to pay the coupons. Thus, until a denial of justice occurred, the relationship between the debtor state and the foreign bondholders was governed by municipal law.

[17] I.C.J. Rep., 31 (1957).

the French nationals could demand payment in gold francs.[18] However, unlike the *Serbian loans* case, Norway disputed the jurisdiction of the International Court of Justice and asserted that the issue was solely within the jurisdiction of Norway.[19] The French government had relied on the compulsory jurisdiction Declarations of the two states whereby disputes concerning the international obligations of the two states could be submitted to the jurisdiction of the Court. The Court held, without providing reasoning, in favour of Norway, thereby accepting that the issue was solely governed by municipal law. The dissenting judges made some interesting observations. Judge Lauterpacht noted that "the treatment by a State of the property rights of aliens ... is a question of international law".[20]

Although the Claims Settlement Declaration established the Tribunal, at least in part, as a substitute forum for United States municipal courts, it also removed the claims to the level of public international law. Article V of the Claims Settlement Declaration confirms this by allowing the Tribunal broad discretion in applying such principles of commercial and international law as it deems applicable. If the Tribunal acted in accordance with the principles of international law established by the *Serbian loans* case, and as expressed by the writers, it could be expected that the Tribunal would apply the appropriate system of municipal law to the claim, unless it is apparent there has been a denial of justice. Since the issue of denial of justice is no longer relevant with the establishment of the Tribunal it would seem that the proper course for the Tribunal is to apply the appropriate system of municipal law unless there is a defect in the substantive municipal law that would constitute a denial of justice of itself.

Awards and decisions of the Tribunal

The difficulty posed by the relatively few awards made thus far in claims for payment of debts is that the Tribunal has not explicitly indicated the applicable law of the claim. Typically, if it finds the factual allegation of non-payment of the debt without good cause proven it will make an appropriate award without further analysis.[21] This is illustrated by the

---

[18] Norway had passed legislation providing that gold debts in kroner could be paid in Bank of Norway notes on the basis of their nominal gold value.

[19] This assertion was on the basis of reciprocity, since the restriction of the Court's jurisdiction on matters within the national jurisdiction was contained in the French Declaration, and not the Norwegian Declaration.

[20] *Ibid.*, 38.

[21] This aspect of the decisions of the Tribunal has caused some frustration for other writers; see Lloyd-Jones, *The Iran–United States Claims Tribunal: Private Rights and State Responsibility*, 51, 76, who noted, "... its rulings on choice of law frequently stand on unstated assumptions as to the role of the Tribunal, and their rationale is frequently difficult to discover," in Lillich (ed.), *The Iran–United States Claims Tribunal 1981–1983* (1984).

Claims arising from debts and contracts 119

case of *Blount Bros* v *Ministry of Housing*.[22] The claimant had entered into a joint venture with the Ministry of Housing and Urban Development in Iran for the construction of a large number of apartments and was to be paid a management fee. Part of the fee was paid but a number of invoices went unpaid. The Tribunal, after reciting the facts in detail, and referring to the terms of the agreement, stated, without further analysis,[23] "Claimant is entitled to compensation in regard to the non-payment of the sums owing."

This approach is also evident in other claims. In *R. J. Reynolds Tobacco* v *Iran*[24] the Tribunal set out the factual background to the claims and counter-claims. The Tribunal stated:[25]

The various invoices and records of payment support Claimant's position ...

Accordingly, the Tribunal must conclude that ITC owes Reynolds US$36,294,667.66 for unpaid tobacco products.

It was sufficient for the claimant to prove that the invoices were unpaid. Unless the respondent could demonstrate a valid reason for non-payment the Tribunal has made its awards on the basis of the factual allegation of non-payment.

Those claims where the Tribunal has referred to specific legal principles show a preference for principles of law that are widely accepted, whether they be derived from municipal law or international law. The case of *Woodward-Clyde Consultants* v *Iran*[26] indicates how the Tribunal frequently fails to make a rigorous analysis of the applicable law but is inclined to support its decisions by reference to both municipal law and international law without considering whether the contract is specifically governed by a particular system of municipal law or by international law. The facts were that Woodward-Clyde Consultants had entered into an arrangement with the Atomic Energy Organisation of Iran (AEOI) to undertake certain consulting work. A number of invoices submitted by Woodward-Clyde Consultants were not paid by AEOI. Chamber Three of the Tribunal, after reciting the facts and the contractual provisions, held that AEOI was liable for the unpaid invoices. However, Woodward-Clyde Consultants also claimed for expenses incurred in trying to collect the unpaid invoices. The Tribunal referred to municipal law and general principles of law to disallow this claim, noting that the claimant had not put forward any legal principles to support the claim.[27] It went on to state:[28]

[22] 3 IRAN–U.S.C.T.R., 225 (1983).
[23] *Ibid.*, 235.
[24] 7 IRAN–U.S.C.T.R., 181 (1984).
[25] *Ibid.*, 190.
[26] 3 IRAN–U.S.C.T.R., 239 (1983).
[27] *Ibid.*, 239.
[28] *Ibid.*, 249.

Moreover it is doubtful that such expenses are generally compensable in municipal legal systems. Finally it appears that other international claims tribunals have explicitly declined to award damages in this regard. See, e.g., *China Navigation Co. Ltd (Great Britain v United States)* 6 R. Int'l Arb. Awards, 64, 68.

The reference by the Tribunal to the terms of contracts and to general principles of law derived from municipal law and international law indicates that the Tribunal liberally applies the provisions of Article V of the Claims Settlement Declaration, without the analysis required by Article V. Although Article V allows the Tribunal to apply such "choice of law rules and principles of commercial and international law as the Tribunal determines to be applicable taking into account... contract provisions", this must be done "on the basis of respect for law". Thus it could be expected that the Tribunal would apply international law as generally expressed by the international tribunals, including the International Court of Justice, and by jurists. The *Woodward-Clyde* award rests largely on contract provisions and general principles of law, an accepted method of determining international law.[29] However, the precedents indicate that under international law the applicable law in respect of debts owed by a state to nationals of another state would be a particular system of municipal law, rather than general principles of law. As a general rule, the Tribunal has confined its analysis of its role, and hence of the law to be applied by it, to issues of general significance in the development of public international law.[30] For claims based on contracts, as is necessarily the case with the claims for debts, the Tribunal is largely concerned with the interpretation and application of the terms of the particular contracts, rather than a rigorous analysis of the applicable law. Since the claims have not been considered as raising issues of general importance the Tribunal has not found any necessity to clearly articulate its views on the appropriate systems of law governing the claims.

Contracts

Introduction

Claims based on contract fall into two categories. First, there are the claims by nationals of one party against the government of the other arising out of "contracts (including transactions which are the subject of

---

[29] Article 38(1)(c) of the Statute of the International Court of Justice.

[30] See the decisions on dual nationality referred to in Chapter Four and the expropriation decisions referred to in Chapter Eight. The important forum selection decisions referred to in Chapter Twelve stand in marked contrast. In those decisions the Tribunal made no explicit references to principles of law or precedent.

letters of credit or bank guarantees)". Secondly, official claims may be made by "the United States and Iran against each other arising out of contractual arrangements between them for the purchase and sale of goods and services".[31]

In respect of the first category, the claims arising from breach of contract between a state and nationals of another state are usually a matter of municipal law in the absence of denial of justice.[32] In the second case, the contractual relationship between states may be a matter of either municipal law or international law, depending on the choice of law and choice of forum by the two states. However, in both cases the Claims Settlement Declaration removes the claims to the international plane. Moreover, the provisions of Article V give the Tribunal wide discretion on the applicable law in determining claims before it.

A number of different issues have arisen in the contractual claims but the most significant is the applicable law, since the resolution of many of the other issues is often dependent on the Tribunal's decision on this issue. It is equally important in claims by nationals of one party against the government of the other party as in the official claims, although it is only explicitly raised in relatively few of the claims.

Applicable law of the contract

The majority of the Tribunal's awards have not specifically referred to the applicable law governing the claim and the awards are usually made on the basis of the facts accepted by the Tribunal and the terms of the contract between the parties. However, a number of decisions have considered the issue of the applicable law in detail.

In the interlocutory award of *Oil Fields of Texas Inc.* v *Iran*[33] the issue before the full Tribunal was whether the second respondent, NIOC, had assumed the liabilities of OSCO, an oil service company incorporated in Iran whose shares were owned by foreign oil companies, thereby incurring the liability of Iran. As a subsidiary issue the Tribunal had to determine whether the relationship between NIOC and OSCO was governed by Iranian municipal law, or by any other system of law. In reference to this issue the Tribunal stated:[34]

From the inception of OSCO in 1973, its relations with NIOC were ... of a complex nature and the circumstances of this case are unique. Not surprisingly,

---

[31] See Article II(2) of *Claims Settlement Declaration*.

[32] The circumstances in which a denial of justice may arise, and a claim therefore be subject to international law, are considered in Debts, *supra*, since the liability of the state stems from the contractual relationship.

[33] 1 IRAN–U.S.C.T.R., 347 (1981–82). The *Oil Field Claim*, and a number of similar claims bear some resemblance to the various oil concession arbitrations.

[34] *Ibid.*, 361.

these circumstances do not fall clearly within well developed and discussed doctrines of law. The controlling rules have therefore to be derived from principles of international law applicable in analogous circumstances or from general principles of law.

In so arguing, the Tribunal was apparently accepting that a denial of justice had taken place, since it saw its role as not merely to provide a forum for a claim otherwise governed by municipal law but also to apply international law to the claim to avoid an injustice that the application of Iranian law might have entailed in view of its silence on the matter.

Mr Mosk, in a concurring opinion, elaborated on the issue of the applicable law. He stated:[35]

> The majority holds NIOC liable with respect of OSCO's obligations to OSCO's creditors by applying international law derived from analogy to municipal law governing mergers and successions. Although respondents suggest that Iranian law should apply there is no clear showing that Iranian law specifically deals with the situation at issue or is inconsistent with the principles of commercial and international law found applicable by the majority. Cf. *Norwegian Shipowners' Claims (USA v Norway)* 1 R. Int'l Arb. Awards 305, 330–33 (1932).

Moreover, Mr Mosk considered the adoption of the principle of *de facto* succession derived from municipal law, legal authorities, general principles of law and international law was justifiable under Article V of the Claims Settlement Declaration "which directs the Tribunal to utilize applicable principles of commercial and international law".[36]

The *Oil Fields* case was not directly concerned with the applicable law of the contract, but with whether NIOC had succeeded to OSCO and thus its liabilities. Although the Tribunal accepted that the relationship between NIOC and OSCO was nominally governed by Iranian law, since both entities are Iranian corporations, the Tribunal seems to have viewed the matter as one of preventing a denial of justice, and international law would be used to supplement the applicable national law to ensure that foreign nationals had a degree of protection that would normally be expected in municipal systems of law.

This supplementation of the applicable municipal law by rules of international law which embody general principles of law by the Tribunal serves two purposes. First, to ensure that the applicable municipal law reaches the appropriate international minimum standard as illustrated by *Oil Fields* and, secondly, because the Tribunal conceives its role as an international tribunal and is therefore able to utilise international law as well as municipal law in any particular case. In this respect the Tribunal

---

[35] *Ibid.*, 374.
[36] *Ibid.*

has relied on Article V of the Claims Settlement Declaration to support this approach.

This latter aspect is well illustrated by the case of *CMI International Inc.* v *Iran*.[37] The claimant alleged breaches of two purchase orders by the Ministry of Roads and Transport of Iran. The purchase orders contained choice of law clauses providing that they should be governed by the laws of the state of Idaho. With regard to the issue of damages the Tribunal stated:[38]

As noted above the purchase orders provided they were governed by the laws of Idaho. The Tribunal does not believe, however, that it is rigidly tied to the law of the contract, at least so far as the assessment of damages is concerned. Article V of the Claims Settlement Declaration provides . . . [not reproduced]

It is difficult to conceive of a choice of law provision that would give the Tribunal greater freedom determining case by case the law relevant to the issues before it . . .

With respect to the assessment of damages, the Tribunal considers its main task to be determining what are the losses suffered by the claimant and to award compensation therefor. Our search is for justice and equity, even in cases where arguably relevant national laws might be designed to further other and doubtless quite legitimate goals. In the present case, while application of the Uniform Commercial Code may not lead to substantially different conclusions from those adopted by the Tribunal (except with respect to accounting for profits on resales, which will be discussed below), the Tribunal prefers to analyse the damage questions in accordance with general principles of law, rather than by reference to the Code as incorporated in the statutory law of Idaho.

The readiness of the Tribunal to override the choice of law of the parties is indicative of the role of the Tribunal as an international tribunal able to apply such law as it determines, rather than as a mere substitute forum for United States municipal courts giving effect to the intention of the parties.

This has not been the case in all claims heard by the Tribunal. In *Queens Office Tower Associates* v *Iran Air*,[39] concerning a lease of offices by Iran Air in New York, Chamber One of the Tribunal determined that the principal issue before it was whether the lease was frustrated by United States Assets Regulations. In considering this issue the Tribunal stated:[40]

The issue must be decided under New York law, which applies to rights and obligations arising out of a New York real estate transaction.

---

[37] 4 IRAN–U.S.C.T.R., 263 (1983).
[38] *Ibid.*, 267–8.
[39] 2 IRAN–U.S.C.T.R., 247 (1983).
[40] *Ibid.*, 250.

In deciding that the United States Assets Regulations were a frustrating measure, the Tribunal referred solely to the United States actions, which were characterised as "sovereign political acts of the Government of the United States which caused the frustration of purposes and impossibility of performance of the lease, not the acts attributed to the Government of Iran".[41]

The dissenting arbitrator, Mr Holtzmann, also agreed that the "real estate transaction took place entirely within New York, [and] thus is governed by the law of that state".[42]

Similarly, in *Economy Forms Corporation* v *Iran*,[43] the Tribunal found that municipal law applied to a contract which was concluded and largely performed in the United States. Economy Forms had entered into a contract in Iowa to manufacture and ship concrete forming materials for companies owned by the government of Iran. On receiving a specific order Economy Forms would make out a "performance invoice" to be used to open a letter of credit. On completion of the order, the goods were delivered to a shipping agent and the shipping papers delivered to the bank for payment of the letter of credit. In some cases the goods were shipped but the letter of credit was dishonoured, in other cases the goods were completed but not shipped owing to the difficulties in Iran. The Tribunal concluded that the applicable law was that of Iowa, stating:[44]

It is a generally accepted principle of private international law that the formation of and the requirements as to the form of a contract are governed by that law which would be the proper law of the contract if the contract was validly concluded. See 2 Dicey and Morris, *The Conflict of Laws*, Rule 146 at 775 and Rule 148 at 784 (10th Ed. 1980); O. Lando, *Contracts* in III *International Encyclopedia of Comparative Law*, chapter 24 at 102–103.

The significant aspect of this decision to apply the law of Iowa to the contract was the reference to "general principles of private international law". The Tribunal had not attempted to apply the law of Iowa by reference to the law of conflicts in Iowa but instead had applied "general principles" of law, one of the sources of international law. Thus the decision is in the same class as the decision of the Permanent Court of International Justice in the *Serbian loans* case.[45] In that case the Court, by reference to a principle of international law, applied municipal law to the substance of the dispute.

---

[41] *Ibid.*, 253.
[42] *Ibid.*, 256. He differed from the majority in whether the Assets Regulations were an event which frustrated the contract. He held that the regulations were a response to the seizure of the hostages, and thus Iran was responsible for the difficulties of Iran Air.
[43] 3 IRAN–U.S.C.T.R., 42 (1983).
[44] *Ibid.*, 47.
[45] P.C.I.J., Ser. A., No. 20 (1929). This case is also referred to earlier in this chapter on Debts, *supra*.

Claims arising from debts and contracts

The case of *DIC of Delaware* v *Tehran Development Corporation*[46] also shows how the Tribunal, when applying municipal law, will ensure that such municipal law conforms to general principles of law. DIC had entered into a number of contracts, along with other contractors, with the Tehran Redevelopment Corporation to construct a large number of apartment buildings.[47] One of the parties, Starrett, had assigned its interest in one of the contracts to DIC. One of the issues before the Tribunal was whether the consent of the respondent was necessary for a valid assignment. The Tribunal noted that the contract contained an Iranian choice of law clause, but that the assignment was presumably made in the United States. The Tribunal stated:[48]

Thus the interpretation and effect of the assignment as between the assignor and assignees is governed by United States law. Issues concerning assignability may be governed by the law of the debt or contract, which could be considered Iranian law. See, e.g., 2 Dicey and Morris on the *Conflict of Laws* 569–572 (10th Ed. 1980). There is no showing that the laws of Iran and the United States are significantly different with respect to the legal principles applicable to this case.

As in *Economy Forms* the Tribunal founded its view of the choice of law on general principles of law. The authority quoted is an English conflicts text. However, it was significant that the same result would be achieved under either Iranian or United States municipal law. Thus, although the Tribunal will apply municipal law to a particular claim it does so on the basis of international law.

There is no fundamental difference between the Tribunal's approach in the first group of claims, where the applicable law is general principles of law, and the second group of claims, where the applicable law is municipal law. The common feature, whether explicitly referred to or not, is Article V of the Claims Settlement Declaration, which allows the Tribunal to apply "such choice of law rules and principles of commercial and international law as the Tribunal determines to be applicable...". Article V does not prioritise each of these three categories of law, and thus the Tribunal is free to support its reasoning by reference to both municipal law and general principles of law. Article V, however, specifically refers the Tribunal to "usages of the trade [and] contract provisions", although such provisions are only to be "take[n] into account" when applying the appropriate law.

The significance of Article V in relation to the applicable law of contracts has been most fully considered in *Anaconda Iran Inc.* v *Iran*.[49] The

[46] 8 IRAN–U.S.C.T.R., 144 (1985).
[47] One of these companies was Starrett, see *Starrett Housing Corp.* v *Iran* 4 IRAN–U.S.C.T.R., 122 (1983), discussed in Chapter Five.
[48] 8 IRAN–U.S.C.T.R., 144, 157 (1985).
[49] 13 IRAN–U.S.C.T.R., 199 (1986).

contract between the parties did not include a choice of law provision. The claimant argued that in the absence of a choice of a particular system of law the doctrine of *pacta sunt servanda* should apply. This would ensure that the Tribunal would have observance to the terms of the contract and usages of the trade. The respondent argued that by virtue of Article V of the Claims Settlement Declaration the Tribunal should apply relevant choice of law rules of international commercial law. The Tribunal agreed that Article V was applicable. However, it observed:[50]

> This Article has a vast scope of application. The Algiers Accords apply to a great number of claims arising out of contracts which may contain very differing provisions regarding applicable law. More importantly, Article V creates a novel system of determining applicable law. Contrary to NICIC's contentions, the Tribunal finds that according to this system the Tribunal is not required to apply any particular national or international legal system. On the contrary, the Tribunal is vested with extensive freedom in determining the applicable law in each case. This freedom is not a discretionary freedom, however, as the Tribunal is given a rather precise indication as to the factors which should guide its decision.

In respect of contract provisions, the Tribunal stated:[51]

> Contract provisions constitute one of the factors, but it is noteworthy that they are not listed first, nor foremost, among the factors nominated. The Tribunal is of course required to take seriously into consideration the pertinent contractual choice of law rules, but it is not obliged to apply these if it considers it has good reason not to do so.

In the particular circumstances of the case where there were no specific provisions in the contract, the Tribunal took into consideration the relevant usages of the trade as well as relevant principles of commercial and international law. It specifically rejected the view that Iranian law is applicable merely because the contract was concluded and executed in Iran. However, it did not finally conclude what the applicable law was, except to the extent that it requested the parties to brief in future pleadings the relevant usages of the trade in respect of the matter in dispute.

As a general rule the Tribunal has tended to rely largely on the terms of the contract, without making it clear what law it is applying. However, where the contract is silent on the matter in dispute the provisions of Article V will be expressly applied. In such cases the Tribunal has taken the view that it has wide discretion under Article V to determine the relevant applicable law of the contract.

---

[50] *Ibid.*, 232.
[51] *Ibid.*

Once the applicable law of the contract has been determined, if at all, the other aspects of the contract can be considered. In most cases, however, the Tribunal does not explicitly consider the applicable law of the contract and it makes its decision on the basis of the facts of the claim and the terms of the contract.

Formation of contract

As a general rule, the contracts which have been the subject of claims were formed by express agreements, usually in writing, and there is no dispute about the existence of the contracts. In some cases, however, there are informal contracts, which have not been reduced to formal written contracts. The existence of the contracts is inferred from the conduct of the parties.

In *Chas T. Main* v *Khuzestan Water and Power Authority*[52] the existence of the contract was inferred from two letters. In the first letter the Ministry of Energy of Iran authorised KWPA to issue a work order for the performance of engineering services. The second letter, signed by KWPA, consented "to the start of engineering services as soon as possible in accordance with the attached details".[53] The Tribunal in considering these two letters stated:[54]

Such letter, which was signed by KWPA, the Claimant and Mahab, reflected more than an intention to contract. It was in reality a contract authorising the Claimant and Mahab to perform the following listed work: ... An invitation to commence preliminary work creates an obligation to pay for that work.

Following this letter, the claimant and respondent exchanged a number of letters and telexes concerning additional work. The Tribunal was concerned to ascertain whether the claimant was entitled to do the work, whether the work had actually been done and, most significantly, if it was not covered by the original contract, whether the undertaking of the work had been ratified by KWPA. In respect of this latter issue the Tribunal noted:[55]

In this connection it should be noted that the law of Iran and the United States both recognise that such subsequent ratification is the equivalent of mutual consent preceding the performance of the work. See The Civil Code of Iran, Art. 193 (M. Sabir trans. 1973); 3A Corbin, *Corbin on Contracts* para. 564 (1960 and Supp. 1982).

[52] 3 IRAN–U.S.C.T.R., 156 (1983).
[53] *Ibid.*, 162.
[54] *Ibid.*
[55] *Ibid.*

This was the only reference to legal authority in the award, and it is notable that the Tribunal did not determine which of Iranian or United States law was applicable, but was concerned to show that the legal principle of part performance had general acceptance.

The case of *Alan Craig* v *Ministry of Energy*[56] also illustrates how undertakings by the parties will amount to contractual obligations. The claimant had alleged that following various oral and telephone discussions he commenced work in Iran as a hydrology consultant for various agencies of the Ministry of Energy. Subsequently a written contract was executed. The Tribunal accepted that all the work performed by the claimant both before and after the execution of the contract was governed by the contract.

Similar principles are evidenced in *Iowa State University* v *Ministry of Culture*.[57] The Ministry had provided a letter to a student indicating that on admission to an American university the university could bill the Iranian embassy for the fees. Iowa State University admitted a student bearing such a letter and proceeded to bill the embassy, which paid the first few accounts rendered to it. The Tribunal stated:[58]

> The Tribunal is of the view that the letter constitutes an offer by the Ministry of Science and Higher Education to purchase services, in the form of educational instruction to the student named therein, from any "leading American University"... The claimant accepted this offer when it permitted the student to continue in its educational program without himself paying the tuition and other fees. The Tribunal holds that a valid contract for the purchase and sale of services was thus concluded.

The decision was subsequently applied in *New York State University* v *Ministry of Culture*.[59]

Employment contracts have been a fruitful source of the requirements for the formation of contracts. Frequently such contracts are not completed by a single document but are evidenced by exchange of letters and the employee actually commencing work. The case of *Hilt* v *Iran*[60] is typical of the many small claims arising from breaches of university employment contracts. Ms Hilt sought a one-year teaching contract at Jundi Shapor University. The offer was made by telegram, with subsequent modifications by letters. Air tickets were provided by the university and Ms Hilt travelled to Iran to take up the appointment in October 1978. She left in January 1979 after the university had closed on the advice of the Chairman of the English Department. The Tribunal was

---

[56] 3 IRAN–U.S.C.T.R., 280 (1983).
[57] 13 IRAN–U.S.C.T.R., 271 (1986).
[58] *Ibid.*, 274–5.
[59] 13 IRAN–U.S.C.T.R., 277 (1986).
[60] 18 IRAN–U.S.C.T.R., 154 (1988).

Claims arising from debts and contracts

satisfied that a contract of employment had been entered into upon the terms set out in the various communications between the parties.

Validity or legality of the contract

In a large number of cases, Iran has argued the contracts are not valid because they do not comply in one or more respects with Iranian law. The argument implies that the contracts are governed by Iranian law, and thus their validity must be governed by Iranian law.

The case of *R. N. Pomeroy* v *Iran*[61] well illustrates the point. The case concerned a contract between the claimant and the Iranian navy. Iran alleged the contract was not valid because the navy official who signed it lacked the authority to do so, that the Pomeroy Corporation was not an eligible contractor approved by the Council of Ministers as required by Iranian statutory law, and that no Farsi language version of the contract was executed. The Tribunal noted that the navy had conducted itself in a manner which indicated that it considered the contract to be valid and thus stated:[62]

> It is both a general principle of law and a principle embodied in Articles 247 and 248 of the Civil Code of Iran that a party may not deny the validity of a contract entered into on its behalf by another if, by its conduct, it later consents to the contract.

Although the contract provided that disputes should be settled "through arbitration according to Iranian laws and regulations"[63] the Tribunal did not restrict itself to applying Iranian law to determine the validity of the contract but also referred to "a general principle of law".

The case of *McLaughlin Enterprises Ltd* v *Iran*[64] is similar. Iran alleged that a contract was invalid since the "Contract was not signed by an authorized representative, that it was unlawful, and that it was contrary to its interests".[65] The person signing the contract was the managing director of the respondent company. The Tribunal stated:[66]

> The Tribunal first determines that the contract forms a valid basis for the legal relationship between ISIRAN and the Claimant. The contract was signed by the managing director on ISIRAN's behalf, and ISIRAN accepted and paid for services pursuant to it. Absent any specific allegation in this respect, the Tribunal has no reason to doubt its lawfulness.

[61] 2 IRAN–U.S.C.T.R., 372 (1983).
[62] *Ibid.*, 380.
[63] *Ibid.*, 378.
[64] 12 IRAN–U.S.C.T.R., 146 (1986).
[65] *Ibid.*, 148.
[66] *Ibid.*, 150.

The Tribunal did not cite any particular principle of law, but it may readily be noted that the finding is consistent with *R. N. Pomeroy*.

Breach and termination of contract

A claimant does not have a cause of action unless there has been a breach of contract by the respondent. This breach can be an actual breach of a particular term of the contract or complete non-performance of the contract. The Iranian revolution meant that contracts between United States companies and Iran were generally terminated. The termination may have been the result of a breach of contract which will lead to liability for the party causing the termination. Alternatively, the termination may have arisen from *force majeure* or frustration making it impossible for the parties to perform the contract.[67]

The Tribunal has largely determined whether or not a breach of contract has occurred after an examination of the facts and the terms of the contracts and has made little reference to the specific legal principles relating to the claim. In part, it is able to rely on Article V for this approach, which requires the Tribunal to take into account the "relevant usages of the trade [and] contract provisions". Moreover, although the Tribunal may not make specific reference to legal authorities and precedents in a particular award, legal principles clearly underlie each award, since "the Tribunal shall decide all cases on the basis of respect for law". This is demonstrated by the awards, which show an adherence to principles of contract law which are accepted in many different legal systems. Without this approach, the awards would merely be decided *ex aequo et bono*.

The case of *Kimberly-Clark Corporation* v *Bank of Markazi Iran*[68] concerned a claim for the non-payment of royalties from 21 September 1978 to 20 March 1986, being the balance of the term of the contract, on the basis that the non-payment of royalties from 21 September 1978 amounted to termination of the contract as a whole, and did not just give rise to the right to claim royalties for the period they were actually unpaid.

The Tribunal noted:[69]

Thus, unless the Claimant can show anticipatory breach of the License as a whole prior to that date, he can recover here only for quarters, prior to and including the one ending 21 December 1980.

[67] See Force Majeure, Frustration and "Changed Circumstances", infra.
[68] 2 IRAN–U.S.C.T.R., 334 (1983).
[69] *Ibid.*, 341.

Claims arising from debts and contracts 131

However, the Tribunal considered that the claimant had not exercised its remedies under the contract to terminate the contract, and therefore could only claim for non-payment of royalties as the non-payment occurred. Accordingly, the Tribunal could only make an award for the non-payment of royalties up to 19 January 1981, the date the Claims Settlement Declaration came into force.[70] Thus the Tribunal not only examined the facts, but also applied recognised legal principles to determine the claim.

In other cases, the Tribunal had to determine when a breach of contract gave rise to a right to damages. In *R. N. Pomeroy v Iran*[71] the claimant had entered into a contract with the Iranian navy for specialist administration services. The contract was terminated by the navy in March 1979 and Pomeroy ceased providing services after this date. However, payments had not been made since November 1978. The Tribunal held:[72]

> The Navy having terminated the contract for no fault of Pomeroy Corporation, the Tribunal finds that the Claimants are entitled to compensation for their losses caused by the termination.

In reaching this conclusion, the Tribunal did no more than set out the terms of the contract and the factual circumstances. Once the facts showed that the contract had been terminated before the date agreed, the Tribunal appeared to consider, without directly stating the position, that a breach of contract had occurred, giving rise to a right to damages. In a concurring opinion, Mr Mosk made plain the reasoning of the Tribunal in stating:[73]

> Thus, the purported termination of the contract by the Navy constituted a breach of that contract.
>
> It is a widely recognized and elementary principle of law that when there has been a breach of a contract, the claimant-obligee is entitled to a remedy which would put it in the economic position it would have occupied had the respondent-obligor performed its obligations. Ryan, *An Introduction to the Civil Law*, 86–87 (1962); 5 *Corbin on Contracts*, para. 992 at 5 (1964); 11 *Williston on Contract*, para. 1338 at 148 (3rd ed. 1968); H. Afchar, "Iran", in Minnatur (ed.), *Contractual Remedies in Asian Countries* 100–01 (1975).

The case of *CMI International Inc. v Iran*[74] concerned purchase orders for construction equipment by the Iranian Ministry of Roads and

---

[70] Article II(1) of the Claims Settlement Declaration requires that the cause of action must arise before January 19, 1981 before it can be entertained by the Tribunal.
[71] 2 IRAN–U.S.C.T.R., 372 (1983).
[72] *Ibid.*, 383.
[73] *Ibid.*, 387.
[74] 4 IRAN–U.S.C.T.R., 263 (1983). This case is also significant for its findings on the applicable law. Refer Applicable Law, *supra*.

Transport. It was a condition of the purchase orders, which fully described the equipment and the delivery dates thereof, that irrevocable letters of credit would be opened by the respondents in favour of the claimants. After setting out the factual circumstances and the terms of the purchase orders, the Tribunal stated:[75]

For the above reasons, the Tribunal holds that two purchase orders at issue in this case were binding contracts from 22 September 1978, the date of their acceptance by the Claimant, and that MORT's failure to establish the required letters of credit at the latest by the first delivery date, 15 November under one order and 30 November under the other, were breaches of contract... Therefore the Claimant is entitled to damages for breach of contract.

In each of these cases, the Tribunal was primarily concerned with the terms of the contract and whether the actions of the respondent were in apparent conflict with the requirements of these terms. Nevertheless, there is an underlying regard for legal principles in reaching a decision. In some cases this is explicitly stated in the award, as *Kimberley Clark Corporation* v *Bank Markazi Iran* illustrates, even though no precedents are cited. In others, the concurring opinion may provide a guide to the Tribunal's reasoning, particularly where, as is frequently the case, the United States arbitrators provide a concurring opinion. Anglo-American legal traditions require fully argued decisions and the United States arbitrators follow this tradition.

The distinction between termination by breach and termination by *force majeure* or frustration is illustrated by the case of *Teichmann Inc.* v *Hamadon Glass Company*.[76] The parties had entered into a turnkey contract for the construction of a glass manufacturing facility. Before the facility was complete the Iranian revolution meant that it became difficult to complete the contract. Teichmann requested a meeting with Hamadon, pursuant to the *force majeure* provision. Several meetings were held during 1979 which finally culminated in Teichmann terminating the contract. The Tribunal considered that it must consider the respective effects of *force majeure* and any breach by either party of its contractual obligation in the period before Teichmann's letter of 15 May 1980 formally brought the contract to an end.[77] The Tribunal noted that:[78]

The characterization of the legal relationship existing between the parties as either *force majeure* or breach of contract may in certain circumstances determine the entitlement of the parties to the amounts claimed.

---

[75] *Ibid.*, 267. The Tribunal considered that the issue of damages was within the context of choice of law; *ibid.*, 267–8. See Applicable Law, *supra*.
[76] 13 IRAN–U.S.C.T.R., 124 (1986).
[77] *Ibid.*, 133.
[78] *Ibid.*

Claims arising from debts and contracts

The Tribunal concluded that the respondent was in continuing breach with respect to its payments obligations, which it did not seek to excuse by reference to *force majeure*.[79] Accordingly the respondent was liable for the unpaid invoices.

The oil claims are particularly useful in providing an analysis of the consequences of terminating long-term contracts. *Mobil Oil Iran Inc.* v *Iran*[80] concerned the termination by Iran of a long-term contract for the production of oil. It was agreed by the parties that conditions of *force majeure* existed at the end of 1978 and the beginning of 1979. However, by March 1979 it was possible for oil exports to be resumed. However, the revolution "could not be without consequences to the contractual relationship between Iran and the Consortium"[81] and it did not continue for its full term. The Tribunal held:[82]

> A close scrutiny of the exchange of letters of 10 and 23 March 1979, as well as of the conduct of the parties prior to and after the exchange, demonstrates that the parties agreed at this time not to revive the Agreement, then suspended by *force majeure*. This agreement, however, was not unconditional. Both parties recognised that a reconciliation of interests was to take place between them... Such negotiations eventually took place and, undoubtedly, would have resulted in compensation for the loss sustained by the Consortium...

Failure to provide compensation would have been a breach of contract. The Tribunal did not cite particular evidence, except to note that failure to provide compensation would have amounted to unjust enrichment of Iran.[83]

Force majeure, frustration and "changed circumstances"

Introduction

The revolutionary circumstances in Iran, the seizure of the hostages by Iran and the United States response could, in some circumstances, readily lead to the conclusion that the performance of contracts became impossible owing to these events, rather than to any voluntary failure to perform the respective obligations by either party in breach of the terms of the contract.

Municipal law takes account of such possibilities by the doctrines of *force majeure* and frustration. The parties of the contracts are excused from further performance of the contracts if supervening events render such performance impossible.

---

[79] *Ibid.*
[80] 16 IRAN–U.S.C.T.R., 3 (1987).
[81] *Ibid.*, 39.
[82] *Ibid.*, 42.
[83] *Ibid.*, 43.

International law has a similar concept in the principle of *rebus sic stantibus*, providing that treaty and contractual provisions may be rendered nugatory as a result of changes of a sufficiently radical nature that the underlying purpose of the agreements are destroyed.[84] This principle was recognised by the drafters of the Claims Settlement Declaration by allowing the Tribunal to take into account "changed circumstances" in deciding cases.[85]

The difference between the municipal law doctrines of *force majeure* and frustration and the international law principle of *rebus sic stantibus* is that in the latter case the change of circumstances may be caused by the voluntary actions of the parties to the agreement. Such changes can encompass revolutionary political changes of governments which result in the new government severing political and economic relationships with erstwhile allies. This will affect not only treaty relationships, but also contractual relationships between the revolutionary state and nationals of the previously friendly state, and vice versa. Similarly, when nations are at war, treaties reflecting friendly relations between them will be terminated or suspended. Of course, not all international obligations of belligerent nations to each other are suspended or terminated, including obligations under the United Nations Charter and various conventions governing the conduct of war and the treatment of nationals, whether civilian or military, of the opposing state.[86] In conflicts less than war but which result in a total breakdown in friendly relationships between states, as occurred with Iran and the United States, a whole range of contractual relationships may be properly terminated, particularly those relating to defence and security matters.[87] However, many other contractual relationships unrelated to matters of state can properly continue, unaffected by the change of circumstances.

---

[84] The concept of "fundamental change of circumstances" is contained in Article 62 of the Vienna Convention on the Law of Treaties. The Convention only covers treaty relations. However, most writers consider that contractual relationships involving state parties are also subject to the principle of *rebus sic stantibus*. The leading modern writer on this principle is Vamvoukos, *Termination of Treaties in International Law* (1985). His study, however, is limited to the termination of treaties, although a comparative study is made of the major municipal legal systems, and of the role of analogous principles such as frustration (English and United States), *imprévision* (French) and *Unzumutbarheit* (German). Thus the doctrine of *rebus sic stantibus* in international law embodies a general principle of law recognised by civilised nations.

[85] Article V of the Claims Settlement Declaration.

[86] In *Diplomatic Staff in Tehran (United States v Iran)* I.C.J. Rep., 3, 28 (1980), the Court noted: "[I]t is precisely when difficulties arise that the treaty assumes its greatest importance."

[87] Brownlie, *Principles of Public International Law*, 617 (1990), gives the example of a change of government incompatible with a military alliance as being a fundamental change to a military alliance involving the exchange of military and intelligence information.

Force majeure

Force majeure is a widely recognised doctrine of contract law and accordingly many contracts contain *force majeure* clauses. The operation of the principle, however, is not dependent upon the parties including such a provision in the contract for the doctrine simply denotes intervening events beyond the control of the parties which render the performance of the contract impossible. The concept is typically applicable to "acts of God". However, it is equally applicable to man-made events such as war, revolution and other forms of violent upheaval. As a rule economic disruption does not allow parties to invoke the doctrine of *force majeure* to terminate or suspend the performance of a contract.

Force majeure has been invoked by one or other of the parties in a number of claims before the Tribunal.

In *Gould Marketing Inc.* v *Ministry of National Defence*[88] the claimant had agreed to supply military radios along with technical assistance over a ten-year period. By mid-1978 the equipment had been largely delivered and the technical and service assistance was being provided. As a result of the revolutionary upheaval, the claimant withdrew its staff from Iran in December 1978. Payments due in June 1979 were not made by the Ministry. The issue considered by the Tribunal was whether the contract had been terminated and the cause of the termination. The Tribunal noted:[89]

By December 1978, strikes, riots and other civil strife in the course of the Islamic Revolution had created classic *force majeure* conditions at least in Iran's major cities. By *force majeure* we mean social and economic forces beyond the power of the state to control through the exercise of due diligence. Injuries caused by the operation of such forces are therefore not attributable to the state for purposes of its responsibility for damages.

Thus delay or cessation in performance of the contract could not lead to liability unless the conditions creating the *force majeure* were attributable to the respondent. With regard to the present contract the Tribunal stated:[90]

During the months February through June 1979, the Islamic Republic was to some extent in control of the revolution, but very little evidence was presented in this case concerning its responsibility for conditions that made return of the FSRS impossible. Such evidence was inadequate to show that the *force majeure* conditions had been transformed during those few months into conditions sufficiently attributable to that Government to make its non-payment in June 1979 a breach of contract.

---

[88] 3 IRAN–U.S.C.T.R., 147 (1983).
[89] *Ibid.*, 152–3.
[90] *Ibid.*, 152–3.

The Tribunal considered that the failure to perform on the part of both parties had by June 1979 "ripened into a termination of the Hoffman–Ministry contract".[91] A discharge of contract, even if caused by *force majeure* conditions not attributable to either party, requires an accounting of the respective parties' liabilities up to the termination. The Tribunal required further evidence on this matter before it could make a final award.[92]

In *Sylvania Technical Systems* v *Iran*[93] the claimant agreed to train intelligence specialists for Iran. Following the Islamic revolution the performance of the contract became difficult, with the Iranian government failing to pay invoices and withdrawing students from the training programme. The claimant invoked the *force majeure* clause in February 1979 to terminate the contract. The claim before the Tribunal was in respect of the unpaid invoices submitted prior to the termination of the contract and for certain termination costs authorised by the contract.

The Tribunal, referring to *Gould Marketing Inc.* v *Ministry of National Defence of Iran*,[94] accepted that *force majeure* conditions existed from December 1978 onward.[95] In particular the Tribunal found "that revolutionary conditions including a general disruption of bank operations ... constituted *force majeure*",[96] delaying payment and disrupting the performance of other aspects of the contract. Owing to the provisions of the contract the respondent was obligated to pay certain post-termination damages as well as damages up to termination.

The Tribunal's decision of *America Bell International Inc.* v *Iran*[97] contains interesting findings on the effect of termination due to *force majeure*. Although the contract contained formal termination provisions they were not invoked by either party. The Tribunal, citing the above two cases, was in no doubt that *force majeure* conditions existed which terminated the contract.[98] The Tribunal found that where the contract provided for allocation of costs on termination due to *force majeure* the contract would apply. However, for costs not covered by the contract the Tribunal considered:[99]

> In such circumstances the determination of the rights and liabilities of the parties is subject "to the Tribunal's equitable discretion using the contract as a framework and reference point". *Queens Office Tower Associates* and *Iran National Airlines Corporation*.

---

[91] *Ibid.*, 154.
[92] *Ibid.*, 155.
[93] 8 IRAN–U.S.C.T.R., 298 (1985).
[94] 3 IRAN–U.S.C.T.R., 147, 152–9 (1983).
[95] 8 IRAN–U.S.C.T.R., 298, 308 (1985).
[96] *Ibid.*, 309.
[97] 12 IRAN–I.S.C.T.R., 170 (1986).
[98] *Ibid.*, 184.
[99] *Ibid.*, 185.

Claims arising from debts and contracts

The approach of the Tribunal was "to reach a result which as closely as possible corresponds with the contractual scheme".[100] However, where the loss was not covered by the contract "the guiding rule concerning costs attributable to *force majeure* situations is that 'the loss must lie where it falls' ".[101]

The oil concession cases consider long-term contracts and the special circumstances which affect the performance and continuation of contracts owing to *force majeure* conditions. The Tribunal accepted in a number of oil concession cases that *force majeure* conditions existed during late 1978 and early 1979 owing to prolonged strikes, interrupted oil supplies and fears for the personal safety of expatriate oil company employees. The *Mobil Oil* case[102] provides an extensive review of *force majeure* on long-term contracts which contemplated the existence of such conditions from time to time. The Tribunal stated:[103]

> Article 27 of the SPA envisioned *force majeure* only as an excuse for failure by a party to comply with the terms of the Agreement. In other words, in this Article . . . *force majeure* conditions were regarded only as causing a suspension of certain provisions of the Agreement. This is in line with the most common practice in contract law. Usually, *force majeure* conditions will have the effect of terminating a contract only if they make performance definitively impossible or impossible for a long period of time.

Since conditions were beginning to normalise by March 1979 it was considered that the contract had not been terminated.

This decision was directly applied by the Tribunal in *Phillips Petroleum Company, Iran. v Iran*.[104] In that case the Tribunal said that if the *force majeure* conditions lasted twelve months or more then the agreement would be extended by a corresponding period of time. Iran also argued that the hostility of the oil workers to resumption of the contract with Phillips constituted a separate *force majeure* condition entitling Iran to terminate the contract. The Tribunal rejected this argument on the facts, noting:[105]

> While there is evidence that the workers did not always trust officials of NIOC to follow the strict nationalistic and anti-Second Party policies pressed by the Workers—and by the highest authorities of the new Islamic regime—there is no evidence for the proposition that they did not ultimately follow the directives of those highest authorities.

---

[100] *Ibid.*, 188.
[101] *Ibid.*, 187, citing *Queens Office Tower Associates* v *Iran National Airlines Corp.* 2 IRAN–U.S.C.T.R., 247 (1983), and *International School Services Inc.* v *National Iranian Copper Industries Co.* 9 IRAN–U.S.C.T.R., 187 (1985).
[102] 16 IRAN–U.S.C.T.R., 3 (1987).
[103] *Ibid.*, 38–9.
[104] 21 IRAN–U.S.C.T.R., 79, 107–8 (1989).
[105] *Ibid.*, 110.

Thus the government could not plead its own policies as *force majeure* conditions terminating the contract.

The oil concession contracts stand apart from ordinary commercial contracts. Firstly, they are long-term and contain provisions to enable them to survive periods of *force majeure* conditions. Secondly, the central importance of oil to the Iranian economy meant the government played an active role in creating the *force majeure* conditions to terminate the contracts. It could not then argue that its own policies removed the obligation to compensate the foreign investors for breach of contract.

Frustration

The doctrine of frustration is well known in municipal law jurisdictions. If a contract is impossible to perform then the parties will be discharged from any further obligations under the contract. The events of the Islamic revolution meant that contracts were most frequently frustrated owing to *force majeure* conditions. Frustration may arise, however, for other reasons such as illegality of performance due to intervening regulation.

The question of frustration was first considered by the Tribunal in *Queens Office Tower Associates* v *Iran Air*.[106] The national Iranian airline, Iran Air, had leased premises in New York in August 1979 for a term of ten years and made rental payments up to December 1979. Queens Tower drew upon a letter of credit established by Iran Air as security for the rental payments for the January and February payments. Between November 1979 and April 1980, as a result of Executive Orders of the United States, Iran Air progressively ceased business in the United States. Iran Air claimed the actions of the United States had frustrated the lease and thus it was discharged from its obligations under it. In response, Queens Tower argued that the actions of the United States were a response to unlawful seizure of the hostages by the Iranian government, and since Iran Air was owned by the Iranian government it could not rely on frustration, since the frustration was ultimately caused by the Iranian government.

In examining the issue of frustration the Tribunal considered four key questions: whether frustration had occurred, whether it could have been foreseen, whether it was attributable to Iran Air and, finally, what were the consequences of frustration. On the first question, the Tribunal found that, as a result of the Executive Orders of the United States, the performance of Iran Air's obligation was "from a practical commercial point of view rendered impossible" by 1 May 1980.[107] Accordingly, Iran

---

[106] 2 IRAN–U.S.C.T.R., 247 (1983). This case has also been considered in respect of the applicable law, see Applicable Law, *supra*.
[107] *Ibid.*, 251.

Air had satisfied the requirements of New York law that the performance of the contract had been frustrated.

However, it is not sufficient to show that performance of the contract is impossible, it is also necessary to show that the frustrating event could not be foreseen or be caused by the party pleading frustration. In respect of these questions, the Tribunal found, first, that at the time the contract had been entered into in August 1979 the events of the hostage crisis could not have been foreseen. Secondly, it characterised the actions of the United States as being the free and independent choice of the United States even if they had been inspired by the hostage crisis. In deciding thus the Tribunal did not have to determine whether the actions of the Iranian government could be attributed to a government-owned commercial entity such as Iran Air.[108] On this issue, Mr Holtzmann, in a dissenting opinion, considered that the hostage crisis was the event that effectively caused the frustration of the contract, notwithstanding that it was the United States' response that actually caused the frustration of the lease. He also considered the actions of the government could be attributed to the airline, since the Iranian government had "assumed responsibility for private as well as public law duties".[109]

Changed circumstances

As noted already the concept of "changed circumstances" is substantially different from *force majeure* and frustration in that the change of circumstances may have been brought about by one of the parties to the agreement. A revolutionary government may consider that it is no longer bound by agreements of the previous government which are directly contrary to the revolutionary imperatives of the new government. The doctrine must, however, be kept within strict bounds if it is not to destroy the integrity of international agreements and contracts.[110] It is noteworthy that the words "changed circumstances" of Article V of the Claims Settlement Declaration have been given only limited consideration by the Tribunal.

One of the first cases in which the Tribunal interpreted the words was *William L. Pereira Associates Iran* v *Iran*[111] concerning non-payment of fees due under a contract. The Tribunal rejected the respondent's contention that it was not liable for non-payment if a project was inappro-

---

[108] *Ibid.*, 253.
[109] *Ibid.*, 259.
[110] The contrary doctrine of *pacta sunt servanda* is given much greater consideration by international jurists. See *Diplomatic Staff in Tehran (United States* v *Iran)* I.C.J. Rep., 7 (1980), and the various arbitral decisons in Chapter Eight, "The legality of expropriation".
[111] 5 IRAN–U.S.C.T.R., 198 (1984).

priate in light of social and economic conditions in Iran. The majority in Chamber Three stated:[112]

> Even if the project was inappropriate, an allegation upon which the Tribunal expresses no view, this would not effect Respondent's liability under the contract.

A more comprehensive analysis of the provision was undertaken by the Tribunal in *Questech Inc. v Ministry of National Defence of Iran*.[113] Questech had supplied the Iranian Ministry of Defence with a training programme for an electronic intelligence-gathering operation known as IBEX. Questech suspended performance of the contract, invoking the *force majeure* clause. The respondent replied, stating that the contact had been terminated owing to "transformations arising from the Islamic Revolution in Iran". In its claims before the Tribunal Questech sought payment of unpaid invoices prior to the suspension of the contract and lost profits for the balance of the term of the contract.

The Tribunal had to determine whether either party had any liability under the contract after its termination. It examined the factual background, noting in particular the sensitive nature of the contractual work and concluded "that the Iranian Government made a deliberate policy decision not to continue with American contractors in a project that related to secret military intelligence operations".[114] Thus the Tribunal stated:[115]

> In this particular situation the political relationship between States concerned was of greater importance than in ordinary commercial relations, and in this case even more than with regard to contracts for the sale of less sensitive military equipment and services. If, during the performance of a contract like the present one, these circumstances undergo fundamental changes which the parties had not foreseen, then a consequence may be that a contract party is not barred from opting for a termination of the contract in such a situation.

The existence of this principle in international law was canvassed by the Tribunal, which noted its existence either directly or by the analogous concept of frustration in the municipal law of several legal systems:[116]

> This concept of *changed circumstances*, also referred to as *clausula rebus sic stantibus*, has in its basic form been incorporated into so many legal systems that it has also found a widely recognised expression in Article 62 of the Vienna Convention on the Law of Treaties of 1969.

---

[112] *Ibid.*, 211.
[113] 9 IRAN–U.S.C.T.R., 107 (1985). This claim arose from a similar factual background; *Sylvania Technical Systems v Iran* 8 IRAN–U.S.C.T.R., 298 (1985). Both claims concerned training of personnel for the IBEX programme.
[114] *Ibid.*, 120.
[115] *Ibid.*, 121–2.
[116] *Ibid.*, 122.

Although the Tribunal considered the principle difficult to apply in practice it was mandated by Article V of the Claims Settlement Declaration to take into account changed circumstances when deciding all cases:[117]

In the context of the Algiers Declaration the inclusion of the term "changed circumstances" means that changes which are inherent parts and consequences of the Iranian Revolution must be taken into account.

Since the sensitive nature of the programme meant that it was going to be affected by the different attitude of the new government, especially toward the United States, the contract was subject to the principle of "changed circumstances". Iran could invoke the principle to terminate the contract despite the absence of a termination clause.[118] The consequences of such termination are similar to those of *force majeure* and frustration. Iran was obligated to compensate the claimant for losses suffered up to and including the termination of the contract. However, there was no obligation to compensate for future profits or lost opportunity, since this would imply an obligation upon Iran to continue the contract.

The restrictive nature of the concept is demonstrated in *Mobil Oil Iran v Iran*.[119] The respondent claimed that a long-term agreement for the exploitation of oil resources was frustrated by changed circumstances, relying on the provisions of Article V of the Claims Settlement Declaration. The Tribunal stated:[120]

In the instant cases, the concept of "changed circumstances", insofar as it can be distinguished from *force majeure*, can refer only to the dramatic political changes brought about in Iran by the success of the Islamic Revolution and the decision of the Islamic Government to follow a policy radically different from that of the previous Government in the oil industry. Changes of such a character and magnitude could not be without consequences to the contractual relationship between Iran and the Consortium. By themselves, however, they could not have had any effect on the validity of the Agreement before materializing in specific measures. As a matter of fact the 10 March 1979 letter was the first expression of such a new policy in relation to the Agreement.

The Tribunal thus rejected the mere fact of the revolution as being a sufficient "change of circumstances" to entitle Iran to terminate contracts.

As noted the *Mobil Oil Iran* case differs from many of the cases where the respondent has pleaded "changed circumstances" since it concerned a long-term agreement for the exploitation of oil resources. It has been a feature of oil exploitation agreements that they are subject to progressive

[117] *Ibid.*, 123.
[118] *Ibid.*
[119] 16 IRAN–U.S.C.T.R., 3, 39 (1087).
[120] *Ibid.*, 3, 39.

change, reflecting the changing balance of power between the companies and the oil exporting nations. The Tribunal referred to the "legitimate expectations" of the parties in respect of the development of the agreement.[121] Such expectations precluded the possiblity that the agreement was frustrated owing to changed circumstances. However, the changed circumstances are not without significance. The revolutionary change in Iran, as was recognised by the Tribunal, was part of the background leading to the modification and ultimate termination, with appropriate compensation, of the agreement. The revolution did not mean that Iran could argue frustration, thereby discharging it from further performance of the contract. The termination was subject to compensation which would include loss of profits.

The award of *Phillips Petroleum Company, Iran* v *Iran*[122] confirmed the reasoning of the *Mobil Oil* case. The Tribunal noted:[123]

As a substantive matter, however, the Respondents appear to rely on "changed circumstances" both in the sense of the dramatic social changes brought about in Iran by the Revolution and in the sense of the change in oil policy applied by the new regime. Changes of such a character and magnitude are not without consequence to contractual relationships, but they do not affect the validity of such agreements. In other words a revolutionary regime may not simply excuse itself from legal obligations by changing governmental policies, nor take for the public benefit without compensation businesses operated by foreign private persons under the previous regime.

The award also distinguished the *Questech* case which related to "military intelligence projects of unique political sensitivity".[124]

Conclusion

Although the consequences of *force majeure*, frustration and "changed circumstances" are similar, the substantial difference is that the former two terminating events do not arise as a result of the actions of the parties to the contract. In the latter case of "changed circumstances", one or other of the parties will have brought about the changes that render performance of the contract inappropriate. Provided these changes were not planned at the time the contract was entered into, no blame will attach to the party invoking the principle.

It is important, however, that the doctrine should be kept within strict limits, since it could undermine the integrity of the contractual relationship. This was recognised by the Tribunal firstly in *William L. Pereira*

---

[121] *Ibid.*, 55.
[122] 21 IRAN–U.S.C.T.R., 79 (1989).
[123] *Ibid.*, 111.
[124] *Ibid.*

Associates v *Iran*[125] and later in the oil concession cases in disallowing economic changes bought about by the revolutionary government as grounds to invoke the doctrine. The doctrine is most appropriately applied to fundamental changes in the areas of defence, security and foreign policy.

Commentary on the debt and contract claims

The distinction between the claims based on contract and debt and those based on expropriation and other measures affecting property rights is essentially the applicable law of the claims. As a general rule the practice of claims commissions and arbitral tribunals indicates that contract and debt claims are governed by a particular system of municipal law unless there has been or will be a denial of justice. In contrast expropriation claims are governed by public international law. The distinction arises from the principle of public international law whereby in the latter case a state's liabilities are determined by the rules of state responsibility toward aliens. In the former case state responsibility does not arise and the claim is governed by the proper law of the contract.

The practice of the Iran–United States Claims Tribunal has not been as clear as the above statements might indicate, especially with regard to the debt and contract claims. The principal reason has been the Tribunal's application of the provisions of Article V of the Claims Settlement Declaration. The Tribunal has interpreted Article V so that any of the sources of law referred to in Article V can be applied to any claim being heard by the Tribunal. Thus "choice of law rules and principles of commercial and international law" have been applied to a variety of claims without regard to whether a particular source of law is appropriate to each category of jurisdiction. Thus the Tribunal has had reference to general principles of law as an equally valid source of law for contracts claim although the parties may have chosen a particular system of law to govern the contract.[126] The Tribunal has indicated that Article V gives it great "freedom in determining case by case the law relevant to the issue before it",[127] and that it is not bound by the choice of law of the parties. The Tribunal's role is to achieve "justice and equity even in cases where

---

[125] 5 IRAN–U.S.C.T.R., 198 (1984).
[126] See especially *CMI International Inc.* v *Iran* 4 IRAN–U.S.C.T.R., 263 (1983); *Economy Forms Corp.* v *Iran* 3 IRAN–U.S.C.T.R., 42 (1983) and *DIC of Delaware* v *Tehran Development Corp.* 8 IRAN–U.S.C.T.R., 144 (1985); referred to in *Applicable Law of the Contract, supra*.
[127] *CMI International Inc.* v *Iran* 4 IRAN–U.S.C.T.R., 263, 267 (1983).

arguably relevant national laws might be designed to achieve other and doubtless quite legitimate goals".[128]

However, while it cannot be disputed that the Tribunal is required to achieve justice and equity, they are best achieved by applying the parties' own explicit or implicit choice of law. In major commercial contracts, such as the Tribunal is deciding upon in the claims exceeding $250,000, the parties can be presumed to have considered the question of the applicable law as part of the bargain.

It is submitted that the reference in Article V providing that the Tribunal should "decide all cases on the basis of respect for law" limits the interpretation of the balance of the clauses of Article V. The Tribunal is required to apply the appropriate system of law to each claim in the various categories of jurisdiction. In many of the awards it is not clear that the Tribunal has gone through this process, particularly where the Tribunal has simply recited the facts of the claim and the provisions of the contract. In other cases the Tribunal has put a liberal interpretation upon Article V without articulating in detail the Tribunal's analysis of the meaning of Article V. It has only been in more recent cases that the Tribunal has provided a more complete analysis of how Article V should be applied by the Tribunal. The approach of the Tribunal in applying the provisions of Article V to the contract and debt claims stands in contrast to its treatment of the expropriation claims which will be considered in the next chapter.

[128] *Ibid.*

CHAPTER EIGHT
Claims arising from expropriation[1]

Introduction

Governing law of expropriation

The claims arising from expropriation are arguably the most important of the four categories of private claims before the Tribunal. Moreover the decisions of the Tribunal in this area may well be regarded as its most significant contribution to international law. Article II(1) of the Claims Settlement Declaration permits claims for expropriation of property of nationals of either party.

As noted in Chapter Six it is well recognised that expropriation of

[1] The literature relating to expropriation is voluminous. The most valuable works which are devoted solely to expropriation include: White, *Nationalisation of Foreign Property* (1961); Wortley, *Expropriation in Public International Law* (1959); Miller and Stanger (ed.), *Essays on Expropriation* (1967); Lillich (ed.), *The Valuation of Nationalized Property in International Law, 1972–75*, (1976). For articles refer to Francioni, *Compensation For Nationalization of Foreign Property: The Borderline between Law and Equity*, 24 I.C.L.Q., 255 (1978); Domke, *Foreign Nationalizations: Some Aspects of Contemporary International Law*, 55 A.J.I.L., 585 (1961), for interesting perspectives of the law. Most general works on international law and state responsibility include substantial sections on expropriation. It is not the writer's intention to give a complete overview of the international arbitral decisions and literature relating to expropriation. The purpose of this section is to highlight those aspects of the law relevant to the expropriations and nationalisations that have been undertaken by Iran. Several writers have considered the Iran–United States Claims Tribunal's decisions on expropriation, including: Bowett, *State Contracts with Aliens: Contemporary Developments on Compensation For Termination or Breach*, 59 B.Y.I.L., 49 (1988); Claggett, *The Expropriation Issue before the Iran–United States Claims Tribunal: is "Just Compensation" Required by International Law or Not?*, 16 Law and Policy in Int. Bus., 813 (1984–85); Gann, *Compensation Standard for Expropriation*, 23 Col. J. Transnat'l. L., 615, especially 639–646 (1985); Swanson, *Iran–U.S. Claims Tribunal: A Policy Analysis of the Expropriation Cases*, 18 Case Western J. of I.L., 307 (1986); Norton, *A Law of the Future or a Law of the Past? Modern Tribunals and the International Law of Expropriation*, A.J.I.L., 474 (1991).

property owned by aliens incurs the responsibility of the state and is thus governed by international law. This is so whether the property being expropriated consists of assets or contractual rights. Moreover, Article V of the Claims Settlement Declaration requires the Tribunal to apply such principles of international law as the Tribunal determines to be applicable to claims. Thus the Tribunal is required, both under the principles of international law and pursuant to Article V of the Claims Settlement Declaration, to ascertain the appropriate rules of international law applicable to the claims arising from expropriation.

The rationale that expropriation of foreign-owned property, whether it be physical assets or contractual rights, incurs the responsibility of the expropriating state to the state of the nationals whose property has been expropriated stems from the fact that the expropriating state has been enriched by the property of another state, even if the property is owned by nationals of the other state rather than directly by the claimant state itself.[2] Thus although the relationship between the foreign nationals and the host state is generally governed by municipal law, such law must comply with international law.[3] This is particularly true if the state expropriates property belonging to such foreign nationals.

The Tribunal has accepted from its very first decision on expropriation that expropriation is governed by customary international law. Moreover both Iran and the United States have argued that public international law governs issues of expropriation.

Thus in *American International Group v Iran*[4] the Tribunal noted that "it is a general principle of public international law that even in a case of lawful nationalization the former owner of the nationalized property is normally entitled to compensation".[5] In *TAMS v TAMS-AFFA*[6] the Tribunal held that when the actions of the government deprive a foreign owner of his property he is "entitled under international law and general principles of law to compensation for the full value of the property".[7]

[2] Generally it is not an issue of international law when a state expropriates the property of its own nationals, since there is no change in property relationships at the international level. Thus the municipal law of the expropriating state governs such transactions. See, however, *Lithgow*, (1986) Yearbook of the European Convention on Human Rights, 165. The European Court of Human Rights noted that the United Kingdom owed a minimum duty to its own citizens to compensate for expropriation. The Court held that it would respect the judgment of the British Parliament in providing compensation unless it was manifestly without reasonable foundation. A taking without compensation would be unreasonable. This case was based on the compulsory jurisdiction of the European Court of Human Rights over signatories to the European Human Rights Convention. The relevant article of Protocol 1 of the Convention permitted expropriation "in the public interest and subject to the conditions provided for by law and by general principles of international law".
[3] *Case of Serbian Loans* P.C.I.J., Ser. A, No. 20 (1929); *Case of Brazilian Loans* P.C.I.J., Ser. A, No. 21 (1929).
[4] 4 IRAN–U.S.C.T.R., 96 (1983).
[5] *Ibid.*, 105.
[6] 6 IRAN–U.S.C.T.R., 219 (1984).
[7] *Ibid.*, 225.

This point has been more directly stated in the recent major decisions arising from the expropriation of contractual rights in respect of the exploitation of Iran's oil resources. In *Mobil Oil Iran v Iran*,[8] concerning the expropriation of contractual rights in a consortium which operated the Iranian oil industry on behalf of NIOC, the Tribunal had no hesitation in deciding the expropriation was governed by international law. The Tribunal stated:[9]

> In these cases, the Tribunal concludes, and the parties agree, that the lawfulness of an expropriation must be judged by reference to international law. This holds true even when the expropriation is of contractual rights. A concession, for instance, may be the object of a nationalization regardless of the law the parties chose as the law of the contract. In the instant cases, the validity under international law of the Single Article Act and of its application to the SBA or any other agreement is not dependent upon the law which the parties chose to govern the Agreement.

However, there has been considerable divergence between the parties and within the Tribunal as to what constitutes the rules of public international law relating to expropriation. The United States arbitrators and, to a lesser extent, the neutral arbitrators have adopted the Western views on the status of the law while the Iranian arbitrators, particularly in their dissenting opinions, have reflected the attitudes of developing nations on the applicable rules of public international law.

The Treaty of Amity

The governing law in relation to expropriation is further complicated by the status of the Treaty of Amity between Iran and the United States.[10] This treaty came into force in 1955, having been entered into by the Imperial government. Nevertheless it was not expressly repudiated by the Islamic government or by the United States, and thus *prima facie* remained in force after the Islamic revolution. The International Court of Justice in *Diplomatic Staff in Tehran (United States v Iran)*[11] referred to the status of the Treaty of Amity, noting:[12]

> Although the machinery for effective operation of the 1955 Treaty has no doubt been impaired by reason of diplomatic relations between the two countries having been broken off by the United States, its provisions remain part of the corpus of law applicable between the United States and Iran.

[8] 16 IRAN–U.S.C.T.R., 1 (1987)
[9] *Ibid.*, 25.
[10] 284 U.N.T.S., 93 (1955).
[11] I.C.J. Rep., 3 (1980).
[12] *Ibid.*, 28.

The relevant provision of the Treaty of Amity states:[13]

Property of nationals and companies of either High Contracting Party including interests in property shall receive protection and security within the territories of the other High Contracting Party in no case less than that required by international law. Such property shall not be taken except for a public purpose nor shall it be taken without the prompt payment of just compensation. Such compensation shall be in an effectively realizable form and shall represent the full equivalent of the property taken; and adequate provision shall have been made at or prior to the time of taking for the determination and payment thereof.

The Treaty of Amity has been considered by the Tribunal in a number of cases. Initially the Tribunal merely noted the contentions of the claimant that the Treaty remained in force and the contentions of the respondent that it was no longer enforceable.[14] In such cases the United States arbitrators, in concurring opinions, have examined the Treaty in detail and have found, particularly on the basis of determination by the International Court of Justice, that the Treaty of Amity was still in force at the time the various causes of action arose, that is, prior to January 19, 1981. In later cases the Tribunal came to the view that the Treaty of Amity was in force at the time the various causes of action arose, that is, after the commencement of the Iranian revolution and before January 19, 1981.

In the decision in *INA Corporation* v *Iran*,[15] the majority opinion of the Tribunal accepted the claimant's contention that the Treaty of Amity remained in force between the two states:[16]

Moreover for the purpose of this case we are in the presence of a *lex specialis*, in the form of the Treaty of Amity which in principle prevails over general rules.

The continued validity and effect of the Treaty have not been contested by the Respondent in any of the written pleadings in this case ... Nor did the Parties invoke any "changed circumstances", or principles of international law, capable of invalidating, suspending or modifying the Treaty, which the Tribunal is bound to take into account or apply in all cases according to the provisions of Article V of the Claims Settlement Declaration. The Tribunal must therefore assume that for the purpose of the present case the Treaty remains binding as it is drafted.

The three most important awards of the Tribunal in respect of the Treaty of Amity are *Phelps Dodge Corporation* v *Iran*,[17] *Sedco Inc.* v *NIOC*[18] and *Amoco International Finance Corporation* v *Iran*.[19]

---

[13] Article IV(2) of the Treaty of Amity.
[14] *American International Group* v *Iran* 4 IRAN–U.S.C.T.R., 96, 105 (1983); *Sealand Service* v *Iran* 6 IRAN–U.S.C.T.R., 149 (1984).
[15] 8 IRAN–U.S.C.T.R., 373 (1985).
[16] *Ibid.*, 378.
[17] 10 IRAN–U.S.C.T.R., 121 (1986).
[18] *Ibid.*, 180.
[19] 15 IRAN–U.S.C.T.R., 189 (1987).

In *Phelps Dodge Corporation* the applicability of the Treaty of Amity, and in particular Article IV(2) of the Treaty, arose in respect of the appropriate standard of compensation. The respondent contended that the Treaty of Amity had "been 'terminated' by implication as a result of economic and military sanctions imposed on Iran by the United States in late 1979 and 1980".[20] The claimant argued that the Treaty remained in force to the present. The Tribunal did not attempt to determine whether the Treaty was in force at present. However, it had no doubt that the Treaty was in force at the time the claim arose, that is, prior to January 19, 1981, noting that the International Court of Justice had reached a similar conclusion in May 1980.[21] The Tribunal came to the same view in *Sedco Inc.* v *NIOC*, citing in support the *Phelps Dodge Corporation* case.[22] The Tribunal also noted that the *Sedco Inc.* claim was in respect of its shareholder interests in Sediran, a company incorporated in Iran.[23]

Amoco International Finance Corporation v *Iran*[24] was the first award arising from the nationalisation of the oil industry. Accordingly the decision is more comprehensive than the previous expropriation decisions, although it reflects the same general view of the current state of international law on expropriation and nationalisation by states.[25]

The applicability of the Treaty of Amity was raised by claimants, since they contended that the Treaty governed Iran's right to nationalise the claimants' property.[26] The respondents argued that the Treaty was not applicable, under three basic heads. First, it was never valid, as it was executed by a government installed as a result of foreign intervention. Second, even if the Treaty was valid it "had ceased to be operative in November 1979 at the latest, by reason of the United States' violations of it by taking measures against Iranian assets, as well as the general change of circumstances".[27] No formal notification of termination was required, "since termination by conduct of the parties is largely admitted in international law".[28] Third, the Treaty did not apply to private parties in respect of the expropriation of their assets.

The Tribunal quickly disposed of the contention that the Treaty was never valid, noting that the two governments were recognised in the international community and that it was never suggested that the Treaty was executed under duress or fraud within the meaning of the Vienna

[20] 10 IRAN–U.S.C.T.R., 121, 131 (1986).
[21] *Ibid.*, 131–2. The Tribunal did not support its finding with any more argument than that set out above.
[22] 10 IRAN–U.S.C.T.R., 180, 184 (1986).
[23] *Ibid.*, 183. See also Chapter Five on the issue of claims in respect of shareholder interests.
[24] 15 IRAN–U.S.C.T.R., 189 (1987).
[25] The Tribunal considers the applicability of the Treaty on pp. 214–22 of the award.
[26] *Ibid.*, 214.
[27] *Ibid.*, 214.
[28] *Ibid.*, 214–15.

Convention on the Law of Treaties.[29] On the question of the Treaty of Amity continuing in force the Tribunal noted that the International Court of Justice had found that the Treaty remained in force after the hostage crisis, notwithstanding United States actions against Iran, with specific reference to "[i]t is precisely when difficulties arise that the [T]reaty assumes its greatest importance".[30] The Tribunal also referred to the previous decisions of the Tribunal referred to above and saw "no reason to depart from these precedents".[31] The Tribunal, however, did canvass whether the change in circumstances, and in particular, the hostage crisis terminated the Treaty. It found that there was no termination by changed circumstances or alleged violations of the Treaty and that the conduct of the parties did not amount to an intention to terminate the Treaty.[32] In respect of the third question, that the Treaty did not apply to expropriation of the claimants' property, the Tribunal rejected the arguments of the respondent. The Tribunal stated:[33]

> It is indisputable, however, that certain provisions of the Treaty, including Article IV, set standards of treatment that each party must accord to the nationals and companies of the other party. The nationals and companies concerned, therefore, are entitled to receive such treatment.

The property rights of the claimants were rights protected by the Treaty.[34]

Although the Tribunal has found in a number of claims that the Treaty of Amity is applicable in cases of expropriation in determining the amount of compensation payable, the interpretation of the words of Article IV(2) of the Treaty, particularly "just compensation" and "the full equivalent of the property taken", have been issues of major importance in the expropriation decisions of the Tribunal.[35]

The main issues of expropriation

The claims before the Tribunal have raised three major substantive issues where there is considerable divergence between Iran and the United States claimants, reflecting an ideological difference between Western states and developing states. Thus the issues of most significance for the Iran-United States Claims Tribunal have been:

---

[29] *Ibid.*, 215–16.
[30] *Ibid.*, 218; from *Diplomatic Staff in Tehran case (United States v Iran)* I.C.J. Rep. 3, 28 (1980).
[31] *Ibid.*, 218.
[32] *Ibid.*, 218.
[33] *Ibid.*, 219.
[34] *Ibid.*, 221–2.
[35] See Chapter Nine, *infra*.

Claims arising from expropriation 151

1 What constitutes expropriation.
2 The limits on the rights of states to expropriate.
3 The standard of compensation.[36]

All of the expropriation claims heard by the Tribunal have been concerned with at least one of these three issues. However, it is the latter issue which is of most concern to investors and where there is the greatest divergence between Western states and developing states. Accordingly the decisions of the Tribunal will have their greatest impact on the development of international law in this area, since the Tribunal has largely rejected the views of developing states, which reached their zenith with the New International Economic Order espoused during the 1970s, and has upheld the traditional view that investors are entitled to full compensation for expropriated property.

What constitutes a taking

International law

An expropriation will have taken place when the state takes title to the property, thereby assuming all the rights and liabilities to the property.[37] However, a state can deprive an owner of some or all of his rights without actually taking title and still be deemed to have expropriated the property. Similarly not every action of the state which detrimentally affects the rights of the owner will constitute a taking.

The two most famous examples of governmental actions which amounted to expropriation despite the fact there was no taking of title are the cases of *German Interests in Polish Upper Silesia (Germany v Poland)*[38] and the *Norwegian Shipowners Claims (Norway v United States)*.[39] The property rights concerned physical property and contractual and other rights associated with the physical property. The *German Interests* case concerned a German-owned factory managed by another German company. The factory was taken over by the Polish government. The management company used certain patents and secret processes

---

[36] This issue will be covered in Chapter Nine, *infra*.
[37] In all cases 'owner' is deemed to refer to 'foreign owners' in which the confiscation of the foreign owners' property will involve international responsibility.
[38] P.C.I.J., Ser. A, No. 7 (1926).
[39] 1 R.I.A.A., 307 (1922). Both of these cases receive special emphasis in the pre-eminent works on this subject: Christie, *What Constitutes a Taking of Property under International Law*, 38 B.Y.I.L., 307, 310 (1962); Higgins, *The Taking of Property by the State*, III Recueil des Cours, 259, 322 (1982); Weston, *"Constructive Takings" under International Law: A Modest Foray into the Problem of "Creeping Expropriation"*, 16 Va. J.I.L., 103 (1975–76).

which it owned to produce nitrates. The Permanent Court of International Justice held that the taking of the physical plant and equipment also amounted to taking of the patents, processes and commercial contracts, although the Polish government had not sought to take these latter property rights. In the *Norwegian Shipowners' Claims* case the United States government requisitioned partially completed ships being built for Norwegian nationals. The United States government offered compensation for the ships themselves, but the Norwegian nationals claimed compensation for the shipbuilding contracts, which were of greater value than partially completed ships, owing to the scarcity of shipping. The Tribunal held in favour of the Norwegian shipowners, stating that the confiscation of the partially completed ships necessarily involved the confiscation of the shipbuilding contracts, and the compensation awarded reflected the value of these contracts.

In both of these cases it was clear that the actions of the government had completely severed the owner from both the physical property and the associated property and contractual rights. Any notional rights retained by the owner were completely valueless.

A government need not go so far for its actions to amount to expropriation. If governmental interference with owners' rights in relation to the property are sufficiently serious to substantially devalue the property or severely restrict the right of the owner to deal with the property, then a taking will be deemed to have taken place. Such interference may take the form of a forced sale, the appointment of managers responsible to the government, the imposition of confiscatory taxes and royalties or a substantial unilateral alteration of contractual rights.

Modern governments of all persuasions are deeply involved in the economic regulation of their societies. All impose taxes and exact measures which restrict the right of owners to use and dispose of their property. Before such actions will be considered to amount to expropriation it must be apparent that the governmental actions have so completely deprived the owners of their property rights that the rights are rendered nugatory. Such findings are more readily made where the government has the avowed intention of socialising the economy and thereby depriving private owners of their property rights.

The forced sale was a device extensively resorted to by the Nazi regime in respect of Jewish property and property owned by persons associated with or sympathetic to Jewish people. The United States Court of Restitution Appeals in *Osthoff* v *Hofele*[40] granted compensation to a former owner of a furniture store who had been forced to sell at a below-market price because of his Jewish sympathies. Similarly in *Poehlmann* v

---

[40] 1 U.S. Ct. Rest. App., 111 (1950).

Kulmbache Spinnerei A.G.[41] compensation was awarded to a hotel proprietor married to a Jewish woman who had been forced to sell as a result of boycotts and threats of violence.

Following the installation of communist governments in Eastern European states a variety of methods were used to an expropriate private property. In *Zwach* v *Kraus Bros & Co.*[42] negotiations were undertaken for the transfer of property in exchange for a passport. In the event Zwach fled the country without a passport and the property was subsequently taken by the Hungarian government.

The appointment of managers responsible to the government has been frequently resorted to by expropriating states.[43] It enables the government to assume control of the property, including the allocation of profit, yet argue that it has not expropriated the property and should thus not be liable for compensation. In the *Lena Goldfields* case[44] the government dismissed the staff employed by the claimant and substituted its own managers. The Tribunal held that this and other actions amounted to an expropriation of the property of the claimant, since the claimant was denied the right to manage and control its property.[45]

Similarly in 1957 the Indonesian government placed property owned by Dutch nationals under the management and control of persons responsible to the Indonesian government, although it specifically denied that it was confiscating the property. The *Netherlands International Law Review* board of editors considered that the actions were so extensive, and so completely deprived the owners of the use and control of the property, that they amounted to expropriation of the property.[46]

In contrast to the appointment of managers responsible to the government instead of the owners are the indigenisation programmes operated in many African and Arab countries. The requirement that foreign enterprises appoint indigenous people to manage and control the enterprise does not amount to a taking, since such persons are chosen by the foreign enterprise and responsible to it. The foreign owner thus retains the overall management and control of its enterprise.

Confiscatory taxes or royalties and rent, price and other regulatory controls may amount to expropriation where it is implicit that the intention of the government is to deprive the owner of his property. Eastern

---

[41] U.S. Ct. Rest. App., 701 (1952).
[42] 237 F. 2d., 255 (2nd Circ.) (1956).
[43] Many of the expropriation cases heard by the Iran–United States Claims Tribunal involve the appointment of managers by the Iranian government to enterprises owned by United States nationals.
[44] 36 Cornell L.Q., 31 (1950).
[45] *Ibid.*
[46] The Board of Editors, *The Measures taken by the Indonesian Government against Netherlands Enterprises*, 5 Netherlands Int. L.R., 227, 242 (1958).

European governments, which had the avowed intention of socialising the economy, were vulnerable to assertions that their actions amounted to confiscation. In the case of *Albert Reet*[47] the Foreign Claims Settlement Commission found that Hungarian laws which prohibited the sale or occupancy of a house amounted to confiscation. The Commission also held that a Czechoslovakian decree requiring owners of rental property to deposit the rent in special accounts, with the owner only being able to withdraw 15 per cent of the income, and specifying that only the government could select the tenants and establish the rent, amounted to expropriation of the property subject to the decree.[48] However, in *Gudmundson v Iceland*[49] the European Human Rights Commission was not prepared to accept that a tax of 25 per cent of the value of property was confiscatory, although it conceded that if such a tax was sufficiently high it could be regarded as confiscatory.[50] Moreover the Commission stated that the general principles of international law in relation to the sanctity of private property only applied to foreign-owned property.[51] A state is free to expropriate the property of its own nationals without being bound to pay compensation. There is a general right to impose taxes and enact regulations for public purposes in respect of foreign property provided such measures are not confiscatory.

More recently the European Court of Human Rights in *Sporring and Lönnroth*[52] held that expropriation permits and building restrictions could amount to sufficient interference with property as to require compensation, even if the permits and restrictions were revoked after a period of time and the owners were able to reassume full rights over the property. In the *Sporring* case the permits and restrictions had been in force for twenty-five years before revocation and during that time the owners had been severely restricted in their dealings with the property.

As already noted, property does not consist only of physical assets but also extends to contractual rights. The most significant expropriation cases relate to oil and mineral concessions, the principal value of which is not the plant and equipment but the right to extract and market the oil or minerals. There has been a tendency on the part of states granting concessions to modify concession rights by increasing royalties and taxes

---

[47] 26 I.L.R., 283 (1958).

[48] Most Western European countries have rent controls and tenancy legislation which significantly restrict the ability of landlords to obtain a market return for their property. It is not generally regarded that such controls amount to expropriation of the property, since the owner retains sufficient rights in the property to be able to exercise his fundamental rights of ownership.

[49] 3 *Yearbook of European Convention on Human Rights*, 390 (1960).

[50] *Ibid.*, 422.

[51] *Ibid.*

[52] 68 I.L.R., 86 (1982).

and expanding the regulatory and licensing powers over the concessions.

If the concessionaire accepts the new conditions the question of taking does not arise.[53] However, in some instances the changes are so extensive that they are an expropriation of the concessionaires property rights. In *Revere Copper* v *OPIC*[54] Revere had entered into a twenty-five-year concession agreement with the government of Jamaica containing stabilisation clauses for the extraction and processing of bauxite. In 1974 the government repudiated the contract and substantially increased the royalties and taxes payable by Revere. As a result Revere made substantial losses and ceased operations in 1975. The Tribunal had to determine whether the government of Jamaica had expropriated the property rights conferred upon Revere by the contract. It found that long-term economic development contracts entered into between foreign companies and government are subject to the principles of public international law governing the responsibility of states for injuries to aliens.[55] The actions of the Jamaican government, particularly with reference to the revocation of existing mining leases, were a repudiation of the concession agreement.[56] With the concession agreement being abrogated the Tribunal held that Revere had lost "effective control" of its total operation in Jamaica, even though it retained ownership of the plant and machinery used to process the bauxite.[57]

Therefore the principal test as to whether actions falling short of a formal taking of title constitute a taking is whether or not the action fundamentally restricts the right of the owner to manage or dispose of the property, or if the property has been rendered virtually valueless. Governmental actions which limit the owner's right in relation to his property but which do not significantly affect the aforementioned fundamental rights generally do not amount to expropriation of the property entitling the owner to compensation.

---

[53] The oil concessions in the Middle East countries usually contain "stabilisation clauses". However, the oil companies have agreed to greater royalties and taxes and increased regulation of the concessions, and have not invoked the arbitration and stabilisation clauses except in very clear cases of expropriation. The Libyan arbitrations took place because it was no longer possible for the oil companies in question to conduct business in Libya.

[54] 56 I.L.R., 258 (1980). The arbitration, which was between Revere and the Overseas Private Investment Corporation, a United States governmental agency established to indemnify United States investors abroad in the event of expropriation, had to determine whether the actions of Jamaica constituted an expropriation. If so, then OPIC would be liable to pay compensation to Revere Copper Inc.

[55] *Ibid.*, 271–2. Extensive reference was made to *Aramco* v *Saudi Arabia*, *Sapphire Oil* v *NIOC* and *Texaco* v *Libya*, on the applicability of international law to concession agreements, with particular emphasis on the "delocalised" nature of such contacts.

[56] *Ibid.*, 290.

[57] *Ibid.*, 292. The Tribunal noted how increased taxes and regulations can amount to "creeping expropriation".

Awards and decisions of the Tribunal

The issue of what constitutes a taking has been considered by the Tribunal in two broad categories. The first relates to claims against respondent companies which were previously privately owned and have since been taken over by the Iranian government and also claims for property and property rights owned by United States nationals which have been expropriated by the Iranian government. The second category concerns breaches of contracts made with state-owned entities, particularly in relation to the oil industry.

State control of privately owned corporations and direct takings
The Tribunal can only hear claims made by nationals of one party against the government, including controlled entities, of the other party. In a number of cases United States nationals entered into contractual relationships with privately owned Iranian companies. Following the revolution, breaches of these contracts occurred, resulting in loss of profits and the loss of property subject to the contracts.[58] In order to make a claim before the Tribunal it was essential for United States claimants to show that the Iranian company had become a controlled entity of the government of Iran and that the breach of contract occurred after the company had become a controlled entity of the Iranian government. In *Raygo Warner Equipment Company* v *Star-Line Iran Company*[59] the claimant had leased machinery to the privately owned Iranian company, Star-Line. Following the revolution the lease payments stopped and the equipment remained in possession of the lessees. It was essential for Raygo Warner to show that Star-Line was, at the time the cause of action arose, a controlled entity of Iran. Chamber Three of the Tribunal, by majority, noted:[60]

... That since the revolutionary events in Iran, Star-Line has not been run by its registered Manager and Board of Directors and that the shareholders have not been in a position to exert their rights and fulfil their duties as shareholders. Furthermore, there are clear indications that Star-Line has been administered by persons who have been appointed by some public authority, although no formal Decree to this effect has been presented.

On the basis of these facts the Tribunal found that *prima facie* the respondent was controlled by the government of Iran.[61] Mr Sani, the

---
[58] In such cases claimants have pleaded breach of contract and expropriation as alternative causes of action. This alternative pleading is only possible if the breach of contract leads to the loss of property or of property rights, as in the termination of oil concessions.
[59] 1 IRAN–U.S.C.T.R., 411 (1981–82).
[60] *Ibid.*, 413.
[61] *Ibid.*, 413. This conclusion was supported by the constitution of the Islamic Republic of Iran, Article 44 of which states that the state sector includes the shipping industry and port and unloading facilities.

Claims arising from expropriation 157

Iranian arbitrator, in his dissenting opinion stated that on many occasions such actions were taken as a result of "the flight of the managers and directors of a number of such companies from Iran after the Revolution".[62] The measures taken by Iran "were to the benefit of the shareholders of such companies, in a sense safeguarding their interests".[63]

Chamber Three of the Tribunal subsequently distinguished control of a company from nationalisation and expropriation of such company. In *Rexnord Inc. v Iran*,[64] the Tribunal, by a majority, noted that the power to appoint managers and directors of the respondent companies since the revolution had been with the government of Iran. It stated:[65]

In view of this, and regardless of whether the two companies were in effect nationalized or expropriated by Iran, the Tribunal holds that both Tchacosh and Siporex are entities controlled by Iran.

These principles were applied when the Tribunal had to determine whether or not property owned by United States claimants had been expropriated by Iran.

One of the most important cases dealing with the nature of expropriation of United States assets is *Starrett Housing Corporation v Iran*,[66] heard by Chamber One of the Tribunal. The claimants had a majority interest in an Iranian corporation, Shah Goli Apartment Company, which was engaged in the construction and sale of 1,600 apartments in the Zomorod apartment complex. Starrett Housing supplied United States managers and technical experts to Shah Goli to manage and design the project. The claimants contended that the Iranian government was responsible for acts which prevented the successful completion of the project. Among the acts complained of were a freeze of Shah Goli's bank accounts, harassment of Starrett personnel by Islamic militants, a governmental requirement that down payments for the apartments must be made to Bank Maskan instead of direct to Shah Goli, and finally in January 1980 the appointment of a temporary manager of Shah Goli by the Ministry of Housing. On reviewing these actions the Tribunal stated:[67]

It has, however, to be borne in mind that assumption of control over property by a government does not automatically and immediately justify a conclusion that the property has been taken by the government thus requiring compensation under international law ... The completion of the Project was dependant upon a

[62] *Ibid.*, 419.
[63] *Ibid.*
[64] 2 IRAN–U.S.C.T.R., 6 (1983).
[65] *Ibid.*, 10.
[66] 4 IRAN–U.S.C.T.R., 122 (1985). The detailed facts of this case have been more fully set out in Chapter Four.
[67] *Ibid.*, 155.

large number of American construction supervisors and subcontractors whom it would have been necessary to replace and the right freely to select management, supervisors and subcontractors is an essential element of the right to manage a project... Indeed the language of [the Completion of Housing Construction] Bill seems to indicate that the right to manage such projects ultimately rests with the Ministry of Housing and Bank Maskan...

It has therefore not been proven in the case that at least by the end of January 1980 the Government of Iran had interfered with the Claimants' property rights in the Project to an extent that rendered these rights so useless that they must be deemed to have been taken.

The Tribunal recognised that although a state need not formally take title in order to expropriate property there must be specific governmental actions which effectively deny the owner the use and control of his property.[68] The Tribunal therefore stated:[69]

There is no reason to doubt that the events in Iran prior to January 1980 to which the Claimants refer seriously hampered their possibilities to proceed with the construction work and eventually paralyzed the Project. But investors in Iran, like investors in all countries, have to assume a risk that the country might experience strikes, lockouts, disturbances, changes of the economic and political system and even revolution. That any of these risks materialized does not necessarily mean that property rights affected by such events can be deemed to have been taken. A revolution as such does not entitle investors to compensation under international law.

The Iranian arbitrator, Mr Kanshani, in his dissenting opinion, took a narrower view of what constituted expropriation. He stated:[70]

... Expropriation or nationalization is attributable to the Government only if it has passed a special law divesting ownership rights, or if it has officially recognised such expropriation. This Chamber cannot interpret its jurisdiction so broadly that it is able to find liable the Government of the Islamic Republic of Iran of expropriation in an instance such as this, where the appointment of a manager was temporary and solely for the purpose of managing the company's affairs. Moreover, the Government of the Islamic Republic of Iran and Bank Omran have disclosed their preparedness to place the company at the disposal of its directors. Obviously there is no compensation greater than the return of a property itself to its owner.

The interlocutory award of *Sedco Inc.* v *NIOC*[71] made by Chamber Three of the Tribunal relied heavily on the *Starrett* decision. A joint venture company between Sedco and NIOC, known as Sediran, owned

---

[68] *Ibid.*, 154.
[69] *Ibid.*, 156.
[70] 7 IRAN–U.S.C.T.R., 119, 165 (1984).
[71] 9 IRAN–U.S.C.T.R., 248 (1985).

ten drilling rigs. Sedco had a 50 per cent interest in Sediran and made a claim for expropriation of the assets of Sediran.[72]

The management of Sediran became increasingly difficult from late 1978 onward owing to the Islamic revolution, although a degree of management was still possible by telephone and telex and by the local Iranian managers. In November 1979 the Iranian Ministry of Industry and Mines appointed three temporary directors in replacement of the existing directors to manage Sediran. The temporary managers sold the assets of Sediran to NIOC, and effectively liquidated Sediran. In August 1980, pursuant to Clause C of the Protection and Development of Iranian Industries Act, the shares of Sediran were transferred to Iran.[73] The Tribunal carried out a thorough review of the facts, the Iranian law which authorised the appointment of the three temporary directors, and the principles of international law governing acts of taking. The Tribunal concluded:[74]

> When, as in the instant case, the seizure of control by appointment of "temporary managers" clearly ripens into an outright taking of title, the date of appointment presumptively should be regarded as the date of the taking. The choice of the date is not without significance because the value of the shareholders' expropriated interest may change dramatically during the surrounding time. Selection of the earlier date of the appointment of government managers as the time of taking is equitably the most appropriate given that the Government of Iran and not SEDCO became the chief architect of SEDIRAN's fortunes at that point.

Not every appointment of managers by the government will constitute a taking by the government.

In *Motorola Inc. v Iran National Airlines Corporation*[75] the claimant contended that its Iranian subsidiary was expropriated through the appointment of a manager by the Revolutionary Council. The manager sought a number of meetings with Motorola, with a view to Motorola being able to continue to exercise its rights of ownership, including appointing a new external management. The Tribunal, on reviewing the facts, held:[76]

> In view of the foregoing the Tribunal finds that neither the events in April 1979 nor, *prima facie*, the events in September 1979 warrant the conclusion that Iran had assumed such control over Milcom that a taking had occurred. On the contrary, they imply that both parties assumed that Motorola was still the owner of Milcom, that it had the right to appoint its own manager and to dispose of it by selling it to I.E.I.

---

[72] The issue of control of Sediran has been considered in Chapter Four.
[73] Clause C stated that where factories and institutions are indebted to Iranian banks, and their debt exceeds their equity, they will be owned by the government.
[74] 9 IRAN–U.S.C.T.R., 248, 278 (1985).
[75] 19 IRAN–U.S.C.T.R., 73 (1988).
[76] *Ibid.*, 87.

In *Sealand Service Inc.* v *Government of Iran*[77] Chamber One of the Tribunal stressed that a taking can only occur if there is some specific act by the government that expropriates the property. In this case Sealand had entered into an arrangement with the Ports and Shipping Organisation to construct and operate a container facility. It was fundamental to the viability of the facility's administrative procedures that the Sealand facility should receive priority treatment. During and after the revolution the usual administrative procedures broke down and the facility could not be operated properly. The Tribunal, in a majority decision, stated:[78]

> A finding of expropriation would require, at the very least, that the Tribunal be satisfied that there was deliberate government interference with the conduct of Sealand's operation, the effect of which was to deprive Sealand of the use and benefit of this investment... A claim founded substantially on omissions and inaction in a situation where the evidence suggests a widespread and indiscriminate deterioration in management, disrupting the functioning of the port of Bandar Abbas, can hardly justify a finding of expropriation.

An example of "deliberate government interference" is found in *TAMS* v *TAMS-AFFA*.[79] The claimant, a United States engineering consultancy firm, had a 50 per cent interest in an Iranian engineering firm, TAMS-AFFA.[80] Following the revolution TAMS-AFFA was placed under government management. The government-appointed manager assumed the right to sign cheques drawn on TAM-AFFA and to make other decisions without consulting TAMS. Subsequently TAMS was able to resume some of its rights in TAMS-AFFA, but once the hostage crisis developed all communication between TAMS and TAMS-AFFA ceased. Chamber Two of the Tribunal, in a majority award, stated:[81]

> While assumption of control over property by a government does not automatically and immediately justify a conclusion that the property has been taken by the government, thus requiring compensation under international law, such a conclusion is warranted whenever events demonstrate that the owner was deprived of fundamental rights of ownership and it appears that this deprivation is

---

[77] 6 IRAN–U.S.C.T.R., 149 (1984).

[78] *Ibid.*, 166. Mr. Holtzmann, the United States arbitrator, dissented, stating that the Iranian government had committed acts which amounted to expropriation.

[79] 6 IRAN–U.S.C.T.R., 219 (1984).

[80] TAMS–AFFA had been established by TAMS and an Iranian engineering consultancy AFFA to perform engineering and architectural services for the Tehran International Airport. This performance was based on a contract between TAMS and AFFA and the Iranian Civil Aviation Organisation.

[81] *Ibid.*, 225–6. This is the most comprehensive statement by the Tribunal as to what constitutes a taking when the legal title to the property is not affected. The Tribunal made reference to Whiteman, 8 *Digest of International Law*, 1006–20; Christie, *What Constitutes a Taking under International Law?*, 38 B.Y.I.L., 307 (1962); and the *Lena Goldfields* arbitration, 36 Cornell L.Q., 31 (1950).

not merely ephemeral. The intent of the government is less important than the effects of the measures on the owners, and the form of the measures of control or interference is less important than the reality of their impact.

Dr Shafeiei, the Iranian arbitrator, in a strongly worded dissent, cited the *Sealand*[82] award with apparent approval.[83] He elaborated on the "elements of expropriation",[84] stating:[85]

The Government must have interfered intentionally with such property rights, and their owner must as a result have been deprived of his property and rights ... Therefore, if an owner personally renounces his right to his property and does not attempt to obtain consideration for it; or if the deprivation of the owner's property rights results from other factors, the Government obviously will not incur responsibility.

Moreover it has been accepted in international law that extraordinary measures taken by a Government in extraordinary situations or in times of crisis in order to safeguard its own national interests will not entail international responsibility.

The *TAMS* award has been cited in subsequent Tribunal awards. In *Phelps Dodge Corporation* v *Iran*[86] the claimant sought compensation for the expropriation of its 19.36 per cent interest in an Iranian company, SICAB. The facts were that Phelps Dodge made an investment in a joint venture company in Iran for the manufacture of electrical cable. It also had the right to appoint key personnel and supervise manufacturing operations. The SICAB factory was constructed by mid-1978 and began production in late 1978. During the Iranian revolution new managers were appointed without prior approval of Phelps Dodge, culminating in a transfer of management of the factory to agencies of the Iranian government in November 1980. Thereafter, Phelps Dodge received no information about the management or finances of SICAB. The Tribunal concluded that as of November 1980 "control of the SICAB factory was taken by the Respondent thereby depriving Phelps Dodge of virtually all of the value of its property rights in SICAB".[87] The Tribunal cited the *TAMS* decision and the *Starrett Housing* decision[88] and considered that taking control of the claimant's interest, even though there had been no formal decree of expropriation, meant Iran "has effectively taken Phelps Dodge's property and is liable to the Claimants for the value of their property".[89]

[82] 6 IRAN–U.S.C.T.R., 149 (1984).
[83] 6 IRAN–U.S.C.T.R., 230, 256 (1984); Dissenting Opinion.
[84] *Ibid.*
[85] *Ibid.* Dr Shafeiei found that the actions of the Iranian government were designed to protect the interests of the shareholders, who had abandoned Iran. These actions prevented the termination of the TAMS-AFFA partnership.
[86] 10 IRAN–U.S.C.T.R., 121 (1986).
[87] *Ibid.*, 130.
[88] *Ibid.*, 130.
[89] *Ibid.*, 131.

162   *The jurisdiction of the Tribunal*

The taking can be achieved by any branch of government, including the courts. In *Oil Field of Texas Inc.* v *Iran*[90] the Tribunal, referring to a decision of the French–Italian Conciliation Commission, stated:[91]

> The interference with the use of the three blowout preventers caused by the Ahwaz Court order amounts to a taking of this equipment... In these circumstances, and taking into account the claimant's impossibility to challenge the Court order in Iran, there was a taking of the three blowout preventers for which the government is responsible.

The crucial test as to whether the actions of a government constitute a taking is whether the foreign owner is denied the ability to exercise his fundamental ownership rights in respect of the property, irrespective of whether there has been a formal taking. If the actions deny the owner these rights for a sufficient period of time there is a taking which gives rise to the right to compensation. Although all members of the Tribunal accept this principle of international law the application of it to particular facts has caused difficulty. The United States arbitrators have taken a liberal view as to what actions constitute expropriation. The Iranian arbitrators have tended to explain the actions of the Iranian government as being necessary for the preservation of the undertaking which cannot, at least at the present, be regarded as a permanent taking entitling the owner to compensation.

Breaches of concession contracts

One of the principal economic objectives of the Islamic revolution was the termination of the foreign oil concessions. The oil workers had been at the forefront of the revolution and acted in concert with the Islamic government.

Typically the oil concessions were organised through a joint structure agreement (JSA) with the NIOC entering into a joint venture agreement to develop and exploit the oilfields. These agreements provided for a fifty–fifty split of the ownership and profits from the oil. However, in 1973 the levy rate and taxes imposed on the oil companies were increased, ensuring that Iran would benefit from the increasing prices for its principal natural resource. The oil companies accepted these modifications to the JSA. The Islamic revolution, however, meant the termination of the JSAs. The termination occurred in a number of ways, including administrative refusal to implement the JSA, nationalising legislation and the appointment of managers.

The *Phillips Petroleum* case[92] illustrates the process. The Phillips JSA

[90] 12 IRAN–U.S.C.T.R., 308 (1986).
[91] *Ibid.*, 318–19.
[92] 21 IRAN–U.S.C.T.R., 79 (1989).

had been entered into in 1964 to develop oilfields in the Persian Gulf. The term of the JSA was twenty-five years from the date of commercial production from various areas of the concession, which occurred in 1969 and 1971, with a renewal of five years. Thus the JSA was due to terminate in 1999. In 1974 in line with all other agreements throughout the Middle East the JSA was varied to take account of the increase in oil prices. The termination of the JSA as a result of the Islamic revolution was "heralded during the days immediately proceeding and following the return of Imam Khomeini to Iran on 1 February, 1979".[93] In relation to the claimant, NIOC unilaterally set production rates far below those prevailing prior to the revolution and did not allow Phillips to lift any oil. All oil production was undertaken by NIOC. Officials appointed by the claimant were dismissed in May 1979. By September 1979 the claimant was notified of the termination of the JSA. The Single Article Act nationalising the oil was passed in January 1980 and written nullification of the JSA was made in August 1980. The Tribunal stated:[94]

> The conclusion that the Claimant was deprived of its property by conduct attributable to the Government of Iran, including NIOC, rests on a series of concrete actions rather than any particular formal decree, as the formal acts merely ratified and legitimized the existing state of affairs.

In the case of concession agreements the actual time of taking is of great importance, since it is the date from which damages will flow. It is in the interests of the claimant that it should be as early as possible and for Iran as late as possible. The claimant suggested the taking was completed by September 1979 and Iran argued for August 1980, when the claimants were formally notified of the termination. The Tribunal held "the Claimant's JSA rights were taken by 29 September 1979, and the Respondents are liable to compensate the Claimant for its loss as of that date".[95] From that date, the taking was an "irreversible deprivation"[96] of the claimant's property and Iran was required to pay damages from that date.

The legality of expropriation

International law

The classical view is that a state cannot expropriate any foreign-owned private property except for public necessity and subject to payment of full

[93] *Ibid.*, 112.
[94] *Ibid.*, 116
[95] *Ibid.*, 118
[96] *Ibid.*, 116. The Tribunal was quoting from *International Technical Products Corp.* v *Iran* 9 IRAN–U.S.C.T.R., 206, 240–1 (1985).

compensation.[97] Early twentieth-century arbitral decisions supported this view. The Permanent Court of Justice in the *Chorzow Factory* case[98] referred to the necessity for "fair compensation" in cases of expropriation, whether or not the expropriation was legally sound.[99] Similarly in the *Norwegian Shipowners' Claim*[100] the Commission stated:[101]

Whether the action of the United States is lawful or not, just compensation is due to the claimants under the municipal law of the United States, as well as under international law, based upon the respect for private property.

Such property need not only be physical assets, it can also be contractual rights. In the *Shufeldt* claim[102] Guatemala had terminated a concession agreement. The arbitrator held that the claimant was entitled to compensation for the breach of contract. The *Delagoa Bay Railway* claim[103] also resulted in an award of damages for the termination of the concession agreement by the Portuguese authorities.

These decisions preceded the large-scale nationalisations that have occurred during the twentieth century, particularly in Eastern Europe and the developing countries. It was quickly accepted by Western governments and jurists that such nationalisations were within the competence of the state and indeed large-scale nationalisations have occurred in a number of Western European countries. The validity of such nationalisations is conditional upon the nationalisations being non-discriminatory. In the event that a nationalisation is discriminatory it will be unlawful *per se*.[104] A valid non-discriminatory nationalization will give rise to a liability on the part of the nationalising state to pay appropriate compensation.

The customary international law on nationalisation is generally regarded as being expressed in the General Assembly Resolution of 1962 on Permanent Sovereignty over Natural Resources.[105] Paragraph 4 of the resolution provides:

Nationalization, expropriation or requisitioning shall be based on grounds or reasons of public utility, security or the national interest which are recognised as overriding purely individual or private interests, both domestic and foreign. In

[97] Refer to Wortley, *Expropriation in Public International Law*, 23–37 (1961).
[98] P.C.I.J., Ser. A, No. 17 (1928).
[99] *Ibid.*
[100] II R.I.A.A., 309 (1922).
[101] *Ibid.*, 334.
[102] *Shufeldt Claim (United States v Guatemala)* II R.I.A.A., 1080 (1930).
[103] The claim was, however, based on a *compromis* in which the only issue before the arbitrator was the amount of damages payable.
[104] This will affect the level of compensation. See *BP v Libya* 53 I.L.R., 297 (1979).
[105] Resolution 1803 (XVII) of the General Assembly of 14 December 1962. It was supported by eighty-seven votes to two, with twelve abstentions. The United States voted for the resolution.

such cases the owner shall be paid appropriate compensation, in accordance with the rules in force in the State taking such measures in the exercise of its sovereignty and in accordance with international law. In any case where the question of compensation gives rise to a controversy, the national jurisdiction of the State taking such measures shall be exhausted. However, upon agreement by sovereign States and other parties concerned, settlement of the dispute should be made through arbitration or international adjudication.

In addition paragraph 8 noted that "Foreign investment agreements freely entered into by, or between, sovereign States shall be observed in good faith".

Since 1962 the consensus reflected in Resolution 1803 has broken down. In 1974 the General Assembly adopted two resolutions which confirmed the right of states to nationalise foreign property but which provided that compensation was to be determined solely under the domestic law of the nationalising state.[106] Although these resolutions were adopted by large majorities, the major investing nations of the West either voted against the resolutions or abstained.[107] Professor Dupuy, the arbitrator in *Topco* v *Libya*,[108] considered that unless General Assembly resolutions were generally accepted by all nations they did not embody customary international law. He stated:[109]

On the basis of the circumstances of adoption mentioned above and by expressing an *opinio juris communis*, Resolution 1803 (XVII) seems to this Tribunal to reflect the state of customary law in this field.

Customary international law embodied in Resolution 1803 has two potentially conflicting strands: first, states have the right to nationalise their natural wealth and resources, subject to compensation, and, secondly, it is an obligation of states to honour agreements which may restrict the right to nationalise. The exploitation of natural resources in developing countries has traditionally been through the vehicle of the concession agreement, frequently with terms of many decades. As the political and economic structures of these nations matured, such agreements were perceived to be an impediment to the ability of states to direct the course of their economic development. The initial response has been to modify the agreements, giving a greater share to the states.

---

[106] Resolution 3281 (XXXIX), 12 December 1974; Resolution 3201 (XXXIX), 1 May 1974. Resolution 3281 did state that other means could be agreed upon to determine the question of compensation, this being a reference to international arbitration.

[107] The voting on Resolution 3281, the Charter of Economic Rights and Duties of States, was 120 for, six against, and ten abstentions. The states voting against were Belgium, Denmark, the Federal Republic of Germany, Luxembourg, the United Kingdom and the United States.

[108] 17 I.L.M., 1 (1978).

[109] *Ibid*.

Eventually this process may lead to the state abrogating the agreement and nationalising the resources. The usual terms of such concession agreements include a stabilisation clause and an arbitration clause.

Thus international arbitrators have had a number of opportunities to determine whether the right of states to nationalise their natural wealth and resources includes the right to abrogate concession agreements and other long-term development contracts.

The *Lena Goldfields* arbitration[110] concerned the nationalisation by the Soviet government of a concession which had twenty-five years to run. The company's claim was made under two heads, breach of contract and unjust enrichment. The arbitrators considered that the action of the Soviet government constituted a breach of contract, thereby entitling Lena to compensation "for the value of the benefits of which it had been wrongfully deprived".[111] Compensation was ordered on the basis of a "fair purchase price for a going concern".[112]

A number of arbitrations between Latin American nations and developed Western nations reflected this concern for the sanctity of the contract. The *Landreau claim (United States v Peru)*[113] concerned a *quantum meruit* claim arising from the failure of the government of Peru to pay a reward agreed to by contract for the discovery of deposits of guano. The arbitral tribunal noted that Landreau had accepted the repudiation of the contract by Peru and was thus only entitled to "the fair value of the communication to Peru of the discoveries of guano".[114] The *Pieri Dominique* case[115] heard by the French–Venezuelan Commission arose from the termination of a tramway concession during revolutionary upheaval in Venezuela.

The circumstances of these early arbitrations were fundamentally different from those of the *ad hoc* arbitrations of the post-war period, particularly those relating to the oil concessions of the Middle East. These oil concession arbitrations can be divided into two categories: those preceding Resolution 1803, and those arbitrations since 1962 which have considered the relevance both of Resolution 1803 and of the 1974 resolutions.

In the first category is the arbitration *Saudi Arabia v Aramco*.[116] This

---

[110] 36 Cornell L.Q., 42 (1950–51). This arbitration is of particular significance because it was the first arbitration arising from a state implementing a comprehensive plan to nationalise the major sources of its economic wealth.
[111] *Ibid.*, 51.
[112] *Ibid.*, 52.
[113] I R.I.A.A., 347 (1922).
[114] *Ibid.*, 364.
[115] X R.I.A.A., 139 (1902).
[116] 27 I.L.R., 117 (1963). Another oil arbitration also falling into this category is *Sapphire Petroleum v NIOC* 35 I.L.R., 136 (1967).

arbitration was concerned with the interpretation and application of the concession agreement granted to Aramco and did not consider the question of compensation. Aramco had been granted an exclusive concession to extract, refine and transport oil from Saudi Arabia. Some years after the commencement of the concession Saudi Arabia entered into an agreement with Mr Onassis giving him first priority to ship oil from Saudi Arabia. This proved to be unacceptable to Aramco and it was agreed that the dispute should be submitted to arbitration. Saudi Arabia argued that the arrangement with Mr Onassis was not in breach of the concession, and that in any event Saudi Arabia retained the sovereign right to make such arrangements for the shipment of oil produced from the Aramco concession as it saw fit.[117] Aramco maintained that the concession agreement gave it the exclusive right to ship oil, and that this right could not be modified without the consent of Aramco. Since both parties accepted the underlying validity of the Aramco concession the tribunal was merely required to determine the proper interpretation of the agreement.

On the preliminary issue of the proper law of the contract the tribunal considered that, owing to the deficiencies of Saudi Arabian law of the time, certain aspects of the concession were to be interpreted in accordance with general principles of law[118] and public international law.[119] However, the tribunal's enquiry was limited to determining whether international law required states to honour the agreements they had entered into. Saudi Arabia argued that the principles of the French "administrative contract" applied generally to oil concessions, enabling the state to modify such concessions.[120] This was rejected by the tribunal, since an oil concession was not a public service. There was no consideration by the tribunal whether international law gave nations the sovereign right to manage their natural resources as they saw fit, even if this meant the modification or abrogation of concession agreements.[121] The principles of *pacta sunt servanda* and vested rights were paramount.

The principle that states should honour the terms of concession agreements is exemplified by *Sapphire Petroleum v National Iranian Oil Company*.[122] This arbitration arose from a failure of NIOC to honour the

---

[117] For a summary of these submissions of the two parties see 27 I.L.R., 117, 132–3 (1963).
[118] *Ibid.*, 166–9.
[119] *Ibid.*, 217.
[120] *Ibid.*, 215. The concept of the "administrative contract" originates in French civil law. It is arguable that the concept is recognised in General Assembly Resolution 1803 as the Permanent Sovereignty over Natural Resources. This resolution recognises the "public" nature of a nation's ownership of natural resources.
[121] The Tribunal interpreted the concession agreement in the same manner as any other contract freely entered into by a nation. It stated that Aramco had acquired or vested rights under the concession capable of enforcement under the terms of the concession. *Ibid.*, 215.
[122] 35 I.L.R., 136 (1967).

terms of the concession agreement. On the issue that agreements must be honoured the arbitrator noted:[123]

> Moreover it is a fundamental principle of law, which is constantly being proclaimed by international courts that contractual rights must be respected. The rule *pacta sunt servanda* is the basis of every contractual relationship.

Sapphire Petroleum was thus able to sustain its claim for loss of profits for breach of contract.[124]

It was not until the three arbitrations arising from the Libyan nationalisations that arbitrators began to consider whether the right of states to nationalise their natural wealth and resources overrode the terms of concession agreements.[125]

The factual background to these arbitrations was that Libya had progressively nationalised its petroleum industry from 1971 onward by abrogating the petroleum concessions granted to foreign oil companies. The circumstances of each nationalisation, however, varied and were impelled by different motives. Thus the nationalisation of the British Petroleum concession was undertaken partly in retaliation for the failure of Britain to protect three islands in the Gulf of Arabia.[126] This particular nationalisation preceded the later widespread nationalisation of all foreign oil concessions. The arbitrator, Judge Lagergren, stated:[127]

> The B.P. Nationalization Law, and the actions taken thereunder by the Respondent, do constitute a fundamental breach of the B.P. concession as they amount to a total repudiation of the agreement and the obligation of the Respondent thereunder ... Further the taking by the Respondent of the property, rights and interests of the Claimant clearly violates public international law as it was made for purely extraneous political reasons and was arbitrary and discriminatory in character. Nearly two years have now passed since the nationalization, and the fact that no offer of compensation has been made indicates that the taking was also confiscatory.

The other two arbitrations were concerned with the nationalisation of concessions owned by United States companies.

In both cases the nationalisations were undertaken directly as part of the Libyan nationalisation programme.[128] The arbitrators could therefore

---

[123] *Ibid.*, 181.

[124] *Ibid.*, 186–7.

[125] For commentaries on the three Libyan arbitrations, see Greenwood, *State Contracts in International Law: The Libyan Oil Arbitrations*, 53 B.Y.I.L., 27 (1982).

[126] *British Petroleum* v *Libyan Arab Republic* 53 I.L.R., 297 (1979).

[127] *Ibid.*, 329. Having found that Libya was in clear breach of international law, Judge Lagergren devoted the greater part of his award to the appropriate remedy for an unlawful nationalisation. See Chapter Nine.

[128] The Libyan government condemned the exploitative aspect of the United States companies when nationalising their concessions, but such condemnations were made against all foreign companies.

Claims arising from expropriation 169

concern themselves with the issue of whether the concession agreement itself prevented the nationalisation of the asset and property rights of the companies.

In *Topco* v *Libya*[129] Professor Dupuy considered that the applicable law was contained in Resolution 1803, noting in particular that "foreign" investment agreements freely entered into by, or between sovereign states should be observed in good faith.[130] He stated:[131]

> Thus in respect of the international law of contracts a nationalisation cannot prevail over an internationalised contract containing stabilisation clauses entered into between a State and a foreign private company.

Professor Dupuy concluded that the Libyan nationalisation was unlawful and he ordered *restitutio in integrum*.[132]

The third arbitration, *Liamco* v *Libya*,[133] was the only one where the views of the developing states on the nationalisation of concessions were given any real recognition. Dr Mahmassani, a Lebanese national, noted that the United Nations resolutions of 1974, although:

> not a unanimous source of law, are evidence of the recent dominant trend of international opinion concerning the sovereign right of States over their natural resources, and that the said right is always subject to the respect for contractual agreements and to the obligation of compensation . . .[134]

Dr Mahmassani made extensive reference to the "principle of respect for agreements".[135] In the context of the nationalisation of natural resources this meant:[136]

> That nationalization of concession rights, even before the expiration of the concession term, if not discriminatory, and not accompanied by a wrongful act or conduct, is not unlawful as such, and constitutes not a tort, but a source of liability to compensate the concessionnaire for said premature termination of the concession agreement.

---

[129] 53 I.L.R., 389 (1979).

[130] *Ibid.*, 491–2; paragraph 1(8) of Resolution 1803.

[131] *Ibid.*, 479; Professor Dupuy also noted the importance of the principle of *pacta sunt servanda* (462) and considered that it was applicable to internationalised contracts. As was held in the *Saudi Arabia* v *Aramco* decision Professor Dupuy did not consider that the theory of administrative contracts was applicable to internationalised contracts (477–8).

[132] *Ibid.*, 509. The appropriateness of this remedy will be considered further in Chapter Nine.

[133] 20 I.L.M., 1 (1981).

[134] *Ibid.*, 53.

[135] *Ibid.*, 56. Dr Mahmassani's consistent use of the words "respect for agreements" implied a different concept from the principle that contracts are binding on the parties. Thus if a nationalising state had terminated a concession agreement, an arbitral tribunal was required to take account of the concession agreement, but was not required to categorise the nationalisation as unlawful.

[136] *Ibid.*, 85. The level of compensation will be considered in the section on *Standard of Compensation*, in Chapter Nine.

The important decision in *Kuwait v Aminoil*,[137] by majority, accepted the right of states to nationalise oil concessions despite the existence of stabilisation clauses. The Tribunal stated:[138]

It seems fair to say that what the Parties had in mind in drafting the stabilization clauses in 1948 and 1961 was anything, which, by reason of its confiscatory character, might cause serious financial prejudice to the interests of the Company... [The clauses] strictly limited all the instances in which the concession can terminate through a forfeiture of the concessionaire's rights (for failure in its obligations), but is silent as to all acts that would lead to the ending of the concession *without* having a confiscatory character. It can be held that the case of nationalization is precisely one of those acts, since as a matter of international law it is subject *inter alia* to the payment of appropriate compensation. The case of nationalization is certainly not expressly provided against by the stabilization clauses... [But] these provisions are far from having lost all their value and efficacity on that account, since, by impliedly requiring that nationalization shall not have any confiscatory character, they reinforce the necessity for proper indemnification as a condition of it.

There is now no doubt among leading jurists, whether they be from Western or developing nations, that states have a general right to expropriate any property situated within their territory, subject to payment of appropriate compensation. Brownlie notes that expropriation will be unlawful *per se* only in limited circumstances, including seizures arising from crimes against humanity, seizures aimed at particular racial groups and seizures of official property of another state.[139] Apart from these limitations expropriation is never illegal, although foreign nationals are entitled to compensation for expropriated property. Thus de Arechaga, former President of the International Court of Justice, has stated:[140]

Contemporary international law recognises the right of every state to nationalise foreign-owned property, even if a predecessor state or previous government engaged itself by treaty or by contract not to do so.

The right of states to expropriate or nationalise foreign-owned property rights or assets may therefore be summarised as follows:

1 Isolated expropriations of assets and contractual rights may be made for lawful public purposes and subject to full compensation.[141]

---

[137] 21 I.L.M., 976 (1982).
[138] *Ibid.*, 1022, 1023.
[139] Brownlie, *Principles of Public International Law*, 538 (1990).
[140] De Arechaga, *State Responsibility for the Nationalization of Foreign Owned Property*, 11 N.Y.U. Int. L. and Pol., 179 (1978–79). See also the references to Bowett and El Chiati in note 142.
[141] Such purposes would include the provision of public utilities such as roads, dams, etc., or for safety and health reasons. In some cases of expropriation for defence or police purposes in times of national emergency, compensation is not necessarily required.

Claims arising from expropriation

2 (a) Large-scale nationalisation of a nation's natural wealth and resources may be made provided such nationalisation is not discriminatory. Appropriate compensation, which may be equivalent to full compensation, must be provided for such lawful nationalization.
 (b) Such nationalisation can terminate concession agreements despite the existence of stabilisation clauses, subject to the provision of appropriate compensation.[142]
3 Any taking, whether an isolated act or part of a large-scale nationalisation, which is discriminatory or for improper purposes is unlawful.[143]

Awards and decisions of the Tribunal

Isolated takings and takings of assets

It has been readily accepted by the Tribunal that states have a general right to expropriate foreign property, unless the action is discriminatory or for an improper purpose. As a consequence relatively few cases deal directly with this issue. The issue was first dealt with by the Tribunal in the case of *American International Group v Iran*,[144] which concerned the expropriation of shares owned by the claimants in an Iranian insurance company. The Tribunal shortly stated:[145]

In the opinion of the Tribunal it cannot be held that the nationalization of Iran America was by itself unlawful, either under customary international law, or under the Treaty of Amity... as there is not sufficient evidence before the Tribunal to show that the nationalization was not carried out for a public purpose as part of a larger reform program or was discriminatory.

---

[142] The *Aminoil* award makes it clear that under certain circumstances a state may nationalise natural resource assets despite the existence of stabilisation clauses in concession agreements. See also Bowett, *State Contracts with Aliens: Contemporary Developments on Compensation for Termination on Breach*, 59 B.Y.I.L., 48, 57–9 (1988), where he notes that international law allows takings for public purposes and that such takings are not made unlawful "by reason of the contract being governed by the contracting State's own law" (p. 59) which contract law provided for the existence of stabilisation clauses. If international law requirements of expropriation in relation to compensation are satisfied then breach of the proper law of the contract (i.e. the state's domestic law) is irrelevant. See also El Chiati, *Protection of Investment in the Context of Petroleum Agreements*, IV Recueil des Cours 9, 160–3 (1987). Mr El Chiati was legal adviser to Amoco. He argues that the power of the state to nationalise in the general interest of the state is *jus cogens* and cannot be abrogated by a stabilisation clause (p. 163). However, such clauses may mean the state is required to indemnify the party for all losses caused by the nationalisation (p. 164).

[143] An improper purpose would be a political retaliation, as in *BP v Libya* 53 I.L.R., 297 (1979).

[144] 4 IRAN–U.S.C.T.R., 96 (1983).

[145] *Ibid.*, 105.

The legality of expropriation was considered by Judge Lagergren in his separate opinion in *INA Corporation* v *Iran*.[146] He stated:[147]

> It is generally accepted that some types of expropriation are inherently unlawful—among these one can cite cases in which foreign assets are taken on a discriminatory basis or for something other than a public purpose. Here it is well settled that the measure of compensation ought to be such as to approximate as closely as possible in monetary terms to the principle of *restitutio in integrum*.

It is clear that other forms of expropriation are lawful although they give rise to a liability to compensate. Thus Judge Lagergren stated in his concluding paragraph:[148]

> I conclude from the foregoing that an application of current principles of international law, as encapsulated in the "appropriate compensation" formula, would in a case of lawful large-scale nationalization in a state undergoing a process of radical economic restructuring normally require the "fair market value" standard to be discounted in taking account of "all circumstances". However, such discounting may, of course, never be such as to bring the compensation below a point which would lead to "unjust enrichment" of the expropriating state.

Oil concession contracts

The preceeding discussion on the current status of international law noted that it is generally accepted that expropriation arising from a premature termination of a contract is not unlawful *per se*, provided that it is not discriminatory or done for an improper purpose.

Nevertheless, the issue of premature termination of contract was extensively dealt with in relation to oil concessions. The first major award of the Tribunal relating to the nationalisation of the oil industry, *Amoco International Finance Corporation* v *Iran*, fully deals with the issue.[149] Amoco had entered into a joint venture agreement with National Petrochemical Company of Iran to establish Khemco to develop natural gas resources. As part of the arrangement Khemco entered into a gas purchase agreement for a period of thirty-five years, the period of the joint venture. The agreement took effect after approval by the Majlis in March 1967 and the plant commenced operation in 1970. As with all other oil companies the operation of the plant was disrupted in 1978 and all expatriates were withdrawn in November 1978. Various discussions of the management of Khemco took place in 1979. However, in January

---

[146] IRAN–U.S.C.T.R., 373 (1985).
[147] *Ibid.*, 385.
[148] *Ibid.*, 390.
[149] 15 IRAN–U.S.C.T.R., 189 (1987). The decision reviews all the major precedents and writings on expropriation and nationalisation, and has been referred to with approval in subsequent important awards of the Tribunal, see *Mobil Oil* v *Iran* 10 IRAN–U.S.C.T.R., 3 (1987); *Phillips Petroleum* v *Iran* 21 Iran–U.S.C.T.R., 79 (1989).

Claims arising from expropriation

1980 the Single Article Act nationalising the oil industry was passed by the Majlis. The Act anulled all existing oil agreements.

The Tribunal accepted that conditions of *force majeure* existed in Iran in late 1978 and that the obligations under the agreement were suspended.[150] However, the agreement was not terminated and the suspension of the obligations under the agreement simply allowed the parties to arbitrate and otherwise resolve the dispute. It was accepted by the parties that Iran had expropriated Amoco's property rights in Khemco and the oil and gas agreements. The key issues were the lawfulness of the expropriation and the degree of compensation payable.[151]

In relation to the lawfulness of the expropriation the Tribunal noted "that the question of the lawfulness or unlawfulness of the expropriation has a direct bearing on the issue of compensation".[152] On this issue it considered the applicability of the Treaty of Amity, the rules of customary international law and the effect of stabilisation clauses in the agreements.

As already noted, the Tribunal considered that the Treaty of Amity was in force at the time of expropriation. The two most important requirements of the Treaty of Amity are that the nationalisation should be for a public purpose and be accompanied by the prompt payment of just compensation. The Tribunal noted that these requirements are accepted as general rules of customary international law.[153] The claimant argued that the failure of Iran to comply with these requirements rendered the nationalisation unlawful. In particular it contended that the nationalisation was discriminatory, was not for a public purpose and was effected without compensation.[154]

The Tribunal noted "that the Single Article Act applied to the entire oil industry irrespective of the nationality of the foreign companies involved in this industry".[155] On the issue of public purpose the Tribunal stated:[156]

An expropriation, the only purpose of which would have been to avoid contractual obligations of the State or of an entity controlled by it, could not, nevertheless, be considered as lawful under international law.

The Tribunal did note, however, that the practice of nationalising the oil industry "to obtain a greater share, or even the totality, of the revenues

---

[150] *Ibid.*, 214. See also Chapter Seven, Frustration.
[151] *Ibid.*, 214. The degree of compensation will be considered in Chapter Nine.
[152] *Ibid.*, 214.
[153] *Ibid.*, 222.
[154] There were other contentions, notably that Iran had not complied with its own domestic law. The Tribunal did not consider that international law required such compliance. *Ibid.*, 225.
[155] *Ibid.*, 232.
[156] *Ibid.*, 233.

drawn from the exploitation of a national resource, which, ... should accrue to the development of the country" has not been denounced as unlawful and illegitimate.[157] The Tribunal also considered that the Single Article Act envisaged compensation being paid and thus it was not in violation of the Treaty of Amity or of customary international law.[158] Accordingly the nationalisation was not unlawful on these grounds.

The contention that the expropriation was unlawful because it violated the agreement is based on the concept of acquired rights, and stands apart from the provisions of the Treaty of Amity and the related general rules of customary international law.[159] The Tribunal analysed the agreement and considered it did not contain "stabilisation clauses" which could prevent the state from nationalising the property interests that were the subject of the agreement. The Tribunal nevertheless considered, no doubt applying the *Aminoil* award, that a state could bind itself by such clauses.[160]

The Tribunal also considered whether a simple breach of contract can render an expropriation unlawful. In this regard the Tribunal firstly noted that Article V of the Claims Settlement Declaration obliges the Tribunal to "decide all cases on the basis of respect for law", and that this required the Tribunal to decide them on the basis of respect for the contracts entered into between the parties. In a notable statement the Tribunal noted:[161]

> It is worthwhile to emphasize that the CSD, concluded in dramatic circumstances between two States with very different political and judicial beliefs and traditions, thus contributed, to a greater extent than any other international compact, to the consolidation of the rule of international law that a state has a duty to respect contracts freely entered into with a foreign party.

However, this rule was not equated with the principle of *pacta sunt servanda*, and unless a state has expressly contracted not to nationalise the claimant's right then the expropriation "cannot be characterised as unlawful as a breach of contract".[162]

The *Amoco* decision was applied by Chamber Two in the *Phillips* case.[163] The Tribunal considered that the lawfulness of the expropriation need not be decided:[164]

> However, the Tribunal need not decide in the present case whether the taking was unlawful, for instance as violative of stabilization clauses or for any other

---

[157] *Ibid.*, 233.
[158] *Ibid.*, 229–31.
[159] *Ibid.*, 229–31.
[160] *Ibid.*, 243.
[161] *Ibid.*, 242.
[162] *Ibid.*, 242–3.
[163] 21 IRAN–U.S.C.T.R., 79, especially at 121–2.
[164] *Ibid.*, 121.

Claims arising from expropriation 175

reason, because whatever the relevance of that question as a matter of customary international law, it is irrelevant under the Treaty of Amity.

The Tribunal accepted that the taking was for a public purpose, as was required by the Treaty of Amity, and that the only compensation standard provided for in the Treaty was "just compensation" representing the "full equivalent of the property taken".

The Tribunal crystallised the lawful/unlawful distinction of the *Chorzow* case to two issues: "whether restitution of the property can be awarded and whether compensation can be awarded for any increase in the value of the property between the date of taking and the date of the judicial or arbitral decision awarding compensation".[165] Since neither of these issues arose in the *Phillips* case the Tribunal did not have any further regard to them in respect of the legality of the expropriation.

Conclusion on the legality of expropriation

Thus far there have not been any cases before the Tribunal where the expropriation has been held to be unlawful. It is unlikely that the Tribunal will make such a finding in future awards, since Iran's programme of nationalisation will be able to be characterised as being for public purposes and not merely directed against United States enterprises. Once expropriation has been determined as lawful the only issue that can arise is the amount of compensation that is payable.[166] This issue is covered in the next chapter.

---

[165] *Ibid.*, 122. These issues do arise in respect of valuation and will be dealt with in detail in Chapter Nine.

[166] Unlawful expropriations may raise the issue of *restitutio in integrum*. See *BP v Libya* 53 I.L.R., 297 (1979) and *Topco v Libya* 53 I.L.R., 389 (1979).

CHAPTER NINE
Entitlement to compensation for expropriation

The standard of compensation

International law

The standard of compensation for expropriated foreign property is now an issue of greater significance than the right to expropriate such property. Since almost all property is ultimately convertible to money it matters less that the property is taken than that the former owner is compensated for the expropriated property by the payment of money. The standard of such compensation has been the source of greater division between the Western and developing nations than the right to expropriate foreign-owned property.[1]

The issue of compensation arises in three different contexts, first where there has been legal expropriation of particular property, secondly where there has been illegal expropriation and thirdly where there has been large-scale nationalisation of a nations' natural wealth and resources.

Particular property

In the case of expropriation of particular property for proper purposes it is generally acknowledged that there must be full compensation according to the traditional principle that compensation should be "prompt, adequate and effective".[2]

---

[1] As noted in the previous chapter there is now some agreement, evidenced by the arbitral awards, especially the *Aminoil* award, of the right of states to expropriate foreign property, even if it results in a breach of contract.

[2] Amerasinghe, *The Quantum of Compensation for Nationalized Property*, in Lillich (ed.), III *Valuation of Nationalized Property in International Law*, 91, 114 (1978); Brownlie, *Principles of Public International Law*, 537 (1990).

Numerous arbitral awards, particularly from the various Latin American arbitrations, were concerned with particular property, usually tangible assets, and in such cases full compensation was provided.[3] Similarly the Mixed Arbitral Tribunals following the two world wars made many awards providing full compensation for loss of particular property. Bowett provides the rationale for this standard, providing a contrast to the compensation standard for large-scale nationalisation. He notes that owners of particular property are singled out for deprivation by the community and other owners of similar property are not affected. Thus "the community compensates him generously, on a going concern value or full market value".[4]

Illegal expropriation

In the case of illegal expropriation there are two possibilities: the owner may receive full compensation, including consequential loss such as loss of profits (*lucrum cessans*), or he may be entitled to *restitutio in integrum*, which may be the monetary equivalent thereof. The latter remedy is particularly controversial. Although it is an appropriate remedy[5] in cases where state territory is involved it is far less appropriate in claims concerning private property where financial compensation is almost always an adequate remedy. Nevertheless the Permanent Court of International Justice ordered restitution of the property or the monetary equivalent thereof in the *Chorzow Factory case (Germany v Poland)*[6] despite the fact that the case concerned commercial property rights. In more recent years Professor Dupuy ordered restitution in the *Topco v Libya* case.[7] On finding that the expropriation was illegal in the circumstances, he concluded that restitution was an available remedy both in Libyan and in international law, stating:[8]

Thus, for the general reasons above, this Tribunal must hold *restitutio in integrum* is, both under the principles of Libyan law and under the principles of inter-

---

[3] Refer to Feller, *Mexican Claims Commissions, 1923–1934*, (1935).

[4] Bowett, *State Contracts with Aliens: Contemporary Developments in Compensation for Termination or Breach*, 59 B.Y.I.L., 48, 73 (1988).

[5] The International Court of Justice ordered restitution of land and temple artefacts in *Temple of Preah-Vihear (Cambodia v Thailand)* I.C.J. Rep., 6 (1962). Similarly in the continental shelf cases the only appropriate remedy is an order on the division of the territory concerned.

[6] P.C.I.J., Ser. A, No. 17, 47 (1928).

[7] 53 I.L.R., 389, 507 (1979).

[8] *Ibid.*, 507–8. Libya never complied with the decision. It was, however, settled by Libya transferring $152 million worth of oil to the companies. Even if the nationalising state does not comply with the order the claimants can commence actions against third parties in municipal jurisdictions claiming title to any minerals or oil produced from the concessions. Topco commenced such actions in France, Switzerland, Sweden and the United States, claiming title to oil allegedly produced from the concession.

national law, the normal sanction for non-performance of contractual obligations and that it is inapplicable only to the extent that the restoration of the *status quo ante* is impossible.

In similar circumstances Judge Lagergren in *British Petroleum v Libya*,[9] although finding that the nationalisation of the British Petroleum concession was illegal, considered, after an extensive appraisal of the precedents and literature, that restitution was not an appropriate remedy, since "an expropriation . . . is an act of finality where a state has exercised its sovereign territorial power to expel a foreign enterprise and appropriate its property and other rights".[10] Moreover the property rights expropriated by Libya were capable of being valued in monetary terms.[11] Judge Lagergren therefore determined that damages were the appropriate remedy.[12]

In the final case of the Libyan trilogy, *Liamco v Libya*,[13] Dr Mahmassani concluded that since restitution "violates the sovereignty of the nationalising state"[14] damages are the proper remedy irrespective of the legality or otherwise of the nationalising measures. In the case of illegal expropriation such damages will cover not just the physical property, but also the loss of expected profits.[15]

Thus where a state has illegally expropriated foreign private property the appropriate remedy is damages, although such damages will be the equivalent of restitution of all the property rights that have been expropriated. They will therefore include the value of any physical property and loss of expected profits. Restitution of physical assets or contractual rights will be ordered only if the property is of unique character not capable of being compensated for in monetary terms.[16]

Large-scale nationalisations and concession agreements

The third context where the level of compensation arises is in cases of large-scale nationalisations. As previously noted, such nationalisations are legal provided they are not discriminatory. However, even if legal

---

[9] 53 I.L.R., 297 (1979).

[10] *Ibid.*, 353.

[11] *Ibid.*, 353.

[12] *Ibid.*, 355. Judge Lagergren did not decide the proper level of the damages in the decision, holding the question over to a subsequent hearing. The case was settled before the issue came to a hearing. In the *Rann of Kutch arbitration (India v Pakistan)* 50 I.L.R., 470 (1968), Judge Lagergren ordered a division of the disputed territory. In cases of state territory financial compensation is clearly inappropriate. The cases concerning state territory do not establish a principle that is applicable to private property, which for the most part can be measured in financial terms.

[13] 20 I.L.M., 1 (1981).

[14] *Ibid.*, 64.

[15] *Ibid.*, 70.

[16] This could include works of art or other unique property.

they give rise to a liability for the payment of appropriate compensation. It is on this issue of appropriate compensation that the Western and developing nations have consistently divided.[17] The Western nations have maintained that compensation must be "prompt, adequate and effective".[18] "Adequate" compensation is traditionally regarded as meaning full compensation.[19] The standard sought by the developing nations is contained in United Nations Resolution 3281 [1974]:

2. Every state has the right . . .
(c) To nationalize, expropriate or transfer ownership of foreign property in which case appropriate compensation should be paid by the State adopting such measures, taking into account its relevant laws and regulations and all circumstances that the State considers pertinent. In any case where the question of compensation gives rise to a controversy, it shall be settled under the domestic law of the nationalizing State and its tribunals, unless it is freely and mutually agreed by all States concerned that other peaceful means be sought on the basis of the sovereign equality of states and in accordance with the principle of free choice of means.

The practice of states, however, is best reflected in the arbitral decisions and lump sum agreements, and United Nations Resolution 3281 (1974) cannot be regarded as embodying customary international law. The arbitral decisions and lump sum agreements, particularly those since 1974, show increasing acceptance of the consensus found in United Nations Resolution 1803 (1962).

The *Kuwait* v *Aminoil*[20] arbitral decision is of particular significance since it was fully argued by both parties before a tribunal of three members having diverse legal backgrounds. The Tribunal referred to United Nations Resolution 1803 (1962) as codifying positive principle.[21] In considering the level of "appropriate compensation", the Tribunal had regard to all the circumstances, including the attitude of Kuwait to foreign investment, the legitimate expectations of the parties entering into the concession agreement and the anticipated profits over the expected life of the concession.[22]

The awards of the International Centre for the Settlement of Invest-

[17] The last time there was a consensus was in Resolution 1803 (1962).

[18] This formula received its most famous exposition by Cordell Hull, the United States Secretary of State, in his note to Mexico in 1938, and has been consistently maintained by Western nations. A number of leading Western jurists have asserted the validity of the formula, e.g. Dawson and Weston, *"Prompt, Adequate and Effective": A Universal Standard for Compensation?*, 30 Fordham L.R., 727 (1962); Doman, *Postwar Nationalisation of Foreign Property in Europe*, 48 Col. L.R., 1125 (1948).

[19] Cf. Restatement (2d), Foreign Relations of the United-States, 188 (1965).

[20] 21 I.L.M., 978 (1982).

[21] *Ibid.*, 1032.

[22] *Ibid.*, 1034. The award of compensation to be paid to Aminoil was $187 million including interest.

ment Disputes (ICSID) arbitration tribunals also reflect this requirement of appropriate compensation. In *AGIP* v *Congo*[23] the tribunal held that the Congo must compensate AGIP for the damage it suffered as a result of the nationalisation of its undertaking, particularly in respect of the value of its share of the company's capital and the amount paid by AGIP or potentially payable by it in its capacity as guarantor of the undertaking.[24]

Since the Second World War large-scale nationalizations have usually been compensated by way of lump sum agreements entered into by the governments of the nationalising state and the claimant state, with the funds to be distributed by national claims commissions.[25] Most often partial compensation has been agreed upon. An indicative recent settlement is the 1979 agreement between the United States and China providing compensation for 40 per cent of the value of the losses suffered by United States nationals following the revolution of 1949.[26] However, the most recent agreement between the United States and Czechoslovakia provided for 100 per cent compensation.[27]

The writings of jurists have reflected and to some extent provided the theoretical justification for the divergence between the standards adopted by Western countries and developing countries.[28]

Nevertheless, some Third World commentators have recognised the need for international standards for international investment acceptable to both capital importing and capital exporting nations. Ijalaye noted that Resolution 1803 "has crippled (if it has not killed) the notion

---

[23] 21 I.L.M., 726 (1982).

[24] *Ibid.*, 736.

[25] For a comprehensive treatment of lump sum agreements refer to Lillich and Weston, *International Claims: Their Settlement by Lump Sum Agreements* (1975).

[26] 18 I.L.M., 551 (1979). The compensation was $80.5 million in full and final settlement of all claims (Article II(a)). See Jackson, *International Settlement: Agreement Concerning the Settlement of Claims, May 11, 1979, United States–People's Republic of China*, 20 Harv. J.I.L., 681, 684 (1979).

[27] 21 I.L.M., 371 (1982). See Pechota, *The 1981 U.S.–Czechoslovak Claims Settlement Agreement. An Epilogue to Postwar Nationalisation and Expropriation Disputes*, 76 A.J.I.L., 639, 640 (1982). This agreement replaced an earlier agreement negotiated in 1974 which provided for 42 per cent compensation. The earlier agreement was rejected by Congress in an amendment to the 1974 Trade Act.

[28] See de Arechaga, *International Law in the Past Third of a Century*, I Recueil des Cours, 1, especially 297–310 (1978); *State Responsibility for the Nationalisation of Foreign Owned Property*, 79 N.Y.U.J. Int. L. and Pol., 179 (1978–79); Garcia-Amador, *The Proposed New International Economic Order: A New Approach to the Law Governing Nationalisation and Compensation by Foreign States for the Taking of Alien Owned Property*, 13 Vanderbilt J. Transnational Law, 51 (1980); Dolzer, *New Foundations of the Law of Expropriation of Alien Property*, 75 A.J.I.L., 553 (1981); Higgins, *The Taking of Property: Recent Developments in International Law*, III Recueil des Cours, 259 (1982); Sornarajah, *Compensation for Expropriation: The Emergence of New Standards*, 13 J.W.T.L., 108 (1979); Weston, *The Charter of Economic Rights and Duties of States and the Deprivation of Foreign Owned Wealth*, 75 A.J.I.L., 437 (1981).

often asserted by representatives of the developing (capital importing) countries that a State ... is at liberty to terminate or abrogate at will, its contractual agreements".[29] He also referred to the requirement of appropriate compensation in the event of nationalisation.[30] The former President of the International Court of Justice, de Arechaga, considered that Article 2(2)(c) of the Charter of Economic Rights did not exclude international law in the event of unilaterally determined compensation.[31] Such compensation must therefore be appropriate having regard to all the circumstances.[32]

Similarly, Sornarajah conceded "the relevance of a residual international standard" to the "new economic order".[33] Since the new economic order is based on notions of justice it would be inequitable to deny appropriate compensation to the foreign investor.[34]

Although there is a consensus that international law requires appropriate compensation in the event of a large-scale nationalisation it is apparent that full compensation has not been required or given in all cases.[35] In determining appropriate compensation, all relevant circumstances may be taken into account including the conduct of the nationalising state and the foreign investor, the legitimate expectations of the parties, the ability of the state to pay, the attitude of the state to foreign investment and any future relationship between the state and the foreign investor.

In recent times, however, there has been increasing evidence that Western nations will insist on full compensation as the only appropriate compensation for expropriation of property. As Norton has noted:[36]

The end of the post-colonial era and the now widely accepted need to encourage investment in the Third World have substantially eroded the rationale for a partial

---

[29] Ijalaye, *Multinational Companies in Africa*, II Recueil des Cours, 9, 47 (1981).
[30] *Ibid.*
[31] De Arechaga, *State Responsibility for the Nationalisation of Foreign Owned Property*, 11 N.Y.U.J. Int. L. and Pol., 179, 188 (1978–79).
[32] *Ibid.*, 187.
[33] Sornarajah, *The Myth of International Contract Law*, 15 J.W.T.L., 187, 216 (1981).
[34] *Ibid.*, 216. Sornarajah refers to de Arechaga and Garcia-Amador as supporting the norm of fair compensation.
[35] This has been recognised by a superior United States court. The United States Court of Appeals (2nd Cir.) considered the meaning of "appropriate compensation" at international law in *Banco Nacional de Cuba* v *Chase Manhattan Bank* 658 F. 2d, 875, 892 (1981). The court stated: "It may well be the consensus of nations that full compensation need not be paid in all circumstances ... and that requiring an expropriating state to pay 'appropriate compensation'—even considering the lack of precise definition of that term–would come closest to reflecting what international law requires. But the adoption of an 'appropriate compensation' requirement would not exclude the possibility that in some cases full compensation would be appropriate".
[36] Norton, *A Law of the Future or a Law of the Past? Modern Tribunals and the International Law of Expropriation*, 85 A.J.I.L. (1991), 474, 475.

compensation standard that appeared so compelling to many observers just a short time ago.

These recent developments have been reinforced by the decisions of the Iran–United States Claims Tribunal.

Awards and decisions of the Tribunal

The awards and decisions of the Tribunal on the issue of the standard of compensation are of particular interest since it is on this issue that the Western nations and the developing nations have shown the greatest divergence, particularly in respect of large-scale nationalisations. The Iranian revolution led to a fundamental reorganisation of the economy with whole sectors being brought under state control.[37]

The cases fall into two broad categories, isolated expropriations and expropriations as part of a major nationalisation scheme. In the latter category a number of the claims concerned the termination of long-term oil concessions and the findings of the Tribunal are of major importance to international investors. The issue of illegal expropriations has not directly arisen, since the Tribunal has not categorised any expropriation of major resources as discriminatingly directed against American citizens and corporations. It is not likely to arise in small claims but such claims rarely involve ongoing contractual rights of any substance.

Until 1987 the cases finalised by the Tribunal had concerned relatively small enterprises and there had been a tendency by the Tribunal to treat each case as if it were an isolated expropriation, whether or not the whole industry had been nationalised. The Tribunal has thus applied the rule of international law that there shall be full compensation for expropriations of particular property. However, these early cases established the precedent for full compensation and this principle has been applied to claims arising from large-scale nationalisations and oil concessions.

Expropriation of assets

The first claim determined by the Tribunal concerning an enterprise nationalised as part of a general scheme of nationalisation was *American International Group* v *Iran*,[38] heard by Chamber Three. The United States claimants had a 35 per cent share in the Iran American International Insurance Company, which had been established in Iran in 1974. Following the revolution all insurance companies in Iran were nationalised pursuant to the Law of the Nationalisation of Insurance and Credit Enterprises. The claimants contended that the nationalisation was a

[37] See Chapter One on the Iranian law nationalising various sectors of the economy.
[38] 4 IRAN–U.S.C.T.R., 96 (1983).

Compensation for expropriation

violation of international law in that it was not accompanied by "prompt, adequate and effective" compensation.[39] As a result of this violation of international law, the claimants argued, they were entitled to just compensation equal to the full value of their interest as at the date of nationalisation, plus interest on the award. Iran argued that the right of nationalisation was an expression of permanent sovereignty of the nation's natural resources and economic activities.[40] Moreover international law did not require prompt adequate and effective compensation.[41] Partial compensation paid within a reasonable time is sufficient.[42]

The Tribunal apparently accepted the contentions of the claimants that they were entitled to full compensation, stating that this meant "the fair market value" of the claimants' shares in the company, valued as a going concern at the date of taking. The Tribunal simply noted the parties' respective views on the current practice of international law.[43]

Chamber One of the Tribunal has also considered the issue of compensation in respect of shares in insurance companies. The case of *INA Corporation* v *Iran*[44] has a similarity of facts with *American International*. A minority shareholding which had been purchased in 1978 in an Iranian insurance company was expropriated together with all other shares in the company as a result of the Law of Nationalisation of Insurance and Credit Enterprises enacted by the Iranian government in 1979. The sole issue to be determined by the Tribunal was the level of compensation, it being agreed that there had been expropriation.

The Tribunal noted the gradual development of the law in relation to compensation for large-scale nationalisations:[45]

In the event of such large scale nationalisations of a lawful character, international law has undergone a gradual reappraisal, the effect of which may be to undermine the doctrinal value of any "full" or "adequate" (when used as identical to "full") compensation standard as proposed in this case.

This statement was the subject of separate opinions by Judge Lagergren and Mr Holtzmann.[46] The Iranian arbitrator, Mr Ameli, dissented from the award as a whole.

---

[39] *Ibid.*, 105.
[40] *Ibid.*, 106.
[41] *Ibid.*, 106.
[42] *Ibid.*, 106.
[43] *Ibid.*, 102–5.
[44] 8 IRAN–U.S.C.T.R., 373 (1985).
[45] *Ibid.*, 378.
[46] The arbitrators forming the majority had divergent views on the significance of the above sentence. Judge Lagergren considered that the traditional rule of "prompt *adequate* and effective" compensation had been superseded, so that *appropriate compensation* is all that is required in the cases of large-scale nationalisations. Appropriate compensation may mean partial or whole compensation, depending on the circumstances. *Ibid.*, 390. Mr

Although the Tribunal made this *obiter* statement, it found on two separate grounds that full compensation was required. Firstly, where there is a small investment shortly before nationalisation "international law admits compensation in an amount equal to the fair market value of the investment".[47] Secondly the Treaty of Amity between Iran and the United States, which so far as the present case was concerned remained binding upon the parties,[48] constituted a *lex specialis*, prevailing over general rules.[49] Article IV of the Treaty requires that in the event of a taking there shall be "prompt payment of just compensation" which "shall represent the full equivalent of the property taken".

In the earlier cases the Treaty of Amity had not been such an issue. Nevertheless, the Tribunal accepted the principle that claimants are entitled to the full value of expropriated property. The case of *TAMS* v *TAMS-AFFA*[50] concerned the expropriation of the claimant's interest in a joint venture firm, TAMS-AFFA, created to perform engineering and architectural services on the Tehran Airport project. The claimant sought its share of the break-up value of TAMS-AFFA after the collection of all its assets, consisting of bank accounts, fixed assets and accounts receivable, and the discharge of all its debts and liabilities. On the general issue of compensation the Tribunal stated:[51]

The Claimant is entitled under international law and general principles of law to compensation for the full value of the property of which it was deprived.

In valuing the assets the Tribunal primarily had to determine the value of the accounts receivable. The Tribunal had considerable difficulty in ascertaining the net dissolution value of TAMS-AFFA, and made "a very rough evaluation of the assets and liabilities involved" and awarded approximately 60 per cent of the amount claimed.

It is noteworthy that in an early case heard by the Tribunal, *ITT Industrial Inc.* v *Iran*,[52] the United States arbitrator had predicated the subsequent decisions of the Tribunal in his concurring opinion dealing

---

Holtzmann, however, considered that arbitral practice showed no deviation from the principle that full compensation was required in all cases. Partial compensation had only found acceptance by a limited number of jurists, and where governments had accepted partial compensation this had been on the basis of a diplomatic compromise. *Ibid.*, 397–9.

[47] 8 IRAN–U.S.C.T.R., 373, 378 (1985).

[48] *Ibid.*, 319. Iran had not pleaded that the Treaty was no longer valid, or was not enforceable owing to "changed circumstances"; cf. Article V of the Claims Settlement Declaration.

[49] *Ibid.*, 378.

[50] IRAN–U.S.C.T.R., 219 (1984).

[51] *Ibid.*, 225.

[52] 2 IRAN–U.S.C.T.R., 348 (1983). This was a settlement award. Mr Aldrich filed a concurring opinion so as to establish the principles of international law relating to compensation for expropriated property, which he believed should be applied by the Tribunal in future cases.

Compensation for expropriation

with the issue of compensation for expropriated assets. He restated the traditional view of international law that a taking of property had to be "accompanied by the prompt payment of just compensation which is effective and adequate to compensate for the value of the property taken".[53] This required the Tribunal to determine the value of the enterprise as a going concern. In determining such value Mr Aldrich noted:[54]

That Iran might experience revolution was a risk assumed by investors in Iran, as in any other country; and any reduction in value of investments as a result of revolution cannot be ignored by the Tribunal. The Islamic Revolution in Iran was not a "wrong" for which foreign investors are entitled to compensation under international law. In computing compensation for expropriated property the Tribunal must find at best only any decline in value resulting from the threat of taking or other acts attributable to the Government itself.

In those cases where the applicability of the Treaty of Amity was fully argued by the parties the Tribunal accepted that the Treaty was binding at the time the cause of action arose.[55] Nevertheless, the parties have continued to dispute the meaning of Article IV(2) of the Treaty of Amity, most notably in *Phelps Dodge Corporation* v *Iran*[56] and *Sedco Inc.* v *NIOC*.[57]

In the more fully reasoned of the two awards, *Sedco Inc.* v *NIOC*, the respondent argued that the Treaty of Amity did no more than "incorporate customary law as it may exist from time to time".[58] The Tribunal apparently accepted this contention.[59]

The Tribunal first examined the status of lump sum agreements which tend to provide for partial compensation and considered that they included "factors other than elements of law" in the determination of the level of compensation.[60] It next examined the status of the various General Assembly resolutions, and confirmed the view of the developed Western nations:[61]

There is considerable unanimity in international arbitral practice and scholarly opinion that of the resolutions cited above, it is Resolution 1803, and not either of

---

[53] *Ibid.*, 354.
[54] *Ibid.*, 355.
[55] See *supra* in Chapter Eight on the applicability of the Treaty of Amity.
[56] 10 IRAN–U.S.C.T.R., 121 (1986).
[57] 10 IRAN–U.S.C.T.R., 180 (1986). For an account of the facts of the case see Chapter Eight.
[58] *Ibid.*, 183.
[59] *Ibid.*, 184.
[60] *Ibid.*, 185. The Tribunal noted the reservations that the International Court of Justice had expressed about the value of lump sum agreements as evidence of custom; *Barcelona Traction* I.C.J. Rep., 3, 40 (1970).
[61] *Ibid.*, 186.

the two later resolutions, which at least reflects, if it does not evidence, current international law.

The Tribunal emphasised the provisions of General Assembly Resolution 1803 that "the owner should be paid *appropriate compensation ... in accordance with international law*".[62] Finally, it considered the level of compensation that the claimant was entitled to in respect of the property that had been expropriated, and concluded:[63]

> Opinions both of international tribunals and of legal writers overwhelmingly support the conclusion that under customary international law in a case such as here presented—a discrete expropriation of alien property—full compensation should be awarded for the property taken.[18] This is true whether or not the expropriation itself was otherwise lawful.
>
> [18] As some of these opinions are expressed in the context of large-scale nationalisation cases, they should *a fortiori* weigh heavily in a case such as the one here presented.

The Tribunal referred specifically to the writings of Brownlie,[64] Amerasinghe[65] and Lauterpacht[66] as jurists who had sympathy with the position of developing nations, that in the case of large-scale nationalisations full compensation is not required, but who also recognised that international law still required full compensation in the case of an expropriation of specific assets.[67] The Tribunal also referred to its own previous decisions on the level of compensation to support its view that the claimant is entitled to compensation for the full value of the property of which it has been deprived.[68]

The award of *Phelps Dodge Corporation* v *Iran* simply applies previous decisions of the Tribunal stating:[69]

> Applying the rule of law set forth in Article IV of the Treaty of Amity to the present case, it is clear that the taking of Phelps Dodge's property, that is, its ownership rights in SICAB, required the prompt payment of "just compensation", which must represent the "full equivalent" of the property taken. Thus, the standard is similar, if not identical, to the standards which the Tribunal has previously applied. See *American Int'l Group Inc. et al.* and *Islamic Republic of Iran et al.*, Award No. 93-2-3 (19 Dec. 1983); *Tippets, Abbott, McCarthy Stratton*, *supra*.

[62] *Ibid*. Emphasis on wording of resolution added by the Tribunal.
[63] *Ibid.*, 187.
[64] Brownlie, *Principles of Public International Law*, 538 (1979). In the fourth edition (1990) Brownlie makes reference to the decisions of the Tribunal, p. 539.
[65] Amerasinghe, *The Quantum of Compensation for Nationalized Property*, in Lillich (ed.), III *Valuation of Nationalized Property in International Law*, 91, 114 (1975).
[66] H. Lauterpacht, *Oppenheim's International Law*, 352 (1955).
[67] 10 IRAN–U.S.C.T.R., 188 (1986).
[68] *Ibid.*, 188; with reference to *TAMS* v *Iran*. The actual amount of the compensation in the *Sedco* case was to be decided in a later award.
[69] 10 IRAN–U.S.C.T.R., 121, 132 (1986).

Both the *Phelps Dodge* and *Sedco* awards confirm the traditional Western view that foreign owners of expropriated property are entitled to full compensation, taking into account the unsettled circumstances in the expropriating states at the time of the expropriation. Not surprisingly, perhaps, the Iranian arbitrators dissented in both cases.

Expropriation of concessionary rights

The partial award of *Amoco International Finance* v *Iran*[70] is of particular significance in the jurisprudence of the Tribunal on compensation payable for expropriated property. The case concerned the termination of a long-term oil concession.[71] Although the Tribunal had determined that the expropriation was lawful, it nevertheless canvassed the "effects of lawfulness or unlawfulness of expropriation on the standard of compensation".[72] It noted that while the Treaty of Amity defines the standard of compensation for lawful expropriation, a nationalisation in breach of the Treaty will be governed by customary law on state responsibility.[73]

Both parties agreed that the *Chorzow Factory* case[74] is the leading authority for determining compensation for unlawful expropriation, and this was accepted by the Tribunal.[75] The standard established by the Court in *Chorzow Factory* was reparation of all damage suffered by the owner. This would require *restitutio in integrum* and damages for any other loss not covered by restitution. The intent is "to wipe out all the consequences of the illegal act and re-establish the situation which would, in all probability, have existed if this act had not been committed".[76]

The Tribunal had already determined that Iran's actions in nationalising the oil industry were not unlawful. However, it considered "that the judgment is also illuminating in analyzing the lawful expropriation before us".[77] It noted the Court's statement that an expropriation may be unlawful "if its wrongful act consisted merely in not having paid...the just price of what was expropriated".[78]

The Tribunal's analysis of this statement was regarded by it as of "paramount importance":[79]

---

[70] 15 IRAN–U.S.C.T.R., 189 (1987).

[71] The reasoning of the Tribunal on compensation is very comprehensive, covering all the major theories and cases. The Tribunal's decision on this part is set out at pp. 244–71 of the partial award.

[72] *Ibid.*, 246.

[73] *Ibid.*

[74] P.C.I.J. Ser. A. No. 17 (1928).

[75] *Ibid.*, 246.

[76] *Chorzow Factory Case* at 47; from award of the Tribunal 15 IRAN–U.S.C.T.R., 189, 247 (1987).

[77] 15 IRAN–U.S.C.T.R., 189, 247 (1987).

[78] *Ibid.*, 189, 247.

[79] *Ibid.*, 247–8. The actual measure of full value is considered in the second section of this chapter on Valuation of Property and Quantum of Compensation.

It means the compensation to be paid in case of a lawful expropriation (or of a taking which lacks only the payment of a fair compensation to be lawful) is limited to the value of the undertaking at the moment of the dispossession, *i.e.* the just price of what was expropriated.

The Treaty of Amity, applicable to lawful expropriations, has a similar concept, that of "just compensation", being "the full equivalent of the property taken". The Tribunal has consistently noted the congruence of the standard imposed by the Treaty of Amity and general principles of international law.[80]

The cases decided since *Amoco International Finance* v *Iran*[81] have relied heavily on the earlier decisions of the Tribunal in holding that full compensation is the standard required by international law. This is best exemplified by *Starrett Housing Corporation* v *Iran*,[82] when the Tribunal had to determine the extent of the liability of Iran to the claimant.[83] The Tribunal's approach was to determine first the appropriate standard of compensation and secondly the principles that would guide it in deciding the weight to be put on the Experts' opinions.[84] In respect of the standard of compensation the Tribunal succinctly stated:[85]

As to the first question, the Tribunal finds that, pursuant to the Treaty of Amity between Iran and the United States, the claimants are entitled to receive compensation which shall be "just" and "shall represent the full equivalent of the property taken" as of the date of taking. As the Tribunal has previously held, the Treaty is "clearly applicable" and thus a "relevant source of law on which the Tribunal is justified drawing". *Phelps Dodge Corp.* v *Islamic Republic of Iran* [10 IRAN–U.S.C.T.R., 121 at 131 (1986)]. See also *Amoco International Finance Corporation* v *Government of Islamic Republic of Iran* [15 IRAN–U.S.C.T.R., 189, at 214 (1987)].

The important decision of *Phillips Petroleum Company* v *Iran*[86] dealt with this issue equally directly. After stating that "the Treaty of Amity is the relevant source of law"[87] the Tribunal stated:[88]

Thus the claimant is entitled by the Treaty to "just compensation", representing the "full equivalent of the property taken". As the Tribunal has previously held,

---

[80] See comments in Summary, *infra*.

[81] 15 IRAN–U.S.C.T.R., 189 (1987).

[82] 16 IRAN–U.S.C.T.R., 112 (1987). This case concerned a building project. The contract for the project was terminated part way through and the claims concerned, among other issues, the value of the uncompleted project.

[83] It had already been decided by the Tribunal that Iran had expropriated the assets of the claimant and was liable to compensate the claimant. See 4 IRAN–U.S.C.T.R., 122 (1983). This aspect is discussed in Chapter Eight.

[84] 16 IRAN–U.S.C.T.R., 112, 195 (1987).

[85] *Ibid.*, 118.

[86] 21 IRAN–U.S.C.T.R., 79 (1989).

[87] *Ibid.*, 118.

[88] *Ibid.*, 119.

Compensation for expropriation

where the property taken was a "going concern", compensation that meets the Treaty standard is compensation that makes the claimant whole for the "fair market value" of the property at the date of taking.

In the case of continuing contractual rights, such as the JSA rights, the compensation should reflect the value of these rights, that is, "the fair market value of the Claimant's interest in the JSA on the date of taking".[89]

The Tribunal rejected the notion that it need consider any developments in international law which prescribed a lesser standard, since the Treaty of Amity governed the case. Accordingly the Tribunal did not need to review whether any such changes had in fact occurred. There is nevertheless an underlying sentiment in the award that the traditional standard of full compensation is still applicable.[90]

Summary

As this review of the awards of the Tribunal shows, the Tribunal in subsequent awards has fully endorsed the traditional view that only full compensation will satisfy the requirements of international law, although admittedly the Tribunal has had recourse to the Treaty of Amity.

Early comment on the decisions has accepted their general significance. Norton noted that the statements on general principles of international law were "technically dicta" but of "greatest interest".[91] He analysed all the decisions on expropriation and found that in every case full compensation was required. This, of course, was the result of the application of the Treaty of Amity, but Norton noted that in a number of cases the majority equated the standard under the Treaty with the standard under general international law.[92] The standard was for fair market value which included physical assets, goodwill and future profits, although this latter point was the subject of dispute in *Amoco*.

Norton also analysed the Iranian dissents, and in particular Ameli's dissent in the *INA* case in which Ameli considered the Tribunal had not taken sufficient account of General Assembly resolutions but instead paid too much attention to judicial and arbitral decisions.

Norton, however, referred to "the limitless opportunities for a tribunal to make factual findings or employ valuation methods that substantially

---

[89] *Ibid.*, 120.
[90] *Ibid.*, 118–22. There are not any particular passages which indicate this statement. It is really contained in a very firm holding that the Treaty of Amity sets the standard of full compensation and that any putative development of international law has not affected in any way the interpretation and application of the Treaty of Amity.
[91] Norton, *loc. cit.*, 483.
[92] *Ibid.*, 484. See in particular *TAMS* 6 IRAN–U.S.C.T.R., 219 (1984); *Sola Tiles* 14 IRAN–U.S.C.T.R., 223 (1982); *Amoco* 15 IRAN–U.S.C.T.R., 189 (1987).

vitiate the impact of its legal rulings".[93] He did not, however, analyse this aspect in depth, except to note the opportunity valuation offered to reduce the award. Norton went on to consider the political economy of the last twenty years, and the shift in the underlying paradigm of rejection of foreign investment to acknowledging the need for foreign investment for the development of the economy and that this was recognised in the arbitral decisions, especially since 1980.[94]

Bowett, prominent as counsel for Iran in a number of cases, has argued that the full compensation standard is not as clearly established as the rubric of the Treaty of Amity would indicate. In his comprehensive analysis of the distinction between compensation for lawful and unlawful nationalisation he notes:[95]

The position towards which the US/Iran claims Tribunal now seems to be moving (and which *Aminoil* supports) is that there are, in fact, three 'standards' of compensation, i.e. (i) for an unlawful taking, (ii) for a lawful *ad hoc* taking, and (iii) for a lawful, general act of nationalisation. And the clear implication is that the third standard is the lowest, which would accord with State practice and the trend in General Assembly resolutions to move towards a concept of 'appropriate' or 'just' compensation.

Bowett notes that a general act of nationalisation is "akin to taxation: it is a form of redistribution of wealth and resources".[96] Accordingly owners of businesses expropriated by a general measure of expropriation cannot expect to be compensated in the same manner as owners whose property is expropriated by an *ad hoc* or singular act of expropriation.[97]

This view preceded the *Phillips* award, which not only awarded full compensation but also, in large measure, considered full compensation to include the contractual right to future earnings.

The Tribunal's decisions are among the most significant legal contributions over the last decade in reversing the trend toward the New International Economic Order espoused by developing states during the 1970s. Moreover the internationalisation of capital markets and investments in recent years may well have the effect of confining the idea that

---

[93] *Ibid.*, 495. However, the Iran–United States Tribunal has made a detailed analysis of valuation techniques and the circumstances of the investment and the country in which it is situate in a number of important cases discussed in this chapter.

[94] *Ibid.*, 497.

[95] Bowett, *State Contracts with Aliens: Contemporary Developments on Compensation for Termination or Breach*, 59 B.Y.I.L., 48, 73 (1988).

[96] *Ibid.*, 73.

[97] *Ibid.*, 73. Bowett does acknowledge that this view is not universally shared. Thus Messen, *Domestic Law Concepts in International Expropriation Law* in IV Lillich (ed.), *Valuation of Nationalised Property in International Law*, 157, 169–71 (1987), rejects the taxation analogy, since a domestic law analogy should not resolve an international law problem.

wealth should be transferred from wealthy nations to poorer nations without the poorer nations incurring a liability in respect of the transfer of such assets to foreign aid that is clearly understood by both parties be such at the time the aid is granted. Commercial relationships will impose on both parties the obligation of honouring the contractual arrangements. In such a climate the notion that states can expropriate assets with little or no compensation has little appeal.

A general trend to full compensation does not, however, eliminate risk which all investors must bear. The valuation of full compensation must assess such risk. The more recent decisions of the Tribunal have primarily focused on the valuation of full compensation, taking into account all factors affecting the value of the expropriated assets.

Valuation of property and quantum of compensation

International law

Although it may be a relatively simple matter for the Tribunal to state a proposition that expropriation gives rise to an entitlement of full compensation, the quantum of full compensation is more difficult to assess. Even the rubric of "fair market value" is of little assistance in the absence of a market for the expropriated assets.

The decisions of the important oil arbitrations have specifically considered the issue of valuation. In the second of the trilogy of Libyan oil nationalisation cases, *Texaco* v *Libya*,[98] the sole arbitrator, Professor Dupuy, made an order for *restitutio in integrum* or the monetary equivalent thereof. This was characterised as "damages which would eventually be the monetary equivalent of specific performance".[99] Unfortunately the award did not specifically value the interests which had been expropriated.

The third of the cases, *Liamco* v *Libya*,[100] provided a rather more full analysis of quantum of compensation, especially with reference to future profits (*lucrum cessans*). Professor Mahmassani, the sole arbitrator, referred to the previous important arbitrations, dividing them into unlawful expropriations and lawful nationalisations. In respect of the former he noted the entitlement to the future profits that would have flowed from the concession. In respect of lawful nationalisations he noted that compensation was frequently less than full compensation. Under the heading in the award "Estimation of Compensation" the Tribunal noted that the claimants had calculated the future profits of the concessions

[98] 53 I.L.R., 389 (1977).
[99] *Ibid.*, 509.
[100] 62 I.L.R., 141 (1977).

on a discounted cash flow basis, estimating the total revenue that would be produced by the concession and applying a discount factor at an annual rate of 12 per cent.[101] The Tribunal, in determining the respondent's position had referred to a speech of the Libyan Oil Minister which postulated compensation on a net book value.[102] The Tribunal concluded:[103]

> For all these reasons and considerations, the Arbitral Tribunal, considering both evaluations as two different exaggerated extremes, and applying the measure of "equitable compensation" hereabove adopted has reached the conclusion that a lump sum of $66,000,000 should be the reasonable equitable indemnification for the nationalisation of the concession rights of LIAMCO's interest in Concession No. 20, Raguba field.

It is noteworthy that apart from reciting the two positions the Tribunal did not enter into a technical discussion for its basis of arriving at $66 million compensation. In addition to this estimate of *lucrum cessans* the Tribunal also awarded full compensation for physical plant assessed on the claimant's valuation.

The very important decision of *Kuwait* v *Aminoil*[104] sought to place a value on the "reasonable rate of return"[105] anticipated by the parties in relation to the concession. The Tribunal assessed various factors, including the level of inflation, the term of the concession and the "reasonable rate of return, assessed on a somewhat more liberal scale".[106] The Tribunal went on to examine the various components of value and stated that:[107]

> [I]t considers it to be just and reasonable to take some measure of account of all the elements of an undertaking. This leads to a separate appraisal of the value, on the one hand of the undertaking itself, as a source of profit, and on the other of the totality of the assets, and adding together the results obtained.

The Tribunal, when assessing the amounts due to Aminoil, concluded:[108]

> These are made up of the values of the various components of the undertaking considered separately, and of the undertaking itself considered as an organic totality—or going concern—therefore as a unified whole, the value of which is greater than that of its component parts, and which must also take account of the legitimate expectations of the owners.

---

[101] *Ibid.*, 212.
[102] *Ibid.*, 208.
[103] *Ibid.*, 214.
[104] 66 I.L.R., 518 (1982).
[105] *Ibid.*, 607. The original concession agreement had been varied by practice.
[106] *Ibid.*, 608.
[107] *Ibid.*, 609.
[108] *Ibid.*, 612.

Compensation for expropriation

The Tribunal relied on a joint report prepared by the international accounting firm Peat Marwick Mitchell & Co., who were the regular auditors of Aminoil, to determine the depreciated replacement value of the fixed assets, and the value of the non-fixed assets, and taking into account the legitimate expectations of the concession determined the compensation payable.[109]

The decision of the ICSID Tribunal in *AGIP* v *Congo*[110] also endorsed the principle of full compensation for losses, including loss of profit. In respect of the latter item the claims were limited by the claimant to a symbolic amount of one franc for each of its three claims for loss of profits. Thus the technique to value loss of profits is not evident in the award.

The important point of these arbitrations is the use of modern accounting techniques to determine the value of the most contentious element of a nationalised asset, that of future profit. The future profit is an essential ingredient in valuing a business asset as a going concern, and it has been the focus of the notable decisions on expropriation of the Iran–United States Claims Tribunal.

Awards and decisions of the Tribunal

Valuation of particular property and assets

The first significant decision of the Tribunal in relation to the quantum of compensation was *American International Group* v *Iran*.[111] The Tribunal stated:[112]

> The Tribunal holds that the appropriate method is to value the company as a going concern, taking into account not only the net book value of its assets but also such elements as goodwill and likely future profitability had the company been allowed to continue its business under its former management. The book value method is used mainly for liquidation purposes.

The Tribunal went on to equate going concern value with the fair market value,[113] and opined that such value must reflect the general political, social and economic conditions.[114] This latter point is of particular significance in a revolutionary situation.

While it is a general principle that the actions of the nationalising government in respect of the nationalisation which have the effect of

[109] *Ibid.*, 613.
[110] 67 I.L.R., 318 (1979).
[111] 4 IRAN–U.S.C.T.R., 96 (1983).
[112] *Ibid.*, 109.
[113] *Ibid.*, 106.
[114] *Ibid.*, 107.

reducing the value of the expropriated assets should be excluded when determining the value of the assets, the overseas investor does assume the risk of social and economic turmoil which may affect the value of his investment. The Tribunal thus considered the fair market value of the shares to be considerably less than had been valued by the experts for the claimant who had taken insufficient consideration of the "changes in general social and economic conditions in Iran which had taken place between the autumn of 1978 and June 1979, or their likely duration".[115]

The case of *INA Corporation* v *Iran*[116] concerned a shareholding interest that had been nationalised as part of a general nationalisation of the insurance industry. In the particular circumstances of the Iranian situation, notably the applicability of the Treaty of Amity between Iran and the United States, full compensation was required.

The Tribunal found that the full value was equal to the fair market valuation of the shares assessed at the date of nationalisation. In determining the fair market value the Tribunal noted that the claimants interest had been purchased only a year before nationalisation and that the company had been gradually increasing in profitability for the three years ending 20 March 1979. There was no evidence to show a decline in value between March 1979 and July 1979, the date of nationalisation, and accordingly the Tribunal made an award equivalent to the purchase price of the shares, plus interest at 8.5 per cent from the date of nationalisation. Unlike Chamber Three, Chamber One made no reference to the changes in the social and economic conditions of Iran which occurred from the middle of 1978 onward, culminating in this instance with the nationalisation of the insurance industry. It cannot be readily disputed that the revolutionary unrest both before and after the destruction of the Imperial government had the effect of reducing the value of virtually all foreign investments in Iran.

The significance of the Islamic revolution on the value of assets is directly considered in *Phelps Dodge Corporation* v *Iran*.[117] In determining the full value of Phelps Dodge's interest in SICAB the Tribunal noted that the company had been founded in 1974 but that production in the factory did not commence until December 1978, at which time the Iranian revolution was well advanced.[118] The Tribunal therefore considered that SICAB had not become a "going concern" by the time it had been expropriated and thus it could not be valued on such a basis. In respect of the effect of the Iranian revolution it stated:[119]

[115] *Ibid.*, 107–8.
[116] 8 IRAN–U.S.C.T.R., 373 (1985).
[117] 10 IRAN–U.S.C.T.R., 121 (1986).
[118] *Ibid.*, 124–5.
[119] *Ibid.*, 133.

Compensation for expropriation

While no diminution in value should be made because of the anticipation of a taking, the Tribunal could not properly ignore the obvious and significant negative effects of the Iranian Revolution on SICAB's business prospects, at least in the short and medium term... SICAB's short-term prospects would certainly have been seen in November 1980 as sufficiently uncertain to require a considerable discounting of the anticipated long-term profits.

On the basis of these findings of fact and law the Tribunal made an award that was equal to the claimant's investment in 1974.

A more recent case, *CBS Inc. v Iran*,[120] also considered the effect of revolution on the value of assets, including future profitability. The case was unusual, involving cultural values. The claimant sought compensation for the expropriation of the CBS Iranian companies. These companies produced records and tapes, mostly of Western music. The Tribunal noted the limited trading history of the company and its lack of profitability. It also stated:[121]

The Claimant's valuations also underestimate the adverse effects of the Islamic Revolution on the music market, and thus on the CBS Iranian Companies' future business. In particular, in view of the policy of the new Iranian Government against music, especially Western music, which constituted a substantial part of the CBS Iranian Companies' field of operations, the expectations for these companies were greatly diminished.

Although *Phelps Dodge Corporation v Iran*[122] and *CBS Inc. v Iran*[123] both consider the value of assets in relation to the future profits of the business, including a discount due to the revolutionary situation, this concept of future profits as being an element of the value of a business receives its fullest consideration only in the claims concerning the expropriation of oil interests where the income is derived from a right to extract oil pursuant to a long-term contract.

Oil concession cases

The first major oil concession case is that of *Amoco International Finance v Iran*,[124] which raised the difficult question of the full value of an ongoing contractual right to extract oil.

The mere recital of the formula of full value provides little guidance to its application in oil concession cases. As a starting point the Tribunal distinguished between lawful and unlawful takings, although it had noted

---

[120] 25 IRAN–U.S.C.T.R., 131 (1990).
[121] *Ibid.*, 148–9. The Tribunal concluded that the CBS Iranian companies had no value and the expropriation claim was dismissed. Claims in relation to debt and contract were upheld.
[122] 10 IRAN–U.S.C.T.R., 121 (1986).
[123] 25 IRAN–U.S.C.T.R., 131 (1990).
[124] 15 IRAN–U.S.C.T.R., 189 (1987).

that the value of an enterprise does not vary accordingly to the lawfulness of the expropriation:[125]

The difference is that if the taking is lawful the value of the undertaking at the time of the dispossession is the measure and the limit of the compensation, while if it is unlawful the value is or may be only a part of the reparation to be paid.

This distinction immediately raises the issue of the additional constituent of compensation due in an unlawful taking: the means of effecting restitution by monetary compensation. The Tribunal analysed this by examining the two questions the Permanent Court had asked in *Chorzow Factory*. The first question looked firstly at the value of the property at the time of taking and secondly at the financial results that would have accrued from the date of judgment had the property remained in the hands of the owners. The Tribunal considered that the first part of the question concerned lawful takings whereas the second part related to unlawful takings. Since the first category has the most relevance to the Tribunal the elements of value were categorised:[126]

They appertain to three categories: corporeal rights (land, buildings, equipment, stocks) contractual rights (supply and delivery contracts) and other intangible valuables (processes, goodwill and "future prospects"). Using today's vocabulary, this would mean "going concern value", which is not a new concept after all.

The Tribunal focused especially on "future prospects", which had to be a different concept from future profits (*lucrum cessans*), since this was compensable only for unlawful expropriation.[127] The distinction drawn by the Tribunal was thus:[128]

The first one [future prospects] clearly refers to the fact that the undertaking was a "going concern" which had demonstrated a certain ability to earn revenues and was, therefore, to be considered as keeping such ability for the future: this is an element of its value at the time of the taking. The second relates to the amount of the earnings hypothetically accrued from the date of taking to the date of the expert opinion had the enterprise remained in the hands of its former owner.

The Permanent Court had also asked a second question, relating to illegal expropriation. The Tribunal saw that this question required the same components of valuation, except that the date of valuation changed from the date of taking to the date of judgment, since this would include accrued profits.[129] Whichever result gave the higher valuation, the

---

[125] *Ibid.*, 248. See also Chapter Eight on the issue of illegality of expropriation.
[126] *Ibid.*, 249.
[127] *Ibid.*, 249.
[128] *Ibid.*, 250.
[129] *Ibid.*, 250. It is noteworthy that in *Phillips*, 21 IRAN–U.S.C.T.R., 79, 122 (1989) the Tribunal found that the *only* difference in the compensation standard for lawful and unlawful expropriation is the timing of when the assets should be valued. In lawful

Compensation for expropriation 197

higher value would prevail. The comparison of the valuation by the two approaches would necessarily include *lucrum cessans* as an element of the valuation, since both questions asked by the Permanent Court concerned unlawful expropriations.

The claim before the Tribunal had been adjudged not to be illegal, therefore the element of *lucrum cessans* was not relevant. Instead there was the element of "future prospects". Thus the Tribunal had the task of translating the formula of "going concern value", which included "future prospects", to the valuation of the expropriated concession rights in *Amoco*.

The Tribunal considered "market value . . . is the most commendable standard since it is also the most objective and the most easily ascertained when a market exists for identical or similar assets".[130] In the present case, however, there was no open market for such large industrial enterprises.

Accordingly, in the process of determining the full value of the business, the Tribunal gave extensive consideration to the submissions of the claimant on the discounted cash flow (DCF) method as the means of determining the true market value of the expropriated assets. The claimant had asserted that the DCF valuation "determines the price at which going concern business assets are bought and sold".[131] In response, Iran contended that "the fair value of the expropriated assets is best represented by net book value".[132]

The Tribunal firstly noted that "the DCF method was specifically proposed by the claimant as a method that would place the foreign investor in as good an economic position as he was before the expropriation".[133] This was rejected, since, as noted in *Chorzow Factory*, it was considered to be applicable only to an illegal expropriation. The Tribunal considered the DCF method to be of most assistance to an investor making a decision to invest who is considering the likely rate of return on the invested funds. The Tribunal, however, was of the view that "The calculation of the revenues expected to accrue over a long period of time in the future which opens a large field of speculation due to the uncertainty inherent in any such projection will probably yield higher results than any other method".[134] Moreover, the method had not been accepted by other Tribunals, including the United States Foreign Claims Settlement Commission.[135]

expropriation the assets would be valued at the time of taking whereas in an unlawful taking account could be taken of increases in value from the time of taking to the date of award.
[130] *Ibid.*, 255.
[131] *Ibid.*, 256.
[132] *Ibid.*, 256.
[133] *Ibid.*, 258.
[134] *Ibid.*, 259.
[135] *Ibid.*, 259.

Notwithstanding its reservations, the Tribunal observed:[136]

> These initial remarks do not necessarily lead to an absolute rejection of the DCF method for any purpose in this case. For the reasons already set out, one element of valuation of a going concern, as was Khemco, is its profitability. This element is not easy to translate into figures and the DCF method could provide the Tribunal with useful information pertaining to profitability if the method is correctly applied.

The Tribunal went on to consider the two elements of the DCF calculation, first the projection of cash flow into the future and second the proper discount rate, taking into account all variables, to arrive at the present value of the future income.

The principal difficulty in both aspects of the DCF calculation is the uncertainty of the future, which, of course, is greatly increased the further one looks into the future. It was these uncertainties, including the future price of oil, civil unrest, war, currency risk and the prospect of lawful expropriation, that the Tribunal was concerned with in making its assessment of the value of Khemco. The Tribunal did not make a formal analysis of the various risks, noting that the information supplied was insufficient to assess the validity of the claimant's assumptions.[137]

In rejecting the DCF method as a means of calculating the market value the Tribunal noted that Khemco was a going concern at the time of the expropriation, and "accordingly is the measure of compensation in this case".[138] The Tribunal amplified this view, stating:[139]

> Going concern value encompasses not only the physical and financial assets of the undertaking, but also the intangible valuables which contribute to its earning power, such as contractual rights (supply and delivery contracts, patent licences and so on), as well as goodwill and commercial prospects.

Since the two parties had not made any submissions on the going concern value of the Amoco subsidiary, Khemco, the Tribunal ordered them to submit data on the value of the undertaking as a going concern before it was prepared to make a final award.[140]

In subsequent cases the Tribunal has given greater credence to the analytical technique of the DCF method in providing a means of quantifying in financial terms such uncertainties as revolution, war and civil or labour unrest. It has to be recognised, however, that there is an element of arbitrariness in providing a discount factor of future earnings of say 5 per cent for the risk of revolution as opposed to an 8 per cent or 9 per

[136] *Ibid.*, 260.
[137] *Ibid.*, 263.
[138] *Ibid.*, 270.
[139] *Ibid.*, 270.
[140] *Ibid.*, 271.

Compensation for expropriation

cent discount factor and this has been noted by Iran as having a greater impact on DCF calculations than any other factor.[141]

Three of the more recent major cases are *Mobil Oil Iran Inc. v Iran*,[142] *Starrett Housing Corporation v Iran*[143] and *Phillips Petroleum* Company *Iran v Iran*.[144]

The *Mobil Oil Iran Inc. v Iran*[145] case considered the important issue of the right of claimants to future profit from a long-term agreement for the exploitation of oil resources. It is a feature of such agreements that they are subject to modification during the term, such modification usually occurring outside the strict terms of the agreement. In this particular case negotiations had been commenced between the parties on the issue of compensation arising from the termination of the agreement. The Tribunal therefore determined its role in the following terms:[146]

In such case, the duty of the Tribunal in ascertaining the damages or compensation to be paid by one Party to the other is to determine what the parties could legitimately have expected from negotiations conducted in good faith on the basis of the March 1979 agreement. In order to assess these legitimate expectations, the Tribunal has to take into account all the relevant factual and legal circumstances of the case. Of primary concern, obviously, are the duties and obligations of both parties under the SPA and all related agreements and arrangements. The Agreement must be construed, not only pursuant to its initial terms, but also as to the manner in which it was performed and *de facto* or *de jure* amended during its life, up to the time it was suspended by *force majeure*.

The second major case, *Starrett Housing Corporation v Iran*,[147] was decided by Chamber One making a final award on the basis of the expert's report arising from an interlocutory award.[148] The expert in making his valuation of the expropriated assets was directed in the interlocutory award to consider "as he deems appropriate the discounted cash flow method of valuation".[149]

This method would lead to a determination of the fair market value of Shah Goli, the apartment company, which had been expropriated. The Tribunal exhaustively considered the expert's report, which extended to twelve volumes. The basic methodology of the expert was accepted, but some of his assessments were revised by the Tribunal, in particular the

---

[141] See *Phillips Petroleum Co. Iran v Iran* 21 IRAN–U.S.C.T.R., 79, 134 (1989).
[142] 16 IRAN–U.S.C.T.R., 3 (1987).
[143] *Ibid.*, 112.
[144] 21 IRAN–U.S.C.T.R., 79 (1989).
[145] 16 IRAN–U.S.C.T.R., 3 (1987).
[146] *Ibid.*, 54.
[147] *Ibid.*, 112.
[148] 4 IRAN–U.S.C.T.R., 122 (1983).
[149] 16 IRAN–U.S.C.T.R., 116 (1987).

number of apartments sold but not settled.[150] The Tribunal made the following observations of the valuation:[151]

> As noted, the Expert made his valuation in three stages. First, he determined Shah Goli's adjusted book value on the date of taking. Then, recognizing that this book value does not represent fair market value, he determined the price a reasonable buyer would pay for the Project. To do this the Expert employed the DCF method, a well known valuation technique based on discounted cash flow ... The use of the DCF method had been foreseen in the Interlocutory Award, in which the Tribunal instructed the Expert to give his opinion "considering as he deems appropriate the discounted cash flow method of valuation". Finally, the Expert determined the Claimants' share of Shah Goli as of the valuation date ... The Tribunal finds that the methods employed by the Expert and the stages by which he made his valuation were logical and appropriate.

In relation to the discount rate the Tribunal adopted the 28 per cent discount rate proposed by the expert, since it accepted that this was within his expertise.[152] The overall result was an award of approximately $36 million plus interest at 8.5 per cent simple interest from the date of taking. This may be contrasted to the claimant seeking $41 million, although it is to be noted that the bulk of the claim related to unpaid loans. The claimant had originally claimed approximately $113 milion, but amended this to the amount reported by the expert, a little over $41 million.

Arguably, the most important of this trio of cases is *Phillips Petroleum Comany Ltd v Iran*,[153] decided by Chamber Two in 1989. The Chamber is presided over by Professor Briner, who was the subject of an unsuccessful challenge by Iran. Iran also requested that the *Phillips* award be annulled, although this request was withdrawn by Iran when the case was settled.[154]

The most significant aspect of the case is the very full consideration of "analytical" methods to determine the fair market value of the assets in question. Such analytical methods have to deal with quantifiable "future profits" rather than the somewhat vague concept of "future prospects". It was perhaps not suprising therefore that the Tribunal had characterised the only difference in valuing assets in unlawful and lawful expropriation as one of timing; "the increase in the value of the property between the date of taking and the date of the judicial or arbitral decision awarding compensation".[155] In the case of unlawful takings the claimant would be

---

[150] *Ibid.*, 201.
[151] *Ibid.*, 201.
[152] *Ibid.*, 220.
[153] 21 IRAN–U.S.C.T.R., 79 (1989).
[154] *Ibid.*, 302.
[155] *Ibid.*, 79, 122.

Compensation for expropriation

entitled to any increase in value from the date of taking to the date of the award. The Tribunal dealt thoroughly with the elements of the analytical methods:[156]

In the absence of an active and free market for comparable assets at the date of taking, a tribunal must, of necessity, resort to analytical methods to assist it in deciding the price a reasonable buyer could be expected to have been willing to pay for the asset in a free market transaction, had such a transaction been possible at the time the property was taken. Any such analysis of a revenue-producing asset, such as the contract rights involved in the present case, must involve a careful and realistic appraisal of the revenue-producing potential of the asset over the duration of its term, which requires appraisal of the level of production that reasonably may be expected, the costs of operation, including taxes and other liabilities, and the revenue such production would be expected to yield, which, in turn, requires a determination of the price, estimates for sales of the future production that a reasonable buyer would use in deciding upon the price it would be willing to pay to acquire the asset. Moreover, any such analysis must also involve an evaluation of the effect on the price of any other risks likely to be perceived by a reasonable buyer at the date in question, excluding only reductions in the price that could be expected to result from threats of expropriation or from other actions by the respondents related thereto.

One such method of analysis, and the method used by the claimant, is the Discounted Cash Flow ("DCF") analysis, which calculates the claimant's prospective net earnings over the term of the JSA [Joint Structure Agreement] and discounts them to give their value at the date of taking, using a discount rate that takes into account the perceived risks. In that connection the Tribunal does not understand the claimant's calculations of anticipated revenues from the JSA as a request to be awarded lost future profits, but rather as a relevant factor to be considered in the determination of the fair market value of its property interest at the date of the taking. The Tribunal recognizes that a prospective buyer would almost certainly undertake such DCF analysis to help it determine the price it would be willing to pay and that DCF calculations are, therefore, evidence the Tribunal is justified in considering in reaching its decision on value.

The Tribunal noted that in *Amoco International Finance* Chamber Three had considered the DCF method inadequate, since it referred only to the financial capitalisation of the revenue generated by the business.[157] In the present case the DCF method was considered to have greater applicability, since the case concerned "contract rights to continue to exploit natural resources previously discovered pursuant to the contract".[158] Accordingly, the DCF method was a relevant contribution to the valuation of the claimant's contractual rights although it was not an

---
[156] *Ibid.*, 122–3.
[157] *Ibid.*, 123.
[158] *Ibid.*, 123–4.

"exclusive method of analysis and all relevant considerations must be taken into account".[159]

The Tribunal proceeded to analyse the various factors that the claimant had considered to be relevant in determining the future profitability of the business, including the quantity of oil in the reservoirs, the future of oil prices, the costs of production and the political risks. Since these were future events they could not be determined with certainty and the claimant and respondent had widely differing projections of these factors. The last factor, political risk, is of great interest in relation to investments in developing nations, which are frequently politically unstable. Thus the respondent noted that there was greater political risk in Iran and the Middle East generally than in the United States or in the North Sea.[160] Such political risks had two dimensions, firstly the risk of further forced modifications to the Joint Structure Agreement, as was common throughout the OPEC nations, and secondly the risk of revolution in Iran which could result in expropriation.

The Tribunal stated it did not intend to make its own DCF calculation but instead would identify the extent to which it agreed or disagreed with the claimant's own assessments.[161] The Tribunal therefore made an assessment of each of the various components, as they would have influenced a potential purchaser of the property in September 1979, the date of expropriation. The principal factors considered by the Tribunal were the risk that not all recoverable oil would be produced, the risk that world oil prices from 1979 to 1999 would be lower than the range foreseen and the risk of coerced revisions of the JSA. The fact that the actual outcome might well be different from the predictions of risk in September 1979 did not affect the Tribunal's assessment of risk, since such an outcome would not be known or anticipated by a purchaser in 1979. A good example of such an outcome was that prices for oil were somewhat lower in the 1980s than might have been anticipated in 1979.

In addition to these factors the Tribunal also examined whether or not there were any equitable considerations which should be taken into account. The Tribunal stated:[162]

The Tribunal notes that, following the exploration and development stages, commercial production began in the Rostam Field on 19 September 1968 and in the Raskhsh Field in February 1971. Thus, at the time of taking, most of the Claimant's exploration and development costs had been amortized, but slightly less than one-third of the thirty-year production period of the JSA had passed. The bulk of the Claimant's investment had been made, but the bulk of the

[159] *Ibid.*, 124.
[160] *Ibid.*, 134.
[161] *Ibid.*, 124, 134.
[162] *Ibid.*, 142.

Compensation for expropriation

financial rewards the Claimant anticipated lay in the future. The Respondents, as the Tribunal has noted *supra*, protected their interests by compelling the Claimant and the other Second Party companies to renegotiate the financial terms of the JSA so as to leave to the Respondents the bulk of the greatly increased revenues that resulted from the 1973 oil price increases. Nevertheless, fundamental policy changes, made possible by a successful revolution, resulted in the taking of the Claimant's interests in the JSA. The Tribunal can discern in the facts of this Case no equitable considerations that would affect the compensation to which the Claimant is otherwise entitled.

The Tribunal went on to determine the effect of all these factors and concluded:[163]

As noted *supra* the Claimant is entitled to compensation equal to the value of its JSA interests as of 29 September 1979, as adjusted for related debts owing between the Parties at that time. Taking into account all the relevant circumstances the Tribunal hereby determines the Claimant is entitled to compensation from the Respondent in the amount of $55 million.

This amount was confirmed by other valuation techniques, including "an underlying asset valuation approach which takes as a starting point previous investment and determines future profitability based on historical performance".[164]

The *Phillips* award is controversial and was the subject of a strongly worded *Statement by Judge Khalilian as to Why it would have been Premature to sign the Award*.[165] The statement was both a protest against the conduct of the deliberations of the majority of the Chamber and in particular of the Chairman, Mr Briner, and an initial dissent from the method of calculating compensation.[166] On the substantive issue of compensation Judge Khalilian disputed that the DCF method was appropriate for the valuation of lawfully expropriated oil exploitation contracts, particularly when they had a long term to run after the expropriation. Judge Khalilian made particular reference to the *Amoco* case, noting that Professor Virally, the Chairman of Chamber Three, "an internationally distinguished authority, clearly rejected the use of the DCF method in cases of nationalisation in the oil industry".[167] However, this praise of Professor Virally does not mean that Iran has now accepted that the methodology adopted by the majority, which included Professor Virally,

---

[163] *Ibid.*, 143.
[164] *Ibid.*, 143.
[165] 21 Iran–U.S.C.T.R., 194 (1989). See also Chapter Three on the challenge to Mr Briner by Iran in respect of his conduct in the *Phillips* case.
[166] Judge Khalilian stated he would elaborate on his reasons in his Dissenting Opinion. *Ibid.*, 198. They are further detailed in his *Second Supplemental Statement of Seyed Khalil Khalilian*, 21 Iran–U.S.C.T.R., 263 (1989).
[167] *Ibid.*, 199.

in the *Amoco International Finance* case[168] is the correct approach in valuing long-term oil exploitation contracts which have been expropriated.

The ultimate conclusion of the *Phillips* award was a settlement award between Phillips and Iran, prior to the Tribunal considering Iran's application to the full Tribunal to annul the award.[169] Included in the Settlement Agreement was a statement that "The English Version... shall be deemed by the Parties as null and void and of no effect whatsoever".[170] The sum to be paid was $92 million, which was approximately 20 per cent less than the award of $55 million plus 10 per cent simple interest awarded from 29 September 1979, the date of expropriation, to the date of payment.

Both the United States and the Iranian arbitrators filed separate opinions on the effect of the settlement on the award. Judge Aldrich stated:[171]

> These actions [by the Parties and Tribunal in relation to settlement], however, cannot change the fact the Award 425-39-2 is the Award that was rendered by the Tribunal following its prolonged deliberations, and it remains the definitive statement of the Tribunal's conclusions and reasoning with respect to this case.

In contrast Judge Khalilian maintained the award was null and void and that Iran would agree to the settlement only if the award was set aside.[172] After reviewing the progress of Iran's application to the full Tribunal to annul the award he stated:[173]

> No reasonable reader of the Award on Agreed Terms (Award No. 461-39-2) can harbour any doubt that as a final and binding award it has unquestionably superseded the English version of Award No. 425-39-2 in its entirety, leaving the latter with no judicial value whatsoever.

The Iranian position in relation to the settlement award with its provision that the award was null and void was emphasised by Judge Ameli in his review of Westberg's book, *International Transactions and Claims involving Government Parties: Case Law of the Iran–United States Claims Tribunal* (1991).[174] Judge Ameli stated:

> Moreover, because the nullification decreased the so-called full compensation by as large a figure as nine million dollars, excluding interest, the whole compen-

---

[168] 15 IRAN–U.S.C.T.R., 189 (1987).
[169] 21 IRAN–U.S.C.T.R., 285 (1990). The application for "Revocation, Setting aside and Annulment of the Award" was made on 30 August 1989; see 21 IRAN–U.S.C.T.R., 283 (1989).
[170] *Ibid.*, 286.
[171] *Ibid.*, 294.
[172] *Ibid.*, 299.
[173] *Ibid.*, 301.
[174] Book review in 24 *Vanderbilt Journal of Transnational Law*, 611 (1991).

sation formula and the resulting sum were so altered that neither the award's validity, nor the compensation formula, could be maintained.

Moreover Judge Ameli is of the view that if the parties decide that the award is null and void "it hardly can be held out as the valid jurisprudence of the Tribunal".[175] It is not apparent that the parties can make such a decision for the Tribunal, even if the Tribunal should record the settlement as an "Award on Agreed Terms". Any such statement by the parties must simply record the position of the parties *inter se* and not in relation to the validity of the award as a valid decision of the Tribunal. Westberg's evaluation is that "[W]hatever arguments might be made as to the technical status of the original award, it was issued by the Tribunal and published and is thus available for whatever use one might want to make of it."[176]

Nevertheless Judge Amelis's review does record the continuing deep division between Western attitudes and those of developing nations in relation to valuation techniques which fully capitalise future profits.

Conclusion on valuation

The valuation of property and the quantum of full compensation have proved to be of greater difficulty than determining the rules applicable to the compensation standard. Although the Tribunal considers that the market value of a going concern offers the most reliable guide, this is extremely difficult to assess when much of the value relates to future rights to extract oil.

It may be argued that the valuation method adopted in the *Phillips* case refines the distinction between unlawful and lawful expropriation. The difference between "future prospects" alluded to in *Amoco* and future profits (*lucrum cessans*) becomes difficult to define when the bulk of the value of an asset is related to its future profitability. The going concern value, especially when assessed by sophisticated purchasers, will necessarily include an element of capitalisation of future profits. It is not surprising that the Tribunal had to characterise the distinction between unlawful and lawful expropriation as only one of timing, that is, of when the asset should be valued rather than of how it should be valued. The sole measure of value then becomes the market value, and the means of the measure will be dependent on the nature of the asset and of the market in which it exists.

However, the assessment of market value including future prospects cannot be easily undertaken where the market is affected by revolu-

---

[175] *Ibid.*, 613.
[176] Westberg, *op. cit.*, p. 233, note 97.

tionary upheavals, and it is not doubted by any arbitrator that a decline in value due to revolution is a proper factor to be taken into account when assessing the value. As a consequence the Tribunal has only been able to provide broad estimates of the value of property taken during a revolution.

Where the property consists of readily ascertainable assets, such as bank accounts, or readily transportable assets, the Tribunal has had a relatively easy task in determining their value. In contrast, where the Tribunal has had to value a going concern, including a contractual right to extract oil in the future, it has virtually had to guess at the future profitability of the venture having regard to the revolutionary changes in Iran. Analytical techniques are not particularly useful predictors of dynamic political and social changes in a revolutionary society.

There is little doubt that the Tribunal has reinforced the traditional view that states must provide full compensation when they expropriate assets belonging to nationals of another state and that the measure of full value is what the market is prepared to pay for assets, which price will include an element of capitalisation of future profits. However, the rejection of the views of the developing states on the rules applicable to compensation has been tempered by the assessment of the value of a going concern in a revolutionary state.

CHAPTER TEN
Other measures affecting property rights

Introduction

The essence of the law of state responsibility is that liability will attach to any act or omission of a state in breach of its international obligations which causes loss to aliens. There is no requirement that the wrongful act need flow from contract or be an expropriation of property.[1] Indeed a mere breach of contract, without more, does not usually engage international responsibility.[2] Neither is there any requirement that the alien should suffer property loss; the claimant state will have a cause of action if its national has suffered personal injury or loss of life, arguably a more serious loss than damage to property.

The fourth category of private claims covers loss suffered by claimants arising from actions which are not a repudiation of debt, a breach of contract or an expropriation of assets or contractual rights. Thus an act or omission not falling into one of the three categories but causing a property loss to the claimant or leading to an unjust enrichment of the respondent state would come within this category of jurisdiction. Claims based on loss due to breach of contract between private parties, which breach was caused by an act or omission of the respondent state, would also come under this head of jurisdiction.

Although tort and unjust enrichment are well established causes of action in international law, they will be of less significance than the

---

[1] Expropriation of property, where it does not involve breach of contractual rights, is a tortious act. However, since it is a separate category of jurisdiction in the Claims Settlement Declaration it will not be covered in this chapter.

[2] A breach of contract is not usually a breach of international law unless there has been denial of justice, or a direct violation of international law. Amerasinghe, *State Responsibility for Injuries to Aliens*, 79–80 (1967); Brownlie, *Principles of Public International Law*, 547–8 (1990). See Chapter Seven, *supra*.

former three categories of jurisdiction, since most claims before the Tribunal fall within the former three categories. Moreover if a claim falls within one of the former categories then causes of action based on *quantum meruit* or unjust enrichment will be excluded by the Tribunal.[3]

The Claims Settlement Declaration, moreover, limits the claims that can be entertained by the Iran–United States Claims Tribunal to those involving property loss. Apart from this restriction the full body of the law of state responsibility is applicable to the claims that can be heard by the Iran–United States Claims Tribunal.

Delictual or tortious responsibility

International law

A great many of the acts and omissions of states giving rise to international claims are essentially delictual or tortious.[4] There is no question in respect of such claims that there has been a breach of a contract, nor is there any unjust enrichment of the respondent state. Nevertheless the act or omission of the state has caused loss to an alien, who is denied a remedy under the respondent state's municipal law. Proof of denial of justice has usually been considered essential before state responsibility is incurred in respect of claims arising from tortious acts.

However, where the claimant and respondent states have established an arbitral tribunal to hear claims for injury to the claimant states' nationals there is usually no need for the claimant to show denial of justice in the sense of the claimant having been unjustly deprived of an effective local remedy. The establishment of the tribunal, as in the case of the Iran–United States Claims Tribunal, is likely to have taken place because of the absence of effective local remedies. The arbitral tribunal will thus have the sole task of determining whether the respondent state is in breach of its international obligations to the claimant state, since not every loss suffered by aliens caused by actions of the respondent state will give rise to a right to damages.

The law of state responsibility in relation to delict or tort has not developed complex rules such as are familiar to Anglo-American jurists. Brownlie notes:[5]

International law is not a system replete with nominate torts or delicts, but the rules are specialised in certain aspects. Thus reference may be made to the source

---

[3] Refer section on Unjust Enrichment, *infra*.

[4] Amerasinghe, *State Responsibility for Injuries to Aliens*, 44–5, 281–2 (1967); Brownlie, *Principles of Public International Law*, 528 (1990); Greig, *International Law*, 568 (1976).

[5] Brownlie, *Principles of Public International Law*, 528 (1990). He refers to denial of justice and expropriation as special topics in the category of delictual responsibility in respect of injury to nationals.

of the harm, such as unauthorised acts of officials, insurrection, and so on, or to the object and form of harm, as, for example, territorial sovereignty, diplomats and other official agents, or injury to aliens.

Accordingly delictual or tortious responsibility is simply an aspect of the law of state responsibility.

Awards and decisions of the Tribunal

The vast majority of claims before the Tribunal arise out of contracts or expropriation. Certainly there are very few claims exceeding $250,000 where there is no question of any contractual, or quasi-contractual remedy.[6]

The first decided claim based on tort was *Hoffland Honey Company* v *NIOC*.[7] The claim was for loss of beehives in Wisconsin due to pesticides made from oil sold by NIOC. Although the claim is startling in the remoteness of damage it was nevertheless based on the tortious liability of Iran in relation to United States nationals. Not surprisingly the Tribunal found that there was no breach of any rule of state responsibility by Iran by virtue of the mere sale of oil by NIOC.[8] Accordingly the claim was dismissed.

The claim in *Grimm* v *Iran*[9] was more firmly based on the rule that a successful revolutionary government is responsible for the acts of the revolutionaries prior to the success of the revolution.[10] Mrs Grimm alleged her husband had been assassinated by Islamic revolutionaries, thereby causing her property loss in that she was deprived of the material support of her husband. The majority considered that she had not suffered property loss within the meaning of the Claims Settlement Declaration and dismissed the claim. The majority, however, did not consider the potential liability of Iran in respect of property loss for acts committed by supporters of the revolution. Mr Holtzmann, in a dissenting opinion, considered that actions of revolutionaries which contributed to the success of the revolution were attributable to the new government.[11] It did not matter that the revolutionaries were not acting according to any specific direction or under a special force organised by the future Islamic government.

It may be expected that many of the small claims which concerned the loss or abandonment of personal property such as motor vehicles and

[6] Many of the claims for less than $250,000, which have yet to be considered by the Tribunal, do involve simple loss of property, such as motor vehicles and other personal property belonging to United States nationals being destroyed by revolutionary guards, or bank accounts belonging to United States nationals being frozen in Iranian banks.
[7] 2 IRAN–U.S.C.T.R., 41 (1983).
[8] *Ibid.*, 42.
[9] *Ibid.*, 78.
[10] Refer to Chapter Eleven on liability for actions of revolutionaries.
[11] For a full discussion of Mr Holtzmann's opinion refer to Chapter Eleven.

personal chattels by United States nationals when they left Iran owing to the revolutionary unrest will be based on the delictual or tortious responsibility of the Iranian government.

This issue was raised in *Kenneth Yeager* v *Iran*.[12] The claimant was forcibly removed from his apartment by Revolutionary Guards during the Islamic revolution. As a consequence he had to abandon his personal property and various bank accounts. The Tribunal summarised his claim:[13]

> The claimant argues that his property was "expropriated" by virtue of his wrongful expulsion, and that expulsion, in any event, is an "other measure affecting property rights". In the Respondent's view a claim based on wrongful expulsion is in the nature of a tort and does not fall within any of these categories.

The Tribunal dealt with these arguments stating:[14]

> It is true that the Tribunal has found that it lacked jurisdiction over claims arising from personal injury in previous cases. [*Grimm* v *Iran*]. This does not mean, however, that all torts fall outside the scope of Article II, paragraph 1, of the Claims Settlement Declaration. A "tort" is commonly defined as a legal wrong committed upon a person *or* property independent of contract. *See Black's Law Dictionary* 1334 (rev. 5th ed. 1979). The term "measures" used in Article II, paragraph 1, of the Claims Settlement Declaration is not limited to contractual relationships and does include "torts", if, and that is the relevant jurisdictional criterion, it affects property rights in a similar way as an expropriation.

The Tribunal found that the wrongful acts of the Revolutionary Guards were attributable to the government of Iran for the claimant's property loss.[15]

Unjust enrichment

International law

The prohibition of unjust enrichment is a well accepted general principle of law found in most recognised legal systems. As such it can be incorporated into international law, being one of the subsidiary sources of international law referred to in Article 38 of the Statute of the International Court of Justice. However, the difficulty that has faced arbitral tribunals and jurists has been the scope and applicability of the concept. International tribunals have given some recognition to the prohibition of unjust enrichment as a general principle of law.

---

[12] Award 324-10199-1 (1987). This case is also considered in Chapter Eleven.
[13] *Ibid.*, 10.
[14] *Ibid.*, 10–11.
[15] The claimant only succeeded in part of his claim. The termination of employment in particular was not attributable to Iran.

Other measures affecting property rights

In *Dickson Car Wheel Company* v *Mexico*[16] the arbitrator referred to the wide use of the doctrine of unjustified enrichment in most systems of municipal law but that it had not become part of the corpus of international law.[17] However, in *General Finance Corporation* v *Mexico*[18] the United States–Mexico General Claims Commission held in respect of a concession agreement for the supply of water which had been terminated by Mexico that "the Government of Mexico, under international law, must reimburse the claimant to the extent that it has been unjustly enriched".[19] In this instance the principle had been applied to determine damages for breach of contract, and had not been perceived as an independent cause of action.

The most widely cited case in support of the principle has been the *Lena Goldfields* arbitration.[20] In this case the claimant had been granted extensive concession rights to exploit minerals in the Soviet Union, which subsequently terminated the concession and nationalised the mines. Although the claim was essentially for breach of contract the tribunal "prefers to base its award on the principle of unjust enrichment".[21]

Support of the principle of unjust enrichment in assessing damages where there has been termination of a concession agreement has been found most recently in *Liamco* v *Libya*.[22] Dr Mahmassani noted the existence of a general principle of law applied by municipal courts and referred to international and arbitral case law and stated:[23]

They thus form a compendium of legal precepts and maxims universally accepted in theory and practice. Instances of such precepts are *inter alia* . . . the prohibition of unjust enrichment.

It is noteworthy that the principle has not been perceived by arbitrators as an independent cause of action, as it has in many systems of municipal law. Instead it has been used to support and justify awards where the respondent state has been in breach of concession or other agreements.

It is accepted by international jurists that the doctrine of unjust enrichment is well entrenched in most municipal legal systems and is a general principle of law.[24] There has, however, been some doubt as to whether it

---

[16] IV R.I.A.A., 669.
[17] *Ibid.*, 676.
[18] From Schreuer, *Unjustified Enrichment in International Law*, 22 Am. J. Comp. Law, 281, 296 (1974).
[19] *Ibid.*
[20] 36 Cornell L.Q., 31 (1950).
[21] *Ibid.*, 51.
[22] 62 I.L.R., 176 (1982).
[23] *Ibid.*, 213.
[24] See O'Connell, *Unjust Enrichment*, 5 Am. J. Comp. Law, 2 (1956); Schreuer, *Unjustified Enrichment in International Law*, 22 Am. J. Comp. Law, 281 (1974).

has independent existence as a principle of international law. Schwarzenberger expressed his reservations when he stated:[25]

On the fringes of international law, the principle tends already to be accepted as a general principle of law, recognised by civilized nations.

Friedman considered that the principle could be "very fruitfully applied to international law"[26] but noted the difficulty of applying the principle in practice owing to the complex nature of international relationships. This uncertainty was also alluded to by Amerasinghe, although he acknowledged that it was accepted as a general principle of law.[27] Schreuer was less certain of the existence of the principle, except as a "decision technique to be applied once the basic policy decisions have been made and not a normative principle or general rule from which specific correct decisions can be logically derived".[28]

Despite these reservations there is sufficient evidence that the principle of unjust enrichment has been incorporated into the body of international law even if only as a general principle of law. The parameters of the concept, however, are still evolving. Although it has been described as a general principle of law it has not been applied as an independent cause of action giving rise to a right to damages as a result of the unjust enrichment of the respondent state at the claimant's expense. Instead it has been used to supplement the existing rules of state responsibility on breach of contract and expropriation as a means of determining the measure of compensation.

Awards and decisions of the Tribunal

A number of claims heard by the Tribunal have been based on unjust enrichment. They have pleaded unjust enrichment either as a separate and independent cause of action, or as a subsidiary cause of action dependent upon subsisting contractual rights. The latter case is particularly applicable where a claim based on the contract has been excluded owing to a forum selection clause. The Tribunal has, in all three Chambers, allowed claims for unjust enrichment only if the cause of action is completely separate from any other causes of action.

Thus in *Isaiah* v *Bank Mellat*[29] the claimant made a claim in respect of a cheque endorsed to him drawn by the International Bank of Iran on

---

[25] Schwarzenberger, *International Law*, 580 (1957).
[26] Friedman, *The Uses of "General Principles" in the Development of International Law*, 263 in *International Law in the Twentieth Century*, Am. Soc. of I.L. (1969).
[27] Amerasinghe, *State Responsibility for Injuries to Aliens*, 148–50 (1967).
[28] Schreuer, *Unjustified Enrichment in International Law*, 22 Am. J. Comp. Law, 281, 301 (1974).
[29] 2 IRAN–U.S.C.T.R., 232 (1983).

Chase Manhattan Bank. The claim for unjust enrichment arose because the bank had received funds, of which Isaiah was the beneficial owner, and retained the funds for its own benefit. Chamber Two of the Tribunal noted the existence of "restitutionary theories" of unjust enrichment in the municipal law of many nations, including Iran, and that it is an "important element of state responsibility".[30] Since it was proved that Isaiah was the lawful owner of the funds in terms of the Claims Settlement Declaration, and that the respondent bank had wrongfully detained the funds, the claim for unjust enrichment was successfully sustained.

A similar case, *Dallal* v *Iran*,[31] also involved a bank cheque drawn by International Bank of Iran on Chase Manhattan Bank. In this case the Tribunal was concerned with two issues before it would consider the claim for unjust enrichment. These issues were whether the transaction breached Iran's currency regulations and the underlying facts that gave rise to the issue of the cheque. On the first issue it found after examining the IMF agreements that they did not prevent members from restricting capital transfers as opposed to payments for technical services or imports. In respect of the second issue the Tribunal found, despite an allegation by the claimant that the sum was a "commission" pursuant to an oral agreement, "that the two cheques must be assumed to be have been issued as part of a capital transfer, intended to merely exchange Rials for Dollars and to transfer the dollar amount to the United States".[32] In this regard it was noteworthy that the Tribunal observed.[33]

Bank Mellat has declared that the Rials could be recovered directly from the bank by the person entitled to them.

On this basis the Tribunal held it was inappropriate to consider an amendment of the claim to include unjust enrichment. In a dissenting opinion Mr Holtzmann noted, "it would be hard to characterize the Respondents' retention of these funds as anything other than unjust enrichment".[34] The ability of the rightful owner of the funds to recover the funds from the bank as rials was considered illusory.[35]

The original forum selection decisions referred to the possibility that claims based on a contract containing an effective provision reserving jurisdiction exclusively to Iranian courts could assert claims "not based on contract".[36] In those cases where the contract contained a valid forum

[30] *Ibid.*, 237.
[31] 3 IRAN–U.S.C.T.R., 10 (1983).
[32] *Ibid.*, 17.
[33] *Ibid.*, 11.
[34] *Ibid.*, 32.
[35] *Ibid.*
[36] *Halliburton Co.* v *Doreen/Imco* 1 IRAN–U.S.C.T.R., 242 (1981–82). See also Chapter Twelve.

exclusion clause the Tribunal has found that unjust enrichment cannot be merely a "derivative" cause of action but must relate to matters beyond the contract.[37] If the finding of unjust enrichment requires a determination of the contractual rights and obligations of the parties the Tribunal has ruled that the "substitute right of action based on unjust enrichment does not arise".[38] In *TCSB Inc.* v *Iran* the Tribunal gave some indication that in some respects the contractual relationship is relevant to claims arising from measures affecting property rights:[39]

> Furthermore, the assets and liabilities of each party in connection with a contract may be relevant for claims arising from measures affecting property rights.

The Tribunal did not indicate the distinction between such claims and claims arising "from performance going beyond the contract or from a situation in which the parties to a contract have, by agreement between them, liquidated their original contractual relationship".[40]

One of the clearest statements of the Tribunal's view of the position of unjust enrichment in international law is found in *Sealand Service Inc.* v *Iran*.[41] The majority in Chamber One stated:[42]

> The concept of unjust enrichment had its origins in Roman Law, where it emerged as an equitable device "to cover those cases in which a general action for damages was not available". It is codified or judicially recognised in the great majority of the municipal legal systems of the world, and is widely accepted as having been assimilated into the catalogue of general principles of law available to be applied by international tribunals.

The Tribunal set unjust enrichment apart from other remedies which could independently found a cause of action. Thus it stated:[43]

> There must have been an enrichment of one party to the detriment of the other, and both must arise as a consequence of the same act or event. There must be no justification for the enrichment and no contractual or other remedy available to the injured party whereby he might seek compensation from the party enriched.

The *Sealand* claim also included expropriation as a cause of action, and apart from the duty to compensate, expropriation is not necessarily a breach of international law. Although there is a close relationship between causes of action founded on expropriation and unjust enrichment they

---

[37] *TCSB Inc.* v *Iran* 5 IRAN–U.S.C.T.R., 160, 172 (1984); see also *Dames and Moore* v *Iran* 4 IRAN–U.S.C.T.R., 212 (1983).
[38] *Ibid.*, 172.
[39] *Ibid.*
[40] *Ibid.*
[41] 6 IRAN–U.S.C.T.R., 149 (1984).
[42] *Ibid.*, 168. The quotation is from Francioni, *Compensation for Nationalisation of Foreign Property: The Borderland between Law and Equity*, 24 I.C.L.Q., 259, 273 (1975).
[43] *Ibid.*, 169.

have been perceived by the Tribunal as quite separate. Thus the Tribunal has awarded compensation to claimants if the respondent state has been enriched at the expense of the claimant, whether or not the respondent state has committed any act of expropriation.[44]

The case of *Futura Trading Inc.* v *Khuzestan Water and Power Authority*[45] provides an interesting insight into the role of the principle of unjust enrichment where it is not possible to prove the existence of a contract between the parties. The claimant had alleged the actual sale, delivery and acceptance of 2,000 wooden poles pursuant to a larger contract for the sale of goods. The Tribunal after evaluating the facts concluded that no contract was formed in respect of the 2,000 wooden poles. However, it was not doubted that the respondent had actually accepted delivery of the poles and had not paid for them. The Tribunal concluded that "KWPA was the party enriched"[46] and held "the invoiced amount of $542,809 to be a reasonable measure of the extent to which KWPA was enriched".[47]

The doctrine of unjust enrichment as an independent cause of action has been progressively developed by the Tribunal. The fullest exposition of the requirement for the application of the principles of unjust enrichment is found in *Schlegel Corporation* v *National Iranian Copper Industries Company*.[48] The Tribunal firstly noted that unjust enrichment does not arise where there is a binding contract, since the obligations of the parties are to be determined by reference to the contract. The Tribunal went on to consider principles of unjust enrichment. It observed that the rule against unjust enrichment represents a principle based on justice and equity and therefore makes it necessary to take into account all the circumstances of each specific situation.[49] Among the principles it noted there must be an enrichment of one party to the detriment of the other. Further, the enrichment must be sufficiently direct. The enrichment of one party and the detriment of the other "both must arise as a consequence of the same act or event".[50] The Tribunal, after examining the facts, stated directly:[51]

The Tribunal finds that the enrichment was and remains unjust. The evidence is clear that the Copper Company has never paid the balance due for Schlegel's work.

---

[44] Refer to the section, What Constitutes a Taking, in Chapter Eight on acts of state which constitute expropriation of assets and contractual rights.
[45] 9 IRAN–U.S.C.T.R., 46 (1985).
[46] *Ibid.*, 57.
[47] *Ibid.*
[48] 14 IRAN–U.S.C.T.R., 176 (1987).
[49] *Ibid.*, 181, from de Arechaga, *International Law in the Past Third of a Century*, Recueil des Cours (1978), 299–300.
[50] *Ibid.*, 182.
[51] *Ibid.*

In one of the more recent cases, *Lockheed Corporation* v *Iran*,[52] the importance of the doctrine being an independent cause of action was reaffirmed. The claimant had supplied technical support for the Iranian Air Force after the termination of the service contract. The Tribunal stated:[53]

First, as the Tribunal has held in other cases, the claimant must establish that there is no valid and enforceable contract on which an action for damages could be based. See *Dames & Moore* v *The Islamic Republic of Iran* [4 IRAN–U.S.C.T.R., 212]. In the present case, this is not in dispute. Secondly, the claimant must establish that the respondent has been enriched at the claimant's expense, the extent of such enrichment and that it would be unfair for the respondent not to pay for the benefits it has received.

The logic of the Tribunal's position is self-evident. If the doctrine of unjust enrichment was merely supplemental or derivative to contract, it could undermine the importance of the contractual bargain and the principles of contract law which serve to uphold the bargain entered into by the parties. If the parties cannot rely on the contract they have entered into, commercial relations would become very precarious. The doctrine of unjust enrichment therefore stands outside and independent of the law of contract, to be applied only where there is no contract between the parties.

The relatively limited number of cases in which the Tribunal has applied or considered the principle of unjust enrichment would appear to significantly advance the establishment of the principle of unjust enrichment as a "normative or general rule"[54] of international law. Previous international tribunals have used the principle for the subsidiary purpose of assessing compensation after liability has been established under some other cause of action. Although some tribunals have acknowledged the existence of the principle as a general rule they have not directly applied it to establish liability.[55] The Iran–United States Claims Tribunal, however, has applied the principle of unjust enrichment to determine liability in the absence of a contractual relationship between the claimant and respondent. Indeed, as has been observed, it has properly considered the principle to be inapplicable where there is a subsisting contract between the claimant and respondent.

---

[52] 18 IRAN–U.S.C.T.R., 292 (1988).
[53] *Ibid.*, 309.
[54] Schreuer, *Unjustified Enrichment in International Law*, 22 Am. J. Comp. Law, 281, 301 (1974).
[55] This was the case in *Liamco* v *Libya* 62 I.L.R., 176, 213 (1982).

CHAPTER ELEVEN

Exclusions from the jurisdiction of the Tribunal: the hostage crisis and the revolution

Introduction

The Algiers Declarations do not permit all claims made by Iranian and United States nationals to be satisfied by recourse to the Tribunal. The jurisdiction of the Tribunal is limited to claims made by nationals of either party against the government and its entities of the other party.[1] The Tribunal does not have jurisdiction to hear claims made by the nationals of one party against nationals of the other. Similarly it cannot hear claims made by the government of either party against the nationals of the other party.[2]

However, even if the claim is made by the nationals of one party against the government of the other party, the claim will fall outside the jurisdiction of the Tribunal unless it arises "out of debts, contracts (including transactions which are the subject of letters of credit or bank guarantees), expropriations or other measures affecting property...".[3]

Moreover, although a claim may fall within these categories, it may nevertheless be excluded from the jurisdiction of the Tribunal. When the Algiers Declarations were being negotiated each government required that certain claims be specifically excluded from the jurisdiction of the Tribunal. These exclusions have a greater impact on United States claimants than on Iranian claimants. There are three exclusions contained in the Algiers Declarations. The first two, dealt with in this chapter, are claims arising from actions by Iran and the United States in connection

---

[1] Article II(1) of the Claims Settlement Declaration. See Chapter Four.
[2] *Iran v United States (Case A/2)* 1 IRAN–U.S.C.T.R., 144 (1981–82).
[3] Article II(1) of the Claims Settlement Declaration. The extent of the jurisdiction of the Tribunal is covered in Chapter Six.

with the seizure of the hostages,[4] and claims arising from actions of popular movements in the course of the Iranian revolution which were not the act of the government of Iran.[5] The third category, dealt with in the next chapter, is claims arising from contracts which provided that all disputes arising therefrom should be settled in competent courts of Iran.[6]

Exclusions arising from the hostage crisis

Article II(1) of the Claims Settlement Declaration and paragraph 11 of the General Declaration contain a series of exclusions from the jurisdiction of the Tribunal for the events occurring during the Islamic revolution and the hostage crisis.

Article II(1) of the Claims Settlement Declaration incorporated the exclusions of paragraph 11 into the Declaration, stating in part:

... excluding claims described in Paragraph 11 of the Declaration of the Government of Algeria of January 14, 1981, and claims arising out of the actions of the United States in response to the conduct described in such paragraph ...

Since Article II(1) only permits claims arising out of debts, contracts, expropriations and other measures affecting property, the exclusions of paragraph 11 of the General Declaration as incorporated by Article II(1) only relate to claims brought under these heads.

The four exclusions of paragraph 11 of the General Declaration relate to events occurring during the Islamic revolution and the hostage crisis. Paragraph 11 of the General Declaration, which sets out the detail of the exclusion, required the United States to:

... thereafter bar and preclude the prosecution against Iran of any pending or future claim of the United States or a United States national arising out of the events occurring before the date of this declaration related to (A) the seizure of the 52 United States nationals on November 4, 1979, (B) their subsequent detention, (C) injury to United States property or property of the United States nationals within the United States Embassy compound in Tehran after November 3, 1979, and (D) injury to the United States nationals or their property as a result of popular movements in the course of the Islamic Revolution in Iran which were not an act of the Government of Iran. The United States will also bar and preclude the prosecution against Iran in the courts of the United States of any pending or future claim asserted by persons other than the United States nationals arising out of the events specified in the preceding sentence.

---

[4] Paragraph 11 of the General Declaration.
[5] Paragraph 11 of the General Declaration.
[6] Article II(1) of the Claims Settlement Declaration.

Article II(1) also prevents Iranian claims in respect of the United States response to these events.

The exclusions of paragraph 11 stemmed from the political imperatives of the two governments. Although the Iranian government recognised that the hostages had to be released it could not accept any legal accountability for their seizure and detention. Such accountability would have been unacceptable to the Iranian people, and any attempt by the United States to make Iran accountable would have rendered the release of the hostages impossible.

Thus the United States agreed to exclude claims arising from the events surrounding the seizure of the hostages. Furthermore, the United States agreed to withdraw all claims pending against Iran before the International Court of Justice despite the fact that the Court had ruled that the United States was entitled to compensation for the seizure of the hostages and the embassy.[7]

Similarly, Iran agreed not to pursue any claims against the United States for actions undertaken in response to the seizure of the hostages. The International Court of Justice had indicated its concern about the military operation to rescue the hostages.[8] Judges Morozov and Tarazi stated that it was a clear breach of international law. Nevertheless it would not have been acceptable to the United States to be accountable to Iran for these actions.

Paragraph 11 can be interpreted as having two parts. The first part relates specifically to the hostages, their property, and the United States embassy and is contained in exclusions (A), (B) and (C) of paragraph 11. The second part, contained in exclusion (D), relates to the actions of "popular movements in the course of the Islamic Revolution" causing loss to United States nationals. This second part covers incidents which occurred during the Islamic revolution which caused loss to United States nationals, excluding the hostages. It should be noted, however, that there is an alternative interpretation of exclusion (D) which limits its application to loss occasioned by the hostages arising from popular movements. This interpretation relies on the inclusion of the word "the" in the phrase "injury to the United States nationals" of exclusion (D) thereby limiting the exclusion to "*the* 52 United States nationals" and "*their* property" as described in exclusions (A) and (B) of paragraph 11.[9]

The Tribunal has thus far dealt with one claim arising from these events. In *Haji-Bagherpour* v *Government of the United States*[10] the claimant sought the recovery of $428,571 as compensation for the destruction of his tanker truck by United States military personnel. The vehicle was

---
[7] Paragraph 11 of the General Declaration.
[8] *Diplomatic Staff in Tehran (United States* v *Iran)* I.C.J. Rep., 3 (1980).
[9] *Grimm* v *Iran* 2 IRAN–U.S.C.T.R., 78 (1983); Dissenting Opinion of Mr Holtzmann.

destroyed on 24 April 1980 in the Iranian desert by United States forces engaged in the abortive rescue mission. The claim was heard in Chamber Two, and in a unanimous decision the Tribunal held the claim was excluded from its jurisdiction:[11]

> The damage suffered by the Claimant occurred because he chanced to come upon the staging area for the rescue operation while the American forces were there. They would not have been there and would not have destroyed his truck if the 52 United States nationals had not been seized and detained. The cause and effect relation is clear. There may be cases where the Tribunal will face difficult questions in interpreting the exclusionary clause in Article II, paragraph 1, of the Claims Settlement Declaration but about the present case there can be no doubt.

Therefore the Tribunal held that this claim was excluded from its jurisdiction as a claim arising out of actions of the United States in response to the conduct described in paragraph 11 of the General Declaration.

The Tribunal has not had to deal with any claims from United States nationals arising directly from the events surrounding the seizure of the hostages. A number of the hostages, however, did make claims against the Iranian government in various United States district courts.

These courts have held that the hostages are barred from making claims against Iran. The implementation of the relevant provisions of the Declarations into United States domestic law by executive order, subsequently approved by the Supreme Court, allowed the district courts to exclude such claims by reference to the executive orders.[12] Furthermore, the doctrine of sovereign immunity, even in its narrowest application under the Foreign Sovereign Immunities Act, 1976, should have precluded the successful prosecution of claims against Iran by hostages.

Thus those individuals, whether of Iranian or of United States nationality, who suffered loss arising directly from the events surrounding the hostage crisis are prevented from making claims against the government causing the loss, either in the Tribunal or in the domestic courts of either nation. The only compensation that they could receive would be from their own government. The hostages have received compensation from the commission established by executive order of the United States President.[13]

Popular movements in the course of the Islamic revolution

The Algiers Declarations

Paragraph 11 of the General Declaration, as incorporated by Article II(1) of the Claims Settlement Declaration, also contained an exclusion from

[10] 2 IRAN–U.S.C.T.R., 38 (1983).
[11] Ibid.
[12] Executive Order No. 12282.
[13] Executive Order No. 12285.

the jurisdiction of the Tribunal for any loss caused to the United States nationals or their property arising from popular movements in the course of the Islamic revolution in Iran which were not an act of the government of Iran.

As noted in "Exclusions Arising from the Hostage Crisis", Iran has argued that although the first three exclusions contained in paragraph 11 of the General Declaration relate to events surrounding the hostage crisis, the fourth exception is general and covers all the actions of popular movements in the course of the Islamic revolution causing loss to any United States nationals.[14] It has been stated by Mr Holtzmann that the fourth exclusion relates only to injury to the fifty-two United States nationals held hostage, or their property, and does not exempt the Iranian government from liability for loss of contractual or property rights of other United States nationals caused by popular movements in the course of the Islamic revolution.[15]

International law relating to revolutionary movements and the interpretation of the Algiers Declarations

Actions of revolutionaries

The discussion in Chapter Six on state responsibility notes that it is an accepted tenet of international law that states must act in a manner sufficient to protect the lives and property of aliens.[16] The standard that must be achieved in providing such protection is established by international law. Thus a state is required to provide sufficient guarantees as are generally considered indispensable for the proper administration of justice. While an alien submits himself to the law of the host state with regard to his property and person, the law of the alien state must provide for the minimum standard of treatment prescribed by international law, and it must be administered without discrimination against aliens of particular states.

These requirements of international law may be supplemented by bilateral treaty between the host state and the state of the alien. In the present case the Treaty of Amity between Iran and the United States sets out the two states' responsibilities.[17] The Treaty required Iran to provide "the most constant protection and security" to the lives and property of United States nationals in Iran in accordance with international law.[18]

[14] *Grimm* v *Government of the Islamic Republic of Iran* 2 IRAN–U.S.C.T.R., 78 (1983).
[15] *Ibid*. Refer to Dissenting Opinion of Mr Holtzmann.
[16] Refer to the discussion and citations on State Responsibility in Chapter Six.
[17] The International Court of Justice held that the Treaty of Amity remained in force between Iran and the United States; *Diplomatic Staff in Tehran (United States* v *Iran)* I.C.J. Rep., 3 (1980).
[18] Articles II(4) and IV(2) of the Treaty of Amity.

Accordingly, the Iran–United States Claims Tribunal, in relation to claims involving state responsibility, must apply the standard established by international law.

It is a general rule of state responsibility that liability attaches only to the acts or omissions of governments or governmental officials which cause loss to aliens.[19] However, successor governments are liable for the actions of predecessor governments, even if the succeeding government has overthrown the former by revolution. Furthermore, a government installed by revolution is liable for the actions of the revolutionaries prior to the success of the revolution. State responsibility, however, does not attach to the actions of private individuals or groups of individuals unless the government adopts the actions as its own.[20] The International Court of Justice accepted that the seizure of the United States embassy and nationals was not an action of the Iranian government, yet the government incurred responsibility once it adopted the actions of the Islamic militants.[21]

The development of the law in this area is largely based on the arbitrations following successive revolutions in Latin American states. The decision of the United States–Venezuela Mixed Claims Commission in the *Dix* case[22] is illustrative. The revolutionary army seized the claimant's cattle. The Commissioner noted:[23]

The revolution of 1899 led by General Cirpiano Castro proved successful, and its acts, under a well established rule of international law, are to be regarded as the acts of a *de facto* government.

This reasoning was applied in the *Henry* case,[24] although the Umpire noted that:[25]

[T]he interruption of the ordinary course of business is an invariable and inevitable result of a state of war under which all the inhabitants, whether citizens or aliens, have to suffer; and whereas losses incurred by reason of such interruption are not subject to compensation by the Government within whose territory the war exists.

---

[19] Refer to Draft Articles 5 to 15 of the *I.L.C. Draft Convention on State Responsibility*, in *Report of the I.L.C.*, in *Yearbook of the I.L.C.* (1980) II, Part II, 31. See also Amerasinghe, *State Responsibility for Injuries to Aliens*, 37–8, 49, 53–4 (1967); Eagleton, *Responsibility of States in International Law*, 77 (1928); Brownlie, *Principles of Public International Law*, 446 (1990).

[20] Brownlie, *Principles of Public International Law*, 452–3 (1990). Brownlie makes specific reference to the ruling of the I.C.J. in the case *Diplomatic Staff in Tehran (United States v Iran)* I.C.J. Rep., 3 (1980). See also Eagleton, *Responsibility of States in International Law*, 77 (1928); Dunn, *The Protection of Nationals*, 136 (1932); Brownlie, *System of the Law of Nations: State Responsibility*, 159–61 (1983).

[21] *Diplomatic Staff in Tehran (United States v Iran)* I.C.J. Rep., 3 (1980).

[22] IX R.I.A.A., 119 (1903).

[23] *Ibid.*, 120.

[24] *Ibid.*, 125.

[25] *Ibid.*, 136.

The acceptance by aliens of such risks was also noted by Sir Henry Strong in the *Rosa Gelbtrunk* claim[26] of the United States–Salvador Claims Arbitration. The claimant had suffered loss from spontaneous looting by revolutionary soldiers without the authority of their officer. Sir Henry Strong stated:[27]

A citizen or subject of one nation who, in pursuit of commercial enterprise, carries on trade within the territory and under the protection of the sovereignty of a nation other than his own is to be considered as having cast his lot with the subjects or citizens of the State in which he resides and carries on business . . . The State to which he owes national allegiance has no right to claim for him as against the nation in which he is resident any other or different treatment in case of loss by war—either foreign or civil—revolution, insurrection, or other internal disturbance caused by organised military forces or by soldiers, than that which the latter country metes out to its own subjects or citizens.

The Mexican Claims Commissions also considered the position of revolutionaries.[28] These commissions have been a major source of precedent to the Iran–United States Claims Tribunal. The Conventions establishing the various commissions contained exclusions from liability for the actions of mutineers, mobs, insurrectionary forces and bandits, other than governmental forces or revolutionary forces opposed to them, unless it could be shown that the government had failed to take reasonable measures to quell them or had treated them leniently.[29]

---

[26] XV R.I.A.A., 454 (1902).

[27] *Ibid.*, 464.

[28] As noted in Chapter One of this work Western states have settled numerous claims with revolutionary states. The usual procedure is for the revolutionary state to make a lump sum payment for all claims. The beneficiary state distributes these sums to the various claimants for which the state has assumed responsibility. Communist governments have particularly used this means of settling claims. Large corporations dealing with Third World states usually provide for binding third party arbitration in their concession and development contracts.

The use of Mixed Claims Tribunals to settle all claims is confined to those instances where the claimant state has some advantage over the other party. Thus, they were established following World War II to settle Allied claims against the Axis powers. The Mexican Claims Commissions were established as a price for the recognition of the government of Mexico. The Iranian government was under similar pressure in relation to United States financial and trade measures.

For a comprehensive review of the Mexican Claims Commissions see A. H. Feller, *The Mexican Claims Commissions* (1935). In view of the lack of more recent precedents the parties and arbitrators in the Iran–United States Claims Tribunal have relied heavily on the decisions of the various Mexican Claims Commissions.

[29] Article III of the United States-Mexican Special Claims Commission stated: "The claims which the Commission shall examine and decide are those which arose during the revolutions and disturbed conditions which existed in Mexico covering the period from November 20, 1910 to May 31, 1920 inclusive, and which were due to any act by the following forces: (1) By forces of a Government *de jure* or *de facto*. (2) By revolutionary forces as a result of the triumph of whose cause governments *de facto* or *de jure* have been established, or by revolutionary forces opposed to them. (3) By forces arising from the

In *Howard (Great Britain v Mexico)*[30] the commissioner awarded damages where "the original seizure of the house of Julon Real was undoubtedly an act committed by a Revolutionary force covered by the Convention, as the said leader was known to have served the cause which afterwards established the Constitutionalist Government".[31] Similarly, the President of the French–Mexican Claims Commission stated in the *Pinson* case[32] that where injury was caused "by offences committed by successful revolutionary forces, the responsibility of the State, in my opinion, cannot be denied".[33]

Nevertheless, aliens are subject to the same risks from war as citizens. In *Lynch (Great Britain v Mexico)*[34] the British–Mexican Claims Commission held that the occupation of a house by government forces, which resulted in its destruction during and after battle, was a lawful act and thus no liability was incurred.

Since these claims commissions, governments have continued to hold that a government installed by revolution is responsible for damage caused by the revolutionaries prior to the success of the revolution.

The proposition that a government installed by revolution is responsible for the acts of the revolutionaries prior to the success of the revolution has been widely accepted by the leading jurists of the twentieth century, both during the early part of the century and in more recent times.[35] The International Law Commission, during its first attempt at codification of the law of state responsibility in the 1950s and early 1960s by Amador and the second attempt by Ago and Riphagen, has specifically recognised the responsibility of revolutionary governments for the acts of revolutionaries prior to their success.[36]

---

disjunction of the forces mentioned in the next preceding paragraph up to the time when the government *de jure* established itself as a result of a particular revolution. (4) By federal forces that were disbanded, and (5) By mutinies or mobs, or insurrectionary forces other than those referred to under subdivisions (2), (3) and (4) above, or by bandits, provided in any case it be established that the appropriate authorities omitted to take reasonable measures to suppress insurrectionists, mobs or bandits, or treated them with leniency or were in fault in other particulars."

[30] V R.I.A.A., 232 (1928).
[31] *Ibid.*
[32] *Ibid.*, 354.
[33] *Ibid.* The original in French is translated by Special Rapporteur Ago in *Report of the I.L.C.*, Yearbook of the I.L.C. (1972) II, 147.
[34] V R.I.A.A., 175.
[35] Borchard, *The Diplomatic Protection of Citizens Abroad*, 213 (1928); Briggs, *The Law of Nations*, 713–20 (1952); Brownlie, *Principles of Public International Law*, 452–3 (1990); Eagleton, *Responsibility of States in International law*, 125–6 (1928); Greig, *International Law*, 138 (1976); Schwarzenberger, *International Law: International Courts*, I, 628 (1957); O'Connell, *International Law*, II, 968 (1970). O'Connell considered that successful revolutionaries are also responsible for their actions where they are "mere mobs".
[36] See especially Draft Article 15 of the I.L.C. Convention on State Responsibility, in *Report of the I.L.C.*, in *Yearbook of the I.L.C.* (1980) II, Part II, 31, originally drafted by

Actions of private individuals

Whilst a revolutionary government may be responsible for the actions of the revolutionaries, it is not responsible for the actions of private individuals during the revolutionary unrest, even though the actions may have been inspired by revolutionary fervour, or committed by revolutionary soldiers acting in a private capacity.[37]

International responsibility will only arise if the actions of such persons are adopted by the government as its own, or if the government fails to act to prevent or punish the offenders. This view has been consistently adhered to by international tribunals of the late nineteenth and early twentieth centuries. The *Sambiaggio* case[38] in the Italian–Venezuelan Mixed Claims Commission clearly states the position. Arbitrator Ralston noted:[39]

> Governments are responsible, as a general principle, for the acts of those they control. But the very existence of a flagrant revolution presupposes that a certain set of men have gone temporarily or permanently beyond the power of the authorities; and unless it clearly appears that the government has failed to use promptly and with appropriate force its constituted authority, it cannot be reasonably said that it should be responsible for a condition of affairs created without its volition.

The corollary of non-responsibility of the government for losses caused to aliens is non-responsibility for damage caused by demonstrators or rioters in support of and by sympathisers of successful revolutionaries. Unless the actions of the "mob" can be attributed to the revolutionary government there is no responsibility on the part of the government. The law in this area owes a great deal to the work of the various Mexican Claims Commissions established in the 1920s to settle the claims of various Western states following the revolutionary upheaval in Mexico from 1910 to 1920.

The Mexican revolutionary period was characterised by several competing revolutionary forces and shifting alliances of revolutionary forces.

Special Rapporteur Ago; see *Yearbook of the I.L.C.* (1972) II, 71, 152. For commentary see *Yearbook of the I.L.C.* (1972) II, 144–51. See also *Draft Convention on International Responsibility for Injuries to Aliens*, reported in 55 A.J.I.L., 545 (1961). This Draft Convention was submitted to the I.L.C. for its consideration. For a fuller account of the work by the International Law Commission on a Draft Convention on State Responsibility see Chapter Six, note 13.

[37] See Draft Article 11 of the I.L.C. Convention on State Responsibility, in *Report of the I.L.C.*, *Yearbook of the I.L.C.* (1980) II, Part II, 31; originally drafted by Special Rapporteur Ago, see *Yearbook of the I.L.C.* (1972) II, 71, 152. The most important and most widely cited judicial precedents are *British Property in Spanish Morocco (Britain v Spain)* II R.I.A.A., 636 (1925) and *Janes Case (United States v Mexico)* IV R.I.A.A., 86 (1925). Special Rapporteur Ago also referred to recent diplomatic practice which confirmed the principle of non-responsibility for acts of private individuals.

[38] X R.I.A.A., 499 (1903).

[39] *Ibid.*, 513.

Hence there were several successive revolutionary governments, both *de facto* and *de jure*, and continual opposition to these governments by competing revolutionary forces. Furthermore, there was mob violence and banditry throughout the revolutionary period which had a greater or lesser degree of political motivation. The claims heard by the commissions encompassed the different categories of revolutionary activity. Although the majority of the cases related to personal injury the principles that can be derived from these cases are applicable to contractual and property claims arising from revolutionary actions causing loss.

In the *Santa Isabel* cases[40] a number of United States mining engineers were killed by a group of armed men from the forces commanded by Pancho Villa. The United States–Mexican Special Claims Commission accepted the Mexican contention that at the time the murders took place the Pancho Villa forces were no longer revolutionary forces opposed to the government but were merely bandits despite the fact that Villa was seeking recognition as head of a *de facto* government.[41] Since the Pancho Villa forces were characterised as bandits, Mexico was not liable unless it could be shown that the government had failed to act properly to protect foreign nationals.

The British–Mexican Claims Commission also considered the status of the Pancho Villa forces and came to a different view.[42] It recognised that even if by 1916 they could no longer be regarded as revolutionary forces they nevertheless had political aims. Moreover, there was an agreement in 1920 granting a general amnesty to the Villa forces. This amounted to lenient treatment within the terms of the convention and thus rendered Mexico liable for acts of banditry and wanton murder committed by the Villa forces without regard to political or military necessity.

There were several claims for property losses arising from mob violence. In the case of *William Russell*, the British–Mexican Claims Commission rejected a claim for injuries resulting from the sacking of a factory by violent demonstrators.[43] The demonstration was not a revolutionary act, or a mutiny, banditry or an insurrection directed against the government. It was a "popular demonstration" directed against foreigners. Under the convention the government was not liable for the loss caused by the demonstrators. Similarly, the Italian–Mexican Commission stated that under general international law Mexico was not liable for acts of mob violence, when rioters had sacked the claimant's shop.[44]

---

[40] From Feller, *Mexican Claims Commissions 1923–1934* (1935).

[41] *Ibid.*, p. 64 of Opinion.

[42] *Buena Tiena Mining Co. Ltd* from Feller, *Mexican Claims Commission 1923–1934* (1935).

[43] Case of *William J. Russell* from Feller, *Mexican Claims Commission 1923–1934* (1935).

[44] Case of *Rafael Ferringo*, Decision No. 10 (unpublished) from Feller, *Mexican Claims Commission*, 170 (1935).

The exclusions for revolutionary actions were more closely defined in the various Mexican claims conventions than in the Claims Settlement Declaration between Iran and the United States. This is due, in part, to the different nature of the revolutionary situations, and also to the circumstances in which the Claims Settlement Declaration was negotiated. Nevertheless, the exclusion for the actions of popular movements of the Algiers Declaration has the same purpose as those of the Mexican Claims Conventions. It specifies in detail the rule of international law relating to state responsibility that Iran will not be responsible for the actions of individuals or groups of individuals unless they had some form of official sanction, either by instigation or by adoption.[45]

The leading publicists have also endorsed the reasoning of the arbitral decisions.[46] Thus liability will arise where the government adopts or encourages the actions of private individuals or groups of individuals, as with the seizure of the United States embassy by Islamic militants. Similarly, liability will be incurred if the government fails to exercise sufficient diligence to protect aliens and their property from the acts of mobs, rioters or individual assailants.

Perhaps the most authoritative work has been that of the International Law Commission.[47] Special Rapporteur Ago, in his fourth report on state responsibility, suggested two draft articles concerning the responsibility for the actions of private individuals or groups of individuals,[48] and for the retroactive attribution to states for the acts of organs of successful revolutionary movements.[49] Although the ILC has not yet submitted a completed draft convention, these two articles, with some modification, have been accepted for inclusion into the proposed draft convention,[50] and must be seen as embodying customary international law. The two draft articles accurately reflect customary international law expressed in the decisions of arbitral tribunals.

---

[45] This is the underlying purpose of Clause D, irrespective of whether the Iranian or the United States arguments as to its scope are accepted. These are set out in *Grimm v Iran* 2 IRAN–U.S.C.T.R., 78 (1983).

[46] Arias, *The Non-liability of States for Damages Suffered by Foreigners in the Course of a Riot, an Insurrection, or a Civil War*, 7 A.J.I.L., 724 (1913); Borchard, *The Diplomatic Protection of Citizens Abroad*, 217 (1928); Briggs, *The Law of Nations*, 697–713 (1952). Briggs particularly notes the responsibility of governments where they fail to provide sufficient protection from the actions of mobs; see also Brownlie, *Principles of Public International Law*, 452–3 (1990); Eagleton, *Responsibility of States in International Law*, 76–94 (1928); Greig, *International Law*, 574 (1976); O'Connell, *International Law*, 1048–56 (1965); Schwarzenberger, *International Law*, 634–6 (1957).

[47] See notes 36 and 37 *supra* for the appropriate references to the work of the I.L.C.

[48] Draft Article 11, *Yearbook of the I.L.C.* (1972) II, 126.

[49] Draft Article, 13, *Yearbook of the I.L.C.* (1972) II, 151.

[50] See Report of the Commission in *Yearbook of the I.L.C.* (1980) II, Part II, 31, for the Draft Articles ultimately adopted by the Commission. The articles have been adopted as Draft Articles 11 and 15.

The interpretation of the Algiers Declarations

The Iranian understanding of exclusion (D) of paragraph 11 is that it is intended to apply to all actions of the Islamic militants affecting all United States nationals. It is submitted that the interpretation of the provisions of the General Declaration and the Claims Settlement Declaration to exclude liability for actions of "popular movements" unless those actions are attributable to the government, either by instigation or adoption, would reflect, in large measure, existing international law. Even if Mr Holtzmann's interpretation of the effect of Clause (D) of paragraph 11 is accepted,[51] the principles of general international law as outlined above are sufficient to exclude the liability of Iran for the actions of "popular movements" unless the actions are instigated or adopted by the government of Iran, or if the actions of the popular movements can be considered in reality to be actions of revolutionaries prior to the successful installation of the Islamic government composed of the revolutionaries. In addition the Islamic government will be responsible, as a successor government, if the Imperial government failed to meet its obligations in providing proper protection for aliens from the depredations of the Islamic militants.

The awards of the Tribunal

Thus far the Tribunal has not been required to directly consider the scope of the exclusion, although it has made reference to the exclusion and to the issue of state responsibility for the actions of revolutionaries.

The Iranian government raised the defence in *Grimm* v *Government of the Islamic Republic of Iran*.[52] The claim was brought by Mrs Grimm for damage suffered as a result of the assassination of her husband in Iran in December 1978, prior to the fall of the Shah. Mr Grimm was the managing director of the Oil Service Company of Iran (OSCO). The claim was based on the words of Article II(1), "other measures affecting property rights". Mrs Grimm contended that the loss of financial support from her husband was the loss of a property right.

This was disputed by the respondent, and the Tribunal, in a majority judgment, noted:[53]

Respondent contended that the Tribunal had no jurisdiction over the claim essentially for two reasons. Firstly, Respondent argued that the claim arose out of events related to "injury to the United States nationals or their property as a result of popular movements in the course of the Islamic Revolution in Iran".

---

[51] See *Grimm* v *Iran* 2 IRAN–U.S.C.T.R., 78 (1983), Dissenting Opinion of Mr Holtzmann.
[52] 2 IRAN–U.S.C.T.R., 78 (1983).
[53] *Ibid.*, 78.

Consequently, the claim was excluded from the Tribunal's jurisdiction under paragraph 11 of the Algeria Declaration of 19 January 1981 and Article II, paragraph 1, of the Claims Settlement Declaration. Secondly, Respondent also argued that the claim did not arise from "debts, contracts, expropriations or other measures affecting property rights" as required in Article II, paragraph 1, of the Claims Settlement Declaration.

The Tribunal dealt only with the second defence and found that damage suffered by persons was a separate category from damage to property, and was not covered by the Claims Settlement Declaration. Once the claim was excluded on this ground the Tribunal did not consider that it was necessary to examine the validity of the defence of paragraph 11 of the General Declaration.

Mr Holtzmann wrote a dissenting opinion in which he considered the scope of the exclusion.[54] He found as an initial premise that Mrs Grimm was entitled to compensation, since the loss of the support of her husband was a property right and therefore covered by Article II(1) of the Claims Settlement Declaration. He was therefore required to determine whether the jurisdiction of the Tribunal would nevertheless be ousted by the exclusion. He found that the exclusion referred to in paragraph 11 of the General Declaration related only to the fifty-two hostages, stating:[55]

Clause (D), read in context, relates only to "*the* United States nationals" who constituted the 52 persons seized on November 4, 1979 and to "*their*" property. Otherwise there would be no meaning for the word "*the*".

Thus he found that the exclusion in paragraph 11 of the General Declaration had no bearing upon the jurisdiction of the Tribunal over the claim by Mrs Grimm.

Mr Holtzmann then considered the wider issue of state responsibility under general international law. He stated:[56]

Moreover, the present Government of Iran is, in my view, responsible for acts in furtherance of the achievement of the goals of the Islamic Revolution. In this case, Mrs Grimm's claim arose out of the alleged assassination by revolutionary forces of her husband, then the most important non-Iranian involved in oilfield operations, in order to further frustrate those operations as a means of achieving the success of the Revolution. By late 1978, in fact, that success was not far away. The assassination of Paul Grimm on December 23, 1978 had a tangible impact on the expatriate community, in leading to a further exodus of companies and personnel ... the acts of the revolutionaries became "attributable to the State in which the group established itself as the government", that is, the new Islamic Republic of Iran.

[54] *Ibid.*, 81.
[55] *Ibid.*, 88.
[56] *Ibid.*, 88–9.

Mr Holtzmann apparently accepted that Mr Grimm's death was occasioned by revolutionaries connected with the new government, for, unless they were associated with the new government, Iran would not be liable. Iran had argued that the assassination resulted from the actions of popular movements in the course of the Islamic revolution which were not an act of the state. Although Iran's defence rested on paragraph 11 of the General Declaration it is also applicable under general international law.

The case of *Sealand Services Inc.* v *Iran*[57] also considered the liability of Iran for loss caused by actions of Islamic militants. Sealand had entered into an arrangement with Ports and Shipping Organisation (PSO) to construct and operate a container cargo facility. Among other matters, it was agreed that Sealand would receive preferential customs, pilotage and berthing services to expedite the turn-round of ships. During the period of upheaval from September 1978 to February 1979 the provision of these services was subject to protracted delays, along with other interference so that the facility was effectively unworkable by December 1978. In respect of the liability of Iran for these actions, the Tribunal noted:[58]

In the Tribunal's view all this tends to indicate a state of upheaval in PSO's internal management which is consistent with the general picture of disruption which characterised Iran in the months leading up to the success of the revolution. It does not suggest that PSO had embarked upon a policy of deliberate disruption or noncooperation directed at Sea–Land in particular. There is no evidence to suggest other carriers fared any better. The difference lies in the fact that the nature of Sea–Land's operation rendered it peculiarly vulnerable to disruption as it depended so totally on the speed and expedition with which PSO had hitherto been able to clear the incoming vessels.

With regard to disruptive actions after the success of the revolution in February 1979, the Tribunal noted:[59]

[T]he state of administrative chaos which prevailed in Iran throughout the first few months of 1979 make it unsafe to attribute any such ostensibly governmental acts to the revolutionary government that subsequently came to power.

The Tribunal therefore concluded:[60]

A claim founded substantially on omission and inaction in a situation where the evidence suggests a widespread and indiscriminate deterioration in management, disrupting the functioning of the port of Bandar Abbas, can hardly justify a finding of expropriation.

[57] 6 IRAN–U.S.C.T.R., 149 (1984).
[58] *Ibid.*, 165.
[59] *Ibid.*, 166.
[60] *Ibid.*, 166.

The hostage crisis and the revolution

Mr Holtzmann, in his dissenting opinion, tended to minimise the effect of the revolutionary disruption and concentrated on the acts and omission of officials of PSO and the local Labour Office, whether authorised or not. Thus he stated in respect of PSO:[61]

> PSO is an Agency of the Government of Iran, and the Government pursued its policies through PSO when contracting with Sea–Land. When the Government changed, its policies changed, and the Government acted not only through PSO but through other agencies to deprive Sea–Land of the benefits of its earlier bargain.

Similarly, with regard to the actions of the Iranian Labour Office, Mr Holtzmann observed:[62]

> There is absolutely nothing in this history to justify the cutting off of responsibility for Government officials acting during the period of February to August 1979. This is particularly true in the absence of any report by Respondents that Sea–Land's complaints were even investigated or that the actions of the labour officials were ever disavowed or countermanded.

Thus Mr Holtzmann was of the clear view that so long as the loss was occasioned by officials, even during the revolution, state responsibility would arise. This approach is consistent with international law, since allowing officials to avoid responsibility for actions ostensibly within their authority committed during a revolution in accordance with the dictates of the revolution would allow revolutionary governments to avoid responsibility for their actions. Moreover, paragraph 11(D) was not intended to apply to the actions of revolutionaries, but rather to the actions of private individuals or groups of individuals caught up in the revolutionary fervour, whose actions may have promoted the installation of the Islamic government, but which were not directed or instigated by the revolutionaries.[63]

In 1987 the Tribunal made a number of awards in respect of claims of less than $250,000. In each case the claimants alleged they had suffered property loss arising from anti-American sentiment at the time of the revolution and from the actions of Islamic militants and Revolutionary Guards.

The three Chambers of the Tribunal have taken a similar approach in these claims, each referring to the decisions of the other Chambers. The award of Chamber One in *Kenneth Yeager* v *Islamic Republic of Iran*[64]

---

[61] *Ibid.*, 200.
[62] *Ibid.*, 201.
[63] If the actions are subsequently adopted by the government it will incur international responsibility, cf. *Diplomatic Staff in Tehran (United States* v *Iran)* I.C.J. Rep., 3 (1980).
[64] 17 IRAN–U.S.C.T.R, 92 (1987). The other relevant awards are *Jack Rankin* v *Islamic Republic of Iran* 17 IRAN–U.S.C.T.R., 135 (1987) by Chamber Two and *Alfred Short* v *Islamic Republic of Iran* 16 IRAN–U.S.C.T.R., 76 (1987) by Chamber Three with a dissenting opinion by Judge Brower, the United States arbitrator.

is illustrative of the decisions. The claimant alleged that, beginning in October 1978, he was harassed by "militant mobs" and was frequently threatened in the streets. In February 1978, after the success of the revolution, he was visited by Revolutionary Guards and forced to leave his apartment. He was taken to the Hilton Hotel, which was controlled by Revolutionary Guards, and was eventually taken to the airport to be evacuated from Iran. He was forced to leave property at his apartment, had money seized from him by Revolutionary Guards at the airport, and his job was terminated by his employer, a United States aerospace firm.

The claimant alleged that the losses were caused by Revolutionary Guards and Islamic militants acting on behalf of the leaders of the revolution, who became the Islamic government. Iran denied responsibility for the actions of the Guards. It also argued that that paragraph 11(D) of the General Declaration absolved it from liability.

The Tribunal accepted that the claim related to property rights.[65] The key issue was whether the acts were attributable to the state. If the acts were the responsibility of Iran then paragraph 11(D) of the General Declaration "does not effectively restrict the Tribunal's jurisdiction"[66] over claims where the acts are attributable to the government. In considering the role of the Revolutionary Guards in the revolution and in the Islamic government the Tribunal concluded "that there were identifiable groups associated with the new government that, in fact, acted for Iran immediately after the victory of the Revolution".[67] The Tribunal set out the extent of the rules of attribution under customary international law:[68]

It is generally accepted in international law that a State is also responsible for acts of persons, if it is established that those persons were in fact acting on behalf of the State. *See* ILC—Draft Article 8(a).

An act is attributable even if a person or a group of persons was in fact merely exercising elements of governmental authority in the absence of the official authorities and in circumstances which justified the exercise of those elements of authority. *See* ILC—Draft Article 8(b).

The Tribunal accepted that the Revolutionary Guards were acting on behalf of the new government and that the new government stood behind them. Iran was liable for their actions to the extent that the Guards exercised elements of government authority if such actions were a breach

---

[65] The Tribunal contrasted the claim with *Grimm* v *Islamic Republic of Iran* 2 IRAN–U.S.C.T.R., 78 (1983), which it considered was a claim arising from personal injury.
[66] 17 IRAN–U.S.C.T.R., 92, 101 (1987).
[67] *Ibid.*, 102. The Tribunal discussed the nature of the revolution and the revolutionary movement in detail, noting the organisation of the revolutionary committees and the Revolutionary Guards.
[68] *Ibid.*, 103.

of international law.[69] The failure of the Guards to allow the claimant time to secure his property and the seizure of the money by the Guards were breaches of customary international law causing property loss. Accordingly Iran was liable to compensate the claimant for the loss.

Commentary on the scope of the exclusions

The revolution in Iran was not the result of armed rebellion by a defined group of revolutionaries who subsequently formed the new government. Rather it was a mass revolution involving many different groups with an Islamic focal point. Although the new government was installed as a result of this revolutionary activity, much of the activity, both before and after the change of government, was neither directed nor controlled by members of the Islamic government.

In respect of acts of revolutionary groups committed prior to the change of government, under general international law Iran is only liable if members of the government instigated, adopted or encouraged such acts. International responsibility is not incurred for illegal acts which promote the revolution unless members of the revolutionary government know of it in advance, or subsequently approve the acts. However, if the Iranian government treated the perpetrators of such acts leniently, Iran would incur international responsibility. Thus, claimants must be able to point to some act or omission on the part of the government before an act is removed from the private realm and becomes an act for which Iran incurs international responsibility.

Furthermore, the Islamic Republic of Iran will only be liable for the acts or omissions of the Imperial government if it can be shown that the Imperial government failed to meet the proper standard in protecting United States nationals and their property. It is not enough for claimants merely to show that loss occurred.

The position concerning acts committed after the change of government is much simpler. Iran is liable if the government directed and controlled the actions of the revolutionaries which caused loss. Where the government subsequently adopted the actions of the popular movements it will be liable for their acts and omissions. The International Court of Justice held Iran responsible for the actions of Islamic militants in light of the later endorsement and inaction by the Iranian government.[70] However, if the Iranian government acted in accordance with the minimum standards prescribed by international law to protect the lives and property

[69] *Ibid.*, 105.
[70] I.C.J. Rep., 3 (1980).

of United States nationals, it will not be liable for the actions of the popular movements which are not acts of the government.

Iran is entitled to rely on these principles of international law, even if Mr Holtzmann is correct in his assertion that the exclusion in paragraph 11(D) of the General Declaration relates only to the fifty-two hostages and not to all United States nationals.

Should the Tribunal accept Mr Holtzmann's view, set out in his dissenting opinion in the *Grimm* case, then the exclusion of the actions of popular movements provides Iran with no greater protection from liability than the exclusions contained in paragraph 11(A) to (C). The first three exclusions covered all possible losses that could be sustained by the hostages. The exclusion in paragraph 11(D) of the actions of popular movements therefore acquires meaning only if it relates to losses incurred by any United States nationals in the course of the Islamic revolution. It would, however, merely confirm customary international law that Iran is not liable for the losses occasioned by any United States nationals caused by popular movements in the course of the Islamic revolution which were not acts of government even though these acts may have materially contributed to the success of the revolution, and from which the present Iranian government gained benefit.

CHAPTER TWELVE

Exclusions from the jurisdiction of the Tribunal: contracts providing for disputes to be settled in competent Iranian courts

Introduction

The jurisdiction of the Tribunal to hear private claims arising out of contract is established by Article II(1) of the Claims Settlement Declaration. However, Article II(1) contains limitations to this jurisdiction in the following terms:

... excluding claims arising under a binding contract between parties specifically providing that any disputes thereunder shall be within the sole jurisdiction of the competent Iranian courts, in response to the Majlis position.

The Tribunal has made a number of decisions in respect of both aspects of this exclusion. The application of the forum selection provision was determined by the full Tribunal and the meaning of the words "in response to the Majlis position" has been separately considered by Chamber Two of the Tribunal.

The forum selection exclusion decisions

A large number of the claimants had contracts with the Iranian government, or government-controlled entities, that included choice of law and choice of forum provisions. In all cases where these clauses contained any reference to the Iranian legal process, even if the connection was as remote as execution of the contract in Iran, the respondent challenged the jurisdiction of the Tribunal.

The respondent stated that in all such cases the provisions of Article II(1) excluded the jurisdiction of the Tribunal. It should be noted, however, that the forum selection issue only arises where the contract has an express provision relating to Iranian jurisdiction. If the contract is silent on the matter, even if it is impliedly subject to Iranian jurisdiction, the issue does not arise.[1]

The Tribunal determined that it would consider this jurisdictional question in a preliminary hearing. In doing so it was acting in accordance with Article 21(4) of the provisionally adopted Tribunal rules, which required the Tribunal to determine matters concerning its jurisdiction as a preliminary question.

In view of the importance of this jurisdictional issue the three Chambers relinquished to the full Tribunal nine separate claims involving nineteen different forum selection clauses so that the Tribunal could determine the application of the exclusion to a representative range of the forum selection clauses.[2] The findings of the Tribunal could then be applied to the large number of other claims where the same issues of forum selection arose.

The Tribunal came to majority decisions in respect of all nineteen forum selection clauses covered by the nine claims, holding that the proviso of Article II(1) did not exclude its jurisdiction in respect of thirteen of the clauses, but that its jurisdiction was excluded by six clauses. The three Iranian arbitrators held that the jurisdiction of the Tribunal was excluded in all nineteen clauses and two of the United States arbitrators, Messrs Holtzmann and Mosk, both of whom wrote separate dissenting opinions, held that the jurisdiction of the Tribunal was not excluded by any of the clauses. Two of the neutral arbitrators, Messrs Bellet and Mangard, and the United States arbitrator, Mr Aldrich, voted with the majority in respect of all nineteen clauses. The President, Judge Lagergren, joined with the three Iranian arbitrators and filed separate dissents in respect of two clauses.[3]

The Tribunal handed down separate decisions for each of the nine claims. The decisions are noteworthy for the lack of legal authority cited in support of the findings.[4]

---

[1] This issue was raised in the preliminary hearing but has not come up in subseqent awards of the Tribunal.

[2] *Dresser Industries Inc. v Iran and NIOC* 1 IRAN–U.S.C.T.R., 280 (1981–82); *Ford Aerospace Communications Corp. v Air Force of Iran* 1 IRAN–U.S.C.T.R., 268 (1981–82); *Gibbs & Hill Inc. v Iran Power Generation and Transmission Company (TAVANIR)* 1 IRAN–U.S.C.T.R., 236 (1981–82); *Howard Neddles Tammen and Bergendoff (H.N.T.B.) v Iran* 1 IRAN–U.S.C.T.R., 248 (1981–82); *George W. Drucker Jnr v Foreign Transaction Co.* 1 IRAN–U.S.C.T.R., 252 (1981–82); *Halliburton Co. v Doreen/Imco* 1 IRAN–U.S.C.T.R., 242 (1981–82); *Stone & Webster Overseas Inc. v National Petrochemical Co.* 1 IRAN–U.S.C.T.R., 274 (1981–82); *TCSB Inc. v Iran* 1 IRAN–U.S.C.T.R., 261 (1981–82); *Zokor International Inc. v Iran* 1 IRAN–U.S.C.T.R., 271 (1981–82).

[3] *Gibbs & Hill Inc. v Iran Power Generation and Transmission Company (TAVANIR)* 1 IRAN–U.S.C.T.R., 236 (1981–82); *Howard Needles Tammen and Bergendoff (H.N.T.B.) v Iran* 1 IRAN–U.S.C.T.R., 248 (1981–82).

[4] Unlike the International Court of Justice, the Tribunal normally cites legal precedent in support of its decisions, including awards and decisions of international courts and tribunals and the writings of jurists.

The Tribunal established three broad principles in respect to forum selection clauses. These are:

1 That the word "binding" used in Article II(1) in reference to "binding contract" is redundant in the context of the forum selection issue.
2 That as a result the Tribunal will not determine the enforceability of the choice of forum clauses in light of "changed circumstances" of Iranian law (Article V of the Claims Settlement Declaration), but will merely apply the clauses as they stand to determine if the jurisdiction of the Tribunal is excluded.
3 That, as a consequence of the application of the above principles, the Tribunal will interpret the plain meaning of the words of such clauses. In so doing, the Tribunal will apply the provisions of Article II(1) in a literal and restrictive sense. Before the Tribunal will surrender jurisdiction the forum selection clause must be all-encompassing, providing for the sole jurisdiction of competent Iranian courts to the absolute exclusion of any other forum.

The reasoning of the Tribunal on the forum selection issue

The opinions of the majority
In several of the claims the plain wording of the choice of forum clause apparently gave exclusive jurisdiction to the Iranian courts. In each of these cases, the Tribunal applied the first two principles referred to above. The Tribunal had to consider only the "plain wording" of the various clauses, and did not have to consider whether there were any "changed circumstances" brought about by the Iranian revolution which might render the clauses inapplicable.

The Tribunal fully discussed the first two principles in *George Drucker v Foreign Transaction Company*[5] and subsequently applied their reasoning in the balance of the test cases before it in which it held that the jurisdiction of the Tribunal was excluded. The claimant was party to a number of different contracts which contained a variety of forum selection clauses.

For each of the contracts, the claimant contended that even if the clause could be construed in such a manner as to confer exclusive jurisdiction upon Iranian courts, the clauses were nevertheless not "binding" upon him. The claimant referred to the words "binding contract" in Article II(1), and also to Article V of the Claims Settlement Declaration providing that the Tribunal shall take into account "changed circumstances" in applying such "choice of law" rules as it considers applicable.

The claimant contended that Iranian law had been changed to such an

[5] 1 IRAN–U.S.C.T.R., 252 (1981–82).

extent following the Islamic revolution that it was unreasonable to expect him to be subject to it. The provisions of the forum selection clause were therefore no longer binding upon the claimant. The Tribunal, in dealing with this argument, did not directly consider the provisions of Article V, but instead focused on the word "binding". After considering both the wording of the Claims Settlement Declaration and the intention of the parties the Tribunal decided the word "binding" was redundant. Thus the Tribunal did not have to consider whether changes in Iranian law affected the enforceability of the forum settlement clause. The Tribunal's reasoning was as follows:[6]

> It is not generally the task of the Tribunal, or any arbitral tribunal, to determine the enforceability of choice of forum clauses in contracts. If the parties wished the Tribunal to determine the enforceability of contract clauses specifically providing for the sole jurisdiction of Iranian courts, it would be expected that they would do so clearly and unambiguously. Thus, the Tribunal would be reluctant to assume such a task in the absence of a clear mandate to do so in the Algiers Declaration.
> The wording of Article II, Paragraph 1, of the Claims Settlement Declaration suggests that the words "binding contract" are intended to refer to the entire contract rather than to the forum selection clause. Although the word "contract" can be interpreted as referring solely to a clause in a contract, it seems likely that the parties to the agreement would have formulated the text so as to refer specifically to an enforceable forum selection clause providing for the sole jurisdiction of Iranian courts had they agreed on such an interpretation. Thus the wording is ambiguous, and the Tribunal is obliged to look beyond the text for other evidence of party intent so as to determine whether, despite the ambiguity of the phrase in question, the parties had nevertheless agreed on its meaning.

Having concluded that it could not adequately interpret the meaning of the clause by simply looking at the plain and ordinary meaning of the words,[7] the Tribunal then considered the mutual understanding of the parties of the reason for the insertion of the word "binding":[8]

> The circumstances at the conclusion of Article II of the Claims Settlement Declaration as well as the text of the article itself indicate clearly that the provision regarding exclusion of certain claims from the Tribunal's jurisdiction represents an attempt to accommodate on the one hand a desire by the United States negotiators to minimise the scope of the exclusion clause and on the other hand a demand from the Iranian negotiators to exclude certain claims as a result of the Majlis position in regard to claims based on contracts which provide for the settlement of disputes by competent Iranian courts. However, there is not sufficient evidence that the two Governments came to an agreement as to the word "binding".

[6] *Ibid.*, 255.
[7] This first step in interpretation is required by Article 31 of the Vienna Convention on the Law of Treaties.
[8] IRAN–U.S.C.T.R., 252 (1981–82).

Since the parties had not agreed on the meaning of the word "binding", and since the Tribunal was unable to give it any sensible meaning in the present context, it determined the word was redundant. The Tribunal therefore concluded:[9]

In these circumstances the Tribunal—which derives its jurisdiction only from the terms of the Declaration—does not reach the question as to whether changes in Iran may have any impact on the enforceability of forum selection clauses in contracts.

The Tribunal applied the same reasoning in all those cases where it determined that the plain wording of the choice of forum clause excluded the jurisdiction of the Tribunal within the meaning of the words of Article II(1): "... *specifically* providing that any disputes thereunder shall be within the *sole* jurisdiction of the competent Iranian Courts..."

The dissenting United States arbitrators' opinions
The two United States arbitrators, Messrs Holtzmann and Mosk, took strong exception to the Tribunal's finding that it did not have jurisdiction in the cases where the plain wording of the clauses apparently excluded the jurisdiction of the Tribunal. Although they both wrote separate opinions the reasoning of both arbitrators was very similar. The opinions covered all nine cases, unlike the approach of the majority, which filed a separate opinion for each case.

Unlike the majority, both arbitrators were able to give meaning to the word "binding" in Article II(1) on the basis of rules of municipal law and international law relating to choice of law by the parties. Once the word "binding" was given a specific meaning the arbitrators were then able to consider the enforceability of the forum selection provisions of each contract. In considering this latter point both arbitrators made reference to established principles of international law, and the provisions of Article V of the Claims Settlement Declaration referring to "changed circumstances". Mr Holtzmann stated:[10]

I would hold that in view of changed conditions in Iran there is no "binding" contract in any of these nine cases which excludes the Tribunal's jurisdiction.

He was therefore able to give meaning to the word "binding" by reference to the wording of Article V of the Claims Settlement Declaration, and by the intention of the parties as expressed by Mr Christopher, the chief negotiator for the United States, in an affidavit presented to the Tribunal. This affadavit was not disputed by Iran.

[9] *Ibid.*, 256.
[10] *Ibid.*, 285.

Mr Holtzmann found that the word "binding" was not redundant, since:[11]

> A "binding contract" is one which is enforceable. That is the ordinary meaning of the term. Moreover, the word "binding" is not surplusage, because not every contract is enforceable at all times. A contract, or one or more clauses therein, may be, or may become, unenforceable for various reasons. One pertinent example of a contract provision which becomes unenforceable is that a contractual choice of forum is no longer binding if conditions have changed so fundamentally since the contract was written that the forum chosen in the contract is no longer the same kind of forum as the parties expected when they signed the contract. That is a recognised principle of international law based on considerations of fairness.

Mr Holtzmann cited the English Court of Appeal decision in *Carvalho v Hull Blythe (Angola) Ltd*[12] as a principal authority in support of this proposition. This case concerned a choice of forum clause in a contract entered into prior to the revolution in Angola, stipulating the choice of forum as Angola. The Court held that the choice of forum provision, as distinct from the balance of the contract, was no longer enforceable owing to the changed circumstances of Angolan law following the revolution. Further support was found in international law. He referred to the requirement of international law that some meaning be given to the word "binding" in Article II(1).[13]

The International Court of Justice in the *Anglo-Iranian Oil Company* case[14] stated "that a reason and meaning would be attributed to every word in the text" of treaties.

Both Mr Holtzmann and Mr Mosk considered, even if the meaning of the word "binding" was not clear from the text of the Declaration, that it was possible to infer the intention of the parties, from the "preparatory work of the treaty and the circumstances of its conclusion", to determine the meaning of it.[15] Thus Mr Mosk stated:[16]

> The word "binding" was inserted, and insisted upon by the United States in order for the Tribunal to be "free to rule" on the enforceability of the Iranian Court clauses. Mr Christopher, in his declaration, also asserts that the "changed circumstances" language in Article V was included at the request of the United States to further ensure that the Tribunal would determine the enforceability of the forum selection clauses in the light of post-contract conditions.

---

[11] *Ibid.*, 289.
[12] [1979] 3 All E.R. 280; at 1 IRAN–U.S.C.T.R., 289 (1981–82).
[13] 1 IRAN–U.S.C.T.R., 289 (1981–82).
[14] I.C.J. Rep., 93, 95 (1952).
[15] See Article 32 of the Vienna Convention on the Law of Treaties; Mr Mosk's opinion, 1 IRAN–U.S.C.T.R., 310 (1981–82).
[16] 1 IRAN–U.S.C.T.R., 311 (1981–82).

On the basis of the foregoing, both arbitrators came to the conclusion that none of the choice of forum clauses was enforceable against the claimants even if on the face of them they provided for Iranian jurisdiction in terms of Article II(1). However, they both contended that none of the clauses in fact satisfied the requirements of Article II(1), "specifically providing that any disputes thereunder shall be within the sole jurisdiction of competent Iranian courts".

In attributing this meaning to the word "binding" the two dissenting arbitrators effectively deleted the forum exclusion provision allowing for exclusive Iranian jurisdiction in Article II(1) from the Declaration. This objection was dealt with by both arbitrators. Mr Mosk set out the United States position when he stated:[17]

At the time of the Treaty, no one could know what Iran's position would be as to whether there were sufficient changed circumstances or conditions such as to render the forum-selection clauses unenforceable. Indeed, Iran has yet to express to the Tribunal a position on these issues. Moreover, at the time of the Treaty no one could know what the situation would be with regard to the Iranian legal system at the time the Tribunal would consider the validity of the forum-selection clauses. Thus by allowing the Tribunal to determine at a future date the validity of the forum-selection clauses, the parties to the Treaty acknowledged the dual possibility that such clauses would or would not be given effect. That is the whole purpose, I submit, of the insertion of the word "binding".

Commentary on the Tribunal's reasoning
The Tribunal's decisions make it apparent that nothing less than an explicit clause will suffice in fulfilling the requirement of Article II(1) of the Claims Settlement Declaration to exclude the jurisdiction of the Tribunal for claims based on contract. Even if claims were centred on contracts which contained forum selection clauses excluding the jurisdiction of the Tribunal, the Tribunal left it open for claimants to establish their claims on other heads, including expropriation and tortious claims.[18]

Thus the majority of claims based on contracts which included forum selection clauses were not excluded from the jurisdiction of the Tribunal. Although it may well have been the intention of the draftsmen of the contracts that disputes should be submitted to Iranian courts in some of the more marginal cases, the Tribunal held that its jurisdiction based on contract was not excluded unless the clause was explicitly drafted to provide exclusive jurisdiction for Iranian courts.

Although the expression of the decision by the majority on the Tribunal can be subject to some criticism it is the writer's opinion that the Tribunal has applied the forum exclusion provision of Article II(1) of the Claims

---
[17] *Ibid.*, 312.
[18] See *Halliburton* claim, note 31.

Settlement Declaration in the manner intended by Iran and the United States.

The application of the dissenting United States arbitrators' reasoning would render the exclusion clause of Article II(1) nugatory, despite Mr Mosk's assertion to the contrary.[19] It cannot be realistically maintained that United States claimants would receive any less favourable consideration in Iranian courts at the time of the Tribunal's decision than they would have when the Declarations entered into force. Furthermore, the United States agreed to the inclusion of the exclusion clause in Article II(1) providing that contracts containing an Iranian forum selection clause would be excluded from the jurisdiction of the Tribunal.

It did so in full knowledge of the nature of the continuing changes in the Iranian legal system, even if it was not aware of the detail of those changes. The United States must have also been aware of the possible difficulties that would face United States claimants in receiving an impartial hearing before Iranian courts. Thus it is not open to the United States after completion of the Algiers Declarations to construe the meaning on the word "binding" so as to negate the effect of the exclusion clause of Article II(1) of the Claims Settlement Declaration. Moreover the provision in Article V of the Claims Settlement Declaration allowing the Tribunal to take into account "changed circumstances" cannot be applied to negate the effect of the forum exclusion clause of Article II(1), and the word "binding" could not have been intended to have such an effect. A general provision such as Article V cannot affect the validity of the specific provision of the forum exclusion clause; the "changed circumstances" must relate to matters not specifically provided for in the Declaration. Thus it would be applicable to choice of law provisions in contracts as envisaged by Dicey and Morris[20] as opposed to forum selection clauses providing for jurisdiction in Iranian courts.

This general view has been maintained by Hakan-Berglin in his analysis of the reasoning of the Tribunal.[21] In particular he considered that the

---

[19] Concurring and Dissenting Opinion, Mr Mosk, 312.

[20] Dicey and Morris, *Conflicts of Laws*, 760 (10th ed.), citing Woolf, *Private International Law*, para. 406 (2nd ed., 1950).

[21] Hakan-Berglin, *Treaty Interpretation and the Impact of Contractual Choice of Forum Clauses on the Jurisdiction of International Tribunals: The Iranian Forum Clause Decisions of the Iran–United States Claims Tribunal*, 21 Tex. I.L.J., 39 (1985–86). This is the most comprehensive analysis of the forum selection decisions, resting, in particular, on the general and supplementary rules of interpretation of treaties in relation to the forum selection clauses. Other authors have tended to the view that the word "binding" in the Claims Settlement Declaration excludes the jurisdiction of Iranian courts in all circumstances owing to "changed circumstances", thus accepting the Holtzmann/Mosk thesis. See Stein, *Jurisprudence and Jurists' Prudence: The Iranian Forum Clause Decision of the Iran–United States Claims Tribunal*, 78 A.J.I.L., 1 (1984); Stewart and Sherman, *Developments at the Iran–United States Claims Tribunal, 1981–1983*, 24 Va. J.I.L., 1 (1983); Note, *Changed*

word "binding" did not relate to the "changed circumstance" of Iranian law following the revolution, but instead that it was attached to the word "contract", and that this interpretation conformed with the ordinary and natural meaning of the choice of forum clause.[22]

The United States' understanding that the word "binding" was inserted in the forum selection clause of the Claims Settlement Declaration so that forum selection clauses in contracts could be challenged, as asserted in the affidavit of Warren Christopher, would effectively render the forum selection provision of the Claims Settlement Declaration nugatory.[23] This clearly could not have been intended by Iran, even if it had been by the United States.

The difficulty, however, facing the Tribunal was to determine the plain and ordinary meaning of the forum selection provision of Article II(1) of the Claims Settlement Declaration. The task was not materially assisted by the submissions of the parties to the Tribunal. The principal difficulty was the purpose of the word "binding" in the forum selection provision. Although Mr Holtzmann considered that the *Anglo-Iranian Oil* case required the Tribunal to attribute a meaning to every word in the text of the Claims Settlement Declaration, this principle cannot be applied to negate the purpose of the forum exclusion provision. Moreover, Mr Holtzmann accepted that there may be a number of reasons why a contract may not be binding, reinforcing the view that the word "binding" is attached to the word "contract" and not to the forum exclusion issue. In the event the Tribunal could not use the "plain and ordinary meaning" rule, but had to determine the meaning of the provision on the basis of effective interpretation of the Claims Settlement Declaration.[24] Such an interpretation is consistent with the letter and spirit of the text of the forum selection provision and enables the Tribunal to apply the provision in a way that takes account of the reason for its inclusion in the Claims Settlement Declaration.

Circumstances and the Iranian Claims Arbitration: Application to Forum Selection Clauses and Frustration of Contracts, 16 Geo. Wash. J.I.L. and Econ., 335 (1982).

[22] Hakan-Berglin, *op. cit.*, 51. The principle that a tribunal interprets the provisions of a treaty according to the ordinary and natural meaning is well established in international law; Article 31(1) of the Vienna Convention on the Law of Treaties, which embodies customary international law.

[23] Hakan-Berglin considered that the United States had failed to demonstrate that the United States had communicated to Iran at the time the Declarations were drafted that this was the reason for the insertion of the word "binding". Moreover, since the United States had drafted the Declaration, the *contra proferentum* rule could be applied against the United States; *ibid.*, 55–64. The Iranian arbitrators have raised the *contra proferentum* rule in the dual nationality case, *Iran v United States (Case A/18)* 5 IRAN–U.S.C.T.R., 251 (1985).

[24] Hakan-Berglin considered this only as a supplementary means of interpreting treaties, since it is not specifically sanctioned by the Vienna Convention on the Law of Treaties. *Ibid.*, 60.

Clauses not excluding the jurisdiction of the Tribunal

The Tribunal has construed the forum exclusion provision of Article II(1) of the Claims Settlement Declaration in a restrictive manner. It must be absolutely clear from the forum selection clause in the contract in question that the parties intended that Iranian courts should have exclusive jurisdiction. There were four categories of claims that the Tribunal considered where the contracts in question did not exclude its jurisdiction. In the first two categories the contracts contained forum selection clauses providing for either arbitration, or resolution of disputes in "competent courts". The third category included contracts which had clauses which referred only one aspect of the contract to the Iranian courts. The fourth category of claims did not have any forum selection clauses in the contracts.

In the first category the Tribunal has held, wherever the forum selection clause provided for arbitration, even if subject to Iranian courts, that its jurisdiction was not excluded. In *Dresser Industries*[25] the contract contained provision for arbitration, with the President of the Supreme Court of Iran having the power to appoint arbitrators should either of the parties fail to do so. The contract also provided that the governing law should be Iranian. The Tribunal stated:[26]

Therefore the Tribunal considers that even though Iranian law provides for a degree of control by the Iranian courts over the arbitral process, such limited control does not, in principle, deprive the arbitrators of their jurisdiction. The limited jurisdiction conferred by Iranian law on the courts with regard to arbitration falls far short of the sole jurisdiction of the Iranian Courts required by Article II, paragraph 1, of the Claims Settlement Declaration.

The claimant, *Gibbs & Hill Inc.*,[27] had two contracts for consideration by the Tribunal. The second contract with the respondent, Atomic Energy Organisation of Iran (AEOI), provided in Article 13:

Any and all disputes, disagreements or questions which might arise between parties in connection with interpretation of any provision of this Agreement or the compliance or non-compliance therewith, which cannot amicably be settled by the parties shall be settled by the arbitration laws of Iran.

As with the *Dresser Industries* claim the Tribunal held that where there is an arbitration provision, albeit subject to Iranian law, no court has sole jurisdiction. The Tribunal stated:[28]

---

[25] 1 IRAN–U.S.C.T.R., 280 (1981–82).
[26] *Ibid.*, 281.
[27] *Ibid.*, 236.
[28] *Ibid.*, 237.

Disputes to be settled in Iranian courts 245

The limited jurisdiction conferred by Iranian law on the courts with regard to arbitration falls far short of the sole jurisdiction of the Iranian courts required by Article II, paragraph 1, of the Claims Settlement Declaration.

Thus in all cases where the parties had provided for arbitration in their forum selection clause the Tribunal determined that it had jurisdiction.[29]

The second category of forum selection clause where the Tribunal considered that its jurisdiction was not excluded was those claims in which the contracts referred disputes for resolution in competent courts.

The first of the *Gibbs & Hill Inc.*[30] contracts was with Tavanir, and provided a two-step method of settling disputes. Thus Article 24 of the contact stated in part:

> All disputes that may arise between parties hereto over this contract or the interpretation of its content, that cannot be settled through negotiation or correspondence in an amicable manner, shall first be referred to a committee consisting of the highest authority of the Client (or his Deputy) and the Consulting Engineer for Settlement, and in case they fail to settle the dispute in accordance with this Contract and current regulations, the dispute shall be settled through competent courts according to Iranian law.

The contract also provided for the choice of the law of the Imperial government of Iran in respect of all disputes. The Tribunal did not consider that the contract unambiguously restricted jurisdiction to the courts of Iran. It stated:[31]

> The Tribunal notes that Article 24 of the TAVANIR contract sets forth that all disputes between the parties regarding the contract or the interpretation of it, failing any settlement of such disputes, shall be settled through competent courts according to Iranian law. Thus, a plain reading of article shows that it only provides that disputes, failing settlement between the parties, shall be solved through court proceedings and that the disputes shall be subject to Iranian law, whatever the court that deals with them.

The Claim was referred back to Chamber Two for further proceedings to determine the validity of the claim under the contract.

The Tribunal maintained a consistent view on the distinction between negotiations and arbitration. Thus in the *Howard Neddles Tammen and Bergendoff (HNTB)*[32] claim, made on behalf of the claimant's Iranian subsidiary, the forum selection clause of the contract stated:[33]

---

[29] Claims which provided for arbitration are: *George W. Drucker Jnr v Foreign Transportation Co., Case 121 Part V (Wheat Contract)* 1 IRAN–U.S.C.T.R., 252 (1981–82) and *Stone & Webster Overseas Inc. v National Petrochemical Co., Part III (FOB Contract)* 1 IRAN–U.S.C.T.R., 274 (1981–82).
[30] 1 IRAN–U.S.C.T.R., 236 (1981–82).
[31] *Ibid.*, 238.
[32] *Ibid.*, 238.
[33] *Ibid.*, 249.

Any disputes which may arise between the two parties in connection with the present contract or change or interpretation of its stipulations and context, which cannot be settled amicably by negotiations or correspondence, shall first be presented for settlement to a committee composed of the Employer's highest authority (or his deputy) and the Consulting Engineer Party to the contract. In case they cannot settle the disputes based on the Contract and the relevant Articles and regulations the case should be settled according to the Iranian Laws by having recourse to the competent courts.

There was a further provision stipulating that the contract would be governed by the law of the Imperial government of Iran. The Tribunal interpreted the clause to mean no more than requiring the parties to attempt an amicable settlement of the disputes. The Tribunal stated:[34]

Thus, a plain reading of this article shows that it only provides that disputes, failing settlement between the parties, shall be solved through court proceedings, and that the disputes shall be subject to Iranian law, whatever the court that deals with them.

The Tribunal also rejected the Iranian contention that contracts between an Iranian corporation and an agency of the government of Iran were necessarily subject to the jurisdiction of Iranian courts. The Tribunal was concerned only with the provisions of the contract, and not the provisions of Iranian law governing the jurisdiction of Iranian courts.[35] The jurisdiction of the Tribunal could be excluded only if the forum selection clause specifically provided for the sole jurisdiction of competent courts of Iran.

The third category covers claims where the contracts provided for the jurisdiction of Iranian courts in certain aspects of contractual disputes. In *Ford Aerospace and Communications Corporation*[36] the contract contained a clause stating:

All disputes and differences between the parties arising out of interpretation of the Contract or execution of the Works which cannot be settled in a friendly way, shall be settled in accordance with the rules provided by the Iranian laws, via referring to the competent Iranian Courts.

The choice of law clause provided that the contract was governed by the laws of the Imperial government of Iran. The Tribunal noted the claimant's contention that settlement in a "friendly way" envisaged arbitration, and that the change in circumstances meant the clause was no longer "binding". However, in determining the application of the clause the Tribunal confined itself to considering the literal wording of the clause. Thus it stated:[37]

[34] *Ibid.*, 250.
[35] *Ibid.* Judge Lagergren and the Iranian arbitrators dissented on this issue, holding that the Tribunal should consider the Iranian law; *ibid.*, 250–1.
[36] 1 IRAN–U.S.C.T.R., 268 (1981–82).
[37] *Ibid.*, 270.

In the present case, the jurisdiction of the Iranian courts has been expressly limited to disputes arising from the interpretation of the contract and the execution of the works. Important aspects of the contract including some of the Claimants' obligations to be performed outside Iran and all the Respondents' obligations such as payment have been left outside the jurisdiction of the selected courts. Such limitation of the jurisdiction places Article 9 of the contract outside the requirement that the Iranian courts must be solely competent for any disputes arising under the contract. Therefore, the Tribunal is not prevented by Article 9 of the Peace Sceptre Contract from asserting jurisdiction over all claims arising under this contract.

The final category comprised those contracts which contained no forum selection clause. Two of the contracts in the *George W. Drucker*[38] claim were in this position. In a contract for the purchase of onions the respondent argued that, since the contract was concluded in Iran, the jurisdiction of the Tribunal was excluded. The Tribunal stated:[39]

The Tribunal notes that it is not alleged that the claims arise under contracts containing a clause providing for the sole jurisdiction of Iranian Courts. Therefore the Tribunal finds there are no grounds under the Claims Settlement Declaration for excluding the . . . claim from its jurisdiction.

Forum selection clauses excluding the jurisdiction of the Tribunal
The range of clauses in which the plain words of the clause excluded the jurisdiction of the Tribunal varied. At one end of the spectrum was the clause in the rice purchase contract entered into by the *George Drucker*.[40] This clause stated:

Any dispute arising from the performance of this contract, not settled amicably, shall be settled by reference to the legal authorities of Iran.

The Tribunal first had to determine whether the words "legal authorities of Iran" were the equivalent of "the competent Iranian Courts". The Tribunal considered that "legal authorities" had the same meaning as "courts", which included administrative as well as judicial tribunals. Furthermore, the Tribunal considered that the words "any dispute arising from the performance of the contract" met the requirement of Article II(1) that all disputes must be subject to the jurisdiction of Iranian courts.[41] Thus on the face of it the clause did provide for the sole jurisdiction of competent Iranian courts.

The forum selection clause in the BHRC contract entered into by *TCSB Inc.*[42] envisaged a two-stage settlement procedure. The relevant clause stated:

[38] *Ibid.*, 252.
[39] *Ibid.*, 259.
[40] *Ibid.*, 253.
[41] *Ibid.*, 256.
[42] *Ibid.*, 261.

All disputes arising out of this subcontract, or the interpretation and understanding of its provisions between parties, which cannot be settled through amicable negotiations or correspondence shall first be referred to a committee composed of a representative of each of the Employer, Housing Organisation, and Subcontractor. In case no agreement can be reached or if one of the parties does not agree with the judgement of the majority of the committee, the dispute will be settled according to the laws of Iran by reference of it to competent courts of Iran.

The claimant contended the dispute resolution procedure of the committee meant that there was an alternative forum to the Iranian courts. The Tribunal rejected this argument, stating:[43]

Thus it does not in essence differ from any general obligation for the parties to a contract to engage in settlement discussions before referring disputes to court proceedings, and it cannot in any respect be compared with an arbitration procedure capable of bringing the contract outside the scope of the exclusion from the Tribunal's jurisdiction provided for in Article II(1), of the Claims Settlement Declaration.

Thus the Tribunal found that the "plain wording" of the clause fulfilled the requirements of Article II(1) to exclude the jurisdiction of the Tribunal. The choice of forum clause in the purchase contract in the claim of *Halliburton Company*[44] also envisaged a two-stage dispute settlement procedure. It stated:

This Purchase Agreement shall be governed and interpreted in accordance with the laws of Iran. All disputes arising in connection with this Purchase Agreement not otherwise amicably settled between the parties shall be settled by submission to the Courts of Iran.

Although providing for amicable settlement as a first step the Tribunal considered all disputes should be submitted to the courts of Iran, thereby excluding the jurisdiction of the Tribunal.

Whilst there was an arguable case in respect of the wording of the clause in the BHRC contract there could be no reasonable argument concerning the wording of the construction contract in the claim lodged by *Stone & Webster Overseas Group Inc.*[45] The relevant clause stated:

All disputes arising out of or in connection with this Agreement, any performance or non-performance thereof, or the consequences of the foregoing shall be settled by a competent Court of Law of Iran.

It was apparently not seriously disputed that on the face of this clause Iranian courts had exclusive jurisdiction in respect of any disputes.

[43] *Ibid.*, 263.
[44] *Ibid.*, 242.
[45] *Ibid.*, 274.

Non-contractual remedies as a basis for jurisdiction

Although the Tribunal found that its jurisdiction was excluded in six contracts by virtue of the specific clauses of the contracts providing for the jurisdiction of Iranian courts it did not determine that it had no jurisdiction over the claims.

Thus the Tribunal in the *Halliburton* claim in relation to the purchase contract stated:[46]

> The Tribunal holds that the instant provision of the Purchase Agreement falls within the scope of the forum clause exclusion contained in Article II(1) of the Claims Settlement Declaration. Consequently, the Tribunal decides that it has no jurisdiction over the claims to the extent that they are based on the Purchase Agreement.
>
> The extent to which the claims asserted in this case are based on this Agreement, and thus outside the Tribunal's jurisdiction, and the extent to which they are based on other contracts or not based on contract, and thus within the Tribunal's jurisdiction, remain to be determined by Chamber Two, the Chamber to which this claim is assigned.

The Tribunal made a similar determination in each of the six contracts which it considered excluded the jurisdiction of the Tribunal. Mr Holtzmann made the observation in respect of the above finding:[47]

> The majority makes clear in each Interlocutory Award denying jurisdiction that the extent to which [claims] are based on other contracts, or are not based on contract, and thus within the Tribunal's jurisdiction remains to be determined by ... the Chamber to which the claim is assigned. Thus claimants are free to assert claims arising out of other contracts, if any, or based on non-contractual grounds such as unjust enrichment in *quantum meruit*, restitution or expropriation. Moreover, each Interlocutory Award denying jurisdiction is limited to a holding that the Tribunal lacks jurisdiction solely because its powers are restricted by the particular words of the Claims Settlement Declaration. The Tribunal does not hold that Iranian courts have jurisdiction.

The Tribunal was only able to make an order that its jurisdiction is excluded to the extent that a claim is based on contract, since the exclusion refers only to contractual claims. The various Chambers will have to determine whether or not the claims can be sustained under any other cause of action.

Application of the forum selection decisions by the Tribunal

The Tribunal has applied the forum selection decisions in a large number of cases.[48] In doing so it has merely interpreted the literal wording of the

---

[46] *Ibid.*, 242, 247.
[47] *Ibid.*
[48] This issue has arisen in most awards of contractual claims following the forum selection decisions. A detailed analysis of particular claims is not warranted, given the nature of the application of the forum selection decisions by the Tribunal to these claims.

clause in question. Having ascribed a particular meaning to the clause, the Tribunal categorises the clause according to the formula set out in the forum selection decisions. On this basis the Tribunal determines whether or not it has jurisdiction over the particular claim under the contract. Thus in every case that the Tribunal has considered on this issue since 1982 the Tribunal has made specific reference to the nine decisions on the nineteen forum selection clauses chosen as test cases. Each clause that has been subsequently considered has been able to be categorised in accordance with the principal forum selection decisions and there has been no necessity to develop new categories.

Depending on the facts of the particular case, the Tribunal may consider the claim under any other of the categories of jurisdiction provided for in Article II(2) of the Claims Settlement Declaration. As a rule the relevant category is "other measures affecting property rights",[49] although a claim based on expropriation may also apply.

Application of non-contractual remedies as a basis for jurisdiction[50]

The case of *Dames & Moore* v *Iran*[51] provided the first opportunity for the Tribunal to consider the scope of alternative remedies. A Venezuelan subsidiary of Dames & Moore had entered into a contract with the Atomic Energy Organisation of Iran.[52] The contract contained an exclusion clause providing that disputes "shall be decided finally by resort to the courts of Iran". Chamber Three of the Tribunal held, on the basis of the decision in *TCSB Inc.* v *Iran*[53] that this clause excluded the jurisdiction of the Tribunal. The claimant had made alternative claims for *quantum meruit* and account stated. The Tribunal, in assessing this claim, stated:[54]

> The *quantum meruit* claim is for the value of services rendered under the contract. That claim clearly arises under the contract. Therefore, the Tribunal finds it has no jurisdiction over that claim. To assume jurisdiction over the *quantum meruit* claim in this case would, in effect, mean circumventing the exclusion provision—Article II(1), thereby rendering it ineffective.

The Tribunal found similarly for the claim based on account stated. In a dissenting opinion the United States arbitrator, Mr Mosk, came to a different view, basing his reasoning on choice of law and the differing

---

[49] Refer to Chapter Ten, for a full discussion of this head of jurisdiction.
[50] Refer to Chapter Ten.
[51] 4 IRAN–U.S.C.T.R., 212, 220 (1983).
[52] Claims by subsidiary companies incorporated in third states may be made pursuant to Article II(1) and Article VII of the Claims Settlement Declaration. See Chapter Five on this issue.
[53] 1 IRAN–U.S.C.T.R., 261 (1981–82).
[54] 4 IRAN–U.S.C.T.R., 212, 221 (1983).

nature of claims based on *quantum meruit* and claims based on contract. Mr Mosk made two points in respect of the applicability of *quantum meruit* to claim. Firstly, he noted that an entitlement based on *quantum meruit* arises out of a debt created by application of the principles of unjust enrichment.[55] Since Article II(1) of the Claims Settlement Declaration gives jurisdiction to the Tribunal over claims arising from debts, the Tribunal has jurisdiction over claims based on *quantum meruit*. On this issue it may be inferred that his reasoning does not differ from that of the majority. However, on the relationship of *quantum meruit* to contract, Mr Mosk noted:[56]

Although a claim for *quantum meruit* may relate to a contract claim, it is, as stated by AEIO itself, "based on completely different and separate bases [sic] ... A *quantum meruit* claim is separate and independent from a breach of contract claim.

It may also be noted that Mr Mosk considered the applicable law of the claim to be international law, rather than a particular system of municipal law. He noted:[57]

Claims based on quasi-contract theories such as *quantum meruit*, restitution and unjust enrichment, have long been recognised under international law as well as the laws of the United States and Iran.

Mr Mosk did not, in this decision, consider *quantum meruit* under the fourth head of jurisdiction in Article II(1) of the Claims Settlement of "... other measures affecting property rights". Instead he considered that the unjust enrichment created a debt and it was upon debt that he held that the Tribunal had jurisdiction. It is submitted that unjust enrichment is sufficient to directly found jurisdiction under the fourth head of jurisdiction, that of "... other measures affecting property rights".[58]

The meaning of "in response to the Majlis position"

The exclusion from the jurisdiction of the Tribunal contained in Article II(1) of the Claims Settlement Declaration has two aspects. The first aspect relates to "the sole jurisdiction of the competent Iranian courts". The Tribunal did not need to consider the exclusion beyond this point in the forum selection decisions.

However, the exclusion goes on to include the words "in response to the Majlis position". Although these words were not referred to by the Tribunal in determining the meaning of the forum exclusion provision,

[55] *Ibid.*, 231.
[56] *Ibid.*, 232.
[57] *Ibid.*, 231.
[58] See the section on unjust enrichment in Chapter Ten.

the Tribunal has had the opportunity to consider the meaning of the words. Chamber Two has issued two interlocutory orders in oil concession nullification cases which consider the meaning of the second aspect of the exclusion. In both cases, *Amoco Iran Oil Company* v *Iran*[59] and *Phillips Petroleum Company* v *Iran*,[60] the Tribunal used identical reasoning and language in determining the application of the words "in response to the Majlis position".

Amoco Iran had the right pursuant to an oil concession agreement to explore for oil in certain areas of the Arabian Gulf. The extraction and sale of the oil would be undertaken together with National Iranian Oil Company. Amoco and NIOC formed the Iran Pan-American Oil Company (IPAC) to conduct the oil operations. Following the Islamic revolution, and before the expiration of the term of various agreements, Amoco was notified by the special committee, which had been established pursuant to the Single Article Act of January 8, 1980, to examine all oil agreements, that the IPAC agreement was "null and void".

The respondents asserted that the Tribunal did not have jurisdiction over the claim, for two principal reasons. The first was that the Single Article Act of January 8, 1980 issued by the Revolutionary Council provided for the exclusive jurisdiction of a special commission to investigate all oil agreements. Secondly, the provisions of Article II(1) of the Claims Settlement Declaration and in particular the words "in response to the Majlis position" excluded the jurisdiction of the Tribunal.

The respondents argued that the last words of Article II(1), "in response to the Majlis position", have a separate meaning from the exclusion from the jurisdiction of the Tribunal of disputes subject to "the sole jurisdiction of competent Iranian courts". In considering the meaning of the words "in response to the Majlis position" the Tribunal would have to take into account all Iranian legislation passed by the Majlis before the completion of the Declarations which provided for exclusive settlement of disputes in Iranian courts. The clause would therefore constitute a separate exclusion from the jurisdiction of the Tribunal. The Single Article Act of January 8, 1980 which established a committee to determine the appropriate compensation for oil companies would be such an exception within the meaning of "in response to the Majlis position".

The Chamber had first to determine which Majlis resolution was being referred to by the Claims Settlement Declaration. It stated:[61]

Two sorts of Majlis Resolutions are invoked by the Respondents, one dated November 2, 1980 and another dated January 14, 1981. The January 1980 Act was an Act of the Revolutionary Council, not the Majlis.

[59] 1 IRAN–U.S.C.T.R., 493 (1981–82).
[60] *Ibid.*, 487.
[61] *Ibid.*, 491.

Thus the Chamber rejected the respondents' contention that the Single Article Act was covered by the words "in response to the Majlis position". The only Iranian legislation in question was the Majlis resolutions of November 1980 and January 1981, both of which related to the settlement of the hostage crisis. The Chamber contrasted the two resolutions:[62]

The November 1980 Resolution, enumerating the conditions upon which the Islamic Republic of Iran then proposed to free the 52 United States nationals, specifies that the United States should take "All legal and administrative proceedings required for the cancellation and annulment of all the claims and demands made by the Government of the United States of America and American companies against Iran under the title whatsoever, . . . and prevent[ion] from instituting new cases whether civil, penal or financial by natural or artificial persons, official or non-official citizens of the States . . .".

It must be admitted that in early November 1980 the Majlis indicated very clearly that its intention [was] to put an end to any judicial claims by United States nationals against Iran in United States courts, presumably including claims by United States oil companies. The Bill enacted by the Majlis on 14 January 1981, however, is narrower in scope than the resolution of 2 November 1980 since it defines in its "Note" the disputes to be excluded from international arbitration as only "those disputes the settlement of which in competent courts of Iran has been provided for in the respective contract". The words "in response to the Majlis position" were included in the Declaration as a result of what has been said by the Majlis, not in November 1980, but in January 1981. Thus the reference to the position of the Majlis also does not affect the jurisdiction of this Tribunal in the present case.

By its decision the Chamber effectively deprived the words of any separate application to claims. Although the Chamber did not refer to United States submissions it is apparent that they were accepted by the arbitrators. The United States memorial accepted that the words referred to the Majlis resolution of January 1981 but argued that they did not add any additional meaning to the exclusion.[63] The words merely signified that the exclusion had been added at the request of the Iranian government. The United States memorial also included a declaration by the United States Deputy Secretary of State, Warren Christopher, who was the chief negotiator for the United States. He stated that the words were added to the Agreement on January 19, 1981 to refer to the Majlis resolution of January 14, 1981. The Majlis resolution confirmed the agreement between the United States and Iran that a claims settlement tribunal should be established. The resolution also required that there should be an exclusion from the jurisdiction of the Tribunal for contracts providing for the settlement of disputes by competent Iranian courts. The

[62] *Ibid.*
[63] Page 10 of United States Memorial.

words "in response to the Majlis position" indicated that the exclusion from the jurisdiction of the Tribunal of contracts "providing for the sole jurisdiction of competent Iranian Courts" was added as a result of the position taken by the Majlis.[64] It also indicated why the Agreement deviated from the resolution of November 2, 1980 which had required the United States to bear financial responsibility for all United States claims. Thus the United States asserted that the words were added as a result of internal Iranian political imperatives, and were not intended to add any additional exclusions to the Agreement.

The United States' attitude stands in contrast to its attitude in the forum selection cases, where it had contended that the word "binding" had to be given an independent meaning in view of its inclusion in the Agreement. The United States had argued it was not then open to the Tribunal to hold that the word "binding" was redundant. However, the meaning given to the word "binding" by the United States had the effect of negating the forum selection provision of Article II(1) of the Declaration excluding the jurisdiction of the Tribunal over contracts providing for the sole jurisdiction of competent Iranian courts.[65]

The Chamber accepted the United States contention. In doing so the Chamber treated the words "in response to the Majlis position" as merely explaining the basis for the forum exclusion provision of Article II(1) of the Claims Settlement Declaration. This is confirmed by subsequent decisions of the Tribunal. The Tribunal in referring to the forum exclusion provision has linked the two parts of the provision together, impliedly accepting the United States argument.[66]

[64] Paragraph 18 of the Declaration of Warren Christopher.

[65] See the opinions of Messrs Mosk and Holtzmann in the forum selection cases.

[66] See *Technology Enterprises Inc. v Foreign Transaction Co.* 5 IRAN–U.S.C.T.R., 118, 119 (1984); *Aeronautic Services Inc. v Air Force of Iran* 7 IRAN–U.S.C.T.R., 217, 219 (1984).

PART THREE
The procedure of the Tribunal and enforcement of awards

CHAPTER THIRTEEN

The procedure of the Tribunal

The rules governing the Tribunal

The Claims Settlement Declaration

As with all aspects of the Iran–United States Claims Tribunal the starting point in an examination of the procedure of the Tribunal is the Claims Settlement Declaration. The relevant provisions of the Claims Settlement Declaration are contained in Articles III, IV and VI.

Article III deals with the composition of the Tribunal,[1] the conduct of the business of the Tribunal in accordance with the UNCITRAL arbitration rules,[2] the method of presentation of claims before the Tribunal,[3] and the time when such claims had to be filed.[4] The most significant of these four paragraphs in the present context is Article III(2), which states:

Members of the Tribunal shall be appointed and the Tribunal shall conduct its business in accordance with the arbitration rules of the United Nations Commission on International Trade Law (UNCITRAL) except to the extent modified by the Parties or by the Tribunal to ensure this agreement can be carried out. The UNCITRAL rules for appointing members of three member tribunals shall apply *mutatis mutandis* to the appointments of the Tribunal.

The adoption of the UNCITRAL arbitration rules to govern the proceedings of the Tribunal means the Tribunal is subject to a comprehensive set of arbitral rules governing all aspects of the proceedings of the

---

[1] Article III(1). The appointment of members of the Tribunal has been covered in Chapter Three.
[2] Article III(2).
[3] Article III(3).
[4] Article III(4).

Tribunal.[5] The UNCITRAL rules, however, were primarily drafted to apply to single *ad hoc* arbitrations. The Iran–United States Claims Tribunal was established to hear a multiplicity of claims, and has been required, in terms of the procedures of the Tribunal, to act more like a municipal court than an *ad hoc* arbitration. Thus the UNCITRAL rules required some modification to take into account this aspect of the Tribunal.

The procedure for presentation of claims is governed by Article III(3) of the Claims Settlement Declaration. It provides that claims of nationals shall be presented to the Tribunal by the claimants themselves, except claims for less than $250,000, which shall be presented by the government of such nationals. The ability of claimants to present claims direct is relatively unusual for arbitral tribunals established pursuant to treaty, although it is not without precedent.[6] As with other aspects of the Tribunal it tends to reinforce the view that the Tribunal is acting as a substitute forum for United States municipal courts.

The states parties do retain some involvement in claims presented by claimants themselves. Article III(2) requires each government to designate an agent to represent it to the Tribunal. The agent, in addition to presenting claims of nationals of less than $250,000 and representing states parties in their own claims, also appears before the Tribunal representing the interests of the state in claims which are presented by the claimant itself.[7] The agent does not control the presentation of the case by the claimant and has no control over the causes of action raised by the claimant, or the evidence presented by the claimant. Instead he simply represents the interest of his state, or of claimants generally where the claim raises issues of general applicability, as in the expropriation or nationality cases.

The third important aspect of the procedure of the Tribunal is the finality of its decisions and awards as provided for by Article IV(1).[8] This is a standard provision in arbitral agreements and signifies two important aspects of the Tribunal; first, that the Tribunal is the only place where claimants can have their cases heard, and secondly that the awards fulfil the requirements of the New York Convention on the Recognition and

---

[5] The rules governing proceedings before the Tribunal are contained in Section III of the UNCITRAL rules. The UNCITRAL rules, as modified by the Tribunal, will be considered in depth in The Tribunals Rules of Procedure, *infra*.

[6] The method of presentation of claims is considered in detail in Presentation of Claims *infra*.

[7] This has occurred in most of the "large" claims. The claims are usually by United States nationals against Iran or its instrumentalities. The claimant is represented by its own attorneys; Iran is represented by its agent and attorneys. The agent of the United States or his representative is also present and may make submissions.

[8] This provision is discussed in detail in Appeals and Reviews of Awards and Decisions of the Tribunal, *infra*.

Enforcement of Foreign Arbitral Awards to be enforced in municipal courts of parties to the Convention.[9]

The final provision of the Claims Settlement Declaration relevant to the procedure of the Tribunal is Article VI. It provides that the seat of the Tribunal shall be The Hague or any other place agreed to by the parties,[10] the appointment of an agent by each government,[11] the equal sharing of the costs of the Tribunal by each government,[12] and the right of each government to request the Tribunal to determine any question concerning the interpretation or application of the Claims Settlement Declaration.[13] This latter provision is of some significance, since much of the Tribunal's work to date has been in deciding questions of the meaning of various provisions of the Claims Settlement Declaration. The determination of the Tribunal on such questions where they relate to issues affecting a number of claimants expedites the handling of the case load of the Tribunal. Perhaps more important is the role of such decisions on the development of international law. Because the decisions affect many claimants they are well argued and researched both by the two governments presenting the cases and by the Tribunal in formulating its decisions. As such the decisions are an important tool in determining the status of various aspects of international law.[14]

The balance of the provisions of the Claims Settlement Declaration pertaining to procedure are mainly technical provisions without significance beyond the Tribunal.

The Tribunal's Rules of Procedure[15]

The Tribunal's Rules of Procedure in Section III, Arbitral Proceedings, provide the basic procedural framework for the prosecution of claims before the Tribunal.[16] Thus Section III of the rules sets out the requirements for filing the documents establishing the claim and the defences

---

[9] Awards can be enforced only if they are final and binding; Article III of the New York Convention. Pursuant to Article IV(2) of the Claims Settlement Declaration awards of the Tribunal can be enforced in the courts of any nation in accordance with the laws of such nation. The issues of recognition and enforcement of decisions and awards of the Tribunal are dealt with in Chapter Fourteen.

[10] Article VI(1).
[11] Article VI(2).
[12] Article VI(3).
[13] Article VI(4).

[14] The dual nationality decision of the full Tribunal discussed in Chapter Four is a good example of a decision of the Tribunal which is an important indicator of the current status of international law.

[15] The Tribunal's Rules of Procedure are reproduced at 2 IRAN–U.S.C.T.R., 405–42 (1983).

[16] The Tribunal's Rules of Procedure consist of three sections. Section I covers the Introductory Rules on Scope of Application, Notice and Calculation of Periods of Time, Notice of Arbitration and Representation and Assistance. These issues have been largely

to it, the evidence necessary to support the claim, the conduct of the hearing, including preliminary matters, and the making of the award, including the awarding of costs.

The international acceptability and comprehensive nature of the UNCITRAL rules meant that they were the obvious choice for the Rules of Procedure of the Tribunal. However, since they had been primarily drafted for *ad hoc* single commercial arbitrations they had to be modified to suit the requirements of the Tribunal.

The Tribunal met in administrative session to amend the UNCITRAL rules to the extent necessary for a Tribunal sitting in three Chambers hearing a large number of claims and to take account of any specific provisions of the Claims Settlement Declaration, including scope of arbitration,[17] notice of arbitration,[18] the requirements of Statements of Claim and Statements of Defence[19] and applicable law.[20] Despite the changes that were made, the essential integrity of the UNCITRAL rules remained intact and the practice of the Iran–United States Claims Tribunal has shown that the UNCITRAL rules are suitable for an international tribunal established by treaty hearing a large number of claims.

Arbitration is usually considered to be a consensual process. Nevertheless, the UNCITRAL rules provide enough powers so that the arbitration cannot be sabotaged by the non-participation or delay of one of the parties. These powers were most important for the Iran–United States Claims Tribunal, having such a large number of claims to deal with. It has been essential for the Tribunal to have the power to compel parties to file various documents, to attend hearings and to complete all interlocutory matters to enable the claims to be heard and awards given. The ability of the Tribunal to expedite the finalisation of claims has depended on the Tribunal being able to issue orders forcing compliance with these various interlocutory matters.[21] In this respect the Tribunal bears considerable resemblance to a municipal court hearing a multiplicity of claims instead of a consensual arbitration.[22] It is a mark of success of the UNCITRAL

---

canvassed in Chapter Two on the establishment of the Tribunal and filing of claims. Section II governs the Composition of the Arbitral Tribunal and has been fully covered in Chapter Three on the appointment of members. Section III, which covers Rules 15 to 41, governing the arbitral proceedings. These rules will be covered in this chapter.

[17] Article 1 of the Tribunal's Rules of Procedure.
[18] Article 2 of the Tribunal's Rules of Procedure.
[19] Articles 19 and 20 of the Tribunal's Rules of Procedure.
[20] Article 33 of the Tribunal's Rules of Procedure.
[21] The provisions of the Tribunal's Rules of Procedure, giving the Tribunal power to issue orders, are Articles 22, 23, 24. These are unchanged from the UNCITRAL rules.
[22] See Simpson and Fox, *International Arbitration*, 154 (1959), where it is stated that claims commissions dealing with large numbers of private claims have rules of procedure intended to ensure cases are dealt with speedily, and that on certain issues the commissions resemble municipal courts with rigid and fixed rules rather than having the more flexible rules of the international tribunals.

rules that they have been successfully applied by the Iran–United States Claims Tribunal.

It is not the writer's intention to examine all aspects of the Tribunal's procedure, set out in both the Claims Settlement Declaration and the Tribunal's Rules of Procedure. Instead selected issues of general significance to international arbitration are discussed in the next section.

Particular procedural issues

Presentation of claims

International practice on the presentation of claims
One of the most interesting aspects of the Iran–United States Claims Tribunal is the right of claimants with claims of more than $250,000 to present claims direct to the Tribunal, instead of the government of the claimant's state presenting the claim on behalf of the claimant.[23] There is nothing to prevent the agent of the claimants' state also appearing before the Tribunal. This has occurred on a number of occasions, particularly where the issues raised by the claim are of general significance, as in the expropriation claims.

Although the right of claimants to directly present claims to the Tribunal is an important development, particularly when coupled with the enforcement provisions, it is not unique in the history of international arbitral tribunals.[24] Those tribunals that have permitted claimants to present their claims direct fall into two distinct categories.

In the early part of this century there were initial moves to develop a comprehensive judicial framework for the peaceful settlement of disputes. The first attempt was made at the Second Hague Peace Conference of 1907. The statute of the proposed International Prize Court would have given private claimants the right to appeal against decisions of national prize courts.[25] National prize courts apply international law, and

---

[23] Claims of less than $250,000 are presented to the Tribunal by the claimant state. Since this has been the norm of claims commissions the presentation of small claims will not be separately considered.

[24] The most useful works on this subject are: Lauterpacht, 1 *International Law: Collected Papers* (ed. E. Lauterpacht) 143–5 (1970); Borchard, *The Access of Individuals to International Courts*, 24 A.J.I.L., 359 (1930); Idelson, *The Law of Nations and the Individual*, 30 Grotius Soc., 50 (1945); St Korowicz, *The Problems of the International Personality of Individuals*, 50 A.J.I.L., 533 (1956); Brownlie, *The Individual before Tribunals Exercising International Jurisdiction*, 11 I.C.L.Q., 701 (1962); Brownlie, *Principles of Public International Law*, 580–94 (1990); Mani, *International Adjudication: Procedural Aspects* (1980). These writers discuss the conceptual base upon which private claimants have direct access to international tribunals.

[25] Lauterpacht, 1 *International Law: Collected Papers* (ed. E. Lauterpacht) 145 (1970). See also Brownlie, *Principles of Public International Law*, 583 (1990).

thus appeals to an international prize court was a logical development. The proposed International Prize Court did not actually come into being. Somewhat more comprehensive in the scope of its jurisdiction was the Central American Court of Justice which functioned between 1908 and 1918. Individual claimants, being nationals of a contracting state, could present their cases against other contracting states for breaches of international law by the other contracting state. It was necessary to show denial of justice, and exhaustion of local remedies, before a claim could be made. Very few claims were presented to the court and it did not add materially to international jurisprudence.

These two tribunals were a first recognition, however, that individuals had certain rights under international law, which were best determined by giving individuals procedural rights in international law.

The next major benchmark in allowing individual claimants access to international tribunals was the Mixed Arbitral Tribunals established by the Treaty of Versailles of 1919. These tribunals gave nationals of the Allied powers right of direct access to present their claims against Germany. Of similar character was the Mixed Claims Commission established to hear claims by United States nationals against Germany. These tribunals are of particular interest in light of their similarities with the Iran–United States Claims Tribunal.

The jurisdiction of the Mixed Arbitral Tribunals was essentially the same as that of the Iran–United States Claims Tribunal, with claims being confined to private property rights. This emphasis on individual property rights was reflected in the ability of individual claimants to present their claims to the Mixed Arbitral Tribunals direct. Claimants could also enforce awards. However, unlike the Iran–United States Claims Tribunal this was not a right to enforce awards in municipal courts of third states, but was a claim against reparations being paid by Germany to the claimants' state pursuant to the Treaty of Versailles.

The emphasis on protecting private property rights in the process of the peace settlement of World War I recognised that the losses concerned had not been borne by the Allied powers but by their nationals. Accordingly it was appropriate that the claimants should have a procedural right to enforce their claims, even though they were claims against a state, being heard by an international arbitral tribunal applying principles of international law.

The ability of private claimants to present their claims direct to international arbitral tribunals has been the subject of considerable academic debate.[26] There is now no doubt that individuals have rights and duties under international law, particularly on issues of human rights, or where

---

[26] The major works on this issue are cited in note 24, *supra*.

The procedure of the Tribunal

the individual has suffered property loss. The traditional view, set out in *the Mavrommatis Palestine Concession* case,[27] that states are the only subjects of international law is not absolute, except where only the interests of the state are concerned, as in boundary disputes. While it is clear that individuals have rights and duties under international law it is also apparent that their procedural rights are limited and are dependent on the discretion of states.

Commentary on the presentation of claims

The interests of the small claimants and large claimants is, apart from the scale of the claims, essentially the same. The fact that the two governments felt that they could permit or deny claimants the right to be heard merely according to the size of the claim is indicative of the limited procedural capacity of individuals and corporations in public international law. Any right to be heard is invariably conferred at the discretion of states and it is exercised on an *ad hoc* basis.

During this century the United States has utilised various mechanisms to settle international claims arising from losses suffered by its nationals. The two basic methods are, first, the setting up of an international arbitral tribunal to hear all claims, usually presided over by a third-country umpire, and secondly, by a lump sum settlement to be distributed by the Foreign Claims Commission, a purely national body.[28] The choice of method is not determined by the claimants, but by international political considerations of the two states in conflict. The settlement of claims is thus an exercise of diplomatic protection.[29]

The choice of an international arbitral tribunal had been extensively resorted to earlier this century, with the Latin American settlements and the post-war settlements following World Wars I and II. In each of these settlements the states parties had a choice whether to allow the claimants to directly present their claims before the tribunals established to settle the claims. There is, however, no apparent trend over time toward allowing private claimants the right to appear before the tribunals, despite the progressive development in international law towards conferring rights and imposing obligations upon individuals as well as states.

The most significant distinction between those tribunals whose claimants could appear and those tribunals where they could not lies in the jurisdiction exercised by the tribunal and the enforcement of the awards.

---

[27] P.C.I.J., Ser. A, No. 2 (1924).

[28] For a comprehensive discussion on the settlement of claims by lump sum agreement see Lillich and Weston, *International Claims: Their Settlement by Lump Sum Agreements* (1975). Lump sum settlements are most commonly used in agreements between Western and communist nations.

[29] De Visscher, *Theory and Reality in Public International Law*, 269 (1957).

Both the Mixed Arbitral Tribunals established by the Treaty of Versailles and the Iran–United States Claims Tribunal can only hear property claims stemming from debt, contract or expropriation. Claims arising from property rights have already been the subject of numerous *ad hoc* arbitration cases between states and private claimants this century. Thus it is a relatively small step for states to confer a procedural capacity upon claimants to present their own claims in an inter-state tribunal, even though it has been established through the exercise of diplomatic protection.

In contrast those international tribunals where claimants have not been able to appear have had a wider jurisdiction. In particular, as in the case of the tribunals established following various revolutions in Latin American states, they have been able to consider claims arising from personal injury and death caused by governmental action or omission. Such claims are no longer in the realm of private international commercial law, but directly raise issues of state responsibility. Moreover the actions or omissions of the respondent government cannot be cloaked with the same economic necessity as claims arising from expropriation. Claims arising from breaches of human rights by states, although arguably more important to individual claimants than economic loss, are central to the notion of state responsibility, since the injury of the claimant state's nationals is tantamount to injury of the state. It is thus inappropriate for the injured national to present the claim. The presentation and control of the claim by the state recognise the public nature of the personal injury to the nationals of the claimant state which has been caused by official action or omission of the respondent state.

Despite the ability of private claimants to directly present their claims before the Iran–United States Claims Tribunal it remains the case that states have the unfettered discretion of conferring procedural rights upon nationals against states. Whilst practice during this century seems to confirm a trend toward conferring substantive rights and duties upon individuals there is a comparatively limited ability of individuals having the procedural capacity to exercise their rights against states. It has only occurred in two categories. First, in respect of property claims where the national who has suffered the loss may have a procedural capacity conferred upon him by the two states establishing a claims settlement tribunal, and secondly, in regional human rights tribunals such as the European Court of Human Rights. The Iran–United States Claims Tribunal fits into the first category.

It is simply another example of *lex specialis*, and does not embody a general principle that individuals who have suffered property loss caused by another state have a right to present their claims. They can only do so if allowed by the states establishing the arbitral forum. The prohibition upon the small claimants presenting their own cases before the Tribunal reinforces this view of the limited and discretionary nature of procedural rights of individuals in international claims.

Evidence

The Tribunal's Rules of Procedure and international law

The Tribunal's Rules of Procedure set out the basic principles to be followed by the Tribunal and the parties in respect of the evidence required to support the contentions of the parties. The two most important rules are contained in Articles 24(1) and 25(6). Article 24(1) states:

Each party shall have the burden of proving the facts relied on to support his claim or defence.

With regard to the evidence presented by the parties to support their claims or defence, Article 25(6) provides:

The arbitral tribunal shall determine the admissibility, relevance, materiality and weight of the evidence offered.

The balance of the Tribunal Rules of Procedure is essentially technical, relating to the filing of written documents,[30] the presentation of oral evidence and written statements of witnesses,[31] the confidential nature of proceedings[32] and the removal of any surprise element in the evidence.[33]

The two key rules set out herein are the only substantive rules of evidence set out in the Rules of Procedure; any other substantive rules of evidence must be derived from the principles of international law relating to evidence presented to international arbitral tribunals.

International law is recognised as allowing the widest discretion in the admissibility of evidence before international tribunals. Sandifer, the acknowledged authority on the rules of evidence before international tribunals, stated that international tribunals "are not bound to adhere to strict judicial rules of evidence".[34] Simpson and Fox also considered that the "greatest liberality" should obtain in the admission of evidence.[35] Mani notes that "Flexibility is, indeed, a virtue of the whole international procedure".[36]

---

[30] Articles 24(2), (3).
[31] Articles 25(2), (3).
[32] Article 25(4).
[33] Article 25(2).
[34] Sandifer, *Evidence before International Tribunals*, 6 (1939). Also cited by Sandifer in the second edition of his work (1975) when he states at p. 9, "No rule of evidence thus finds more frequent statement in the cases than the one that international tribunals are not bound to adhere to strict judicial rules of evidence."
[35] Simpson and Fox, *International Arbitration*, 192 (1959).
[36] Mani, *International Adjudication: Procedural Aspects*, 192 (1980).

The practice of international tribunals, consistent with the liberality of international law in this area, has been to give wide scope for the admission of evidence. Thus evidence is seldom rejected by international tribunals.[37] Once evidence is admitted by the Tribunal its relevance and weight can be considered by the Tribunal. Sandifer cited the Swiss memorial in the *Interhandel case (Switzerland* v *United States)*:[38]

[I]t is necessary to start from the principle already developed in the jurisprudence of the International Court of Justice ... that the Court is free to appreciate the evidence and the allegations of the Parties. The Parties are thus in a large measure free to present any evidence that they consider necessary and opportune.

The reason for this liberality was considered by the International Court of Justice in *Corfu Channel (merits) case (United Kingdom* v *Albania)*.[39] The Court noted that states exercise exclusive territorial control within their frontiers and thus the claimant state is not usually in a position to "furnish direct proof of facts giving rise to responsibility".[40] This is equally true of claimants before the Iran–United States Claims Tribunal, since claimants of either state would find it extremely difficult to obtain any evidence beyond what they had in 1979 from the territory of the respondent government.

Although specifically provided for by Article 24(1) of the Tribunal's Rules of Procedure it is trite law in any legal system, be it international or municipal, that the party seeking to prove a fact must submit sufficient evidence for the Tribunal to be satisfied of the veracity of the fact sought to be proved. Thus the more significant evidential issues are those referred to in Article 25(6) of the Tribunal's Rules of Procedure, particularly in respect of the admissibility, relevance and weight of the evidence presented to the Tribunal.

The Tribunal has confirmed existing international practice in having few restrictions, apart from time limits, on the admission of evidence. There has, however, been greater acceptance of oral testimony than is usual in inter-state international tribunals. This undoubtedly reflects the fact that large claimants are able to present their cases direct to the Tribunal.

Tribunal decisions

Every award of the Tribunal involves the consideration of the evidence presented by the parties. However, the Tribunal has dealt only with the

---

[37] *Ibid.*, 193.
[38] I.C.J. Rep., 6 (1959); from Sandifier, *Evidence before International Tribunals*, 180 (1975).
[39] I.C.J. Rep., 4 (1949).
[40] *Ibid.*, 18.

specific issues of admissibility, relevance and weight of evidence referred to in Article 25(6) of the Tribunal's Rules of Procedure in a limited number of awards and decisions. Nevertheless these awards and decisions confirm the relative liberality of the rules of evidence in international law.

The approach of the Tribunal is particularly well illustrated by the decisions on corporate nationality. These decisions deal with the general principles of evidence as well as the specific rules for proof of corporate nationality. Accordingly examination of the practice of the Tribunal will be confined to the corporate nationality decisions.

General principles of proof of corporate nationality
The important issue of proof of corporate nationality illustrates the liberal and pragmatic approach in respect of the degree of proof and the nature of the evidence that the Tribunal has considered sufficient to satisfy itself that claimants have the nationality of either party in accordance with Article VII(2) of the Claims Settlement Declaration.[41] This was the first major issue in which the Tribunal gave detailed consideration to an evidentiary question. The decisions of the Tribunal on this issue have set the pattern followed by the Tribunal in respect of other issues of evidence.

The question of proof of nationality has arisen in all corporate claims but the approach of the Tribunal and of the parties has differed according to whether the claim has been settled or has been defended by Iran.

In claims which have been settled, a simple assertion by the claimant in its Statement of Claim that it is a United States national within the meaning of the Claims Settlement Declaration, which has not been disputed by Iran, has been sufficient for the Tribunal to conclude that it has jurisdiction.

This approach was established in the first case dealt with by the Tribunal. In *Iran v United States (Case A/1)*[42] the Tribunal had been requested to define the conditions of settlement between a United States claimant and Iran to be recorded as an award on agreed terms. The relevant sub-issue concerned the extent to which the Tribunal must establish that it has jurisdiction over the claim being settled.[43]

Therefore, if requested to make an award on agreed terms, the Tribunal will make such examination concerning its jurisdiction as it deems necessary. However, the Tribunal holds that it would be neither appropriate nor feasible to establish, *in abstracto*, without reference to the situation in any particular case, a general rule concerning the extent of the examination as to jurisdiction that may

---

[41] The question of proof of nationality was noted in Chapter Five.
[42] 1 IRAN–U.S.C.T.R., 144 (1982).
[43] *Ibid.*, 152.

be needed, given the large variety of situations in which matters of jurisdiction may arise and the detailed nature and complexity of the provisions on jurisdiction in the Algiers Declarations.

Thus in *B. F. Goodrich Company* v *Kian Tire Manufacturing Company*,[44] *White Westinghouse International Company* v *Sepah-Iran*[45] and a number of other cases the Tribunal accepted the claimant's assertion in its Statement of Claim that it was a United States national, stating:[46]

> The Tribunal has satisfied itself that it has jurisdiction in this case.

These early decisions established a pattern which the Tribunal has followed in a large number of settlements.

The Tribunal is not prepared to allow the parties to have any reservations in respect of a settlement recorded as an award. However, it has accepted that a position taken by a party for the purposes of a settlement would not bind the party in contested cases. This is illustrated by the award on agreed terms in *Daniel, Mann Johnson and Mendenhall* v *Iran*.[47] The parties had agreed to the settlement, but Iran reserved its position on jurisdiction, since a clause in the contract provided for arbitration with final reference to the appropriate court of Iran. The Tribunal issued a final award, noting:[48]

> Nor is it necessary to delineate any further the standards to be applied to the acceptance of awards on agreed terms. See Decision of May 14, 1982 in *Case A-1*.
>
> The Respondent's concern appears to be that a settlement in this case not prejudice their contention in other cases that the presence in a contract of a clause referring disputes to Iranian courts removes claims based on that contract from the Tribunal with no prejudice to the Respondents' contention in other cases ... the Tribunal accepts the settlement for recording as an award on agreed terms.

In cases where the two parties agreed that the Tribunal did not have jurisdiction the Tribunal has accepted without examination the claimant's view of its own nationality. Thus in *Aeromaritime Inc.* v *Iran*[49] an assertion by the claimant in its Statement of Claim that it was owned by Lebanese nationals, which was accepted by Iran, was deemed sufficient for the Tribunal to decide the claim was not within its jurisdiction. Such a decision is important if the claimant is to pursue its remedies in municipal courts, for it must be able to show that it was not entitled to bring a claim before the Tribunal.[50]

---

[44] *Ibid.*, 123.
[45] *Ibid.*, 169.
[46] *Ibid.*, 123.
[47] *Ibid.*, 160.
[48] *Ibid.*, 161.
[49] *Ibid.*, 135.
[50] See Chapter Fourteen, and in particular the discussion of *Dallal* v *Bank Mellat* [1986] 1 All E.R., 239.

The procedure of the Tribunal

The approach of the Tribunal in contentious cases where proof of corporate nationality has been put in issue by Iran has been substantially different. Although international law imposes the burden of proof upon a party to prove the essential elements of a claim it provides little guidance on the nature of the evidence that the claimant must adduce so that the Tribunal can be satisfied that the claimant possesses the nationality of the claimant's state.[51] In proving nationality the rule is that the claimant must adduce "*prima facie* evidence sufficent to ... raise a presumption of nationality leaving it open to the respondent state to rebut the presumption".[52]

The generality of the rules of international law has meant that the Tribunal has had to formulate its own rules as to what constitutes *prima facie* evidence that a corporate claimant has United States nationality within the meaning of the Claims Settlement Declaration.

Iran has argued that corporate claimants should provide the birth certificates or passports of individual shareholders as the only acceptable proof that at least 50 per cent of the stock of the claimant is held by United States citizens. United States claimants argued that such a requirement would place an impossible burden upon them. Furthermore, such evidence was unnecessary for the Tribunal to draw a reasonable inference that the claimants had United States nationality. In line with the practice of various United States regulatory agencies the claimants relied on statistical data to show they possessed United States nationality.[53]

In support of the corporate claimants the agent for the United States sent a letter to the President of the Tribunal containing additional statistical materials to assist the Tribunal in establishing a satisfactory test for proving corporate nationality. Mr Rovine, the agent, referred to the confidentiality of shareholder lists, the expense of assembling them, and their limited usefulness. They could only show the names and addresses of the legal owners of the shares but not their nationality. He also referred to the United States Government Reports to Congress on the total foreign ownership in United States corporations.[54]

---

[51] Seidl-Hohenveldern, *The Austrian–German Arbitral Tribunal*, 91 (1972).

[52] *Lynch (Great Britain v Mexico)* V R.I.A.A., 17, 19 (1929).

[53] This evidence primarily consisted of the percentage of stock held by shareholders with United States addresses, and the numbers of persons with United States addresses who were citizens of the United States. A collation of these two facts enabled an inference to be drawn as to the United States nationality of corporate claimants.

[54] The two reports showed a very small degree of foreign ownership of stock, being 6 per cent in 1974 and 7.1 per cent in 1978, although the value of investments increased from $23.7 billion to $79.7 billion. The 1980 report indicated that of the 7.1 per cent of stock in publicly listed corporations held by foreign parties in 1978, 2.8 per cent of the stock was held by foreign parties with a 10 per cent or greater interest in a given corporation, and 4.3 per cent of the stock by foreign parties with lesser holdings (Report to the Congress on Foreign Portfolio Investment in the United States [1980]). In addition the Securities and Exchange Commission requires all corporations to make publicly available reports of the

The President of the Tribunal replied that there was no case before the full Tribunal which warranted the United States presenting written submissions. Thus the letter "was not made in accordance with the applicable provisions of the Rules, and would be deemed not to have been received". However, before arriving at this conclusion, the president provided copies to Mr Bellet and Mr Mangard, and subsequently to all members of the Tribunal and the agent for Iran. It appears that the contents of the letter were relied upon in subsequent decisions of the Tribunal.[55]

The Flexi-Van Leasing decision
The claim of *Flexi-Van Leasing Inc.* v *Iran*,[56] heard by Chamber One with Judge Lagergren as Chairman, has established the precedent for proving corporate nationality where it has been contested by Iran. The claimant alleged in its Statement of Claim that it was a United States corporation wholly owned by Flexi-Van Corporation, also a United States corporation.[57] Iran, in its Statement of Defence, challenged the jurisdiction of the Tribunal, stating that the claimant had not provided sufficient evidence showing it was a national of the United States.

The Chamber, in its order, rejected forthwith the Iranian proposal that passports or birth certificates be produced, and similarly rejected the suggestion that the claimant should produce a list of its shareholders. Judge Lagergren did so "particularly because the identity of shareholders in the United States is safeguarded to protect confidentiality".[58] Moreover, the Tribunal considered that the Iranian proposal would place excessive burdens on the parties, and on the Tribunal. Nevertheless it was concerned to ensure that sufficient evidence was placed before it to *prima facie* establish corporate nationality. In taking this approach, it pointed to the decisions of other international claims tribunals.

The Tribunal noted that the Mexican–United States General Claims Commission had held:[59]

When the claimant has established a *prima facie* case and the respondent has offered no evidence in rebuttal, the latter may not insist that the former pile up

names and addresses of all persons holding 5 per cent or more of the stock of the corporation. More recent statistics show an increasing degree of foreign ownership in United States corporations.

[55] See *infra* on the question of the Tribunal taking judicial notice of official United States statistics of foreign ownership in United States companies.
[56] 1 IRAN–U.S.C.T.R., 455 (1982). This case has since been settled.
[57] The claimant submitted an affidavit showing that 96 per cent of its common shares were held by shareholders with United States addresses. However, owing to the large number of shares and shareholders it could not produce evidence of the nationality of individual shareholders.
[58] 1 IRAN–U.S.C.T.R., 455, 457 (1982).
[59] *Parker Case* IV R.I.A.A., 39 (1926); from *Flexi-Van Leasing*, 457.

The procedure of the Tribunal 271

evidence to establish its evidence beyond a reasonable doubt without pointing out some reason for doubting.

Similarly, Judge Lagergren referred to the statement by Judge Lauterpacht in the International Court of Justice in *Case concerning certain Norwegian Loans* that "the degree of burden of proof thus to be adduced ought not be so stringent so as to render the proof unduly exacting".[60]

On the basis of the foregoing principles the Tribunal set out the requirements for *prima facie* proof of corporate nationality, to be applied to all publicly held corporations.[61]

Since the claimant, Flexi-Van Leasing Inc., was alleged to be a wholly owned subsidiary of Flexi-Van Corporation the Tribunal required the claimant to produce "sufficient evidence that its parent, Flexi-Van Corporation, is a national of the United States within the meaning of the Declaration".[62] First, as agreed by the claimant and respondent, the claimant had to produce a certificate of "a government official of the State of New York" that Flexi-Van Corporation is incorporated under the law of New York, and that it was in existence from the date the claim arose to January 19, 1981". The Tribunal will draw the "reasonable inference" of continuous ownership of the claim from the date it arose until the date of the Declarations, unless the respondent can produce convincing rebuttal evidence.[63] Secondly, and more important, the claimant had to produce evidence that 50 per cent or more of the stock of Flexi-Van Corporation was ultimately held by citizens of the United States. This degree of ownership must continue from the date the claim arose until the date of the Declaration. The Tribunal took judicial notice of the official statistics published by the United States government showing that the percentage of foreign ownership in the United States is very small,[64] although these statistics had been introduced by the United States arbitrator, and not by the claimant.[65] The Tribunal also noted the requirement to report to the Securities and Exchange Commission the names and addresses of all persons holding more than 5 per cent of the shares in corporations.

In light of these facts, and the reporting requirements, the Tribunal determined that:[66]

---

[60] I.C.J. Rep., 39–40 (1957); from *Flexi-Van Leasing* 458.
[61] 1 IRAN–U.S.C.T.R., 455, 458 (1982).
[62] *Ibid.*, 458.
[63] *Ibid.*, 458. Refer also to Chapter Five on Continuous Ownership of Claims.
[64] *Ibid.*, 459–60.
[65] Dissenting Opinion, Mr Kashani, 480. These were the reports referred to in Mr Rovine's letter to President Lagergren.
[66] *Ibid.*, 461 (Tribunal's majority opinion).

Examination of the specific information as to holders of 5 per cent or more of the voting stock of a corporation, as already reported in the proxy statements for the relevant annual meetings, and consideration of official statistics as being applicable to the other small shareholders provides a practical and appropriate basis for reaching conclusions as to the percentage of foreign ownership.

On the basis of the foregoing evidence, if the percentage of voting stock held by persons with 5 per cent or more of such stock is less than 40 per cent then the Tribunal:[67]

Will draw the reasonable inference that more than 50% of such stock holders are citizens of the United States. That is a reasonable inference because even if as much as 40% of all voting stock were owned by large shareholders who are not citizens the remaining shares held as "portfolio investments" by small shareholders could not reasonably be expected to exceed 10%. For as the treasury reports show, less than 4.3% of "portfolio investments" in United States corporations are foreign. Thus, adding 4.3% to 40% there would still be only 44.3% foreign ownership.

In the event that the voting stock owned by holders of 5 per cent or more of such stock is greater than 40 per cent the Chamber would require additional evidence concerning the nationality of these holders to enable it to draw a reasonable inference regarding the nationality of the corporate claimant.

In making these calculations the Tribunal was concerned solely with voting stock, despite the fact that a significant percentage of ownership in corporations is held in non-voting stock. Judge Lagergren gave two reasons for this: the intent of the Claims Settlement Declaration and pragmatism. In respect of the first reason he stated:[68]

Thus, Article VII, paragraph 1, refers to ownership of 50% of capital stock and paragraph 2 establishes the test of "control". This indicates that the only capital stock referred to is voting stock.

This finding also implies that "control" is 50 per cent or more ownership of voting stock. It is, however, possible to control a public corporation with less than 50 per cent ownership of stock.[69] Secondly, Judge Lagergren found it would not be "practical, or necessary, to include other classes of stock".[70] The proxy statements identifying holders of 5 per cent or more stock related only to voting stock. He went on to state:[71]

---

[67] *Ibid.*, 461.
[68] *Ibid.*, 461.
[69] See Chapter Five, Shareholder Claims in Respect of Corporations not Incorporated in the Claimant State: the Nature of Control.
[70] 1 IRAN–U.S.C.T.R., 455, 461 (1982).
[71] *Ibid.*, 462.

The procedure of the Tribunal 273

Also, any attempt to base calculations on both voting and non-voting shares would require complex valuation hypotheses and computations. Moreover, there is no reason to believe that foreign ownership of non-voting stock is greater than that of voting stock. On the contrary the Treasury Report states that most foreign investments (87%) are in voting stock.

The Tribunal reviewed the practices of various governmental agencies in the United States in determining the percentage of foreign shareholdings in United States corporations, and to some extent had based its own requirements upon these:[72]

The procedures and evidence required by this Order, while similar in some respects to certain governmental procedures, have been established to accord best with the circumstances and needs of this Tribunal.

To satisfy the evidential burdens imposed by Article VII of the Claims Settlement Declaration the Tribunal therefore ordered Flexi-Van Leasing to submit the specific evidence upon which it determined the nationality of the claimant. It was, however, open to Iran to submit written evidence in rebuttal.

The Iranian arbitrator, M. Kashani, filed a dissenting opinion. Mr Kashani noted the difference between municipal administrative procedures for proving nationality and international adversary proceedings. Thus he considered the requirements of various United States federal and state authorities to be inapplicable to the requirements of an international arbitral tribunal. Moreover, the requirements of a number of these authorities, including the Federal Communications Commission, the Maritime Administration and the Department of Agriculture were more stringent than those imposed upon Flexi-Van Leasing Inc.

Mr Kashani referred to the *Barcelona Traction* case, stating that Judges Fitzmaurice and Jessup did not accept certificates by chartered accountants or shareholder lists as sufficient of proof of Belgian nationality. He further stated:[73]

It is incredible to base the reasoning on *Parker* and *Pinson* cases, decided in 1926 and 1928 by the Mexican Claims Commission, while a 1970, almost unanimous, judgement of the International Court of Justice, the highest source of international law, is left unnoted, i.e., *Barcelona Traction*.

Relying on the authority of Judges Fitzmaurice and Jessup in the *Barcelona Traction* case, Mr Kashani rejected the documentation to be presented by Flexi-Van Leasing as satisfactorily establishing United States nationality. The proxy statements could not prove the nationality of the owners of stock, they could only indicate the names and addresses

[72] *Ibid.*, 460.
[73] *Ibid.*, 475.

of the owners of the stock.[74] The application of the statistical material in the Treasury report of the proxy statements in order to determine the nationality of the claimant was "a presumption made on the basis of other presumptions".[75] Furthermore, it was not appropriate in an international tribunal to apply the concept of judicial notice to accept reports prepared by a government which was a party to the Claims Settlement Declaration.

Mr Kashani, however, recognised the difficulties facing large public corporations in proving nationality. Although he did not indicate the nature of the documentation that the claimant ought to produce, he did note the readiness of *General Motors Inc.* to produce its shareholder list and made the comment:[76]

How, without the shareholders' list and other documents, [could] the opposing party or the Tribunal sufficiently search into nationality of Claimants shareholders in order to ascertain their majority United States citizenship?

Mr Kashani concluded his dissenting opinion stating that the Tribunal should request the two governments to settle the matter by negotiation and modification of the Claims Settlement Declaration if the claimants could not prove United States nationality by a simpler method.

The third member of the Chamber, Mr Holtzmann, did not sign the order or provide a separate opinion. He apparently provided the Chamber with the Treasury and Securities and Exchange Commission reports which the President referred to in the order.[77]

Subsequent decisions of the Tribunal on corporate nationality
Following the order in the *Flexi-Van* case, Chamber One made a number of orders on the evidence to be presented by corporate claimants to prove their United States nationality where it had been contested by Iran. In addition to the materials to be submitted by Flexi-Van Leasing, these claimants were also required to submit a signed statement of a corporate official sworn before a notary public, "stating the percentage of voting stock which is held by stockholders of record with addresses in the United States as shown on the stockholders list used in connection with the corporation's Annual Meeting closest to 19 January 1981".[78]

Flexi-Van Leasing had voluntarily submitted an affidavit showing the percentage of its stockholders who resided in the United States. The respondent had objected to the affidavit as a basis for drawing a reasonable inference as to corporate nationality. Mr Holtzmann filed a dissent

---
[74] *Ibid.*, 479.
[75] *Ibid.*, 480.
[76] *Ibid.*, 475.
[77] Mr Kashani's dissenting opinion, 480.
[78] Dissenting Opinion of Mr Holtzman, 2 IRAN–U.S.C.T.R., 33 (1983).

The procedure of the Tribunal

from the additional requirements, stating that only one separate and independent basis was necessary from which a reasonable inference could be drawn. He also noted:[79]

> The terms of the Flexi-Van Order were widely reported and claimants in various other cases, believing that they could rely on consistency in the Tribunal's rulings, have already proposed and submitted their evidence following its terms. In my view, it is inappropriate for the Tribunal to change its rulings unless there are compelling reasons; there are none in these cases.

The principles of the Flexi-Van order are also applicable to cases where the Tribunal has to determine whether a foreign corporation is controlled by United States citizens. In the *Alcan* claim[80] evidence was submitted on behalf of the claimant to show that United States citizens controlled Alcan, a corporation incorporated in Canada. The only evidence submitted was a declaration by Alcan's Assistant Secretary that between 52.1 per cent and 52.8 per cent of Alcan's voting shares were owned by shareholders reporting United States addresses. The claimant also referred to statistics showing that 98 per cent of the residents of the United States are also citizens. Thus the claimant contended that if the Tribunal applied the same ratio to its shareholders it could infer that between 51.06 per cent and 51.74 per cent of Alcan's shareholders were United States citizens.[81] In ruling on this submission the Tribunal stated:[82]

> In view of the practical difficulties inherent in attempting to directly prove the exact percentage of shares of widely-owned corporations which are held by United States nationals, it may, in the Tribunal's opinion, be necessary in certain cases to draw reasonable inferences concerning such percentage from the evidences before the Tribunal based upon probabilities. In the present case, however, the facts do not provide an adequate basis to draw the inference suggested by claimants. The proportion of shareholders with United States addresses is only very marginally above 50%. Also, it must be recognised that Alcan is a Canadian corporation.

The board of directors of Alcan in fact contained a majority of non-United States citizens. Mr Mosk, the United States arbitrator, filed a concurring opinion in which he referred to the additional evidence that could have been filed by the claimant in support of its contention that a majority of its shares were owned by United States nationals. In doing so he referred to the material to be filed in the *Flexi-Van* decision, including "statistical and sampling results" and "governmental filings".[83]

---

[79] *Ibid.*, 33.
[80] *Ibid.*, 294.
[81] *Ibid.*, 297.
[82] *Ibid.*, 297.
[83] *Ibid.*, 300.

In closely held corporations the claimants have generally produced direct evidence of United States nationality. In *Pomeroy Corporation* v *Iran*[84] the claimant submitted the passports and birth certificates to show that its three shareholders were United States citizens. This type of evidence has also been presented by claimants whose stock is publicly traded if there is a small group of people holding 50 per cent or more of the stock. Thus, in *Starrett Housing Corporation* v *Iran*[85] evidence was presented by a certified public accounting firm and the corporate secretary that 50 per cent and more of the stock was held at all relevant times by a limited group of persons along with passports and other evidence to show that these persons had United States nationality.[86]

Although the orders and decisions following the *Flexi-Van* case required additional evidence to be presented, the Tribunal must still draw an inference of United States nationality. The claimants of widely held public corporations have not been required to present the best evidence of nationality—the birth certificates or passports of shareholders—to show that not less than 50 per cent of the shares are held by United States citizens. The Tribunal recognised that imposing this requirement upon large public corporations would be to effectively deny them any reasonable prospect of receiving compensation. It is noteworthy that Mr Kashani also accepted that this would be an unreasonable requirement.

Decision of the full Tribunal on corporate nationality
Following the *Flexi-Van* decision and the subsequent decisions based on it, Iran made a "request for the decision of the Full Tribunal as to 'the criteria for the proper application' of Article VII of the Claims Settlement Declaration concerning the evidence required to establish the nationality of corporate claimants".[87]

The full Tribunal dealt briefly with the request, stating:[88]

[T]he Tribunal holds that the request does not pose a question concerning the interpretation or application of the Declaration. The questions raised by Iran relate to burden of proof, to the evidence required to establish to the satisfaction of the Tribunal the existence of the facts on which its jurisdiction is based, and to the weighing of such evidence by the Tribunal. These issues are obviously not questions concerning the interpretation or application of the Declaration, but, rather, relate to the application of the Tribunal Rules governing burden of proof and evidence.

---

[84] *Ibid.*, 391, 396.
[85] 4 IRAN–U.S.C.T.R., 122 (1983).
[86] *Ibid.*, 132.
[87] I.A.L.R., 12658 (1986).
[88] *Ibid.*, 12660.

The Tribunal, however, did accept that the term "capital stock" in Article VII(1) included both voting and non-voting stock,[89] reversing the interpretation of "capital stock" by Judge Lagergren in the *Flexi-Van* decision. Nevertheless the Tribunal left it to the Chambers to decide in each particular case whether "it is sufficient to rely solely on evidence of ownership of voting stock as in *Flexi-Van*, or if further evidence is needed".[90]

The Tribunal noted that the Chambers had not adopted a general rule on the evidence to be submitted "but have approached the question flexibly and pragmatically".[91] Adopting the language of the Tribunal's first decision, it stated:[92]

[I]t would be neither appropriate, nor feasible to establish, *in abstracto*, without reference to the situation in any particular case, a general rule concerning the extent of the examination as to jurisdiction that may be needed.

In any event both states parties agreed at the hearing that the "requirements laid down in the *Flexi-Van* and *General Motors* orders can constitute a useful basis for the examination of the corporate nationality of a Claimant".[93]

Conclusion on evidence of corporate nationality

The Tribunal has only required claimants to place before it sufficient evidence to *prima facie* draw the inference of United States nationality. It is open to the respondent to submit evidence in rebuttal.

International law does not indicate the nature of documentary evidence to be produced to prove corporate nationality. Although Judges Fitzmaurice and Jessup were not satisfied with the evidence presented on behalf of *Barcelona Traction*, they did not suggest that birth certificates or passports should be produced. It is noteworthy that various United States regulatory authorities, able to confer substantial financial benefits upon corporations having United States nationality, have imposed higher standards of proof than those laid down by the Tribunal.

The pragmatic and liberal approach of the Tribunal on the nature of evidence to be presented to the Tribunal to prove corporate nationality is an endorsement of the customary international law in this area. It recognises the difficulties that parties before international tribunals have in proving the facts supporting their claim. To apply standards common to many municipal systems of law, especially those of the Anglo-American

---

[89] *Ibid.*, 12660.
[90] *Ibid.*, 12660.
[91] *Ibid.*, 12661.
[92] *Ibid.*; from *Iran v United States (Case A/1)*, 1 IRAN–U.S.C.T.R., 144, 152 (1982).
[93] *Ibid.*

common law tradition, would in many cases be a substantial cause of injustice in international arbitration. Unless the respondent is able to produce rebuttal evidence claimants are only expected to produce such evidence to support their case as they can reasonably obtain.

Expert evidence

The Tribunal's Rules of Procedure and international law

The use of experts is envisaged at two separate stages of a claim by the Tribunal rules. First, the claimant or respondent may present as part of its case the evidence of experts. Such evidence is not precluded by the rules, except that:[94]

The arbitral tribunal shall determine the admissibility, relevance, materiality and weight of evidence offered.

Second, the Tribunal itself may, pursuant to Article 27 of the Tribunal rules, appoint one or more experts to report to the Tribunal on specific issues determined by the Tribunal. The report of such experts may be challenged by expert witnesses of either party.[95]

The use of experts by international tribunals, particularly in the latter case, is well established in international law.[96]

As noted by White the principal role of an expert appointed by an arbitral tribunal is "to obtain any technical information that might guide it in its search for the truth".[97] The experts are not usually given a judicial role, but are confined to applying their expert knowledge to specific issues of fact beyond the competence of the tribunal. In claims concerning property this most often resolves to being a question of the value of the property or the amount of compensation due, should the tribunal decide that there is a justifiable claim.[98]

Use of experts by the Tribunal

The Tribunal has on a number of occasions referred specific questions to be determined by experts appointed by it pursuant to Article 27 of the Tribunal's rules. The most important question concerns the valuation of

[94] Article 25(6).
[95] Article 27(4).
[96] The pre-eminent work on the subject is White, *The Use of Experts by International Tribunals* (1965). See also Simpson and Fox, *International Arbitrations* (1959), and Sandifer, *Evidence before International Arbitrations*, 325, 343 (1975).
[97] White, *The Use of Experts by International Tribunals*, 180 (1965), from *Corfu Channel case (Merits)* I.C.J. Rep., 20 (1949).
[98] See *Lighthouses arbitration (France v Greece)* 12 R.I.A.A., 155 (1956); 23 I.L.R., 659 (1956); *Delagoa Bay Railroad* from Moore, *History and Digest of the International Arbitrations to which the United States has been a Party*, 1865. See also White, *The Use of Experts by International Tribunals*, which refers to a number of such cases at 128–49.

expropriated businesses as going concerns. Experts, however, have been appointed to advise the Tribunal on a variety of matters.

In *Starrett Housing Corporation* v *Iran*[99] the Tribunal appointed an accounting expert to value the expropriated assets of the claimant. The terms of reference were quite detailed, specifying the method of valuation and the factors to be taken into account in making the valuation.[100] It was anticipated that the expert would hold a meeting with the parties. The comprehensiveness of the experts report was indicated by the provision of $80,000 "as advances for the costs of the expert advice".[101] The sum was to be paid equally by the two parties.

The Tribunal has also appointed experts to advise it on other technical issues where it would not be appropriate to rely on the assistance or evidence of the parties. In *Behring International Inc.* v *Iranian Air Force*[102] the claimant was in possession of property belonging to the respondent. An interim award was made to prevent the sale of the equipment by the claimant.[103] The parties had agreed that a representative of Iran would be able to inspect the property. However, Iran considered it could be essential to ascertain the exact condition of its property and requested the appointment of an expert to undertake this check. The Tribunal, after hearing argument, decided:[104]

Having considered the Parties' submission in this case, the Tribunal finds that the advice of independent expertise with regard to the status of the goods would assist the Tribunal in the adjudication of this case.

The evidence of experts is not conclusive, whether they be experts appointed by the Tribunal or experts giving evidence on behalf of the parties. In *International Technical Products Corporation* v *Iran*[105] the Tribunal noted that:[106]

Classic references to experts, under Article 27 of the Tribunal Rules, ordinarily require an adversary proceeding.

Thus the Tribunal gave the parties an opportunity to comment on a translation provided by the Tribunal's Division of Language Services.[107]

---

[99] 4 IRAN–U.S.C.T.R., 122 (1983).
[100] The terms of reference of the expert are set out at 4 IRAN–U.S.C.T.R., 157–8 (1983).
[101] *Ibid.*, 158.
[102] 4 IRAN–U.S.C.T.R., 89 (1983); 6 IRAN–U.S.C.T.R., 30 (1984); see also the Tribunal's interim award in this case, 8 IRAN–U.S.C.T.R., 238, 276, note 51 (1985).
[103] 3 IRAN–U.S.C.T.R., 173 (1983).
[104] 4 IRAN–U.S.C.T.R., 89, 91 (1983).
[105] 9 IRAN–U.S.C.T.R., 10 (1985).
[106] *Ibid.*, 34.
[107] *Ibid.*, 35.

Interim measures of protection

Introduction

The protection of the legal interests subject to the arbitration prior to the making of the award is of profound importance in preserving respect for the arbitral process. If either party could irrevocably alter the position between the two arbitrating parties before the award was made, the value of the award to the successful party would be substantially or completely reduced. There would be little incentive to settle disputes by arbitration.

The necessity for international tribunals to be able to preserve the situation prior to the making of the award has long been recognised in international law.[108] Generally the power to make such measures is specifically provided for in the treaty establishing the tribunal, or in the tribunal's rules of procedure.[109] The Statutes of the International Court of Justice and its predecessor, the Permanent Court of International Justice, provided powers to the Court to make interim orders protecting the rights at issue in their respective statutes.[110] In the present context the interim decision in *United States Diplomatic Staff in Tehran (United States v Iran)*[111] provides the most pertinent example of the Court protecting the rights at issue prior to final determination of the case. The Court, on application from the United States, indicated provisional measures prior to the hearing on the merits, to preserve the rights claimed, namely the release of the hostages.

However, the question arises whether an international tribunal can have inherent jurisdiction to order interim measures if the parties have not provided such powers to the Tribunal in the *compromis* or the rules of procedure. Even if such powers have been provided there may be an issue as to the scope of the powers. Fitzmaurice, citing the dissenting judges in the *Anglo-Iranian Oil*[112] case considered that the arguments against tribunals having inherent powers must probably prevail in the present state of international affairs, although he considered that on the basis of logic and of principle tribunals should have such inherent

---

[108] The writings in this area are largely concerned with the powers of the I.C.J. to make interim measures. See Dumbauld, *Interim Measures of Protection in International Controversies* (1932); Elkind, *Interim Protection: A Functional Approach* (1981); Fitzmaurice, *The Law and Procedure of the International Court of Justice*, 533–50 (1986); Mani, *International Adjudication: Procedural Aspects*, 276–301 (1980); Rosenne, *The Law and Practise of the International Court*, (1965); Simpson and Fox, *International Arbitration*, 162–9 (1959). However, in all of these works reference is made to the powers of tribunals other than the I.C.J.

[109] Fitzmaurice, *The Law and Procedure of the International Court of Justice*, 542 (1986).

[110] Article 41 of the Statute of the International Court of Justice, and Article 66 of the Rules of the Court.

[111] I.C.J. Rep., 7 (1979).

[112] I.C.J. Rep., 89 (1951).

jurisdiction.[113] The arguments of Fitzmaurice that tribunals ought to have inherent jurisdiction to make interim measures are compelling, and there is some precedent for tribunals to order interim measures in the absence of specific provision. The Mixed Arbitral Tribunals considered that they had the power to order certain interim measures. These powers were derived from their power to adopt rules of procedure "in accordance with justice and equity".[114] The *Trail Smelter* arbitration is considered by most writers as indicating interim measures being a temporary regime, pending a final award.[115]

The Tribunal's Rules of Procedure

The Tribunal has considerable powers to take interim measures to protect the rights claimed by the parties. The Tribunal's Rules of Procedure provide in Article 26 as follows:

1. At the request of either party, the arbitral tribunal may take any interim measures it deems necessary in respect of the subject matter of the dispute, including such as ordering their deposit with a third person or the sale of perishable goods.
2. Such interim measures may be established in the form of an interim award. The arbitral tribunal shall be entitled to require security for the costs of such measures.
3. A request for interim measures addressed by any party to a judicial authority shall not be deemed incompatible with the agreement to arbitrate, or as a waiver of that agreement.

The article gives wide discretion to the Tribunal in respect of the nature of interim measures it may take. Although there is specific reference to deposit of goods, or sale of perishable goods, clearly the powers of the Tribunal to take interim measures extend beyond such actions. The practice of international arbitral tribunals would indicate that the Tribunal will have wide scope in taking interim measures even if the specific nature of the measures is not specified in Article 26 of the Rules of Procedure.

Decisions of the Tribunal

The Tribunal has exercised its power to take interim measures at the application of claimants on a number of occasions. The measures taken include orders to municipal courts in Iran and the United States to withdraw attachments on goods, restraints on the misuse of trade marks,

---

[113] Fitzmaurice, *The Law and Procedure of the International Court of Justice*, 542 (1986).
[114] From Mani, *International Adjudication: Procedural Aspects*, 288 (1980).
[115] 3 R.I.A.A., 1907, 1934 (1938); see Fitzmaurice, *The Law and Procedure of the International Court of Justice* (1986); Mani, *International Adjudication: Procedural Aspects*, 289 (1980).

and requesting a stay of proceedings. The latter action is probably of most interest, since the request of the Tribunal effectively overrides the jurisdiction of the municipal courts of Iran and the United States. Moreover, the request for a stay of proceedings is an interim measure not specifically provided for in the Tribunal's rules.

The case of *E-Systems Inc. v Iran*,[116] decided by the full Tribunal, is the most important of these cases, if only for the reason that it was the first case in which the Tribunal requested one of the parties to move for a stay of proceedings in its municipal courts.

The claimant, E-Systems Inc., had filed claims in the Tribunal alleging breach of contract for non-payment and non-delivery of equipment by the government of Iran in respect of the installation of electronic equipment aboard aircraft. Iran counterclaimed that E-Systems had failed to perform the contract and deliver the aircraft as required by the contract. The Iranian Ministry of Defence also filed a claim against E-Systems in the Public Court of Tehran in 1982, after E-Systems had filed its claim with the Tribunal. The Iranian Ministry of Defence relied on the fact that the contract provided that differences arising out of the interpretation of the contract or the execution of the work should be settled in accordance with the law of Iran in competent Iranian courts.

E-Systems applied to the Tribunal for the proceedings in the Iranian court to be stayed. Its motion referred to General Principle B of the General Declaration, which stated that the parties intended all claims between the parties to be settled by binding arbitration before the Tribunal, and Article VII(1) of the Claims Settlement Declaration, which excluded claims filed with the Tribunal from the jurisdiction of the courts of either country. This motion would only be effective, however, if the claim by E-Systems was within the jurisdiction of the Tribunal.

The Tribunal had to determine whether the claim was within its jurisdiction. The Tribunal found that the claim was within its jurisdiction, since the forum selection clause in the contract did not provide for the exclusive jurisdiction of Iranian courts as required by Article II(1) of the Claims Settlement Declaration. However, the Tribunal concluded that "the wording of the Algiers Declarations does not support the argument that the Tribunal's jurisdiction over Iran's counterclaims is exclusive".[117] Thus, Iran was free to initiate claims before Iranian courts even though the counter-claims were being heard by the Tribunal as well. Nevertheless, the Tribunal was concerned that the "Tribunal's jurisdiction and authority are made fully effective",[118] since its award "will prevail over

[116] 2 IRAN–U.S.C.T.R., 51 (1983).
[117] *Ibid.*, 56.
[118] *Ibid.*, 56.

any decision inconsistent with it rendered by Iranian or United States courts".[119] Accordingly:[120]

The Tribunal requests the Government of Iran to move for a stay of the proceedings before the Public Court of Tehran until the proceedings in this case before the Tribunal have been completed.

It is apparent that the Tribunal considered that the Ministry of Defence could continue its action in the Tehran Public Court once the Tribunal had made its award on the counter-claim, provided that the Tehran Public Court's decision did not conflict with the award of the Tribunal.

This determination is reasonably similar in concept to President Reagan's executive order which "suspended" litigation commenced by United States nationals against Iran in United States courts prior to the Claims Settlement Declaration coming into force.[121] The suspension of the litigation was effectively a termination of the litigation in the event that the Tribunal made an award in respect of the claim, irrespective of whether the award upheld or rejected the claim. However, if the Tribunal determined that it did not have jurisdiction over the claim then it could be revived in the United States courts. The Tribunal's request for the stay of proceedings is of the same nature, since the Tribunal is only concerned about the effectiveness of its jurisdiction if the Iranian courts made decisions inconsistent with the awards of the Tribunal. So long as the decisions of the Iranian courts do not conflict with those of the Tribunal, there is no inherent difficulty in the Iranian courts having jurisdiction. The request for the stay of proceedings has the same effect as President Reagan's suspension of proceedings, since in both cases the purpose is to freeze proceedings pending the outcome of the claims before the Tribunal. Once this is known, the respective municipal courts can proceed in hearing the claims, provided their decisions do not conflict with the Tribunal's awards.

The decision of the Tribunal in *E-Systems* set the precedent to be followed by the Tribunal in a number of claims.[122] In all similar cases the Tribunal requested Iran to stay proceedings before Iranian courts until the Tribunal had disposed of the claim before it.

However, the Tribunal has not granted a stay of proceedings in all

---

[119] *Ibid.*, 56.

[120] *Ibid.*, 57. In a concurring opinion arbitrators Holtzmann and Mosk considered that instead of the Tribunal making a "request" it should have made an "order", although they accepted that "'request' is tantamount to and has the same effect as an order". 2 IRAN–U.S.C.T.R., 64 (1983).

[121] Executive Order No. 12294. See Chapter One for further discussion of this order.

[122] See, among many cases, *Questech Inc.* v *Iran* 2 IRAN–U.S.C.T.R., 96 (1983); *Ford Aerospace* v *Iran* 2 IRAN–U.S.C.T.R., 281 (1983); *Rockwell International Systems Inc.* v *Iran* 2 IRAN–U.S.C.T.R., 310 (1983).

cases where a claim has been filed with the Tribunal. In *Boeing Company v Iran*[123] Boeing had filed claims against Iran for breach of contract. These claims had also been filed as counter-claims to a claim by the Iranian Air Force in the United States district court in Washington. The United States court dismissed the Iranian claim and entered judgment in favour of Boeing on the counter-claims. Following the judgment Iran filed a request with the Tribunal for an order requiring the United States to refrain from any action for execution of the judgment. The Tribunal refused the request, since the execution of the judgment would not result in irreparable harm to Iran. Any monetary losses arising from execution of the judgment could be rectified by the Tribunal in any future award it might make.[124] A similar result also occurred in *McHarg and others v Iran*.[125] The United States, appearing on behalf of the claimants, requested the Tribunal to direct Iran to dismiss complaints filed by the Environmental Protection Organisation of Iran against the claimants in the Public Court of Tehran. Prior to the Tribunal considering the request the Public Court of Tehran entered a default judgment against the claimants. The Tribunal in its decision "concluded that the interim relief requested by the Government of the United States has become moot and must be denied".[126]

The principal consideration of the Tribunal in determining whether to make an order requesting a stay of proceedings appears to be the efficacy of such a request. It will make the request if the Iranian or United States court has not made a judgment, thereby ensuring that there will not be any conflict between judgments of the municipal courts and awards of the Tribunal. Once the municipal court has made a judgment the Tribunal will not make a request to stay the proceedings but will take account of the judgment in any award of the Tribunal. The net result in both cases should be the same, unless the request of the Tribunal is ignored by the government of the respondent state. However, even if the request is ignored and the case before the court proceeds to judgment the Tribunal should be able to take account of this in the award. The only situation where this would not apply is where a request for a stay of proceedings is honoured by the respondent government until the Tribunal makes an award, but thereafter the respondent government pursues its case before the municipal court to obtain a judgment which is inconsistent with the award of the Tribunal. In such a case the respondent government would be in breach of its obligations under the Algiers Declarations and the

---

[123] 5 IRAN–U.S.C.T.R., 152 (1984).
[124] This was subsequently confirmed by the Tribunal in an interim award, 6 IRAN–U.S.C.T.R., 47 (1984).
[125] 7 IRAN–U.S.C.T.R., 277 (1984).
[126] *Ibid.*, 278.

other state party could bring a claim before the Tribunal pursuant to paragraph 17 of the General Declaration and Article VI(4) of the Claims Settlement Declaration in respect of such a breach.

Interest on awards

General principles

This book has not examined the nature of the award of damages as a separate issue, except in relation to the expropriation cases. There is, however, one issue in regard to the award of damages which is worthy of separate consideration. The events which led to the creation of the Tribunal occurred more than a decade ago. Thus the importance of interest on an award for losses that occurred many years ago is of great significance to the claimants. Over the space of a decade a rate of 5 per cent simple interest will add 50 per cent to an award and a more commercial rate of 10 per cent simple interest will double an award.

The award of interest is designed to compensate the claimant for the loss of income that would have been earned by the sum of damages for the loss from the date of the loss to the date of payment. Interest rates typically compensate an investor both for the declining value of the capital sum caused by inflation and to provide a real rate of return on the capital. The rate of interest will be determined by the security of the investment. The greater the risk, the higher the yield. It is accepted that the safest investments are government bonds of the major Western nations and United States Treasury bonds are usually recognised as the most secure and most convertible national bonds. Accordingly, they tend to provide a minimum interest rate. All other interest rates tend to be higher. Over the decade of the 1980s United States Treasury bonds have had interest rates ranging from 14.62 per cent in 1980 to 8.12 per cent in 1989.[127] Thus a conservative investor could have reasonably expected to earn 84.09 per cent simple interest over the decade and 123.51 per cent on a compound basis.

It would be quite unjust if claimants were unable to be awarded interest. The principle that interest should be paid on awards of damages is widely accepted in municipal law, with all major jurisdictions providing for the award of interest on damages. The major exceptions are the Muslim countries, with the prohibition on interest prescribed by the Koran. Interest is commonly awarded by international arbitral tribunals, including the various *ad hoc* tribunals concerning the expropriation of oil concessions in the Middle East.

---

[127] *Federal Reserve Bulletin*, United States Treasury three-month bills, annualised interest rates for year end.

Thus in *Sapphire Petroleum Ltd v NIOC*[128] the sole arbitrator awarded interest on the award "at the usual rate of 5 per cent per annum from the date of the first step taken in the arbitration procedure".[129] No further consideration was given by the arbitrator to this issue. The question of interest did not arise in the three Libyan arbitrations with the exception of *Liamco v Libya*.[130] The arbitrator referred to Libyan law and international law, noting that the Tribunal "takes into consideration the proper law of the contract which is international law only when consistent with Libyan domestic law".[131] Article 229 of the Libyan Civil Code provided for interest at 5 per cent by way of compensation for delay. The arbitrator noted that:[132]

Interest in Islam is prohibited if it has a usurious (*ribâ*) character.

Pursuant to that trend and to general equitable principles of law, and taking into consideration the discount rate which was applied by the claimant in its evaluations, the Arbitral Tribunal has reached the conclusion that it is just and equitable to consider the interest claimed not as usury (*ribâ*), but as a compensatory equivalent consideration of the said discount rate, after reducing it, in harmony with the Libyan Code, to the most usual rate of 5% applicable to commercial matters.

The case of *Kuwait v Aminoil*[133] is quite different in that the reasoning was based on economic analysis of the loss of value of money rather than on a legal analysis. In such a calculation inflation assumes great importance, particularly in a time of high inflation such as prevailed at the time of the award. The Tribunal stated:[134]

... [T]he sum total of the amount due to Aminoil as at 19 September 1977 came to $206,041,000 less the liabilities of $123,041,000, that is to say $83,000,000. This represents the outcome of the balance sheet of the rights and obligations of the Parties as at 19 September 1977.

In order to establish what is due in 1982, account must be taken both of a reasonable rate of interest, which could be put at 7.5%, and of a level of inflation which the Tribunal fixes at an overall rate of 10%—that is to say at a total annual increase of 17.5% on the amount due over the amount due the preceding year.

Capitalising the above mentioned figure of $83,000,000 at a compount rate of 17.5% annually gives the amount specified in the Operative section (Dispositif) below.[135]

[128] 35 I.L.R., 136 (1963).
[129] *Ibid.*, 190.
[130] 62 I.L.R., 140 (1977).
[131] *Ibid.*, 215.
[132] *Ibid.*
[133] 21 I.L.M., 976 (1982).
[134] *Ibid.*, 1042.
[135] The figure was thereby increased from $83,000,000 to $179,750,764.

This splitting of "interest" into "interest and inflation" has been interpreted as being a recognition of the controversial nature of high rates of interest in Islamic countries.[136] Redfern noted the more usual practice of building inflation into the principal sum awarded and bringing the sum up to date by the award of interest.[137]

This type of analysis is not traditional. The more common approach is to apply a particular legal rule. Thus in *SPP v Egypt*[138] the arbitration applied the rules of the governing law of the contract, Egyptian law, stating:[139]

To this sum [$12.5 million in damages] must be added interest at the statutory rate of 5% from the date of the commencement of the arbitration proceedings, namely 1st December 1970, until the date of payment (Article 226 Egyptian Civil Code).

However, there is some indication that the economic approach evidenced in *Aminoil* is gaining ground. In *Liberian Eastern Timber Corporation v Liberia*,[140] a relatively recent ICSID arbitration, the arbitration awarded interest on the award accruing at the annual rate of LIBOR at three months, starting with the date of the award.[141] The award of interest was made after a determination of damages corrected to reflect the value of the money at the date of the award. The award would therefore appear to have applied a compound interest rate to the award in the accruing of interest at the LIBOR rate as well as compensating for inflation as an element of damages.

The awards of the Tribunal

The Tribunal has consistently awarded interest as part of the award of damages. This occurred as early as awards handed down in 1982 in *White Westinghouse International Company v Bank Sepah-Iran*.[142] In this case interest was awarded on a cheque issued by the respondent in New York. The law of New York provided for interest on judgments and the Tribunal simply applied the New York law, including the rates of interest prescribed by New York statute.

The Tribunal has had a general practice of awarding interest as an element of damages. However, varying rates of interest have been awarded, ranging from 8.5 per cent to 12 per cent, which different

---

[136] Redfern, *The Arbitration between the Government of Kuwait and Aminoil*, 55 B.Y.I.L. 65, 109 (1984).
[137] *Ibid.*
[138] 22 I.L.M., 753 (1983).
[139] *Ibid.*, 783.
[140] 26 I.L.M., 647 (1987).
[141] *Ibid.*, 676.
[142] 1 IRAN–U.S.C.T.R., 169, 170–2 (1981–82).

Chambers have determined to be fair rates. This problem was noted by the Tribunal in *Sylvania Technical Systems Inc. v Iran*.[143] Chamber Three of the Tribunal noted:[144]

> This Chamber finds it in the interest of justice and fairness to develop and apply a consistent approach to the awarding of interest in cases before it. Unless there are special circumstances the rates stipulated in a contract will be accepted by the Tribunal. In the absence of a contractually stipulated rate of interest, the Tribunal will derive a rate of interest based approximately on the amount that the successful claimant would have been in a position to have earned if it had been paid on time and thus had the funds available to invest in a form of commercial investment in common use in its own country. Six month certificates of deposit in the United States are such a form of investment for which interest rates are available from an authoritative source.

The Tribunal rejected the use of borrowing rates, since they varied according to the creditworthiness of the borrower. Moreover not all claimants who suffered loss would have been borrowers.

The rationale for awarding interest was more fully explained in *McCollough & Co. Inc. v Ministry of Post*.[145] The claimant sought 12 per cent simple interest on the unpaid invoices until February 1979 and 15 per cent compound interest thereafter.

The first issue was the applicable law. The contract provided that disputes should be settled in accordance with the laws of Iran, and Iranian law, in common with the law of other countries applying Islamic principles, provided that interest was not payable. The Tribunal did not consider that it was bound by this contractual provision but relied on the practice of relevant judicial institutions.[146] It noted the practice of most municipal legal systems in awarding interest as an element of compensation. It also examined the practice of international tribunals in some detail, noting the variation of rates of interest that had been awarded, which ranged from 5 per cent to 6 per cent through to 14.5 per cent.[147] Most often simple interest has been awarded but compound interest was awarded in the important case of *Kuwait v Aminoil*.[148] The Tribunal drew two principles of general import from international practice:[149]

> The first principle is that under normal circumstances, and especially in commercial cases, interest is allocated on the amounts awarded as damages in order to

---

[143] 8 IRAN–U.S.C.T.R., 298, 320–2 (1985).
[144] *Ibid.*, 320.
[145] 11 IRAN–U.S.C.T.R., 3, 26–31 (1986).
[146] *Ibid.*, 27.
[147] *Ibid.*, 27–8.
[148] 21 I.L.M., 1042 (1982).
[149] *Ibid.*, 29.

compensate for the delay with which the payment to the successful party is made. This delay, however, varies in relation to the date determined to be the time when the obligation to pay arose. This date can be the date when the underlying damage occurred, the date when the debt was liquidated, the date of the formal notice to pay, the date of the beginning of the arbitral or judicial proceedings, the date of the award or of the judgment determining the amount due, or the date when the judicial or arbitral decision reasonably should have been executed.

The second principle is that the rate of interest must be reasonable, taking due account of all pertinent circumstances, which the Tribunal is entitled to consider by virtue of the discretion it is empowered to exercise in this field.

These two principles, drawn from international practice, are principles of commercial and international law, within the meaning of Article V of the Claims Settlement Declaration. By virtue of the nature of the arbitral tribunals which apply these principles and of the cases involved, they qualify as general usages of trade. They are particularly relevant to this Tribunal.

The Tribunal referred to the practice of the Chambers, noting that the rate of interest is usually "a moderate rate, labelled as 'fair', or 'reasonable', and in some cases, supported by express reference to the discretion of the arbitrator".[150] The importance of consistency in the decisions of the Tribunal has been emphasised in a number of contexts. In the present case the Tribunal stated:[151]

To the extent that the diversity of rates applied by the different Chambers is not traceable to the varying circumstances of each case, a higher degree of uniformity is certainly desirable. On the other hand, the diversity of the cases submitted to the Tribunal renders difficult the application of an inflexibly determined interest rate in all cases. For the same reason, the date from which the interest will be calculated is best determined on a case by case approach, taking due account of all relevant factors.

The importance of the *McCollough & Co. Inc.* case has been recognised in a number of subsequent decisions of the Tribunal. Thus in *Exxon Corporation v Iran*[152] the Tribunal stated:

In the absence of any contractual provisions for the payment of interest, the Tribunal finds it reasonable to fix the interest rate at 10% per annum pursuant to the principles established by the Tribunal in *McCollough and Company Inc. v Ministry of Post Telegraph and Telephone*, Award No. 225-89-3 (22 April 1986).

As a general rule the Tribunal has awarded simple interest, in keeping with practice of both municipal and international tribunals. The issue of

---

[150] *Ibid.*, 30.
[151] *Ibid.*, 31.
[152] 17 IRAN–U.S.C.T.R., 3, 17 (1987).

compound interest was raised in *Starrett Housing Corporation* v *Iran*.[153] The claimants had requested compound interest at the average annual rate charged by banks to the claimants. The Tribunal noted:[154]

> With respect to the rate of interest, the Tribunal cannot agree to the Claimants' request to calculating interest on a compound basis. As noted in *Sylvania Technical Systems* v *Government of the Islamic Republic of Iran*, Award No. 180-64-1 p. 31 (27 June 1985), the Tribunal has not made any award of interest on a compound basis. The Tribunal is not persuaded to depart from that practice in this case.

In a concurring opinion on the substantive issue, Mr Holtzmann diverged from the majority on the issue of compound interest. Mr Holtzmann referred to an opinion of Professor Mann, the pre-eminent legal scholar in this field, who noted that the decisions which had established the "rule" that compound interest was not awarded "were decided many years ago when economic conditions and commercial practices were less developed, and in the absence of profound argument and discussion".[155] In contrast the recent *Aminoil* arbitration awarded compound interest to compensate for the lost oportunity to use the assets to earn income. Mr Holtzmann referred to Professor Mann's opinion that municipal and international law evidence a trend to award compound interest, especially where the injured party has incurred compound interest charges as a direct result of the wrongful acts of the party.[156] Thus he concluded:[157]

> Modern economic reality as well as equity demand that injured parties who have themselves suffered actual compound interest charges be compensated on a compound basis in order to be made whole. International Tribunals and respected commentators have come to recognise this principle; it is unfortunate that the Final Award does not.

Notwithstanding the failure of the Tribunal to award compound interest the general practice of the Tribunal to award simple interest is consistent with modern municipal and international tribunals. The only significant exception is the *Aminoil* award. Moreover the interest awarded by the Tribunal has had some regard to the rates that could have been earned by a conservative investor over this period of time. The existence of the Security Account has meant that successful United States claimants are guaranteed the interest on the amount awarded as damages.

---

[153] 16 IRAN–U.S.C.T.R., 112, 234 (1987).
[154] *Ibid.*, 234.
[155] *Ibid.*, 253.
[156] *Ibid.*, 254.
[157] *Ibid.*

Appeals and reviews of awards and decisions of the Tribunal

The Claims Settlement Declaration states:[158]

All decisions and awards of the Tribunal shall be final and binding.

This provision is certainly effective in ensuring that parties cannot have claims or issues reconsidered by the Tribunal once the Tribunal has made an award or decision in respect of the claim or issue. The question that arises, however, is the effectiveness of this provision in preventing parties turning to other courts or tribunals to have claims heard once the Tribunal has made an award or decision on the claim.

In so far as Iran and the United States are concerned, claimants are barred from prosecuting claims in the courts of these countries owing to legislation or executive decree in these countries.[159] However, there is no legislation in third countries barring claims before the courts of such countries. Iran filed applications with The Hague District Court, challenging ten of the awards of the Tribunal, although the proceedings were withdrawn before the court could consider the issues.[160]

One of the claimants, Dallal, also considered that municipal courts of third countries were not bound by awards of the Tribunal. The case, *Dallal v Bank Mellat*,[161] heard by the English High Court, concerned an action by Dallal against the bank in respect of two cheques issued by the bank. The Tribunal had already made an award in favour of Bank Mellat on the same issue.[162]

The question before the Court was whether the award of the Tribunal could be recognised by English courts. Bank Mellat raised two basic defences, firstly that the action was "an abuse of the process of the Court" and secondly the defence of *res judicata*.[163] These defences could succeed only if the awards could be recognised by English courts. The problem facing the Court in recognising the awards was that they are a

---

[158] Article IV(1). As noted in Chapter Fourteen this provision is essential, not only to ensure that the Tribunal will be the final arbiter of claims, but also to ensure that the awards of the Tribunal can be enforced in courts of third countries pursuant to the New York Convention on the Recognition and Enforcement of Foreign Arbitral Awards.

[159] In the United States litigation before the courts was suspended pending the Tribunal making an award; see Chapter One on Executive Order 12294. In Iran there have been a number of claims before Iranian courts on the same issues as before the Tribunal; see Interim Measures of Protection, *supra*.

[160] See Chapter Fourteen for a full consideration of these applications and Dutch law on arbitration.

[161] [1986] 1 All E.R., 239. For comment on the decision see Kunzlik, *Public International Law—Cannot Govern a Contract, Can Authorise an Arbitration*, C.L.J., 377 (1986), and Crawford, *Decisions of British Courts during 1985–86 involving Questions of Public or Private International Law*, 57 B.Y.I.L., 405 (1986).

[162] See *Dallal v Iran* 3 IRAN–U.S.C.T.R., 10 (1983) for the award of the Tribunal.

[163] [1986] 1 All E.R., 239, 247.

nullity under Dutch law. For the defendant to be able to invoke the principle of *res judicata* in English courts the rights of the parties under the Claims Settlement Declaration "must exist as part of some municipal legal system".[164] The defendant was unable to show such a connection. The Court noted the problems of recognition "of proceedings which exist solely at a supra-national level and have no relationship at all to any system of municipal law".[165] However, both the municipal law of Iran and that of the United States have "give[n] validity to the arbitration proceedings".[166] Thus the Court was prepared to recognise the competence of the Tribunal, since the Tribunal was established "by competent international agreement between the relevant states, but also [recognised] by the municipal laws of those states".[167] Moreover, a series of decisions of English courts had recognised decisions of consular courts, including "the application of the principle of *res judicata* in respect of decisions of a foreign consular court".[168] Thus the Court concluded:[169]

> These decisions clearly illustrate that competence can be derived from international law and that international comity requires that the courts of England should recognise the validity of the decisions of foreign tribunals whose competence is so derived. It would be anomalous and contrary to justice and comity if I were to decline to recognise the decision of the Hague tribunal between the present parties. In my judgment, where two sovereign states have chosen to set up a tribunal to determine disputes between nationals of their respective states in respect of choses in action for which the situs lies within the jurisdiction of those two states, there can be no warrant for the courts of this country to fail to recognise and treat as fully competent the decisions of that tribunal.

The recognition of the award of the Tribunal gave effect to the provisions of the Claims Settlement Declaration that awards of the Tribunal shall be final and binding. However, the finding of the High Court that the Tribunal's competence is "found in international law and practice"[170] poses considerable problems for the enforcement of awards of the Tribunal in "the courts of any nation in accordance with its laws",[171] which issue will be dealt with in the next chapter.

---

[164] *Ibid.*, 250.
[165] *Ibid.*, 251.
[166] *Ibid.*, 251.
[167] *Ibid.*, 252.
[168] *Ibid.*, 254.
[169] *Ibid.*, 255.
[170] *Ibid.*, 253.
[171] Article IV (3) of the Claims Settlement Declaration.

CHAPTER FOURTEEN
Satisfaction, recognition and enforcement of the awards and decisions of the Tribunal

Provisions of the Algiers Declarations

Introduction

Perhaps the most interesting features of the Iran–United States Claims Tribunal are the mechanisms for the satisfaction and enforcement of the decisions and awards of the Tribunal. There are two means of satisfaction and enforcement of decisions and awards, first, payment of awards from the Security Account[1] and secondly, in the event that payment from the Security Account is not possible, the enforcement of awards against the respondent government in the courts of any state in accordance with the law of such state.[2]

The Security Account

The Security Account was established pursuant to paragraph 7 of the General Declaration from Iranian funds that had been frozen by the United States. The payment of funds into the Security Account was completed by the Algerian central bank (Banque Centrale d'Algérie) directing the Bank of England (the central bank) to transfer Iranian funds received from United States banking institutions into the Security Account to be held by the central bank in escrow.[3] The Security Account was required to have a balance of US$1 billion. A minimum balance of US$500 million has to be maintained in the Security Account by Iran. If

---

[1] Paragraph 7 of the General Declaration.
[2] Article IV(2) of the Claims Settlement Declaration.
[3] See also Chapter One for further information on the establishment of the Security Account in the central bank.

the balance falls below US$500 million Iran is required to make further deposits into the account. Thus far Iran has made substantial deposits totalling several hundred million dollars into the Security Account to maintain a minimum balance of US$500 million.[4] The source of these funds was the interest earned on the Security Account.[5]

The funds in the Security Account "are to be used for the sole purpose of securing payment of, and paying, claims against Iran in accordance with the Claims Settlement Agreement".[6] Awards in favour of Iranian nationals or the Iranian government against the United States government, which are not otherwise satisfied, must be enforced in accordance with Article IV(2) of the Claims Settlement Declaration.

The requirements of paragraph 7 of the General Declaration had to be supplemented by further agreements. It was agreed by Iran and the United States that the central bank of the Netherlands (De Nederlandsche Bank), should assume management of the Security Account.[7] However, while De Nederlandsche Bank is the Depositary the account is held in the name of Banque Centrale d'Algérie as Escrow Agent. Withdrawals can only be made at the behest of the Escrow Agent.[8]

Enforcement of awards in the courts of any country

Awards made against the United States which are not voluntarily satisfied, and awards against Iran once the Security Fund has been exhausted and which Iran does not honour, will have to be enforced in accordance with Article IV(2) of the Claims Settlement Declaration, which states:

Any award which the Tribunal may reach against either government shall be enforceable against such government in the courts of any nation in accordance with its laws.

Moreover Articles 16 and 17 of the General Declaration, concerning the return to Iran of the assets of the family of the former Shah and the interpretation or performance of any of the provisions of the General Declaration, state that all awards and decisions of the Tribunal in respect

---

[4] These deposits were first made in 1986 and have continued on a periodic basis since then. See I.A.L.R., 12135, 12396 (1986).

[5] This issue will be covered in Maintenance of the Security Account, *infra*.

[6] Paragraph 7 of the General Declaration.

[7] Exchange of notes between Netherlands and the United States, July 10, 1981, with annexed agreement; from 1 IRAN–U.S.C.T.R., 26 (1981–82). The central bank of the Netherlands manages the account and the N.V. Settlement Bank of the Netherlands is the Depositary.

[8] The operation of the Security Account will be covered in Satisfaction of Awards from the Security Account, *infra*.

of such matters shall be enforceable in the courts of any nation in accordance with its laws.

The issue that these provisions raise is whether municipal courts of third states will in fact recognise and enforce awards and decisions of the Tribunal.[9] The mere inclusion of such provisions in a treaty between Iran and the United States does not obligate courts of third states to enforce awards of the Tribunal. Whether such courts recognise and enforce the awards will be dependent on the characterisation of the awards.

Satisfaction of awards in favour of United States nationals

Satisfaction of awards of international arbitral tribunals

As a general rule international tribunals have no compulsory means of satisfying the awards of the tribunal. The treaties establishing the tribunal simply provide for payment of the awards by the respondent government to the claimant government, with no means for the claimant government to enforce such payment. The respondent government simply pays the claimant government the amount awarded. The sums paid in satisfaction of the awards are then distributed to individual claimants by the claimant government, usually through national claims commissions.

In at least one instance, however, there have been more substantial means of enforcement. The Mixed Arbitral Tribunals established by the Treaty of Versailles following World War I did not simply rely on German integrity to settle awards.[10] The awards of the tribunals were to be a charge against German assets and would form part of the reparations.[11] Thus awards in respect of debts, contracts and other property losses were to be recovered through the clearing office in the same manner as the reparations.

While there were substantial powers of enforcement of awards of the Mixed Arbitral Tribunals there is no international precedent for the establishment of an independently controlled security fund specifically set up to satisfy awards of an international arbitral tribunal. In this respect the Iran–United States Claims Tribunal is unique. The insistence of the United States on the provision of such a fund was only possible because United States banks were in possession of substantial Iranian funds prior to the hostage crisis.[12] The freezing of the funds by the United States

---

[9] See Recognition and Enforcement of Arbitral Awards *infra* for discussion on this issue.
[10] Articles 296 to 303 of the Treaty of Versailles. See also Thorpe, *International Claims*, 138 (1924).
[11] Article 297(e) of the Treaty of Versailles.
[12] See Chapter One on the regulatory action taken by the United States government against Iranian assets as a result of the hostage crisis.

government meant that the United States could insist on the establishment of the Security Account to satisfy awards of the Tribunal in favour of United States nationals.

Satisfaction of awards of the Iran–United States Claims Tribunal from the Security Account

Payment of awards from the Security Account

The method of satisfying awards of the Iran–United States Claims Tribunal is unparalleled in modern arbitration. Iran, the respondent government in the vast majority of awards, agreed to establish a Security Account of $1 billion to be used to satisfy awards in favour of United States claimants.[13]

The procedure for payment of monies from the Security Account to successful claimants follows the management of the Security Account. On the making of an award the Secretary General of the Tribunal notifies the Banque Centrale d'Algérie as Escrow Agent. The Escrow Agent then notifies the depositary of the Security Account, the N.V. Settlement Bank of the Netherlands, to make payment to the Federal Reserve Bank of New York, which then makes payment to the claimants.[14] This procedure is followed whether the award is made on agreed terms or is an adjudicated claim.

It is essential that the Tribunal should make awards in respect of settlements between the parties, since the Security Account is available only for satisfaction of awards of the Tribunal.[15] Originally Iran had disputed that the Security Account could be used to satisfy settlement awards.[16] It was agreed that this issue would be resolved by the Tribunal.[17] However, prior to the Tribunal deciding this issue the two states parties had come to an agreement that settlement awards could be paid from the Security Account.

The issue that had to be decided by the Tribunal was the standard to be applied by the Tribunal in recording a settlement as an award on agreed terms.[18] The Tribunal stated:[19]

Therefore, the Tribunal must determine that the claim which has been settled is within its jurisdiction. The Tribunal must also review the settlement and satisfy

[13] Paragraph 7 of the General Declaration.
[14] Clause 1(e)(i) of the N.V. Settlement Bank of the Netherlands, Technical Agreement, at 1 IRAN–U.S.C.T.R., 38, 41 (1981–82).
[15] Paragraph 7 of the General Declaration.
[16] See Clause 4 of Appendix 1 to the N.V. Settlement Bank of the Netherlands, Technical Agreement, at 1 IRAN–U.S.C.T.R., 53 (1981–82).
[17] *Iran v United States (Case A/1)* 1 IRAN–U.S.C.T.R., 144, 149 (1981–82).
[18] *Ibid.*, 144, 149.
[19] *Ibid.*, 151.

itself that it represents a reasonable determination of the claim. The critical element of the Security Account—the security it affords—would otherwise be destroyed. In the case of an adjudicated claim, access to the Security Account is determined by a procedure which guarantees consistency and fairness.

The integrity of the Security Account has thus been protected by the Tribunal so that only claims coming within the jurisdictional limits of the Claims Settlement Declaration can be satisfied from the Security Account.

Maintenance of the Security Account

It is a requirement of paragraph 7 of the General Declaration that the Security Account be maintained at a minimum balance of $500 million. In the event that the balance falls below this sum Iran is required to replenish the account. As noted previously Iran has made several deposits into the account since 1986 to maintain the minimum required amount.

To date the replenishment of funds has been made from the interest earned upon the Security Account. This interest had been deposited in an escrow account held with the N.V. Settlement Bank of the Netherlands. As with the Security Account the Escrow Agent is the Banque Centrale d'Algérie.

This escrow account had been established as a result of a decision of the Tribunal in respect of the establishment and operation of the Security Account.[20] One of the four issues had been the disposition of interest earned on the Security Account. The United States had argued that the interest should be retained in the Security Account, while Iran had argued that it should be remitted to Iran as it accrued, since the funds in the Security Account were Iranian property. The Tribunal, in ensuring that the "equilibrium" of the agreements was maintained,[21] decided that the interest was to be credited to a separate interest-bearing account as it accrued and that Iran could use the funds to replenish the Security Account as the need arose.[22] The Tribunal required the parties to meet to determine any technical arrangements necessary to carry out the Tribunal's decision.

The arrangements are essentially the same as for the Security Account, with the N.V. Settlement Bank of the Netherlands holding the accrued interest account. There were difficulties in making the first replenishment of the Security Account from the accrued interest account.[23] Iran had notified the N.V. Settlement Bank to pay the funds into the account. However, the N.V. Settlement Bank indicated that it could not act

---

[20] *Iran v United States (Case A/1)* 1 IRAN–U.S.C.T.R., 189 (1981–82).
[21] *Ibid.*, 191–2.
[22] *Ibid.*, 191–2.
[23] *Ibid.*, 192.

without an instruction from the Escrow Agent. Iran was unwilling to give such an instruction, since it considered it had absolute power to give the instruction. The difficulty was resolved by the banks agreeing to the transfer being made on the instruction of Bank Markazi.[24] Subsequent transfers have been made on the same basis.

Thus far there have been no fundamental difficulties in the replenishment of the Security Account. However, problems are anticipated once the escrow account is exhausted and Iran has to make replenishment from another source.[25]

Satisfaction of awards in favour of Iran and Iranian nationals

Introduction

The claims made by United States nationals against Iran have often been met by a counter-claim by Iran. While such counter-claims are rarely successful, there have been a number of net awards in favour of Iran against the United States claimant. Moreover, Iranian nationals may make claims against the United States which may result in an award in favour of the Iranian national.

The Security Account is not available to satisfy such awards, since it has been established solely to satisfy United States claimants. The issue then arises: how are awards in favour of Iran and Iranian nationals satisfied? The key provision is Article IV(3) of the Claims Settlement Declaration, providing:

Any award which the Tribunal may render against either government shall be enforceable against such government in the courts of any nation in accordance with its laws.

This provision, however, is applicable only in respect of awards rendered against governments. The only relevant provision that would allow enforcement of awards arising from a successful counter-claim in favour of Iran is Article IV(1) of the Claims Settlement Declaration, which states:

All decisions and awards of the Tribunal shall be final and binding.

This provision is essentially the same as that contained in all instruments governing international commercial arbitrations. It is an essential requirement of the Convention on the Recognition and Enforcement of Foreign Arbitral Awards that an arbitral award should be final and

[24] See I.A.L.R., 12396 (1986).
[25] *Ibid.*, 12397.

binding before it can be enforced in the municipal courts of contracting states. Thus it can be argued that awards of the Iran–United States Claims Tribunal are enforceable in courts of third states in the same manner as awards of other international commercial arbitration.[26]

Awards and decisions of the Tribunal

The most important decision of the full Tribunal on this issue is the "Request for Interpretation by the full Tribunal of the Algiers Declarations with respect to whether the United States is obligated to satisfy promptly any award of this Tribunal rendered in favour of Iran against nationals of the United States", *Iran* v *United States, Case A/21*.[27] The essence of the Iranian case was that the Algiers Declarations established a "reciprocal system of commitments" that obligated the United States to pay awards if its nationals refuse to do so.[28] Such payment could either be direct by the United States or through the enactment of special legislation enabling the enforcement of Tribunal awards on a "full faith and credit" basis, as has been done in the case of awards rendered pursuant to the ICSID Convention.[29] The United States refuted the Iranian case, noting in particular that the Algiers Declarations do not relieve Iran of the necessity to seek enforcement in the United States or other national courts in the event of a United States national failing voluntarily to satisfy such an award.

The Tribunal essentially accepted the United States position, stating:[30]

The Tribunal notes at the outset that the Algiers Declaration contains no express provision obligating the United States to pay a Tribunal award made against one of its nationals.

Indeed, in all the awards at issue, the disposition obligates named United States nationals—not their Government—to make payments . . . Thus when a party fails to comply voluntarily with a final and binding arbitral award the other party is free to seek enforcement of the award through municipal court proceedings.

The Tribunal, relying on the dual nationality decision of *Iran* v *United States, Case A/18*,[31] emphasised that the Tribunal was not established as a result of diplomatic protection and thus the awards recognise that no espousal of claims by the United States is involved in the cases before it.[32] Accordingly, the awards requiring payment by United States nationals

---

[26] See Recognition and Enforcement of the Awards of the Iran–United States Claims Tribunal in Municipal Courts, *infra*.
[27] 14 IRAN–U.S.C.T.R., 324 (1987).
[28] *Ibid.*, 326.
[29] *Ibid.*, 326.
[30] *Ibid.*, 328–9.
[31] 5 IRAN–U.S.C.T.R., 251 (1984).
[32] *Ibid.*, 330.

are specifically directed against those nationals and not against their governments.

The Tribunal, however, did note the obligation of the United States to implement the Algiers Declaration in good faith. Thus the Tribunal stated:[33]

> The Parties to the Algiers Declarations are obligated to implement them in such a way that the awards of the Tribunal will be treated as valid and enforceable in their respective national jurisdictions ... It is therefore incumbent on each State Party to provide some procedure or mechanism whereby enforcement may be obtained within its national jurisdiction, and to ensure that the successful Party has access thereto. If procedures did not already exist as part of the State's legal system, they would have to be established, by means of legislation or other appropriate measures. Such procedures must be available on a basis at least as favourable as that allowed to parties who seek recognition or enforcement of foreign arbitral awards.

At the time of the decision Iran had not sought enforcement of any of the awards in the United States courts and thus it was "premature to make any pronouncement as to whether the mechanisms currently existing in municipal law are adequate".[34]

The three Iranian arbitrators provided separate opinions. In a joint opinion, Arbitrators Bahrami-Ahmadi and Mostafavi noted that the Tribunal had in effect granted Iran's request, since it was open to Iran to seek further relief from the Tribunal in the event that United States courts refused to enforce the Tribunal's awards or there was undue delay in the enforcement of the awards.[35]

It appears that the Tribunal has, without dissent, concluded that the principal enforcement procedure for the awards is through United States courts in accordance with the Convention on the Recognition and Enforcement of Foreign Arbitral Awards. This is expressly contemplated by Article IV(3) of the Claims Settlement Declaration in relation to awards rendered against a government party which are enforceable against such government in the court of any state in accordance with the law of such state.[36] The Tribunal has effectively ensured that Article IV(1), providing that all awards shall be final or binding, allows enforcement of awards against nationals under the same procedure as awards rendered against the government of either state. This procedural mechanism is the Convention on the Recognition and Enforcement of Foreign Arbitral Awards.

Since this decision Iran has sought enforcement of the Tribunal's

---

[33] *Ibid.*, 330–1.
[34] *Ibid.*, 331.
[35] Separate opinion of Hamid Bahrami-Ahmadi and Mohsen Mostafavi, 333, 335.
[36] Article IV(3).

awards in the United States. In *Ministry of Defence of Iran* v *Gould Inc.*[37] the United States Court of Appeals affirmed a district court decision that awards of the Tribunal are enforceable in the the United States by virtue of the New York Convention on the Recognition and Enforcement of Foreign Arbitral Awards. The objection that the awards of the Tribunal were not connected with the municipal law of any country did not preclude their enforcement in United States courts.[38] The court, after a detailed analysis of the provisions of the New York Convention, held:[39]

> Thus we conclude that an award need not be made "under a national law" for a court to entertain jurisdiction over its enforcement pursuant to the Convention.

It would seem that the decision of the district court lays the foundation for the effective enforcement of awards of the Tribunal in favour of Iran against United Sates nationals in United States courts. This will be sufficient compliance by the United States with the Tribunal's decision in *Iran* v *United States, Case A/21*.

Recognition and enforcement of arbitral awards

Nature of international arbitral awards

The enforceability of international arbitral awards in municipal courts is traditionally regarded as being dependent on the awards being subject to the jurisdiction of the states in which they are made. Article V(1)(e) of the New York Convention on the Recognition and Enforcement of Foreign Arbitral Awards[40] requires that the awards "... are made in the territory of a state ...".[41] Whether or not the awards of an international arbitral tribunal are awards made in the territory of a state depends on the nature or characterisation of the tribunal. If it is an international tribunal dealing with inter-state disputes it will normally be completely separate from any municipal law. Conversly the tribunal may be subject to a system of municipal law, and in the case of the Iran–United States

---

[37] 887 F. 2d 1357 (9th Cir. 1989). See also Caron, *The Nature of the Iran–United States Claims Tribunal and the Evolving Structure of International Dispute Resolution*, 84 A.J.I.L., 105, 107 (1990), and Lewis, *What Goes Around Comes Around: Can Iran Enforce Awards of the Iran–U.S. Claims Tribunal in the United States?*, 26 Colum. J. Transnat'l L., 515 (1988).

[38] See Convention on the Recognition and Enforcement of Foreign Arbitral Awards, *infra*, for a more complete analysis of this decision particularly in relation to the *lex arbitri* of the arbitration.

[39] 887 F. 2d., 1365.

[40] See Convention on the Recognition and Enforcement of Foreign Arbitral Awards, *infra*.

[41] Article V(1)(e) of the Convention.

Claims Tribunal this is most likely to be the law of the Netherlands, the *lex loci arbitri*.

The enforceability of awards of the Iran–United States Claims Tribunal, pursuant to the New York Convention, at least in states other than Iran or the United States, will therefore be dependent on the characterisation of the Tribunal.

Lex loci arbitri

It is widely accepted that in international commercial arbitrations established by private agreement between two disputing parties the *lex arbitri* will be a system of national law.[42] Moreover the applicable system of national law will be the law of the place where the arbitration takes place, the *lex loci arbitri*. The doctrine of *lex loci arbitri* has been most forcefully argued by Dr Mann, who stated:[43]

> The *lex arbitri* cannot be the law of any country other than that of the arbitration tribunal's seat. No act of the parties can have any legal effect except as the result of the sanctions given to it by a legal system.

Dr Mann's exposition of the doctrine of *lex loci arbitri* was fully endorsed by Professor Wetter, who noted that "this, universally, is sound law".[44] Even those writers who question the sweeping application of the doctrine of *lex loci arbitri* concede its essential validity.[45] Dr Mann, however, was not content to argue that there was residuary jurisdiction in

---

[42] The characterisation of international commercial arbitrations is the subject of considerable academic debate. The leading proponents of the proposition that international commercial arbitrations are subject to the law of the place of arbitration, the *lex loci arbitri*, include Mann, *Lex Facit Arbitrum*, in Sanders (ed.), *International Arbitration: Liber Amicorum for Martin Domke*, 157, 160 (1967); Wetter, II *The International Arbitral Process*, 394 (1976); Park, *Lex Loci Arbitri and International Commercial Arbitration*, 32 I.C.L.Q. 21, 23 (1983). There has been an increasing trend toward the view that the parties may agree that the international commercial arbitral tribunal established by them shall not be subject to any particular system of national law, that the *lex arbitri* is "delocalised"; see Szasy, *Recognition and Enforcement of Foreign Arbitral Awards*, 14 Am. J. Comp. Law, 658, 663 (1966); Sanders, *Trends in International Commercial Arbitration*, 145 Recueil des Cours, 243, 270 (1975–II); Luzzatto, *International Arbitration and the Law of States*, 157 Recueil des Cours, 17, 198 (1977–IV); Broches, *Arbitration in Investment Disputes*, in Schmitthoff (ed.), III *International Commercial Arbitration*, 6 (1981); Paulsson, *Arbitration Unbound: Award Detached from the Law of its Country of Origin*, 30 I.C.L.Q. 358, 360 (1981). A proponent of the latter view, Toope, *Mixed International Arbitration* (1990), has considered the position of the Iran–United States Claims Tribunal in detail and his views are noted further in this chapter.

[43] Mann, *Lex Facit Arbitrum*, in Sanders (ed.), *International Arbitration: Liber Amicorum for Martin Domke*, 167, 160, (1967).

[44] Wetter, II *The International Arbitral Process*, 394 (1979).

[45] Park, *Lex Loci Arbitri and International Commercial Arbitration*, 32 I.C.L.Q., 21, 23 (1983).

the municipal courts to ensure fundamental fairness; rather the *lex arbitri* governed the tribunal's fundamental existence:[46]

The law of the arbitration Tribunal's seat initially governs the whole of the Tribunal's life and work. In particular it governs the validity of the submission, the creation and composition of the Tribunal, the rules of the conflicts of law to be followed by it, its procedure, the making and publication of its awards. This does not mean the *lex arbitri* will invariably be applied to all these matters as well as to others that may fall to be considered. On the contrary, most legal systems, when called upon to function as *lex fori* of arbitrations, allow much room for the application of the rules of other legal systems. The scope of such reference, however, is in principle determined by the *lex arbitri* from which any enquiry must start and to which it will revert at many points.

The essential point made by Dr Mann, that the *lex loci arbitri* governs the tribunal's life, is undoubtedly correct. The municipal courts of the place of the arbitration have the overriding power to control arbitrations taking place within their jurisdiction.

In recent years there has been a trend by municipal systems of law to reduce the degree of control exercised by municipal courts over international commercial arbitration. Thus in the principal arbitration forums the *lex loci arbitri* is restricted to ensuring the fundamental fairness of international commercial arbitration; in all other respects there is complete party automony. Moreover, the right of municipal courts in the place of the arbitration to ensure fundamental fairness is a generally accepted principle of law.[47] A tribunal must comply with a certain minimum standard of procedure if it wishes to conduct its business unfettered by the courts of the place of its seat, and if its awards are to be enforced by the courts of other states.[48] The loosening of the grip of municipal courts upon international commercial arbitrations has led to the view that the awards of such tribunals are "delocalised", with municipal courts having only the power to ensure fundamental fairness and to enforce the awards of such tribunals. However, once an international commercial arbitration is deemed to be subject to the *lex loci arbitri*, the award of the tribunal will have the nationality of the *lex loci arbitri*. The municipal law will determine the degree of control that the municipal courts may exercise over such an award.

[46] Mann, *Lex Facit Arbitrum*, in Sanders (ed.), *International Arbitration: Liber Amicorum for Martin Donke*, 157, 161, (1967).

[47] Cf. Section 23 of the United Kingdom Arbitration Act, 1950, and Section 3 of the United Kingdom Arbitration Act, 1979; Articles 484 and 502 of French Code of Civil Procedure; Section 10 of the United States Arbitration Act, 1925. UNCITRAL has prepared a "model law" to achieve consistency on the grounds upon which courts may refuse the enforcement of foreign arbitral awards.

[48] Article V(2)(b) of the New York Convention, 1958, permits states to refuse enforcement of foreign arbitral awards if such "enforcement of the award would be contrary to the public policy of that country".

Denationalised arbitral awards

The position of international commercial arbitrations may be contrasted with international claims tribunals established to settle inter-state disputes. International claims tribunals have three primary features setting them apart from most international commercial arbitrations. First, they are established pursuant to a treaty between sovereign states. Secondly, they generally do not allow claimants to present their claims direct to the Tribunal, which must be done through the agency of the claimant's state.[49] Thirdly, they do not provide for the enforcement of awards in the domestic courts of third states.[50] Each of these features is indicative that the rights being protected are those of the state rather than those of the nationals of the state.

It has traditionally been argued that the espousal of claims by a state on behalf of its nationals against another state is the protection of the state's rights rather than of the rights of the nationals who have suffered the loss.[51] Since the claims are considered to be claims of the state it is inappropriate for them to be presented by the nationals as their own claims. The presentation of the claims by the state ensures that they remain entirely within the domain of public international law.[52]

In the present context the most important distinguishing feature between international arbitral tribunals established by treaty and international commercial arbitrations undertaken pursuant to contract is the enforcement of their respective awards. In the former case the municipal courts of the contracting states are obliged to comply with the judgment of the arbitral tribunal no less than any other organ of state.[53] However, since the national whose claim has been espoused by his state has not participated in the international proceedings, as a rule, it is not open to the national to enforce the award or decision. In *Socobel* v *Greek State*[54] the Belgian Tribunal Civil de Bruxelles held that a private company could not rely on the decision of the Permanent Court of International Justice

---

[49] There have been some claims tribunals that have allowed direct access by the nationals holding the claim.

[50] While there are no precedents for the enforcement of awards of an international claims tribunal by domestic courts of third countries there have been provisions for the enforcement of claims by the contracting states. Thus the German assets seized by the United States were security for claims heard by the United States–German Mixed Claims Commission; Section 5 of the Resolution of Congress, 1921, from Thorpe, *International Claims*, 138 (1924).

[51] Borchard, *Diplomatic Protection of Citizens Abroad* 351 (1915); Phillimore, II *Commentaries upon International Law*, 4 (1879). See also Harvard Convention on the International Responsibility of States for Injuries to Aliens, Explanatory Notes to Article 1 at 50–1 (Draft No. 12, 1961).

[52] Borchard, *Diplomatic Protection of Citizens Abroad*, 357 (1915).

[53] Schreuer, *The Implementation of International Judicial Decisions by Domestic Courts*, 24 I.C.L.Q., 153, 157 (1975).

[54] 18 I.L.R., 3, 4–5 (1957).

in a case between Belgium and Greece. An arbitral award between Greece and the company was obligatory to subsequently enforce the award in the Belgian courts. The decision of the Permanent Court of International Justice was binding only between the two states parties. In *La Abra Silver Mining Company* v *United States*[55] the United States Supreme Court held the money received in performance of an award of the United States–Mexico Commission of 1875 was the property of the United States, since the national who suffered the loss was not a party to the arbitration, which was between two states. Accordingly the money could be withheld from the national who had suffered the loss if it appeared that the award had been procured by fraud, since the national never acquired title to the money of the award even if it was properly made.

Domestic legislation can resolve the difficulty. Following the First World War, a Mixed Arbitral Tribunal was established to resolve claims between Hungary and Czechoslovakia. Legislation was enacted in Czechoslovakia providing for the execution of awards of the tribunal. The Supreme Court of Czechoslovakia held that an award in favour of a Czechoslovak national against Hungary could be enforced against Hungarian property located in Czechoslovakia.[56]

Whilst awards may be executed by the courts of the contracting states, the courts of third states are not bound by the judgments of such tribunals. Article 59 of the Statute of the International Court of Justice provides that "the decisions of the Court have no binding force except between the parties". In *Steinberg et al.* v *Custodian of German Property*[57] the applicant sought to enforce an award in Israel that had been made by the Germano-Roumanian Mixed Arbitral Tribunal. The Supreme Court of Israel refused to recognise the award, since it was not made by a competent court that could be recognised under the law of Israel.[58]

Although municipal courts of third states will not enforce such arbitral awards they may hold that the awards are *res judicata*. In *Société Vinicole de Champagne* v *Mumm Champagne & Importation Co. Inc.*[59] the Federal District Court in New York held that an award of the Franco-German Mixed Arbitral Tribunal was *res judicata* against the defendant corporation. The court recited the history of the award of the Franco-German Mixed Arbitral Tribunal in some detail. However, in holding

---

[55] 175 U.S., 423 (1899).
[56] *Enforcement of International Award (Czechoslovakia) Case* 4 Annual Digest, 174 (1927–28). The property against which the award was executed turned out to be the premises of the Hungarian Legation. Consequently the Supreme Court discharged the execution order.
[57] 24 I.L.R., 771 (1957).
[58] *Ibid.*, 772–3.
[59] 13 F. Supp., 575 (1935).

that the award was *res judicata* it merely noted that the defendant was "bound by judgments by which he is bound".⁶⁰ This approach is essentially the same as in the English decision of *Dallal* v *Bank Mellat*,⁶¹ concerning recognition of the awards of the Iran–United States Claims Tribunal in English courts. To hold that a decision of an international tribunal is *res judicata* is to effectively recognise the decision in municipal courts.⁶² Such recognition will prevent the unsuccessful parties pursuing their claims in municipal courts. However, a successful claimant cannot otherwise seek enforcement of the decision in municipal courts.

Enforceability of awards

In contrast awards made by international commercial arbitral tribunals established pursuant to contract can be enforced, as opposed to merely being recognised, by courts in third states, since the award will be governed by the *lex loci arbitri*.

In *N. V. Cabolent* v *NIOC*⁶³ the award of the *Sapphire Petroleum* arbitration was enforced against NIOC in the Netherlands. The Hague Court of Appeal made the distinction between *acta jure imperii* and *acta jure gestionis* and held that when NIOC concluded the agreement with Sapphire Petroleum it acted as a commercial entity. Thus the doctrine of sovereign immunity was not a bar to the enforcement of the award in the Netherlands. Moreover, the court went on to state:⁶⁴

> A judicial award is by its nature enforceable and if immunity constitutes no bar to jurisdiction it can in principle neither constitute a bar to enforcement.

In respect of international arbitration, Schreuer notes that where a "state has consented to international judicial proceedings the considerations militating against interference by domestic courts should not apply to the implementation of the international decision".⁶⁵

There is increasing recognition that awards of international commercial arbitrations involving states parties should be capable of enforcement. This is exemplified by the awards of *British Petroleum* v *Libya*,⁶⁶ *Liamco* v *Libya*,⁶⁷ *Topco* v *Libya*⁶⁸ and most recently *Kuwait* v *Aminoil*.⁶⁹ These

---

⁶⁰ *Ibid.*, 595.
⁶¹ [1986] 1 All E.R., 239. This decision is separately considered in this chapter, see Recognition of the Tribunal and its Awards in Courts of Third States, *infra*.
⁶² See also Toope, *Mixed International Arbitration*, 102 (1990).
⁶³ 47 I.L.R., 138 (1965).
⁶⁴ *Ibid.*, 147.
⁶⁵ Schreuer, *The Implementation of International Judicial Decisions by Domestic Courts*, 24 I.C.L.Q., 153, 176 (1975). He made this observation in respect of enforcement of the *Sapphire International Petroleum* award.
⁶⁶ 53 I.L.R., 297 (1979).
⁶⁷ 62 I.L.R., 140 (1982).
⁶⁸ 53 I.L.R., 389 (1979).
⁶⁹ 21 I.L.M., 976 (1982).

four arbitrations illustrate the importance of an award being connected with a particular system of municipal law if there is to be certainty that the award will be enforceable in third states, since there will be no doubt that it is "made in the territory of a state".[70]

This issue was most succinctly put by Judge Lagergren, formerly the President of the Iran–United States Claims Tribunal, in the first of the arbitrations, *British Petroleum v Libya*,[71] when he stated:[72]

> By providing for arbitration as an exclusive mechanism for resolving contractual disputes, the parties to an agreement, even if one of them is a State, must, however, be presumed to have intended to create an effective remedy. The effectiveness of an arbitral award that lacks nationality—which it may if the law of the arbitration is international law—generally is smaller than that of an award founded on the procedural law of a specific legal system and partaking of its nationality. Moreover, even where the arbitrators do, as the Tribunal does in this instance, have full authority to determine the procedural law of the arbitration, the attachment to a developed: legal system is both convenient and constructive.

Judge Lagergren did not accept the reasoning of the award in *Aramco v Saudi Arabia*, which held that international arbitrations involving a state party are governed by public international law.[73] Instead he preferred the reasoning of the arbitrators in *Alsing Trading Company v Greece*[74] and *Sapphire International Petroleum v NIOC*.[75] Judge Lagergren noted that the arbitrators in both cases "held that the relevant procedural law was the law of the seat of the arbitration".[76] In the latter case, which involved the Iranian state oil company, the sole arbitrator stated "the rule was that an arbitration is subject to the judicial sovereignty of the state where the proceedings take place".[77]

Since the Tribunal had its seat in Copenhagen, and Danish law allowed a "wide scope of freedom and independence" to arbitral tribunals, Judge Lagergren considered the procedural law of the Tribunal to be Danish.[78] He recognised that the Tribunal could not conclusively determine the nationality of its award, for that was within the competence of the Danish courts or other jurisdictions where the award might be enforced. Nevertheless, Judge Lagergren deemed the award to be subject to Danish law.[79]

The second arbitration was *Liamco v Libya*,[80] which took place in

---

[70] Article V(1)(e) of the New York Convention.
[71] 53 I.L.R., 297 (1979).
[72] Ibid., 309.
[73] Ibid., 309.
[74] 23 I.L.R., 136 (1956).
[75] 35 I.L.R., 136 (1967).
[76] 53 I.L.R., 297, 310 (1979).
[77] Ibid., 297, 310.
[78] Ibid., 309.
[79] Ibid.
[80] 62 I.L.R., 140 (1982).

Geneva. The arbitrator, Dr Mahmassani, did not specify a *lex arbitri* in the award. However, he did note that it is an accepted principle of international law that the arbitral rules of procedure shall be determined by agreement of the parties or, failing such agreement, by the arbitral tribunal independently of the local law of the seat of the arbitration.[81] He had previously indicated in his preliminary decision that the procedure of the arbitration would be governed as far as possible by the general principles contained in the Draft Convention on Arbitral Procedure elaborated by the International Law Commission of the United Nations in 1958.[82] Liamco sought enforcement of the award in the United States,[83] Sweden[84] and Switzerland.[85]

The United States District Court noted that the award was granted in a foreign jurisdiction but that enforcement was sought in the United States. The agreement of Libya to arbitration constituted a waiver of sovereign immunity and thus the court had jurisdiction to recognise and enforce the award under the New York Convention. However, since Article V(2)(a) of the New York Convention allowed a court to refuse recognition and enforcement if the subject matter of the arbitration was not capable of being arbitrated in the country in which enforcement was sought, the court refused enforcement of the award. Liamco appealed to the Court of Appeal. Although the case was settled prior to the hearing, the Court of Appeal vacated the district court's order as moot, and not to be treated as a precedent in other cases.[86]

In Sweden, the Svea Court of Appeal held that the award could be enforced. Libya had waived its right of sovereign immunity by accepting the arbitration clause, and there were no circumstances that would render the execution of the award manifestly incompatible with the fundamental principles of Swedish law.[87]

The Federal Supreme Court of Switzerland refused attachment of the Libyan assets on the ground that there was insufficient connection between the arbitration and the assets sought to be attached.[88] The only connection was the fact that the arbitration took place in Switzerland.

In the third arbitration arising from the Libyan nationalisations, between *Topco and Calasiatic* v *Libya*[89] the sole arbitrator, Professor

---

[81] *Ibid.*, 180.
[82] *Ibid.*
[83] 482 F. Supp., 11775 (1980).
[84] 62 I.L.R., 225 (1982).
[85] 62 I.L.R., 228 (1982).
[86] 62 I.L.R., 224 (1982). The District Court had held that under United States law it was not possible to question the validity of Libyan nationalisation laws, and therefore an arbitration award on such matters could not be enforced in the United States.
[87] 62 I.L.R., 225, 227 (1982).
[88] 62 I.L.R., 228 (1982).
[89] 53 I.L.R., 389 (1979).

Dupuy, held that the arbitration was entirely divorced from municipal law, and was therefore governed by public international law. In contrast to Judge Lagergren, he considered that the *Aramco* award correctly stated the position, since one of the parties in the *Aramco* arbitration was a sovereign state. In the *Sapphire Petroleum* arbitration neither of the parties was a sovereign state and thus the arbitration was not applicable to the present case.[90] Moreover, the arbitral rules of procedure, including the appointment of the arbitrator by the President of the International Court of Justice, excluded reference to municipal law. Thus it was appropriate for the Tribunal to declare that the arbitration was governed by international law "because—the parties wanting to remove the arbitration from any national sovereignty—one cannot accept that the institution of arbitration should escape the reach of all legal systems and be somewhat suspended *in vacuo*".[91] Professor Dupuy conceded that an award linked to a system of municipal law would be easier to enforce, but held that considerations relating to enforcement were not within his jurisdiction, a fact stressed by the plaintiff.[92] He therefore filed the award with the Registry of the International Court of Justice, which has no effective means of enforcement.

These three awards illustrate the difficulty, inherent in international commercial arbitrations involving states parties, of determining whether the arbitral tribunal is governed by municipal law or international law. The three arbitrators had three different approaches to the question of the *lex arbitri*, indicating the uncertain state of the law in this area.

The later decision in *Aminoil* v *Kuwait*[93] shed greater light on the question of the applicable law. This arbitration concerned an American-owned oil company and the Kingdom of Kuwait following the nationalisation of the Aminoil oil concession. The parties entered into an arbitration agreement. Article IV(1) of the agreement provided that the proceedings were to be subject to "any mandatory provisions of the law of the place where the arbitration is held (namely Paris)".[94]

In a unanimous decision the three arbitrators held "the Parties themselves by their mutual arbitral commitments have defined with adequate clarity what the applicable law is".[95] There was no doubt that the parties had chosen the French legal system as "the law governing the arbitral

---

[90] *Ibid.*, 431–6.
[91] *Ibid.*, 436.
[92] *Ibid.*, 432; Professor Dupuy ordered restitution of the assets of the two companies, instead of monetary compensation. The case was settled in 1978, with Libya agreeing to supply $152 million worth of crude oil to Topco and Calasiatic. Municipal courts were therefore never requested to enforce the award.
[93] 21 I.L.M., 976 (1982).
[94] *Ibid.*, 999.
[95] *Ibid.*, 999.

procedure in the broadest sense".[96] The Tribunal recognised that this did not imply that there was a general submission to French law, since the parties had provided the means of settling the essential procedural rules and the substantive law to be applied by the Tribunal.[97] Moreover, the arbitrators noted that French law "befriended arbitrations the transnational character of which has been well in evidence".[98] This attitude has been enhanced by the new French legislation governing international commercial arbitration.[99]

It is therefore possible to draw some conclusions on the question of the *lex arbitri*. There is now little doubt that where the arbitration involves not a state party but a commercial entity of the state such as a state corporation, or where the arbitration involves two private parties, the *lex arbitri* will be a system of municipal law, usually the law of the place of the arbitration. Professor Dupuy, in deciding that a sovereign state could not be subject to another state's municipal law, considered that the decision of the arbitrator in *Sapphire International Petroleum* v *NIOC*,[100] that the arbitration was governed by Swiss law, was "completely justified", since NIOC was not a sovereign state but "only an emanation" of Iran.[101]

In cases where one of the parties to arbitration is a sovereign state the crucial issue appears to be the intention of the parties. If the parties intend the award to be capable of effective enforcement then it is desirable for the award to be attached to a system of national law. This does not pose too great a theoretical difficulty if the arbitration is derived from a contract with a private party. However, as with the Iran–United States Claims Tribunal, the arbitration may be established pursuant to a treaty between sovereign states. Unless there is some compelling evidence to indicate that the states parties intended that the arbitral tribunal should be subject to a system of national law, then it is the usual rule that such an arbitration remains completely within the realm of public international law.

However, where sovereign states have agreed, whether by treaty or by contract, that awards may be enforceable in municipal courts of third states which are not party to the treaty or contract, the courts of such states where enforcement is sought are entitled to take notice of this agreement between the states and enforce the award according to their own domestic law. Moreover, the enforcement of awards pursuant to the

---

[96] *Ibid.*, 999.
[97] *Ibid.*, 999, 1000.
[98] *Ibid.*, 999.
[99] *Ibid.*
[100] 35 I.L.R., 136, 164 (1967).
[101] 53 I.L.R., 389, 431–6 (1979).

New York Convention can be certain only if the awards are attached to a system of municipal law. It will therefore be necessary for the courts of third states where enforcement is sought pursuant to the New York Convention to determine whether the awards are subject to a system of municipal law, or whether they remain in the realm of public international law. A finding that the Tribunal, and hence its awards, are subject solely to public international law will mean that the New York Convention is probably not applicable. Enforcement of awards of such a tribunal in the courts of third states will be, at best, uncertain.

Convention on the Recognition and Enforcement of Foreign Arbitral Awards[102]

The only general international convention for the recognition and enforcement of arbitral awards in countries other than where the awards are made is the New York Convention of 1958 on the Recognition and Enforcement of Foreign Arbitral Awards.[103] The Convention has wide application, having been ratified by all the major trading nations, including the United States and the Netherlands. However, Iran is not a party to the Convention.[104]

The New York Convention is applicable only if the parties themselves have not established a code for the enforcement of awards. The Claims Settlement Declaration does not provide such a code, except to the extent that it states that the awards of the Tribunal shall be enforceable in the courts of any nation in accordance with the laws of such nation.

Thus *prima facie* it would appear that the New York Convention is applicable. The key issue is whether the awards of the Iran–United States Claims Tribunal are "awards made in the territory of a state other than the state in which recognition and enforcement of such awards are sought".[105]

Connection of arbitral awards with a system of municipal law
If the awards of the Iran–United States Claims Tribunal are considered

---

[102] The most comprehensive discussion of the Convention is found in Van den Berg, *The New York Arbitration Convention of 1958* (1981).

[103] There are the older conventions on arbitration. These are the Geneva Protocol on Arbitral Clauses, 1923, 27 L.N.T.S., 158, and the Geneva Convention on the Execution of Foreign Arbitral Awards, 1927, 92 L.N.T.S., 301. However, these conventions have limited acceptance and are largely supplanted by the New York Convention of 1958.

[104] The United States has been a party to the Convention since 1970, reserving the jurisdiction of the Convention to awards "which are considered commercial under the national laws of the United States". It also made the reciprocity reservation so that it will apply only to awards made in the territory of another contracting State. In all, sixty-two nations have ratified the Convention; from Sanders (ed.), VIII *Yearbook: Commercial Arbitration*, 335 (1983).

[105] Article I of the New York Convention.

to be awards made in the Netherlands, and therefore subject to the law of the Netherlands, then the awards will be considered to have been "made in the territory of a state" that is a party to the Convention. Conversely if the Tribunal is considered by the courts of states where enforcement of awards is sought to be an international tribunal divorced from the law of the state where it is located, then the awards would not be "made in the territory of a state" for the purposes of the New York Convention and such awards could not be enforced in that state pursuant to the New York Convention.

There is, however, an indication in the Convention that "denationalised" awards may be enforceable under the New York Convention.[106] Article V(1)(e) states that enforcement may be refused if the party can show that the award has been "set aside or suspended by a competent authority of the country in which, or under the law of which, the award has been made". The words "under the law of which" may envisage that the award can be subject to a system of law other than that of the country where the award is made. Such law may be the municipal law of a third country or may be public international law or international commercial law (*lex mercatoria*).

This view has received some support in municipal courts. The Court of Appeal of Paris in the decision of *Gotaverken* v *Libya*[107] held that it had jurisdiction over awards of international commercial arbitrations taking place in France only if the parties sought to enforce the awards in France. The court held that since neither of the parties was French and French procedural law did not govern the award, the fact that the arbitration took place in France could "not be considered an implicit expression of the parties' intent to subject themselves, even subsidiarily, to the *loi procédure française*".[108] Moreover, the provisions of the New York Convention allowing courts to review awards were not applicable since the action had been brought for the enforcement of the award. Paulsson concluded that the award was "denationalised", and that the Court of Appeal of Paris had determined it could only intervene if asked to enforce the award.[109]

---

[106] See *Delocalised Arbitrations and the New York Convention*, paper presented to International Law Association Montreal Conference 1982 by the British Branch Committee on the Enforcement of International Arbitral Awards, 10 (1982).

[107] Clunet, 660 (1980); from VI *Yearbook: Commercial Arbitration*, 221 (1981); Gotaverken had contracted to construct three tankers for Libya Maritime Co. Upon completion of the vessels Libya Maritime refused delivery on the grounds that there was a breach of the contract not to use components manufactured in Israel, and that the vessels did not meet specification. The dispute went to ICC arbitration in Paris. The arbitrators held that Libya had to accept delivery with a 2 per cent reduction in price as a result of the breaches of contract by Gotaverken. The award is published in VI *Yearbook: Commercial Arbitration* 221, 222 (1981).

[108] *Gotaverken* v *Libya* VI *Yearbook: Commercial Arbitration*, 221, 222 (1981).

[109] Paulsson, *Arbitration Unbound: Award Detached from the Law of its Country of Origin*, 30 I.C.L.Q. 358, 367 (1981). Paulsson did consider the problem of enforcing awards

Denationalised or international awards

The decision of the English High Court in *Dallal* v *Bank Mellat*[110] considered the recognition of arbitral awards which are governed by international law. Although the court was prepared to recognise an award of the Iran–United States Claims Tribunal on the basis of comity and English precedents, the court considered that the award was not enforceable pursuant to the New York Convention, since the Convention requires that the agreement be subject to some system of municipal law.[111] The court considered the proper law of the arbitration agreement between the two private parties was Dutch law.[112] The New York Convention requires that the "arbitrators shall have acquired their jurisdiction pursuant to an arbitration agreement which is valid according to its proper law".[113] However, the agreement was a nullity under Dutch law and thus the New York Convention was not applicable.

The court drew a distinction between the competence of an international tribunal established by treaty between states and private law rights which must exist as part of a municipal law system. The court stated:[114]

If public international law is to play a role in providing the governing law which gives an agreement between private law individuals legal force it has to do so by having been absorbed into some system of municipal law.

Any enforcement of an award governed by international law in English courts would have to take place outside the auspices of the New York Convention.

The courts of Iran and the United States have greater incentive to extend the application of the New York Convention to awards governed by international law should it be regarded that awards of the Iran–United States Claims Tribunal are governed solely by international law. This issue was fully canvassed in the decision of the United States Court

which were not made under the law of a particular country (cf. Article V(2) of the New York Convention), and saw no bar to such enforcement. Professor Park questioned whether French courts would have been so quick to hold that the award was not subject to the control of French courts if the contract was in some way in breach of French public policy, e.g. if the contract was for the sale of heroin instead of ships; Park, *Lex Loci Arbitri and International Commerial Arbitration: A Study in Liberal Civilian Judicial Creativity*, 55 Tulane L.R., 1 (1980), for a summary of French judicial practice. The article was published prior to the promulgation of the Decree of 1981 on International Commercial Arbitration.

[110] [1986] 1 All E.R., 239. This decision is discussed more fully in Recognition of Awards of the Tribunal, *infra*.

[111] *Ibid.*, 250.

[112] *Ibid.* The arbitration agreement between the two parties was deemed to be the parties' written pleadings and the demand by Mr Dallal to have the dispute referred to arbitration by the Tribunal. The agreement was not the Claims Settlement Agreement, which is a treaty between states.

[113] *Ibid.*

[114] *Ibid.*

of Appeals in *Ministry of Defence of Iran* v *Gould Inc.*[115] The court considered two aspects of the New York Convention: firstly whether or not there was a written agreement to arbitrate and secondly that the Convention only applies to awards subject to a "national" arbitration law. On the first issue the court held that the United States government had the authority to enter into the Algiers Accords. It thereby acted on behalf of Gould Inc. in entering into a written agreement to submit its claims against Iran to arbitration. Moreover, Gould Inc. ratified the actions of the United States by submitting the claim to arbitration.[116] This finding set up the second argument, that, even if the arbitration was properly entered into, the award was not enforceable under the New York Convention, since it was not made under the national arbitration law of any state. The court did not determine under which law the arbitration was conducted but dealt with the issue of whether the Convention covered awards not subject to the national law of a state. It held that there is no requirement in the Convention that awards must be subject to a national law, particularly in "Article I which lays out the Convention's scope of applicability".[117] Indeed the court held that "the fairest reading of the Convention itself appears to be that it applies to the enforcement of non-national awards",[118] and referred to a decision of the Dutch Supreme Court, the Hoge Raad, in *Société Europénne d'Etudes et d'Entreprises* v *Socialist Federal Republic of Yugoslavia*.[119] The court cited a particular passage:[120]

The relationship between the award and the law of a particular country need only be examined in the framework of an investigation to be carried out following a plea that the impediments mentioned in Article V(1) exist... in respect of which questions may arise which can be answered only with reference to the law of a particular country.

This passage demonstrated that the attachment of the award to a national arbitration was only necessary if Article V(1) was to be invoked to deny enforcement of the award. The court, in dealing with this issue, stated:[121]

Finally, as they are laid out, the defenses seem to apply to arbitral awards made pursuant to municipal domestic law or those made pursuant to law of the parties' choosing, as in this case. In particular, Article V(1)(d) allows a party against whom enforcement is sought to defend against enforcement if "the arbitral pro-

---

[115] 887 F. 2d, 1357 (1989).
[116] *Ibid.*, 1364.
[117] *Ibid.*, 1365.
[118] *Ibid.*
[119] H.R.N.J. 74, 361 (1974) from 887 F. 3d, 1357, 1365 (1989).
[120] *Ibid.*, 1365.
[121] *Ibid.*

cedure was not in accordance with the agreement of the parties, or, failing such agreement, was not in accordance with the law of the country where the arbitration took place".

Although this language seems to be at loggerheads with that of Article V(1)(e) concerning "the country... under the law of which [the] award was made", it is possible to reconcile the two provisions in accordance with an interpretation that holds that the Convention applies to "non-national law" awards. That is, if the parties choose not to have their arbitration governed by a "national law", then the losing party simply cannot avail itself of certain of the defenses in subparagraphs (a) and (e).

Thus, we conclude that an award need not be made "under a national law" for a court to entertain jurisdiction over its enforcement pursuant to the Convention.

At least in relation to awards of the Iran–United States Claims Tribunal there are policy reasons why United States courts would endeavour to allow enforcement of such awards under the New York Convention, even if the Court of Appeals did not specifically determine whether the awards were connected to a national system of arbitration law. Instead the court took the more innovative step of extending the application of the New York Convention to awards not made under a national law. It must be conceded, however, that this reasoning would not be generally applicable to all arbitral awards which are not connected with a system of national law.

It is submitted that the applicability of the New York Convention to arbitral awards which are governed by public international law, or which are "denationalised", is uncertain. Both the language of the Convention and international practice indicate that an award is more readily ensured of being enforced in third countries if it is governed by the *lex loci arbitri*.

Recognition and enforcement of arbitral awards not governed by the New York Convention[122]

As is well illustrated by *Dallal* v *Bank Mellat*[123] municipal courts may determine that an arbitral award cannot be recognised or enforced pursuant to the New York Convention of 1958. Furthermore, an arbitral award may have to be enforced in a state which is not a party to the Convention.[124] In both of these instances, however, arbitral awards may still be recognised, and, depending on the circumstances, be enforced by municipal courts.

The first situation will arise if the arbitral award does not meet the

---

[122] See especially Kennedy, *Enforcing International Commercial Agreements and Awards not Subject to the New York Convention*, 23 Va. J.I.L., 75 (1982).
[123] [1986] 1 All E.R., 239.
[124] Iran is not a party to the New York Convention.

requirements of the New York Convention as enacted in the state where the award is sought to be enforced. Depending on the reservations of the states adopting the New York Convention, it may be impossible to enforce an award pursuant to the Convention that would otherwise be enforceable under the Convention.[125] In addition the arbitral agreement under which the award is made may not conform with the requirements of the Convention, as was the case in *Dallal* v *Bank Mellat*.[126] In such cases recognition and enforcement need not necessarily be denied, although the latter procedure poses theoretical difficulties. Municipal courts have recognised awards of arbitral tribunals which are governed by public international law only as *res judicata* and have not enforced such awards.

Where reservations by states to the Convention preclude enforcement under the Convention, the arbitral award may still be enforceable under other provisions of municipal law providing for the enforcement of arbitral awards. An alternative is to convert the award into a judgment in the country where the award was made and then enforce the foreign judgment. Neither of these options will apply, however, for awards that fall completely outside the regime of the New York Convention or other treaty. A basic premise of the New York Convention is that it is only applicable to arbitral awards which are subject to the law of the state in which they are made or otherwise comply with a system of municipal law.[127] Unless a court can construct a cogent theory for the recognition and enforcement of such awards, as Hobhouse J. was able to do in *Dallal* v *Bank Mellat*,[128] and as the French court was able to do in the *Gotaverken* case,[129] then such awards will be unable to be recognised and enforced by municipal courts.

The second situation that arises is where the award is made in a country which is not a party to the New York Convention or any other treaty. In well developed legal systems this will not generally be a problem. Courts will be able to recognise and enforce foreign awards made in such countries pursuant to appropriate statute, codified law or precedent.[130] Alternatively the award can be converted into a judgment in the state where it was made and the judgment can be enforced by municipal courts of other states in accordance with their laws.

It can be seen from the above that arbitral awards that are outside

---

[125] As an example the United States has reservations limiting the application of the New York Convention to commercial disputes and on the basis of reciprocity.

[126] [1986] 1 All E.R., 239.

[127] Article IV of the New York Convention.

[128] [1986] 1 All E.R., 239.

[129] From VI *Yearbook: Commercial Arbitration*, 221 (1981).

[130] In the United States the appropriate law would be the 1925 Arbitration Act. In the Netherlands Article 1076 of the new arbitration law will be applicable.

municipal law are uncertain of enforcement, although they may be recognised under theories such as enunciated by Hobhouse J. in *Dallal* v *Bank Mellat*.[131]

Recognition and enforcement of the awards of the Iran–United States Claims Tribunal in municipal courts

Introduction[132]

The recognition and enforcement of the awards of the Iran–United States Claims Tribunal in municipal courts, whether pursuant to the New York Convention or otherwise, will depend on the characterisation of the awards of the Tribunal. In turn this requires a determination of the law governing the Tribunal; that is, what is the *lex arbitri* of the Tribunal? There are three possibilities:

1. That the *lex arbitri* is public international law and thus the Tribunal is completely divorced from any system of municipal law.
2. That the *lex arbitri* is a system of municipal law, most probably the law of the place of arbitration, the *lex loci arbitri*.
3. That the Tribunal is a "hybrid", with the *lex arbitri* dependent on the jurisdiction being exercised by the Tribunal in any particular claim.

The provisions of the Claims Settlements Declaration indicate that the Tribunal cannot be characterised as a traditional inter-state arbitral tribunal subject solely to public international law. The ability of private claimants to present their claims direct to the Tribunal and the provision for the enforcement of awards in courts of third countries are of particular significance in this regard. Moreover, the registration of the Tribunal awards with the Hague District Court and the Iranian applications in the Hague District Court challenging ten of the awards further support the view that the Tribunal is not solely governed by public international law. In addition the proposed legislation by the Netherlands government indicated that the Netherlands government considered that the Tribunal was governed, at least in part, by the *lex loci arbitri*. This proposed legislation only related to awards made in respect of claims and counter-claims by nationals of either party against the government of the other party, and did not extend to inter-state claims.

While the Tribunal *prima facie* would appear to be subject to Dutch

---

[131] [1986] 1 All E.R., 239.
[132] This issue has been dealt with at length in Toope, *Mixed International Arbitration* (1990) especially at 265–319.

law in respect of claims by nationals of either party against the government of the other party, even if the proposed Dutch legislation is never enacted, such claims are only one part of the jurisdiction of the Tribunal. The Tribunal also has to interpret treaty obligations between the two sovereign states and to decide whether these states have fulfilled their obligations under the treaty. Many of these obligations are concerned with high state policy, including the United States' pledges not to intervene in the internal affairs of Iran, the removal of economic and trade sanctions against Iran and the withdrawal of proceedings against Iran in the International Court of Justice. It is noteworthy that Iran and the United States considered that awards of damages of the Tribunal to compensate for a loss arising from a failure to fulfil the requirements of the Declaration with regard to such matters could be enforced by the prevailing party in the courts of any nation in accordance with its laws.[133] Nevertheless it seems unlikely that the two states intended that courts of third states should have the right to review the awards of the Tribunal in respect of such matters. Moreover the proposed Dutch legislation did not attempt to bring such awards within the purview of Dutch courts.

There is a third category of claims arising from commercial contracts between the governments of the two states. The proposed Dutch legislation did not extend to these claims and it may therefore be considered that the Netherlands government took the view that these awards were not subject to the *lex loci arbitri*. Accordingly the enforcement of awards in respect of such claims in courts of third states pursuant to the New York Convention would be uncertain. However, the *Gotaverken*[134] decision envisaged that awards not governed by municipal law could be enforced in municipal courts. The Court of Appeal of Paris stated that it did not have jurisdiction over the award except in the event of the court being requested to enforce the award.[135] Thus the actions of the arbitral tribunal in the *Gotaverken* case were not subject to judicial control by municipal courts until enforcement was requested. However, it must be recognised that, if an award lacks a nationality, enforcement of it under the New York Convention becomes less certain.[136]

It is submitted that the Iran–United States Claims Tribunal is properly characterised as a "hybrid", being both an international tribunal dealing with inter-state claims and a conventional arbitral tribunal dealing with private claims, albeit under a special regime. Thus the awards made in

[133] Paragraph 17 of the General Declaration.
[134] VI *Yearbook: Commercial Arbitration*, 221 (1981).
[135] *Ibid.*
[136] See *BritishPetroleum* v *Libya* 53 I.L.R., 297 (1979), and *Topco* v *Libya* 53 I.L.R., 389 (1979), for confirmation that an award must have a nationality to be certain of enforcement in municipal courts.

Recognition and enforcement of awards

respect of claims by nationals of either party against the government of the other party are, *prima facie*, subject to the *lex loci arbitri*, that is, Dutch law.[137] The awards made in respect of inter-state commercial claims are "denationalised" but capable of enforcement under the New York Convention in accordance with the *Gotaverken* decision. However, the awards in respect of the treaty obligations of the two states are subject solely to public international law and are not capable of enforcement in the courts of third states. Toope has characterised the Tribunal as "'mixed' econompassing elements of private and public law".[138] However, he considered that the nature of the Tribunal is "so mixed as to preclude legal clarity".[139] This view is confirmed by the actions of the parties and the Tribunal, and by the proposed Dutch legislation relating to the Tribunal.

Iranian challenges to the awards of the Tribunal[140]

The challenges to awards of the Tribunal by Iran meant that the issue of the *lex arbitri* of the Iran–United States Claims Tribunal was apparently going to be resolved, at least to the satisfaction of the Dutch Courts.

As already noted, Iran filed applications in the Hague District Court challenging ten of the awards of the Tribunal.[141] The challenges were based on the alleged non-participation of the Iranian arbitrator in the "deliberations in which the decision was taken and the finding pronounced".[142]

This issue of the non-participation by Iranian arbitrators had already arisen in Chamber Two of the Tribunal when the majority of the Chamber

---

[137] See the discussion in The Dutch Law of Arbitration, *infra*, on the requirement that arbitrations subject to Dutch law must satisfy, and the views expressed by Hobhouse J. in *Dallal v Bank Mellat* [1986] 1 All E.R., 239 on the proper law of the Tribunal in Recognition of the Tribunal and its Awards in Courts of Third States, *infra*.

[138] Toope *Mixed International Arbitration*, 277 (1990).

[139] *Ibid.*, 278.

[140] The most comprehensive discussion of these applications is found in Lake and Dana, *Judicial Review of Awards of the Iran–United States Claims Tribunal: Are the Tribunal's Awards Dutch?*, 16 Law and Policy in Int. Bus., 755, 759–82 (1984–85). See also Hardenberg, *The Awards of the Iran–United States Claims Tribunal Seen in Connection with the Law of the Netherlands*, Int. Bus. Law, 337 (1984).

[141] Iran challenged the following awards and decisions in the Hague District Court: *Blount Bros Corp. v Ministry of Housing* 3 IRAN–U.S.C.T.R., 225 (1983); *Woodward Clyde Consultants v Iran* 3 IRAN–U.S.C.T.R., 239 (1983); *Warnecke & Assocs v Bank Mellat* 3 IRAN–U.S.C.T.R., 256 (1983); *C. T. Main International Inc. v Mahab* 3 IRAN–U.S.C.T.R., 270 (1983); *Gruen Assocs Inc. v Iranian Housing Co.* 3 IRAN–U.S.C.T.R., 97 (1983); *Intrend v Iran Air Force* 3 IRAN–U.S.C.T.R., 10 (1983); *Esphahanian v Bank Tejarat* 2 IRAN–U.S.C.T.R., 157 (1983); *Rexnord v Iran* 2 IRAN–U.S.C.T.R., 6 (1983); *Raygo Wagner Equipment Co. v Star Line Iran Co.* 1 IRAN–U.S.C.T.R., 411 (1982); from Lake and Dana, *op. cit.*, 759, note 15.

[142] Lake and Dana, *op. cit.*, 760.

made awards in the *Raygo Wagner* and *Rexnord* claims without Judge Sani being present or available at the signing.[143] Judge Sani subsequently filed documents stating the reasons for his non-signature, which were replied to by Mr Mosk. In both cases it was alleged by Judge Sani that the decisions were rendered without him taking part in any deliberative sessions, which was denied by Mr Mosk.

The challenges remained before the Hague District Court for several months, during which time there was only a preliminary formal hearing. After the applications had been filed, and before any substantive progress had been made in respect of them, the Netherlands government presented a Bill into the Dutch Parliament concerning the jurisdiction of Dutch courts over awards made by the Tribunal.[144] The Bill made it clear that the Dutch courts had jurisdiction, albeit limited, over certain of the awards of the Tribunal. Iran, however, objected to the Bill, despite the fact that Iran had already accepted the jurisdiction of the Dutch Courts by filing its applications in the Hague District Court in respect of the objections. After an apparent reconsideration of its view of the status of the Tribunal, Iran withdrew the ten applications from the Hague District Court.

The Dutch law of arbitration

Introduction

Prior to the establishment of the Iran-United States Claims Tribunal in the Netherlands, discussions had been held between the government of the Netherlands and representatives of Iran and the United States. The Netherlands government proposed that there should be an agreement between all three parties stipulating that "the Tribunal would operate as an arbitral Tribunal hearing civil disputes and that Dutch law on arbitration would apply".[145]

The government of the Netherlands recognised that the principal jurisdiction of the Tribunal was over claims by nationals of either party against the government of the other party, and as such were "disputes of

---

[143] This issue was also raised in connection with the resignation of arbitrators; refer to Chapter Three on this issue.

[144] For a discussion of the Bill refer to The Proposed Dutch Law on the Iran-United States Claims Tribunal, *supra*.

[145] *Applicability of Dutch Law to the Awards of the Tribunal sitting in the Haque to hear Claims between Iran and the United States*, 4 IRAN-U.S.C.T.R., 308, 309 (1983). A paper prepared by the Ministry of Foreign Affairs of the government of the Netherlands as a commentary on the Bill on the Iran-United States Claims Tribunal presented to the Dutch Parliament, August 1983, 3. Hereinafter the paper will be referred to as *The Commentary on the Bill*. Both the paper and the Bill are reproduced in 4 IRAN-U.S.C.T.R., 305-16 (1983).

a civil law nature".[146] Furthermore the awards of the Tribunal could be enforced in the courts of any nation. Since the parties envisaged this connection with municipal law the Netherlands government considered it desirable to provide "legal certainty concerning the nature of the arbitral proceedings, the Tribunals' judicial proceedings and the awards made by the Tribunal".[147] Since these awards would be arbitral awards within the meaning of Dutch law there would be no doubt that they could be enforced in the Netherlands and, in principle, in other countries pursuant to the New York Convention.[148]

It was not possible to reach agreement. However, the Tribunal and Iran have acted as if the Tribunal is subject to Dutch law. The Tribunal has deposited its awards with the Hague District Court in accordance with Article 639 of the Dutch Code of Civil Procedure.[149] As noted previously Iran had submitted ten applications pursuant to Article 649 of the Code of Civil Procedure to the Hague District Court, challenging the awards made by the Tribunal.[150]

In light of these actions and "to remove all possible doubt as to the nature of the proceedings" the government of the Netherlands has submitted legislation to the Dutch Parliament providing that the Tribunal is subject to Dutch law as if it were a civil arbitral body having its seat in Dutch territory, and that its awards are arbitral awards within the meaning of Dutch law. The proposed legislation has been the subject of discussion between the Netherlands government and the governments of Iran and the United States. At the time of writing the Bill has not, and is unlikely to be, passed into law. It was intended that the Bill would supplant the existing Dutch law on applications for review of arbitral awards. However, the new Dutch law on arbitration has largely obviated the need for a special enactment for the Tribunal, although the Bill has some advantages over the new law of arbitration.

The Dutch law of arbitration[151]

On December 1, 1986 the old Dutch arbitration law was replaced by an entirely new Arbitration Act, set out as Articles 1020 to 1076 of the Code of Civil Procedure. The new Arbitration Act reflects a modern approach to arbitration, providing much greater freedom to the parties than did the old law. Van den Berg notes that the law is compatible with the

---

[146] *The Commentary on the Bill*, 4 IRAN–U.S.C.T.R., 308, 310 (1983).
[147] *Ibid.*, 309.
[148] *Ibid.*, 310.
[149] *Ibid.*, 310.
[150] Refer to Iranian Challenges to the Awards of the Tribunal, *supra*.
[151] This discussion is largely drawn from the report by Dr van den Berg entitled *National Reports: The Netherlands*, in XII *Yearbook: Commercial Arbitration*, 3 (1987). An English translation of the articles is provided at XII *Yearbook: Commercial Arbitration*, 370 (1987).

UNCITRAL Model Law on International Commercial Arbitration of 1985.[152]

The points of particular interest in the present context are the provisions on the arbitration agreement, the arbitral award, the grounds for setting aside an award and arbitration outside the Netherlands.

The articles on the arbitration agreement are perhaps the most significant in light of the decision of the English High Court in *Dallal v Bank Mellat*[153] that the arbitral proceedings before the Iran–United States Claims Tribunal were a nullity under the old Dutch law on arbitration. The new articles avoid this difficulty by requiring that an arbitration agreement must be in writing "provided that this instrument is expressly or impliedly accepted by or on behalf of the other party".[154]

It is not clear that a treaty between states requiring their nationals to submit certain disputes to an arbitral forum established by the treaty, as is the case with the Claims Settlement Declaration, is an agreement envisaged by Articles 1020 and 1021. It can be argued that the arbitrating parties before the Tribunal have impliedly accepted the Claims Settlement Declaration as an agreement to arbitrate. Similarly the Statements of Claim and Defence filed by the parties may constitute such agreement to arbitrate. In any event courts are not placed in the difficult situation of Hobhouse J. of having to declare that the arbitral proceedings are a nullity under Dutch law if they do not comply in every particular with the requirements of Articles 1020 and 1021.

The articles on the recognition and enforcement of arbitral awards further indicate the freedom of the parties. The courts will not entertain a plea that a tribunal lacks jurisdiction on the ground that there is no valid arbitration agreement if a party has appeared before the tribunal and submitted a defence.[155] The applicable law provision, however, is essentially the same as under the old rules.[156]

The grounds for setting awards aside are now more limited, although they are still more extensive than in other jurisdictions.[157] In particular the ability of a party to set awards aside on the basis of the absence of a valid arbitration agreement, or on the grounds that the tribunal has been improperly constituted or that it has not complied with its mandate is

---

[152] *Ibid.*, 3.
[153] [1986] 1 All E.R., 239. In particular Hobhouse J. stated that because there was no written agreement to arbitrate as per the requirements of Article 623 of the pre-1986 code, the arbitration proceedings before the Iran–United States Claims Tribunal were a nullity under Dutch law. The old articles are reproduced in 4 IRAN–U.S.C.T.R., 299–304, (1983).
[154] Article 1021.
[155] Article 1052(2).
[156] Article 1054.
[157] Article 1065.

restricted by preceding provisions.[158] Thus if a party accepted these breaches without demur during the arbitration he cannot subsequently seek to have the award set aside.

The provisions in respect of arbitration outside the Netherlands are essentially similar to the previous law covering enforcement under the New York Convention.[159] A similar procedure also applies to enforcement of awards where the Convention or other treaty is not applicable.[160]

The key feature of the new arbitration law is the greater degree of freedom allowed to the parties, especially on the fundamental issue of submitting disputes to arbitration. As a result of these provisions it can be reasonably argued that the Iran–United States Claims Tribunal and its awards, especially in respect of claims of nationals, are governed by Dutch law.

The proposed Dutch law on the Iran–United States Claims Tribunal

The Netherlands government was aware that, since the Tribunal was established pursuant to treaty between the two sovereign states for the settlement of disputes between Iran and the United States, it "cannot be entirely put on a par with a regular arbitral agreement under civil law".[161] The Bill presented to the Dutch Parliament therefore limits the applicability of the provisions of the Code of Civil Procedure governing arbitrations.[162]

The Bill applies only to awards of the Tribunal made in respect of claims and counter-claims by nationals of either party against the government of the other.[163] These awards are deemed to be arbitral awards within the meaning of Dutch law.[164] However, they may not be challenged in Dutch courts on the grounds of the lack of jurisdiction of the Tribunal.[165]

Awards made in respect of claims between the governments of Iran and the United States are not to be subject to Dutch law. Accordingly it would appear that these awards are subject only to public international law, although Article IV(3) of the Claims Settlement Declaration states that *all* awards of the Tribunal may be enforced in the courts of any

---

[158] See Article 1052 referred to above.
[159] Article 1075.
[160] Article 1076.
[161] *Commentary on the Bill*, 4 IRAN–U.S.C.T.R., 308, 311 (1983).
[162] The appointment of arbitrators and the conduct of the settlement proceedings are governed solely by the Claims Settlement Declaration and the UNCITRAL rules. This was accepted by the Netherlands government, see *Commentary on the Bill*, 4 IRAN–U.S.C.T.R., 308, 311 (1983).
[163] Section 2 of the Bill.
[164] *Ibid.*
[165] *Ibid.*

nation. Thus awards made in respect of claims between the two governments may not be readily enforceable in national courts other than those of Iran and the United States.[166]

Although awards made in respect of claims by nationals of one party against the government of the other are arbitral awards within the meaning of Dutch law, the Bill severely limits the application of the provisions of the Code of Civil Procedure relating to arbitrations in respect of these awards. The only provisions of the Code of Civil Procedure that remain applicable are those relating to the depositing of awards in the Dutch courts[167] and the enforcement of awards by Dutch courts pursuant to the New York Convention.[168] In place of the provisions of the Code of Civil Procedure for challenging awards of the Tribunal the Bill provides limited grounds for the challenge of awards of the Tribunal to which the Bill applies.[169] There are two grounds upon which challenges may be made:[170]

1. That the proceedings leading to the award have been conducted in a manner which constitutes a manifest breach of the principles of proper judicial procedure or;
2. That the award is manifestly contrary to public order or morals.

The government of the Netherlands limited the grounds to "essential requirements, which are incorporated in all arbitral legislation".[171] Moreover, the inclusion of the word "manifest" was to make it apparent that only in very clear cases could awards be successfully challenged.[172] The procedure for challenging awards is also prescribed in the Bill.[173] The application to challenge the award must be filed in the Hague District Court within three months of the award being deposited with the registry of the court. The Hague District Court has jurisdiction to hear the application in the first instance, but parties can make appeals and appeals

---

[166] These awards would be enforceable in the courts of Iran and the United States, since those courts would be bound by the ratification by their respective governments of Article IV(3) of the Claims Settlement Declaration providing for the enforcement of the awards in the courts of any nation. Courts of other nations would not be bound by the Claims Settlement Declaration, and since it appears that these awards do not have a nationality they may not be enforceable pursuant to the New York Convention.

[167] Section 3 of the Bill. Article 639 provided for the depositing of awards in the Dutch courts. The Tribunal has already been depositing its awards with the Registry of the Hague District Court. This article has been replaced by a provision of the 1986 Arbitration Act.

[168] Section 3 of the Bill. Articles 642, 644 and 645 of the Code of Civil Procedure contained the provisions for the enforcement of arbitral awards. These articles have been replaced by provisions of the 1986 Act.

[169] Section 4 of the Bill.

[170] Unofficial translation of the Bill, from 4 IRAN–U.S.C.T.R., 305, 306–7 (1983).

[171] *Commentary on the Bill*, 4 IRAN–U.S.C.T.R., 308, 314 (1983).

[172] *Ibid*.

[173] Section 5 of the Bill.

in cassation against the judgment of the Hague District Court. It is the view of the Netherlands government that matters of such importance should be decided at the highest judicial level.[174]

It is recognised by the Netherlands government that the Tribunal has exclusive jurisdiction to determine whether it will hear a case in which an award of the Tribunal has been set aside by the Dutch courts. Nevertheless it was considered desirable for the Bill to specify that it should not be construed as preventing the Tribunal from deciding whether a case might be resubmitted for rehearing.[175] A second award made as a result of such a rehearing could be enforced in Dutch courts in the same manner as any other award of the Tribunal.[176]

The final provision of the Bill states that it shall be retrospective to July 1, 1981.[177] However, any final and irrevocable judgment of the court in respect of an award of the Tribunal made before the Bill becomes law will be unaffected by the Bill.

The Bill was approved by the Dutch Cabinet in March 1983. The Bill was then presented to the Second Chamber of the Netherlands Parliament and passed in February 1984. The final step for the Bill to become law was its passage through the First Chamber, due to take place in March 1984.

The Iranian government, however, had reconsidered the characterisation of the Tribunal, and apparently decided that it ought to be outside the scope of municipal law to the maximum extent possible. The Iranian agent, Eshragh, wrote to the Dutch Ministry of Foreign Affairs protesting about the Bill, and requested that it should be withdrawn to "protect Iran's rights and to respect Iran's stand in respect of the Algiers Declarations".[178] Subsequently Eshragh and the Iranian arbitrator, Kashani, held meetings with the First Chamber Justice and Foreign Affairs Committee to further dissuade the Chamber from passing the Bill.[179] Their principal representation was that the enactment of the Bill into law would prejudice the international character of the Tribunal.

Since the Bill had largely been motivated by the Iranian applications in the Hague District Court to review decisions of the Tribunal, the applications were withdrawn by Iran, thereby removing the need for the Bill. As

---

[174] *Commentary on the Bill*, 4 IRAN–U.S.C.T.R., 308, 315 (1983).
[175] *Ibid.*, 315.
[176] *Ibid.* Section 6 of the Bill.
[177] Section 7(1) of the Bill.
[178] Letter from Eshragh to Dutch Ministry of Foreign Affairs, from 5 IRAN–U.S.C.T.R., 405, 413 (1984). This letter contains detailed argument on the status of the Tribunal as an international tribunal governed by international law. See also Dana and Lake, *Judicial Review of Awards of the Iran–United States Claims Tribunal: Are the Tribunal's Awards Dutch?*, 16 Law and Policy in Int. Bus., 755, 786 (1984).
[179] Mealys L.R.: Iranian Reports, 306 (1984).

a result the First Chamber did not vote on the Bill, which remains pending before it. Moreover unless there are any future applications to review awards of the Tribunal, or applications to enforce awards of the Tribunal in Dutch courts, it is unlikely that the Bill will proceed.

The enactment of the new Dutch law of arbitration has made the Bill less necessary, since it can now be more readily maintained that the Tribunal is governed by Dutch law. Nevertheless a case can still be made for the Bill to be enacted as law. The ability of Dutch courts to intervene in the Tribunal and its awards would be much less under the provisions of the Bill than under the new law on arbitration.

Recognition of the Tribunal and its awards in the courts of third states

The status of the Tribunal and its awards has been considered in the courts of England and Switzerland. The decisions, although giving opposite results, both seem to indicate that the Tribunal is governed by international law.

The English decision in *Dallal v Bank Mellat*[180] is of particular significance in any discussion of the characterisation of awards of the Tribunal, in view of its finding that although the agreement to arbitrate, the Claims Settlement Declaration, is a nullity under Article 623 of the Dutch law on arbitration in force prior to December 1, 1986, comity requires English courts to recognise the awards of the Tribunal.[181]

The Tribunal had previously made an award, *Dallal v Iran*,[182] in which it had rejected Dallal's claim in respect of the dishonour of two cheques drawn by the International Bank of Iran, the predecessor of Bank Mellat. The cheques were made out in United State dollars and were payable in Dallal's bank in the United States. The Tribunal was in some doubt as to whether the cheques were in payment for services or were a simple capital transfer of rials into dollars. In the latter case they would infringe Iranian currency regulations, which required such payments to be approved by Bank Markazi. The International Monetary Fund (IMF) permitted and obligated members of the IMF to respect such currency regulations. The Tribunal considered that it was necessary for the claimants to prove that the transaction was an approved transaction, rather than for the respondent to show that it infringed currency regulations,

---

[180] [1986] 1 All E.R., 239. The decision has been the subject of comment in Kunzlik, *Public International Law—Cannot Govern a Contract, Can Authorise an Arbitration*, C.L.J., 337 (1986), and Crawford, *Decisions of British Courts during 1985–6 Involving Questions of Public or Private International Law*, 57 B.Y.I.L., 405 at 410–14 (1986).

[181] The relevant part of Article 623 was not enacted in the new law and accordingly had the court decided on this issue in respect of an award made after December 1, 1986 the court might have reached its decision on quite different reasoning.

[182] 3 IRAN–U.S.C.T.R., 10 (1983).

Recognition and enforcement of awards 327

since the necessary information was in the possession of the claimant. Since the claimant did not show that the transaction satisfied the requirements of Iranian currency regulations it stated:[183]

The Tribunal therefore reaches the conclusion that the two cheques must be assumed to have been issued as part of a capital transfer, intended merely to exchange Rials for Dollars and to transfer the dollar amount to the United States. The Tribunal therefore concludes that it is unable to issue an award in favour of the Claimant.

Dallal then issued proceedings in England against Bank Mellat. The issue before the court was whether it could recognise the award of the Tribunal and thereby strike out the proceedings in the English court as being an abuse of process. The approach of Hobhouse J. throws considerable light on the status of awards of an international tribunal established by treaty which are made in respect of claims by private claimants. As noted previously Hobhouse J. recognised the award on the grounds of comity, since:[184]

If under international law such a tribunal is competent, its competence ought to be recognised by the English courts.

The court referred to a number of points which were relevant to recognition of the award.[185] First, the competence of a tribunal can be found in international law and practice. Second, competence under international law can be conferred by treaty. Third, where a tribunal has been set up by a subject's own sovereign government, the subject cannot say that the act of his own government was incompetent. Fourth, once a person has voluntarily submitted to the jurisdiction of a tribunal he has made the tribunal competent by his own act.

On the basis of these points, and a number of precedents of superior English courts in respect of the recognition of decisions of foreign consular courts, in particular *The Laconia*[186] and *Messina* v *Petrococchino*,[187] Hobhouse J. stated:[188]

These decisions clearly illustrate that competence can be derived from international law, and that international comity requires that the courts of England

---

[183] *Ibid.*, 17.
[184] *Ibid.*, 253. Professor Crawford considers that "The decision is an intriguing mixture of dualistic premisses and a willingness to give effect to decisions which were, in a certain sense, taken at the international level"; from Crawford, *Decisions of British Courts during 1985–86 Involving Questions of Public or Private International Law*, 57 B.Y.I.L., 405, 413 (1986).
[185] These points are covered at pp. 253–4 of the report of the judgment.
[186] (1863) 2 Moore P.C. (N.S.) 161; 15 E.R., 862.
[187] (1872) L.R. 4 P.C., 144.
[188] *Ibid.*, 255.

should recognise the validity of the decisions of foreign tribunals whose competence is so derived.

The finding of Hobhouse J. that the Tribunal acquired its competence under public international law poses significant problems for the enforcement of the awards of the Tribunal under the municipal law of third states. The mere recognition of an award of an international tribunal by a municipal court does not mean that the award can be enforced by that court. Under the Arbitration Act, 1975, ratifying the New York Convention on the Recognition and Enforcement of Foreign Arbitral Awards, recognition and more importantly enforcement will be denied unless the award is made in the territory of a state other than where the award is sought to be enforced.[189] Thus if the award is not subject to the law of the Netherlands, but is governed by international law, then it will not comply with the requirements of the Convention and will not be enforceable pursuant to the Convention.

Any enforcement or recognition of the awards prior to December 1, 1986 of the Tribunal in English courts can only be achieved outside the regime of the New York Convention.[190] So far as recognition is concerned Hobhouse J. was able to find an avenue based on precedents for the recognition of decisions of foreign consular courts and on the doctrine of comity. Thus the principle of *res judicata* meant that Dallal could not commence proceedings in an English court since the Tribunal had already made an award in favour of Iran.

The new Dutch law on arbitration will eliminate the problem of nullity faced by Hobhouse J. in *Dallal* v *Bank Mellat*. Since awards made by the Tribunal in respect of claims of nationals will be governed by Dutch law there should be no difficulty in recognising and enforcing such awards pursuant to the New York Convention.

The Swiss case concerned the review of an International Chamber of Commerce arbitration award made in Switzerland in respect of a claim, *Textron Inc.* v *Iran*.[191]

The facts were that a United States corporation had concluded an agreement with the Iranian government for the establishment of a helicopter industry in Iran, including arbitration under the ICC rules in the event of a dispute. In December 1978, during the Islamic revolution, the Iranian government terminated the agreement. In August 1979 the claimant submitted a request for arbitration and in December 1979 the ICC Court of Arbitration decided that the arbitration should proceed.

---

[189] Article IV of the Convention.

[190] At this stage the old Dutch law of arbitration was applicable.

[191] Arbitral Award, 6 IRAN–U.S.C.T.R., 328 (1984); Arbitral Order, 6 IRAN–U.S.C.T.R., 347 (1984); Judgment of the Court of Appeal of the Canton of Zurich, 6 IRAN–U.S.C.T.R., 350 (1984).

After a series of correspondence with various Iranian authorities the single arbitrator, in an award dated 12 February 1981, some three weeks after the Algiers Declarations had entered into force, concluded that the arbitrator had the competence to hear the case. The status of the Algiers Declarations was not considered in the award.

Following this award the Iranian government made a submission to the ICC Court of Arbitration that the arbitration proceedings should be stayed pending a decision of the Iran–United States Claims Tribunal. The Court of Arbitration informed the arbitrator that he alone had to decide the effect of the Algiers Declarations on the ICC arbitration. The arbitrator in his order noted, firstly, that at the time of the original proceedings the existence of the Algiers Declarations was known to both parties and no objection to the arbitrator's jurisdiction on this ground was raised at that time.[192] Second, the Algiers Declarations were an agreement between states and its effects are limited to the two states and their courts and institutions. The arbitrator stated:[193]

> The Arbitration Tribunal, established in Switzerland by the ICC and on the basis of a valid agreement between the conflicting parties, does not fall under the jurisdiction of international instruments binding on the contracting states only. An Arbitration Tribunal established in a third state cannot be an addressee of the "Algiers Declaration".

Moreover the arbitrator noted that Principle (B) of the General Declaration confirmed this view, since it only required the United States to terminate all legal proceedings in United States courts, and did not extend to proceedings in third countries.[194]

Finally, the arbitrator noted that even if the Algiers Declarations were applicable the ICC Arbitration Tribunal complied with the requirements of Article I of the Claims Settlement Declaration, since "the term 'settlement' includes settlement through arbitration which the parties expressly agreed upon as the means for settling disputes between them".[195]

Following this order the Iranian government commenced proceedings in the Court of Appeal of the Canton of Zurich, requesting the court to negate the jurisdiction of the arbitrator, or at least to stay the proceedings until after a final decision of the Iran–United States Claims Tribunal. After a series of orders and decisions in the Swiss courts, including the Court of Cassation, the issue before the Court of Appeal was "whether the Algiers Declaration indeed excludes the jurisdiction of the single arbitrator".[196]

---

[192] 6 IRAN–U.S.C.T.R., 347, 348 (1984).
[193] *Ibid.*, 349.
[194] *Ibid.*, 349.
[195] *Ibid.*, 350.
[196] 6 IRAN–U.S.C.T.R., 350, 352 (1984).

The Iranian government contended that the Algiers Declaration applies to all claims of United States nationals without any geographical or jurisdictional limitation.[197] Furthermore Swiss courts and Swiss arbitral tribunals were bound to recognise the Algiers Declaration, since "International law has precedence over municipal law".[198]

The court accepted that the:

Algiers Declaration determined that claims brought before the Iran–United States Claims Tribunal would be deemed to be excluded from the jurisdiction of the tribunals not only of Iran or the U.S.A. but also from the jurisdiction of any other courts (Article VII(2) of the Claims Settlement Declaration).[199]

However, the court considered that the Declaration did not have any legal force in Switzerland even if the arbitrating parties in Switzerland would otherwise be bound by the Treaty. The court stated:[200]

Contrary to the Appellant's contention, there is no principle of public international law according to which a treaty between two States should be respected by all other states. On the contrary, there is a principle in public international law according to which a treaty does not create any rights or obligations for a third party without the latter's express consent. The single arbitrator therefore correctly pointed out that in its effect the Algiers Declaration is an agreement between states; its effects were limited to those courts, institutions and administrative agencies which are under the jurisdiction of the two contracting states.

Moreover, Swiss precedent held that provisions of treaties were not part of Swiss law in cases involving nationals of the contracting states if Switzerland was not a party to the treaties. Accordingly, the single arbitrator retained jurisdiction, irrespective of whether the Iran–United States Claims Tribunal also had jurisdiction.

The Swiss case did not consider the status of awards of the Tribunal, but merely whether an international treaty to which Switzerland was not a party, the Algiers Declarations, excluded the jurisdiction of Swiss courts. In the event of the Iran–United States Claims Tribunal making an award the question of whether the Swiss arbitral proceedings should be annulled or stayed would arise.[201] The grant of an annulment or stay of proceedings would not depend on whether the Iran–United States Claims Tribunal was governed by international or municipal law. As with the English court in *Dallal* v *Bank Mellat* the principle of *res judicata* could be invoked even if the Tribunal was considered to be governed solely by international law. However, this principle stops short of allowing the

[197] *Ibid.*, 353.
[198] *Ibid.*, 353.
[199] *Ibid.*, 354.
[200] *Ibid.*, 354.
[201] *Ibid.*, 355.

enforcement of the awards of the Tribunal, notwithstanding the expectations of the parties to the Claims Settlement Declaration.

Conclusion on the recognition and enforcement of awards of the Iran–United States Claims Tribunal

The two decisions of the English and Swiss Courts would appear to indicate that courts of third states will hold that the Tribunal is governed solely by international law, at least until December 1986, when the new Dutch law of arbitration came into effect, and that it has no connection with municipal law, apart from that of Iran and the United States. In particular the English High Court considered that if the Tribunal was governed by Dutch law then it must be a nullity. However, the English court was prepared to recognise awards of the Tribunal on the basis of comity. Since December 1, 1986 it can be argued, the Tribunal, at least in respect of claims of nationals, is governed by the new Dutch law of arbitration.

The Tribunal, however, has acted at all times as if it is subject to Dutch law by depositing its awards with the Hague District Court. Moreover, the Dutch government considered that it was appropriate that the Tribunal should be subject to Dutch law, albeit to a limited extent only, both with the proposed Bill on the Tribunal, and as a result of the new Dutch law on arbitration.

The most interesting feature of the Dutch Bill was the distinction between the different categories of jurisdiction that can be exercised by the Tribunal. As noted at the outset the Tribunal has jurisdiction over three categories of claims: claims of nationals of one party against the government of the other party, claims by one government against the other government arising from commercial contracts, and disputes between the two governments concerning the interpretation, performance and application of the two Algiers Declarations. However, only those awards made in respect of claims by nationals of one party against the government of the other are deemed to be awards within the meaning of Dutch arbitral law. By implication all other awards are considered by the Netherlands government to be subject to public international law, as in *Aramco v Saudi Arabia*[202] and *Topco and Calasiatic v Libya*.[203] The arbitrators in these awards were more ready to find that the arbitrations were subject to public international law, since they held that enforcement of the awards was not a matter that they need consider. The Claims

[202] 27 I.L.R., 117 (1963).
[203] 53 I.L.R., 389, 431 (1979).

Settlement Declaration, however, states that "*all* awards shall be enforceable in the courts of any nation in accordance with the laws of that nation".[204] No distinction is drawn between awards made under the different categories of jurisdiction.

It is the writer's view that the Tribunal is a "hybrid", with its characterisation dependent on the jurisdiction which it exercises in any particular award or decision. For the first two categories of jurisdiction the Tribunal ought to be subject to Dutch law in the same manner as any other international commercial arbitration tribunal having its seat in the Netherlands. Until December 1, 1986 there were the potential problems posed by Article 623 of the Dutch Code of Civil Procedure that had been identified in *Dallal* v *Bank Mellat*.[205] The new Dutch law on arbitration removes these difficulties and a strong case can be made that the Tribunal is now subject to Dutch law in respect of these two categories of jurisdiction. In respect of the third category of jurisdiction, concerning the implementation and interpretation of the Algiers Declarations and matters of high state policy, the Tribunal should be subject only to public international law, with municipal courts having no power to review or enforce such awards or decisions.

The provisions of the Dutch Bill governing the Tribunal were more satisfactory than the new Dutch law on arbitration. First, it drew a distinction between various categories of jurisdiction. Second, the Bill limited the involvement of Dutch courts to a greater extent than the new Dutch law on arbitration.

The Bill provided that awards arising from disputes between nationals of one party and the government of the other party are subject to Dutch arbitral law. The Bill therefore correctly stated the position in respect of the various categories of jurisdiction. It recognised that these claims are essentially civil claims, such as would be dealt with by international commercial arbitration. The two governments intended that such awards should be enforceable in the courts of nations which are not parties to the Declaration. To make this intent effective it is desirable that the awards should have a nationality. Moreover, the Tribunal and Iran have already acted as if the awards are subject to Dutch law. The limits placed on Dutch courts by the proposed legislation to review such awards are in accordance with modern practice and with the terms of the Claims Settlement Declaration. Moreover, a strong case can be made that awards made prior to December 1, 1986 in these two categories are already subject to Dutch law on the basis that the parties' pleadings are sufficient compliance with Article 623 of the Dutch Code of Civil Procedure.

---

[204] Article IV(3) of the Claims Settlement Declaration.
[205] [1986] 1 All E.R., 239.

Awards made prior to December 1, 1986 in respect of government-to-government claims will be in the same position as the award in the *Gotaverken* case.[206] It is clear from the Claims Settlement Declaration that Iran and the United States intended that such awards should be enforceable in the courts of any nation. The Court of Appeal of Paris recognised that the award in the *Gotaverken* case could be enforced pursuant to the New York Convention, but that it did not have jurisdiction over the award, except in the event of the court being asked to enforce it. Thus the actions of the arbitral tribunal were not subject to any judicial control until enforcement was requested. Under the current French law on arbitration all international commercial arbitration taking place in France is subject to the ultimate control of French courts.[207]

The position in the Netherlands is now quite similar. Awards of the Tribunal made since December 1, 1986 would apparently be covered by the new Dutch law of arbitration and thus able to be enforced pursuant to the New York Convention.

It is the view of the writer that awards made in respect of government-to-government contract claims are also subject to Dutch law on arbitration. Ideally they should have also been covered by the proposed legislation. Although the Claims Tribunal was established by treaty between two sovereign states to resolve claims between them, the second category of jurisdiction relates solely to claims of a commercial nature. Furthermore, Iran and the United States intended that the awards made in respect of such claims should be enforceable in the courts of any nation. The exclusion of such claims in the Bill from being reviewed or enforced by Dutch courts was contrary to the intentions of the parties as expressed in Article IV(3) of the Claims Settlement Declaration.[208] Moreover the jurisdiction of the Dutch courts was in any event limited by the legislation to matters of fundamental fairness "incorporated in all arbitral legislation".[209] The proposed legislation should therefore have properly covered the government-to-government claims.

In its final category of jurisdiction, that of the interpretation, performance and application of the Algiers Declarations, the Tribunal should be considered as an international arbitral tribunal subject only to

---

[206] Clunet, 660 (1980); from VI *Yearbook: Commercial Arbitration*, 133 (1981).

[207] Craig, Park and Paulsson, *French Codification of a Legal Framework for International Commercial Arbitration: The Decree of May 12, 1981*, in VII *Yearbook: Commercial Arbitration*, 407, 411 (1982).

[208] Under Section 2 of the Bill only awards made in respect of claims by nationals of one party against the government of the other party are "arbitral awards within the meaning of Dutch law". Under Section 3 of the Bill these awards can be enforced in Dutch courts pursuant to Articles 642, 644 and 645 of the Dutch Code of Civil Procedure, provisions since replaced by provisions of the Arbitration Act, 1986.

[209] *Commentary on the Bill*, 4 IRAN–U.S.C.T.R., 308, 31 (1983).

public international law. The Tribunal has to interpret treaty obligations between two sovereign states and to determine whether these states have fulfilled their obligations under the treaty.[210] Many of these obligations are concerned with high state policy, including the United States' pledges not to intervene in Iran's internal affairs, the lifting of sanctions against Iran, and the withdrawal of proceedings against Iran in the International Court of Justice.[211]

It is noteworthy that Iran and the United States agreed that only awards and not decisions or orders of the Tribunal could be enforced in the courts of any nation in accordance with its laws. In respect of this third category of jurisdiction the Tribunal has, thus far, only made decisions, not awards.[212]

However paragraph 17 of the General Declaration envisages that the Tribunal can make awards of damages to compensate for any breaches of the Algiers Declarations causing loss. Presumably, such breaches could be in respect of the political and state policy undertakings of the two states. Thus the two states intended that such awards should be able to be enforced by the prevailing party in the courts of third states. The difficulty is that the Convention on the Recognition and Enforcement of Awards would be unlikely to apply to such inter-state awards, for which the governing law is public international law. It is therefore doubtful that these awards could be enforced in municipal courts of third countries pursuant to the Convention. The only possibility of recognition and enforcement is by an extension of the reasoning of the *Dallal* case so that the principle of comity could also be applied by municipal courts of third states in respect of inter-state awards.[213] The award could only be used as a defence to an action in a municipal court by either state against the other, provided that in any event such actions were not excluded by the doctrine of sovereign immunity.

It is unlikely that either Iran or the United States would wish to have

---

[210] Iran has commenced proceedings in the Tribunal against the United States under this head and is making eighteen claims of non-performance by the United States of its obligations under the Algiers Declarations; *I.A.L.R.*, 5389 (1982).

[211] All of these obligations are set out in the General Declaration.

[212] All volumes of the IRAN–U.S.C.T.R. include an Editorial Note, which states in part: "*Decisions* are rendered by the Tribunal in cases arising directly between the Governments of Iran and the United States." However the governments of the contracting parties can raise cases concerning the interpretation and application of the Algiers Declarations, and the Tribunal can make awards of damages in respect of the third category of jurisdiction which are enforceable by "the prevailing party in the courts of any nation in accordance with its laws"; paragraph 17 of the General Declaration.

[213] [1986] 1 All E.R., 239. See discussion of this case in *Recognition of the Tribunal and its Awards in Courts of Third States*. Refer also to *Société Vinicole de Champagne* v *Mumm Champagne & Importation Co. Inc.* 13 F. Supp. 575, in which it was held that a decision of an international arbitral tribunal, the Franco-German Mixed Arbitral Tribunal, was *res judicata* against the defendant in the proceedings in United States municipal courts.

Recognition and enforcement of awards

the issues which are the subject of such awards being reviewed by the municipal courts of third countries, or indeed by their own municipal courts, which could occur if they were to be enforced in such courts. It is therefore probable that awards in the third category are not enforceable in municipal courts of third states despite the provisions of paragraph 17 of the General Declaration. These awards are governed solely by public international law. Nevertheless such awards may be recognised in municipal courts of third states on the principles of comity and *res judicata*, to prevent claims by either state against the other if the claim would otherwise be justiciable. Most of the issues in the third category, however, would not be justiciable in any municipal courts and would remain solely in the domain of public international law.

PART FOUR

Conclusion

CHAPTER FIFTEEN

An assessment of the contribution of the Tribunal to international arbitration

Introduction

The Iran–United States Claims Tribunal was established in unique circumstances. Both states had interests they wished to preserve. In the case of the United States they were the release of the hostages and protection of United States property interests. For Iran the guarantee against intervention and release of the frozen assets were the motivating factors. In the balancing of these competing interests the Claims Tribunal was established. To the extent that Iran was compelled to agree, the establishment of the Tribunal recalls the circumstances that led to the establishment of the various claims commissions between the Latin American states and the European powers at the end of the nineteenth and beginning of the twentieth centuries. Since the end of World War II, states have tended to settle claims by lump sum agreement, usually providing payment for less than 100 per cent of the actual loss. It is only when the claimant state is able to exercise military, economic or other coercive power that it has been able to insist on the establishment of a claims settlement tribunal.

Nevertheless the constitution of the Tribunal does reflect, to a degree, the interests of both states. This may be contrasted with the establishment of the United Nations Compensation Commission arising from losses caused by Iraq's unlawful invasion and occupation of Kuwait. Iraq had no say in the jurisdiction of the Commission and up to 30 per cent of Iraqui petroleum sales will be used to establish the compensation fund. However, it cannot be doubted that, despite appearances to the contrary, in the struggle between Iran and the United States, the freezing of the substantial deposits held by Iran in United States banks and the litigation commenced by United States claimants against Iran in United States courts meant that the United States could insist on a settlement that reflected its interests more than those of Iran. It is only where a revolutionary state has few contacts with Western powers, or has an alternative sponsor, that it can proceed on a revolutionary path without paying heed to overseas ownership interests in the economy. Even if a state chooses this approach there may be substantial costs.

The unwillingness of Cuba to settle the claims of United States nationals has undoubtedly imposed substantial costs on the Cuban economy through the denial of the United States market to Cuba. Despite the improbability of a developing state agreeing to the establishment of an arbitral tribunal to settle claims except under circumstances where the claimant state is able to exert a high degree of leverage, the experience of the Iran–United States Claims Tribunal is of general significance for states and international lawyers.

There are three aspects that are worthy of discussion. Of foremost importance is the development of public international law through the awards and decisions of the Tribunal. In this respect the expropriation decisions are of greatest interest. Secondly, the nature of the relationship between the decisions of the Tribunal and particular systems of municipal law is of some significance, especially having regard to the growth of international commercial arbitration to resolve disputes between governments and multinational corporations. Finally, the Tribunal underscores the limits of the ability of arbitration to settle inter-state disputes and thus establish a new relationship between the arbitrating states, untainted by the dispute that led to the establishment of the arbitral tribunal.

In respect of the latter point the present relationship between Iran and the United States is particularly illustrative. Where there are major tensions between states stemming from fundamentally different perspectives of each other's roles and interests then international arbitration will be of limited usefulness. Although arbitration may settle specific limited disputes it cannot resolve the fundamental conflict. So long as sovereign states remain the paramount actors in the international arena, international arbitration will be of marginal significance. States will be reluctant to surrender their freedom of action *vis-à-vis* one another by handing over the resolution of disputes to independent legal tribunals, thus exemplifying the fundamental weakness of the international order.[1] Nevertheless, as is shown by the Iran–United States Claims Tribunal, international arbitration has a useful, albeit limited, role to play in the relations between states. The final section of this chapter examines the prospects and role of international arbitration between states.

[1] The refusal of the United States to recognise the decision of the International Court of Justice in *Case Concerning Military and Paramilitary Activities in and around Nicaragua (Nicaragua v United States) (Merits)* I.C.J. Rep., 14 (1986), is a particularly good illustration of this feature of state behaviour.

The development of international law by the Tribunal

The jurisdiction of the Tribunal is limited to claims arising from debt, contract, expropriation and other measures affecting property rights.[2] Despite the limited jurisdiction of the Tribunal, its jurisprudence is of great importance to the international legal community.

The major theme of the Tribunal, identifiable at the very early stage of the Tribunal's existence when Iran objected to Mr Mangard,[3] has been the Tribunal's observance of traditional "Western" norms of legal reasoning, with extensive use of precedent and literal interpretation of the governing rules of law and contract. Although the Iranian agents and the Iranian arbitrators have perceived this as being adverse to Iranian interests and the interests of developing states generally, such an approach did not necessarily have to lead to such a result.

Nevertheless there is some basis for arguing that the reasoning of the awards, and the compensation payable thereunder, have been generally favourable to United States claimants. This can be largely attributed to three reasons. The first reason is explicit and is the extensive use of precedent by the Tribunal in its decisions. The second reason stems from the fact that the neutral arbitrators have been schooled in the "Western" legal tradition. This fact underpins the extensive use of precedent by the Tribunal. The final reason is the recognition of the internationalisation of the world economy and the need to protect capital.

The importance of precedent in the decisions of the Tribunal has reinforced a conservative view of international law. Most of the available precedents are the decisions of the claims commissions arising from the Latin American revolutions at the end of the nineteenth century and the beginning of the twentieth century, and the decisions of the commissions established by the victorious Allies after the First and Second World Wars. As may be expected the decisions of these commissions primarily reflect the views of the Western European states. Thus in using these precedents the Iran–United States Claims Tribunal has reinforced a Euro-American view of international law. This feature is well illustrated in the dual nationality decision of the Tribunal.[4] This decision applied the *Mergé* case[5] of the Italian–United States Conciliation Commission, thereby enabling claimants having the nationality of both Iran and the

[2] Article II(1) of the Claims Settlement Declaration.
[3] For a full review of the Tribunal's decision and Dr Moons's decision as appointing authority, refer to Chapter Three.
[4] *Iran v United States (Case A/18)* 5 IRAN–U.S.C.T.R., 251 (1984). See Chapter Four for a full discussion of the case.
[5] XIV R.I.A.A., 236 (1955). It is recognised that the *Mergé Case* is an application of the decision of the International Court of Justice in the *Nottebohm Case*. However, the *Merge Case* extended the *ratio* of *Nottebohm* by applying to claims of dual nationals against a state whose nationality the claimant also possesses.

United States to make claims against Iran provided they could demonstrate that their closest and most real connections were with the United States.[6]

This approach to precedent by the Tribunal is also shown in the decisions on arguably the most important category of jurisdiction, that of expropriation. The Tribunal has had substantial recourse to the awards of the *ad hoc* arbitrations arising from nationalisation programmes, particularly of oilfields, and to early Permanent Court of International Justice decisions. In relying on these decisions the Tribunal has consistently upheld "Western" views on the nature of expropriating events and the degree of compensation claimants are entitled to. This is most comprehensively demonstrated in the very fully argued decisions of *Amoco International Finance* v *Iran* and *Phillips Petroleum* v *Iran*.[7] In the first case the Tribunal, after examining all the major international judgments and arbitral awards, with particular emphasis on the *Chorzow Factory* case,[8] determined that "appropriate compensation was the just price of what was expropriated",[9] being "the full equivalent of the property taken".[10] The decision rejected the views of developing states that appropriate compensation could be less than the full value of the assets expropriated, depending on the circumstances of the expropriating state and of the investor. The decision is a major rejection of the concept of the "New International Economic Order" as expressed in the Charter of Economic Rights. More recently the decision in *Phillips Petroleum* v *Iran*[11] has established that the DCF method of valuation is appropriate in determining the value of an oil concession. This method of valuation was strongly opposed by the Iranian arbitrator, Judge Khalilian, in the *Statement by Judge Khalilian as to Why it would have been Premature to Sign the Award*.[12] In doing so he made some approving remarks about the *Amoco* decision and the high reputation of the Chairman, Professor Virally, of the Chamber which made the *Amoco* decision.[13]

These two decisions of the Tribunal, and the general approach of the expropriation decisions, illustrate the use of precedent by the Tribunal.

---

[6] *Iran* v *United States (Case A/18)* 5 IRAN–U.S.C.T.R., 251 (1984).

[7] 15 IRAN–U.S.C.T.R., 189 (1987) 21 IRAN–U.S.C.T.R., 79 (1989). See Chapters Eight and Nine for a full discussion of these cases.

[8] P.C.I.J., Ser. A. No. 17 (1928).

[9] 15 IRAN–U.S.C.T.R., 189, 247–8 (1987).

[10] *Ibid.*, 252.

[11] 21 IRAN–U.S.C.T.R., 79 (1989).

[12] *Ibid.*, 194. The award was settled and the settlement agreement between the parties held the award to be null and void, 21 IRAN–U.S.C.T.R., 285 (1990). Judge Aldrich in his separate opinion stated that the award remained "the definitive statement of the Tribunal's conclusions and reasoning with respect to this case"; 21 IRAN–U.S.C.T.R., 285, 294 (1990).

[13] *Ibid.*, 199.

However, they do not of themselves fully explain why the Tribunal has been so heavily wedded to precedent, thereby reinforcing a "Western" view of international law.

It is submitted that part of the answer lies in the selection of the neutral members of the Tribunal. In every case the neutral members have been Western European nationals educated and practising in Western legal traditions and philosophy. The process of selection, either by agreement between the two states or by the appointing authority, has inevitably disqualified jurists whose opinions might be considered to strongly favour the perspectives of either state party.

Whilst the writer is not claiming that there is any overt preference for "Western" views of international law by neutral arbitrators, the techniques of legal reasoning used by arbitrators, and in particular the extensive use of precedent, have acted as a conservative force in evaluating the current status of the rules of international law.[14] Much of the precedent came into existence prior to the process of decolonisation, or as a result of an unequal position between claimant and respondent. The use of these precedents, and of the writings of jurists based on the precedents, is reflected in a traditional view of international law in the decisions of the Tribunal. Moreover the presentation of claims by United States lawyers, schooled in the common law tradition of the reliance on precedent, has further emphasised this approach and had the effect of requiring Iranian respondents to reply in kind. It is recognised that Article V of the Claims Settlement Declaration requires the arbitrators to confine themselves to deciding "cases on the basis of respect for law" and applying "principles of international law". These requirements should not have precluded the arbitrators from more fully considering the changing nature of international law, as had been done by Dr Mahmassani in *Liamco* v *Libya*,[15] and more persuasively by the majority in the *Aminoil* v *Kuwait*[16] arbitration.

The techniques of legal reasoning used by the Tribunal ought not, however, to blind one to the reality of the task of the Tribunal. The Tribunal was established primarily to determine claims of United States nationals stemming from breach of contract, non-payment of debt and expropriation. Notwithstanding the complexity of the legal issues before the Tribunal its essential task was to provide some meaningful relief to the United States claimants. In doing so the Tribunal was essentially required to determine the meaning of contractual arrangements, debt

---

[14] It may be noted, however, that Judge Lagergren has been more ready to take into account the views of developing states on the current status of international law, particularly in the field of expropriation. See his separate opinion in *INA Corporation* v *Iran* 8 IRAN–U.S.C.T.R., 373, 390 (1985).
[15] 62 I.L.R., 140 (1982).

instruments and to ascertain the rules of international law applicable to expropriation.

The necessity for the Tribunal to provide meaningful relief, coupled with the composition of the Tribunal and the limitations of Article V of the Claims Settlement Declaration, has imposed some constraints on the judicial creativity of the Tribunal. The majority of the claims based on contract and debt are not of a nature that permit the Tribunal to embark on a bold course of law-making. In the case of the expropriation claims the Tribunal has been able to explore the legal issues in greater depth. However, the methodology of the Tribunal and its underlying purpose have resulted in a conservative approach that is favourable to the claimants. It is nevertheless noteworthy that this approach is in line with the recent trend in state practice towards providing full compensation.[17]

The third reason is related to the progressive internationalisation of the world economy and the need to protect the free flow of capital. It must be conceded that direct consideration of this issue has been obscured by the application of the Treaty of Amity. Nevertheless there has been some consideration of the balance of interests between capital-exporting and capital-importing states and the respective attitudes of these two groups of states as reflected in United Nations General Assembly resolutions and arbitral practice. An important element reflected in all the resolutions is the ability of states to enter into agreements for the exploitation of natural resources. The awards of the Tribunal have tended to focus on the agreements entered into by Iran and the expectations of parties under them.[18] Since premature termination is a breach of an investor's "legitimate expectations",[19] it has been necessary to provide an analytical technique to assess the quantum of the legitimate expectations. The DCF approach is such a means and can be used to measure the anticipated profitability of an agreement, especially of a long-term oil concession. The application of the technique, and in particular of the discount factor, can take account of the risk of revolution and expropriation which serves to reduce the value of the concession.

The use of the DCF technique with the appropriate discount factor should result in full compensation, even if such compensation is less than might be anticipated from investments made in countries where the risk of expropriation and revolution is significantly less. The rubric "appropriate compensation" used by a number of jurists and commentators as

[16] 21 I.L.M., 978 (1982).

[17] The Czechoslovakia–United States Lump Sum Agreement of 1981 provided for 100 per cent compensation, 21 I.L.M., 371 (1982).

[18] General Assembly Resolution 1803, Article 8; The Charter of Economic Rights and Duties of States, 1974, Article 2(2)(c).

[19] *Mobil Oil* v *Iran*, 16 IRAN–U.S.C.T.R., 354 (1987).

justifying a standard of compensation that is less than full compensation, particularly in the case of general nationalisations of long-term concession rights, can be subsumed into a sophisticated analytical assessment of full compensation in such cases.[20] As Norton notes, there has been a fundamental shift in attitudes to foreign investment:[21]

> The end of the post-colonial era and the now widely accepted need to encourage investment in the Third World have substantially eroded the rationale for a partial compensation standard that appeared so compelling to many observers just a short time ago.

The contribution of the Tribunal to the development of contemporary international law therefore has to be seen in the light of the particular purpose and methodology of the Tribunal. Although the Tribunal is a judicial body applying principles of law it is not divorced from its underlying purpose of providing a forum for United States claimants, whose compensation is secured by a $1 billion security fund. The purpose of the Tribunal means that it differs from the International Court of Justice, both in its composition and in its constitution. Any analysis of the contribution of the Tribunal to international law must take into account that these aspects of the Tribunal have ensured a conservative approach to the interpretation of principles of the law.

This is most evident in the contract claims. The analysis of the Tribunal has been the least satisfactory for scholars of the awards in these claims. As noted by Lloyd-Jones the decisions often do not provide any direct indication of the Tribunal's legal analysis.[22] Frequently the Tribunal has simply recited the facts of the claim, including the provisions of the contractual document or debt instrument, and made its decision on the basis of applying the plain wording of the document or instrument to the particular factual situation. Where the Tribunal is required to refer to principles of law it has tended to choose principles of law common to a number of legal systems rather than determine whether the contract is governed by a particular system of law.[23]

---

[20] See as among the leading authorities of the view that appropriate compensation means partial compensation especially in large-scale nationalisations: Judge Lagergren in *INA* v *Iran* 8 IRAN–U.S.C.T.R., 373, 385–90 (1985); U.S. Court of Appeals; *Banco Nacional de Cuba* v *Chase Manhattan Bank* 658 F. 2d 875, 892 (1981); *Kuwait* v *Aminoil* 21 I.L.M., 976 (1982) Reuter and Sultan (Fitzmaurice dissenting); Bowett, *State Contracts with Aliens: Contemporary Developments on Compensation For Termination or Breach*, 58 B.Y.I.L., 48 (1988); Brownlie, *Principles of Public International Law*, 544 (1990); de Arechaga, *State Responsibility for the Nationalisation of Foreign Owned Property*, 11 N.Y.U. Int. L. and Pol., 179 (1978–79).

[21] Norton, *A Law of the Future or a Law of the Past? Modern Tribunals and the International Law of Expropriation*, 85 A.J.I.L., 474, 475 (1991).

[22] Lloyd-Jones, *The Iran–United States Claims Tribunal: Private Rights and State Responsibility*, in Lillich (ed.), *The Iran–United States Claims Tribunal 1981–1983* (1984).

[23] Refer to Chapter Seven for a discussion of this aspect of the decisions of the Tribunal.

Where the Tribunal has been faced with a question of state responsibility, as in expropriation, or an issue clearly governed by public international law such as dual nationality, the stance of the Tribunal is more satisfactory. In these cases the Tribunal has clearly articulated its reasoning on the applicable rules of law. While the actual determinations of the law may not meet with the accord of developing states, the pronouncements of the current position of the principles of law, especially in the area of expropriation, are not without importance. The awards and decisions will form an important body of precedent, useful not only to future claims tribunals but, perhaps more significantly, for *ad hoc* international commercial arbitrations between states and multinational corporations. Moreover the decisions will influence choice of law provisions in international contracts and the numerous commercial treaties entered into between states.

The Tribunal's contribution to international law is not confined to its awards and decisions. The Claims Settlement Declaration establishing the Tribunal contains significant provisions enhancing the attractiveness of international arbitration. Two aspects are notable, first the use of the UNCITRAL arbitration rules, and, second, the access of individual claimants to the Tribunal. The third aspect of enforcement of awards will be considered in the next section of this chapter.

The adaptability of the UNCITRAL arbitration rules to a Tribunal sitting in three chambers hearing a large number of claims is confirmation of the utility of the rules. They were originally drafted for *ad hoc* arbitrations hearing a single claim, but have proved to be acceptable with modification for a Tribunal acting like a court hearing a large number of claims. The success of the Iran–United States Claims Tribunal has in large measure depended on those provisions in the UNCITRAL arbitration rules which ensured that the Tribunal could continue hearing claims even if one of the state parties did not participate.[24] Neither state could sabotage the Tribunal by simply not attending. The participation of both states in the Tribunal will increase the importance of the decisions of the Tribunal in ascertaining the rules of international law, even if the role of the Iranian arbitrators has often been to provide dissenting opinions. The widespread acceptability of the UNCITRAL arbitration rules should be substantially enhanced by the experience of the Iran–United States Claims Tribunal.

The second important feature of the Claims Settlement Declarations is the provision for individual claimants having claims exceeding $250,000 to present their own claims direct to the Tribunal.[25] Whilst this is not unique

---

[24] See Chapter Three.
[25] Article III(3). For further information refer to Chapter Thirteen.

The contribution of the Tribunal 347

in the history of arbitral tribunals established by states, it does reinforce the view that nationals of states have procedural as well as substantive rights and duties under international law. Whilst it is still true that these procedural rights only exist if states specifically agree in each case to grant such rights, the Iran–United States Claims Tribunal will be an important precedent for procedural rights to be granted to claimants in future inter-state arbitral tribunals.

The right of persons to present their own cases in municipal courts has long been recognised as a fundamental right. The argument for claimants being able to present claims directly against a respondent state is no less compelling. The prospect of a state being brought to account for its actions will be the greatest inhibitor against wrongdoing by states. Although international law does not offer the certainty of a forum for hearing claims, it is nevertheless a progressive step that the persons most directly injured can present their claims when circumstances allow the establishment of a claims commission in particular cases.

The relationship of the Tribunal to municipal law

The essence of the distinction between an arbitral tribunal governed solely by public international law and one governed by a system of municipal law is the independence of the tribunal and its awards. If a tribunal is governed solely by international law then its decisions are not subject to review by any other judicial organ. Equally, however, the awards and decisions of such a tribunal cannot be enforced under any other system of law. The only method of enforcement is that provided for in the agreement establishing the tribunal; in the case of the Iran–United States Claims Tribunal, the $1 billion Security Account. If on the other hand the tribunal is governed by a system of municipal law then its awards can be enforced under that system of law, and pursuant to the New York Convention of 1958 on the Recognition and Enforcement of Foreign Arbitral Awards, under the municipal law of other states. However, since the tribunal is subject to a system of municipal law both the tribunal and its awards are subject to review by superior courts of the jurisdiction governing the tribunal. The modern approach in municipal law is to synthesise the advantages of both systems of law. Thus modern arbitral statutes allow considerable freedom to the parties and the tribunal, while still ensuring that the awards can be recognised and enforced.

The paradox of the Iran–United States Claims Tribunal is that it cannot easily be characterised as being exclusively subject to public international law or to a system of municipal law, notably that of the Netherlands. The Claims Settlement Declaration points in both directions. As noted in Chapter Fourteen the governing law of the Tribunal is best determined by examining the jurisdiction that the Tribunal is exercising in each particular award or decision.

It is recognised, however, that to a large extent the issue is a theoretical one. It only becomes important if municipal courts are required to enforce awards of the Tribunal or to bar litigants whose claims are subject to the jurisdiction of the Tribunal. Moreover the one municipal court which has had the opportunity to consider the issue did not deem it necessary to reach a definitive finding on this issue, although the court indicated that it would have been prepared to hold that the Tribunal's award was a nullity under Dutch law.[26] Nevertheless, on grounds of comity the court considered that an adverse determination by the Tribunal would bar litigants from pursuing a remedy in English courts. The new Dutch law on arbitration would eliminate the difficulty faced by Hobhouse J. in finding that the Tribunal's award was a nullity under Dutch Law.[27] Accordingly, under the new Dutch law on arbitration, awards made in respect of claims of nationals against either of the states parties may be considered to be subject to Dutch law and recognised and enforced under the New York Convention of 1958.

The ability of individual claimants to present their claims direct to the Tribunal may also be seen as indicative of the characterisation of the Tribunal. If, as is submitted in Chapter Fourteen, awards made in respect of claims of nationals are governed by Dutch law then the ability of claimants to present their claims direct is of less significance than may be at first apparent. Since the awards in respect of claims of individuals would not be governed by international law, the rule that only states have procedural rights under public international law remains intact. Moreover, irrespective of the characterisation of the Tribunal, the ability of the individual claimants to present their claims direct was reliant on the discretion of Iran and the United States to grant the claimants procedural rights in the Claims Settlement Declaration.

It was noted at the outset of this section that the important issue of the characterisation of the Tribunal is the independence of the Tribunal. It is significant that when the issue of the independence of the Tribunal came before a municipal court, as in *Dallal v Bank Mellat*, the independence of the Iran–United States Claims Tribunal was preserved. The court did not impliedly overturn the award by granting a new forum to the claimant.

An objective of the Dutch law on arbitration is to minimise the ability of courts to interfere with the arbitral process, thereby allowing parties freedom to conduct arbitration as they see fit. Thus the principal effect of

---

[26] *Dallal v Bank Mellat* [1986] 1 All E.R., 239. For a full discussion of this case refer to Chapter Fourteen.
[27] *Ibid*. See Chapter Fourteen for a discussion on this point.

The contribution of the Tribunal

the Dutch law which ensures that the awards of the Tribunal in respect of claims of nationals are subject to the municipal law of the Netherlands is to ensure the recognition and enforcement of the awards in Dutch courts, and in third countries under the New York Convention of 1958. This is achieved without significantly affecting the independence of the Iran–United States Claims Tribunal. However, enforcement of the awards will only be necessary in the event that there are insufficient funds in the Security Account to satisfy the award, or if the award is made in favour of an Iranian national.

Prospects for international arbitration

As noted at the beginning of this chapter the circumstances that led to establishment of the Iran–United States Claims Tribunal were unique. Since the Second World War international arbitration between states to settle claims of nationals had largely gone out of favour, although it has grown in popularity in respect of commercial disputes between large corporations and states, as witnessed by the ICSID and the ICC.

While the Tribunal may demonstrate the efficacy of arbitration in resolving claims of nationals against states it will not necessarily encourage other states to settle such claims by arbitration. As demonstrated by the Czechoslovakia–United States Claims Agreement of 1981, lump sum agreements are still an attractive option in settling claims.

However, for certain types of inter-state disputes arbitration remains the best answer. Where relations between the two states are so strained that direct negotiations are not possible, arbitration is a means of ensuring that certain aspects of the dispute, in particular claims of nationals, can be removed to a neutral forum for resolution. Although the essential differences between the states will remain, at least one impediment to improved relationships between the two states will have been removed. Frequently the issue of claims, as shown by the dispute between Cuba and the United States, is the most difficult to resolve by direct negotiation. The removal of this aspect of the dispute between the two states to an arbitral tribunal could permit improvements in the overall relationship between the two states.

In this respect the most important success of the Iran–United States Claims Tribunal is that it has continued to function notwithstanding the continuing tensions between the two states. This can of course be attributed, at least in part, to the inability of either state to terminate the Tribunal by withdrawal of its arbitrators or agent and to the existence of the Security Account, which ensured that the awards of the Tribunal could be met. The participation of all arbitrators in most of the decisions of the Tribunal has provided an important insight into the development and application of international law by a modern international claims tribunal. However, as noted previously, the determinations of the Tribunal on the principles of international law may in fact deter some developing states from agreeing to the establishment of a claims tribunal as an acceptable means of resolving claims disputes, except where the claimant state is able to exercise sufficient leverage to encourage the respondent state to agree. The circumstances of the establishment of the Iran–United States Claims Tribunal, with Iranian assets being frozen by the United States, illustrate the degree of pressure required to force a recalcitrant state to agree to arbitration.

Certainly the United States has not been able to exercise sufficient leverage upon Cuba to bring about the establishment of a claims tribunal to settle the claims of United States nationals. The prospect of future claims commissions being able to settle such claims is therefore quite limited except in special circumstances.

The enduring value of the Iran–United States Claims Tribunal, however, does not rely on the establishment of future claims commissions. The precedent value of the awards and decisions of the Tribunal is available to all international commercial arbitral tribunals. The issues dealt with by such tribunals, being the interpretation of contracts and expropriation, are similar. The choice of law provisions in arbitral agreements are also often similar. The awards and practice of the Iran–United States Claims Tribunal are therefore an important contribution to the law and procedure of international arbitration, irrespective of the nature of the tribunal.

APPENDIX I

The Algiers Declarations

Reproduced from 1 IRAN-U.S.C.T.R., 3-15 (1981-82)

The General Declaration

Declaration of the Government of the Democratic and Popular Republic of Algeria (General Declaration), 19 January 1981

The Government of the Democratic and Popular Republic of Algeria, having been requested by the Governments of the Islamic Republic of Iran and the United States of America to serve as an intermediary in seeking a mutually acceptable resolution of the crisis in their relations arising out of the detention of the fifty-two United States nationals in Iran, has consulted extensively with the two governments as to the commitments which each is willing to make in order to resolve the crisis within the framework of the four points stated in the Resolution of November 2, 1980, of the Islamic Consultative Assembly of Iran. On the basis of formal adherences received from Iran and the United States, the Government of Algeria now declares that the following interdependent commitments have been made by the two governments:

General principles

The undertakings reflected in this Declaration are based on the following general principles:

A. Within the framework of and pursuant to the provisions of the two Declarations of the Government of the Democratic and Popular Republic of Algeria, the United States will restore the financial position of Iran, in so far as possible, to that which existed prior to November 14, 1979. In this context, the United States commits itself to ensure the mobility and free transfer of all Iranian assets within its jurisdiction, as set forth in Paragraphs 4-9.

B. It is the purpose of both parties, within the framework of and pursuant to the provisions of the two Declarations of the Government of the Democratic and

Popular Republic of Algeria, to terminate all litigation as between the government of each party and the nationals of the other, and to bring about the settlement and termination of all such claims through binding arbitration.

Through the procedures provided in the Declaration relating to the Claims Settlement Agreement, the United States agrees to terminate all legal proceedings in the United States courts involving claims of United States persons and institutions against Iran and its state enterprises, to nullify all attachments and judgments obtained therein, to prohibit all further litigation based on such claims, and to bring about the termination of such claims through binding arbitration.

Point I: Non-intervention in Iranian affairs

1 The United States pledges that it is and from now on will be the policy of the United States not to intervene, directly or indirectly, politically or militarily, in Iran's internal affairs.

Points II and II: Return of Iranian assets and settlement of United States claims

2 Iran and the United States (hereinafter "the parties") will immediately select a mutually agreeable Central Bank (hereinafter "the Central Bank") to act, under the instructions of the Government of Algeria and the Central Bank of Algeria (hereinafter "the Algerian Central Bank") as depository of the escrow and security funds hereinafter prescribed and will promptly enter into depositary arrangements with the Central Bank in accordance with the terms of this Declaration. All funds placed in escrow with the Central Bank pursuant to this Declaration shall be held in an account in the name of the Algerian Central Bank. Certain procedures for implementing the obligations set forth in this Declaration and in the Declaration of the Democratic and Popular Republic of Algeria Concerning the Settlement of Claims by the Government of the United States and the Government of the Islamic Republic of Iran (hereinafter "the Claims Settlement Agreement") are separately set forth in certain Undertakings of the Government of the United States of America and the Government of the Islamic Republic of Iran with Respect to the Declaration of the Democratic and Popular Republic of Algeria.

3 The depository arrangements shall provide that, in the event that the Government of Algeria certifies to the Algerian Central Bank that the fifty-two U.S. nationals have safely departed from Iran, the Algerian Central Bank will thereupon instruct the Central Bank to transfer immediately all monies or other assets in escrow with the Central Bank pursuant to this Declaration, provided that, at any time prior to the making of such certification by the Government of Algeria, each of the two parties, Iran and the United States, shall have the right on seventy-two hours' notice to terminate its commitments under this Declaration. If such notice is given by the United States and the foregoing certification is made by the Government of Algeria within the seventy-two hour period of notice, the Algerian Central Bank will

Appendix I

thereupon instruct the Central Bank to transfer such monies and assets. If the seventy-two hour period of notice by the United States expires without such a certification having been made, or if the notice of termination is delivered by Iran, the Algerian Central Bank will thereupon instruct the Central Bank to return all such monies and assets to the United States, and thereafter the commitments reflected in this Declaration shall be of no further force and effect.

Assets in the Federal Reserve Bank

4 Commencing upon completion of the requisite escrow arrangements with the Central Bank, the United States will bring about the transfer to the Central Bank of all gold bullion which is owned by Iran and which is in the custody of the Federal Reserve Bank of New York, together with all other Iranian assets (or the cash equivalent thereof) in the custody of the Federal Reserve Bank of New York, to be held by the Central Bank in escrow until such time as their transfer or return is required by Paragraph 3 above.

Assets in foreign branches of United States banks

5 Commencing upon the completion of the requisite escrow arrangements with the Central Bank, the United States will bring about the transfer to the Central Bank, to the account of the Algerian Central Bank, of all Iranian deposits and securities which on or after November 14, 1979, stood upon the books of overseas banking offices of U.S. banks, together with interest thereon through December 31, 1980, to be held by the Central Bank, to the account of the Algerian Central Bank, in escrow until such time as their transfer or return is required in accordance with Paragraph 3 of this Declaration.

Assets in United States branches of United States banks

6 Commencing with the adherence by Iran and the United States to this Declaration and the Claims Settlement Agreement attached hereto, and following the conclusion of arrangements with the Central Bank for the establishment of the interest-bearing Security Account specified in that Agreement and Paragraph 7 below, which arrangements will be concluded within thirty days from the date of this Declaration, the United States will act to bring about the transfer to the Central Bank, within six months from such date, of all Iranian deposits and securities in U.S. banking institutions in the United States, together with interest thereon, to be held by the Central Bank in escrow until such time as their transfer or return is required by Paragraph 3.

7 As funds are received by the Central Bank pursuant to Paragraph 6 above, the Algerian Central Bank shall direct the Central Bank to (1) transfer one-half of each such receipt to Iran and (2) place the other half in a special interest-bearing Security Account in the Central Bank, until the balance in the Security Account has reached the level of U.S. $1 billion. After the U.S. $1 billion balance has been achieved, the Algerian Central Bank shall direct all funds received pursuant to Paragraph 6 to be transferred to Iran. All

funds in the Security Account are to be used for the sole purpose of securing payment of, and paying, claims against Iran in accordance with the Claims Settlement Agreement. Whenever the Central Bank shall thereafter notify Iran that the balance in the Security Account has fallen below U.S. $500 million, Iran shall promptly make new deposits sufficient to maintain a minimum balance of U.S. $500 million in the Account. The Account shall be so maintained until the President of the arbitral tribunal established pursuant to the Claims Settlement Agreement has certified to the Central Bank of Algeria that all arbitral awards against Iran have been satisfied in accordance with the Claims Settlement Agreement, at which point any amount remaining in the Security Account shall be transferred to Iran.

Other assets in the United States and abroad

8 Commencing with the adherence of Iran and the United States to this Declaration and the attached Claims Settlement Agreement and the conclusion of arrangements for the establishment of the Security Account, which arrangements will be concluded within thirty days from the date of this Declaration, the United States will act to bring about the transfer to the Central Bank of all Iranian financial assets (meaning funds or securities) which are located in the United States and abroad, apart from those assets referred to in Paragraphs 5 and 6 above, to be held by the Central Bank in escrow until their transfer or return is required by Paragraph 3 above.

9 Commencing with the adherence by Iran and the United States to this Declaration and the attached Claims Settlement Agreement and the making by the Government of Algeria of the certification described in Paragraph 3 above, the United States will arrange, subject to the provisions of U.S. law applicable prior to November 14, 1979, for the transfer to Iran of all Iranian properties which are located in the United States and abroad and which are not within the scope of the preceding paragraphs.

Nullification of sanctions and claims

10 Upon the making by the Government of Algeria of the certification described in Paragraph 3 above, the United States will revoke all trade sanctions which were directed against Iran in the period November 4, 1979, to date.

11 Upon the making by the Government of Algeria of the certification described in Paragraph 3 above, the United States will promptly withdraw all claims now pending against Iran before the International Court of Justice and will thereafter bar and preclude the prosecution against Iran of any pending or future claim of the United States or a United States national arising out of events occurring before the date of this Declaration related to (A) the seizure of the fifty-two United States nationals on November 4, 1979, (B) their subsequent detention, (C) injury to the United States' property or property of the United States' nationals within the United States Embassy compound in Teheran after November 3, 1979, and (D) injury to the United States' nationals or their property as a result of popular movements in the course of the Islamic Revolution in Iran which were not an act of the Government of Iran. The United States will also bar and preclude the prosecution against

Appendix I 355

Iran in the courts of the United States of any pending or future claim asserted by persons other than the United States' nationals arising out of the events specified in the preceding sentence.

Point IV: Return of the assets of the family of the former Shah

12 Upon the making by the Government of Algeria of the certification described in Paragraph 3 above, the United States will freeze, and prohibit any transfer of, property and assets in the United States within the control of the estate of the former Shah or of any close relative of the former Shah served as a defendant in U.S. litigation brought by Iran to recover such property and assets as belonging to Iran. As to any such defendant, including the estate of the former Shah, the freeze order will remain in effect until such litigation is finally terminated. Violation of the freeze order shall be subject to the civil and criminal penalties prescribed by U.S. law.
13 Upon the making by the Government of Algeria of the certification described in Paragraph 3 above, the United States will order all persons within U.S. jurisdiction to report to the U.S. Treasury within thirty days, for transmission to Iran, all information known to them, as of November 3, 1979, and as of the date of the order, with respect to the property and assets referred to in Paragraph 12. Violation of the requirement will be subject to the civil and criminal penalties prescribed by U.S. law.
14 Upon the making by the Government of Algeria of the certitication described in Paragraph 3 above, the United States will make known, to all appropriate U.S. courts, that in any litigation of the kind described in Paragraph 12 above the claims of Iran should not be considered legally barred either by sovereign immunity principles or by the act of state doctrine and that Iranian decrees and judgments relating to such assets should be enforced by such courts in accordance with U.S. law.
15 As to any judgment of a U.S. court which calls for the transfer of any property or assets to Iran, the United States hereby guarantees the enforcement of the final judgment to the extent that the property or assets exist within the United States.
16 If any dispute arises between the parties as to whether the United States has fulfilled any obligation imposed upon it by Paragraphs 12–15, inclusive, Iran may submit the dispute to binding arbitration by the tribunal established by, and in accordance with the provisions of, the Claims Settlement Agreement. If the tribunal determines that Iran has suffered a loss as a result of a failure by the United States to fulfil such obligation, it shall make an appropriate award in favour of Iran which may be enforced by Iran in the courts of any nation in accordance with its laws.

Settlement of disputes

17 If any other dispute arises between the parties as to the interpretation or performance of any provision of this Declaration, either party may submit

the dispute to binding arbitration by the tribunal established by, and in accordance with the provisions of, the Claims Settlement Agreement.

Any decision of the tribunal with respect to such dispute, including any award of damages to compensate for a loss resulting from a breach of this Declaration or the Claims Settlement Agreement, may be enforced by the prevailing party in the courts of any nation in accordance with its laws.

Initialled on January 19, 1981
by Warren M. Christopher

Deputy Secretary of State of the Government of the United States By virtue of the powers vested in him by his Government as deposited with the Government of Algeria.

The Claims Settlement Declaration

Declaration of the Government of the Democratic and Popular Republic of Algeria Concerning the settlement of Claims by the Government of the United States of America and the Government of the Islamic Republic of Iran (Claims Settlement Declaration), 19 January 1981

The Government of the Democratic and Popular Republic of Algeria, on the basis of formal notice of adherence received from the Government of the Islamic Republic of Iran and the Government of the United States of America, now declares that Iran and the United States have agreed as follows:

Article I

Iran and the United States will promote the settlement of the claims described in Article II by the parties directly concerned. Any such claims not settled within six months from the date of entry into force of this Agreement shall be submitted to binding third-party arbitration in accordance with the terms of this Agreement. The aforementioned six months' period may be extended once by three months at the request of either party.

Article II

1 An international arbitral tribunal (the Iran–United States Claims Tribunal) is hereby established for the purpose of deciding claims of nationals of the United States against Iran and claims of nationals of Iran against the United States, and any counter-claim which arises out of the same contract, transaction or occurrence that constitutes the subject matter of that national's claim, if such claims and counter-claims are outstanding on the date of this Agreement, whether or not filed with any court, and arise out of debts, contracts (including transactions which are the subject of letters of credit or bank guarantees), expropriations or other measures affecting property rights, excluding claims described in Paragraph 11 of the Declaration of the Government of Algeria of January 19, 1981, and claims arising out of the actions of the United States in response to the conduct described in such paragraph, and

Appendix I

excluding claims arising under a binding contract between the parties specifically providing that any disputes thereunder shall be within the sole jurisdiction of the competent Iranian courts, in response to the Majlis position.
2 The Tribunal shall also have jurisdiction over official claims of the United States and Iran against each other arising out of contractual arrangements between them for the purchase and sale of goods and services.
3 The tribunal shall have jurisdiction, as specified in Paragraphs 16–17 of the Declaration of the Government of Algeria of January 19, 1981, over any dispute as to the interpretation or performance of any provision of that Declaration.

Article III

1 The Tribunal shall consist of nine members or such larger multiple of three as Iran and the United States may agree are necessary to conduct its business expeditiously. Within ninety days after the entry into force of this Agreement, each government shall appoint one-third of the members. Within thirty days after their appointment, the members so appointed shall by mutual agreement select the remaining third of the members and appoint one of the remaining third President of the Tribunal. Claims may be decided by the full Tribunal as the President shall determine. Each such panel shall be composed by the President and shall consist of one member appointed by each of the three methods set forth above.
2 Members of the Tribunal shall be appointed and the Tribunal shall conduct its business in accordance with the arbitration rules of the United Nations Commission on International Trade Law (UNCITRAL) except to the extent modified by the Parties or by the Tribunal to ensure that this Agreement can be carried out. The UNCITRAL rules for appointing members of three-member tribunals shall apply *mutatis mutandis* to the appointment of the Tribunal.
3 Claims of nationals of the United States and Iran that are within the scope of this Agreement shall be presented to the Tribunal either by claimants themselves or, in the case of claims of less than $250,000, by the government of such national.
4 No claim may be filed with the Tribunal more than one year after the entry into force of this Agreement or six months after the date the President is appointed, whichever is later. These deadlines do not apply to the procedures contemplated by Paragraphs 16 and 17 of the Declaration of the Government of Algeria of January 19, 1981.

Article IV

1 All decisions and awards of the Tribunal shall be final and binding.
2 The President of the Tribunal shall certify, as prescribed in Paragraph 7 of the Declaration of the Government of Algeria of January 19, 1981, when all arbitral awards under this Agreement have been satisfied.
3 Any award which the Tribunal may render against either government shall be enforceable against such government in the courts of any nation in accordance with its laws.

Article V

The Tribunal shall decide all cases on the basis of respect for law, applying such choice of law rules and principles of commercial and international law as the Tribunal determines to be applicable, taking into account relevant usages of the trade, contract provisions and changed circumstances.

Article VI

1. The seat of the Tribunal shall be The Hague, The Netherlands, or any other place agreed by Iran and the United States.
2. Each government shall designate an Agent at the seat of the Tribunal to represent it to the Tribunal and to receive notices or other communications directed to it or to its nationals, agencies, instrumentalities, or entities in connection with proceedings before the Tribunal.
3. The expenses of the Tribunal shall be borne equally by the two governments.
4. Any question concerning the interpretation or application of this Agreement shall be decided by the Tribunal upon the request of either Iran or the United States.

Article VII

For the purpose of this Agreement:

1. A "national" of Iran or of the United States, as the case may be, means (a) a natural person who is a citizen of Iran or the United States; and (b) a corporation or other legal entity which is organised under the laws of Iran or the United States or any of its states or territories, the District of Columbia or the Commonwealth of Puerto Rico, if, collectively, natural persons who are citizens of such country hold, directly or indirectly, an interest in such corporation or entity equivalent to fifty per cent or more of its capital stock.
2. "Claims of nationals" of Iran or the United States, as the case may be, means claims owned continuously, from the date on which the claim arose to the date on which this Agreement enters into force, by nationals of that state, including claims that are owned indirectly by such nationals through ownership of capital stock or other proprietary interests in judicial persons, provided that the ownership interests of such nationals, collectively, were sufficient at the time the claim arose to control the corporation or other entity, and provided, further, that the corporation or other entity is not itself entitled to bring a claim under the terms of this Agreement. Claims referred to the Arbitration Tribunal shall, as of the date of filing of such claims with the Tribunal, be considered excluded from the jurisdiction of the courts of Iran, or of the United States, or of any other court.
3. "Iran" means the Government of Iran, any political subdivision of Iran, and any agency, instrumentality, or entity controlled by the Government of Iran or any political subdivision thereof.
4. The "United States" means the Government of the United States, any political subdivision of the United States, and any agency, instrumentality or entity controlled by the Government of the United States or any political subdivision thereof.

Appendix I 359

Article VIII

This Agreement shall enter into force when the Government of Algeria has received from both Iran and the United States a notification of adherence to the Agreement.

Initialled on January 19, 1981
by Warren M. Christopher

> Deputy Secretary of State of the Government of the United States By virtue of the powers vested in him by his Government as deposited with the Government of Algeria.

Undertakings

Undertakings of the Government of the United States of America and the Government of the Islamic Republic of Iran with respect to the Declaration of the Government of the Democratic and Popular Republic of Algeria.
19 January 1981

1   At such time as the Algerian Central Bank notifies the Governments of Algeria, Iran, and the United States that it has been notified by the Central Bank that the Central Bank has received for deposit in dollar, gold bullion, and securities accounts in the name of the Algerian Central Bank, as escrow agent, cash and other funds, 1,632,917.779 ounces of gold (valued by the parties for this purpose at U.S. $0.9397 billion), and securities (at face value) in the aggregate amount of U.S. $7.955 billion, Iran shall immediately bring about the safe departure of the fifty-two U.S. nationals detained in Iran. Upon the making by the Government of Algeria of the certification described in Paragraph 3 of the Declaration, the Algerian Central Bank will issue the instructions required by the following paragraph.

2   Iran having affirmed its intention to pay all its debts and those of its controlled institutions, the Algerian Central Bank acting pursuant to Paragraph 1 above will issue the following instructions to the Central Bank:

(A)   To transfer U.S. $3.667 billion to the Federal Reserve Bank of New York to pay the unpaid principal of and interest through December 31, 1980 on (1) all loans and credits made by a syndicate of banking institutions, of which a U.S. banking institution is a member, to the Government of Iran, its agencies, instrumentalities or controlled entities and (2) all loans and credits made by such a syndicate which are guaranteed by the Government of Iran or any of its agencies, instrumentalities or controlled entities.

(B)   To retain U.S. $1.418 billion in the Escrow Account for the purpose of paying the unpaid principal of and interest owing, if any, on the loans and credits referred to in Paragraph (A) after application of the U.S. $3.667 billion and on all other indebtedness held by United States banking institutions of, or guaranteed by, the Government of Iran, its agencies, instrumenalities or controlled entities not previously paid, and for the purpose of paying disputed amounts of deposits, assets, and interest, if any, owing on Iranian deposits in U.S. banking institutions.

Bank Markazi and the appropriate United States banking institutions shall promptly meet in an effort to agree upon the amounts owing. In the event of such agreement, the Bank Markazi and the appropriate banking institution shall certify the amount owing to the Central Bank of Algeria which shall instruct the Bank of England to credit such amount to the account, as appropriate, of the Bank Markazi or of the Federal Reserve Bank of New York in order to permit payment to the appropriate banking institution. In the event that within thirty days any U.S. banking institution and the Bank Markazi are unable to agree upon the amounts owed, either party may refer such dispute to binding arbitration by such international arbitration panel as the parties may agree, or failing such agreement within thirty additional days after such reference, by the Iran–United States Claims Tribunal. The presiding officer of such panel or tribunal shall certify to the Central Bank of Algeria the amount, if any, determined by it to be owed, whereupon the Central Bank of Algeria shall instruct the Bank of England to credit such amount to the account of the Bank Markazi or of the Federal Reserve Bank of New York in order to permit payment to the appropriate banking institution. After all disputes are resolved either by agreement or by arbitration award and appropriate payment has been made, the balance of the funds referred to in this Paragraph (B) shall be paid to Bank Markazi.

(C) To transfer immediately to, or upon the order of, the Bank Markazi all assets in the Escrow Account in excess of the amounts referred to in Paragraphs (A) and (B).

Initialled on January 19, 1981
by Warren M. Christopher

Deputy Secretary of State of the Government of the United States By virtue of the powers vested in him by his Government as deposited with the Government of Algeria.

Subsequent amendment by exchange of letters

The Deputy Secretary of State, Washington
Algiers, January 19, 1981

Dear Mr Minister

You have drawn my attention to the omission of the words "not less than" before the figure of U.S. $7.955 in the Declaration of the Government of Algeria designated: "Undertakings of the Government of the United States of America and the Government of the Islamic Republic of Iran with respect to the Declaration of the Government of the Democratic and Popular Republic of Algeria."

Appendix I 361

I agree and authorise you on behalf of the United States to issue this correction.

Sincerely yours,

(Sgd) Warren M. Christopher

Mr M. Benyahia
Minister of Foreign Affairs
of the Government of the Democratic and Popular
Republic of Algeria

APPENDIX II
List of members

Reproduced from 25 IRAN–U.S.C.T.R. (1990)

Appendix II

I. Present members

Name	Appointed by	Country	Date of appointment	Chamber
Karl-Heinz Bockstiegel	Appointing Authority, pursuant to Tribunal Rules	Federal Republic of Germany	1 October 1984	1
Robert Briner	Mutual agreement of Government-appointed members	Switzerland	1 June 1985	2
Michel Virally	Mutual agreement of Government-appointed members	France	1 July 1985	3
P. Ansari Moin	Government of the Islamic Republic of Iran	Iran	14 September 1983	3
Howard M. Holtzmann	Government of the United States of America	United States	1981 (Original member)	1
George H. Aldrich	Government of the United States of America	United States	1981 (Original member)	2
Assodollah Noori	Government of the Islamic Republic of Iran	Iran	5 July 1987	1
Seyed Khalil Khalilian	Government of the Islamic Republic of Iran	Iran	1 January 1988	2
Richard C. Allison	Government of the United States of America	United States	1 April 1988	3

II. Former members

Seyyed H. Enayat	Government of the Islamic Republic of Iran	Iran	1981 (Original member)	3
Pierre Bellet	Mutual agreement of Government-appointed members	France	1981 (Original member)	2
M. Jahangir Sani	Government of the Islamic Republic of Iran	Iran	1 March 1982	3
Richard M. Mosk	Government of the United States of America	United States	1981 (Original member)	1
Gunnar K. Lagergen	Mutual agreement of Government-appointed members	Sweden	1981 (Original member)	1
Mahmoud Kashani	Government of the Islamic Republic of Iran	Iran	1981 (Original member)	1
Shafie Shafeiei	Government of the Islamic Republic of Iran	Iran	1981 (Original member)	2
Willem Riphagen	Appointing Authority, pursuant to Tribunal Rules	Netherlands	1 August 1983	2
Nils Mangard	Mutual agreement of Government-appointed members	Sweden	1981 (Original member)	3
Seyyed Mohsen Mostafavi Tafreshi	Government of the Islamic Republic of Iran	Iran	29 November 1984	1
Charles N. Brower	Government of the United States of America	United States	16 January 1984	3
Hamid Bahrani Ahmadi	Government of the Islamic Republic of Iran	Iran	29 November 1984	3

III. Members appointed by agreement between the agents

Koorosh Hossein Ameli	(Agents agreement *ad hoc*)	Iran	1 August 1985 Cases Nos. 111, 134, 161, 174, 480 12 December 1985 Cases Nos. 18, 24, 36, 37, 61, 231 2 April 1987 Cases Nos. A19, B1, (Claims Nos. 2 and 3), 184, 484, 10172	1
Richard M. Mosk	(Agents agreement *ad hoc*)	United States	1 August 1985 Cases Nos. 52, 53 12 December 1985 Cases Nos. 43, 198, 769	1

IV. Substitute members (note to Article 13 of the Tribunal rules)

C. F. Salans	Government of the United States of America	United States	17 February 1984	—
W. H. Levit	Government of the United States of America	United States	14 March 1984	—
Richard M. Mosk	Government of the United States of America	United States	26 January 1984	—

V. Former members under III and IV

Charles N. Brower	Government of the United States of America	United States	7 March 1983	—
Mohsen Aghahosseini	Government of the Islamic Republic of Iran	Iran	6 December 1983	—

Bibliography

Statement of sources

The principal primary sources for this work have been the awards and decisions of the Tribunal. These are reported in permanent form in the *IRAN–U.S.C.T.R.* They are also reported in two bimonthly publications, the I.A.L.R. and the Mealy's L.R.: Iranian Claims, no more than two weeks after being handed down by the Tribunal, along with many of the pleadings and submissions of the parties. These bimonthly publications also include a commentary on the administration of, and political events at, the Tribunal.

The list of secondary references refers primarily to books and articles cited in the work. However, the writer has also had extensive reference to other books and articles, particularly on general international law, international arbitration, expropriation and nationalization, and on the Tribunal and its awards and decisions. With respect to the latter materials the Tribunal has published a list of all legal publications about the Tribunal and its awards and decisions. The writer has had access to, and considered all the publications listed that have been published in the English language. These references are also listed in the bibliography.

Primary references

Iran–United States Claims Tribunal

Reports of Awards, Decisions and Orders of the Tribunal
IRAN–U.S.C.T.R., Vols 1 to 9 (1981–82 to 1985).
I.A.L.R., 1981 to 1987.
Mealy's L.R.: Iranian Claims, 1983 to 1986.

Annual Reports of the Tribunal, 1981–83 to 1986–87

Various press releases, Orders, and correspondence of the Tribunal and the Governments of Iran and the United States reported in the above publications

Treaties

Multilateral

Hague Convention Concerning Certain Questions Relating to the Conflict of Nationality laws, 1930. Statute of the International Court of Justice. Vienna Convention on the Law of Treaties, 1969. New York Convention on the Enforcement and Recognition of Foreign Arbitral Awards, 1958. Geneva Prorocol on Arbitral Clauses, 1923. Geneva Convention on Execution of Foreign Arbitral Awards, 1927. Treaty of Versailles, 1919.

Bilateral

Iran and the United States
Algiers Declarations, 1981.
Treaty of Amity, 1955.

United States with other states
United States–China Agreement, 1979.
United States–Yugoslavia Agreement, 1948.
United States–Hungary Agreement, 1973.
United States–Czechoslovakia Agreement, 1981.
United States–Mexican Special Claims Commission.

Reports of awards, decisions and judgments of courts and tribunals other than the Iran–United States Claims Tribunal

International

P.C.I.J. Rep.
I.C.J. Rep.
R.I.A.A.
Annual Digest.
T.A.M.
Moore, *History and Digest of the International Arbitrations to which the United States has been a Party*, 6 vols.
Yearbook of European Convention on Human Rights, (1960).
I.L.R.
I.L.M.
Yearbook: Commercial Arbitration, vols. 1–XII, I (1976–87).

National

United States
Supreme Court Reports.

Bibliography

Federal Reports.
Federal Supplements.

English
A.C.
All E.R.

Official documents

International organisations

European Convention on Human Rights, Yearbooks.
League of Nations, Treaty Series.
United Nations, General Assembly Official Records.
United Nations, Security Council Official Records.
United Nations, Treaty Series.
United Nations, Yearbooks of the International Law Commission.

National organisations

United States
Iran Agreements, Hearings of Committee of Foreign Relations: United States Senate (1980). *Iran: The Financial Aspects of the Hostage Settlement Agreement*, Committee on Banking, Finance and Urban Affairs; House of Representatives, 97th Congress (1981). Restatement (2d) Foreign Relations of the United States (1965).

Netherlands
Applicability of Dutch Law to the Awards of the Tribunal sitting at the Hague to hear claims between Iran and the United States, Ministry of Foreign Affairs (1983).

Secondary references

Books

Amerasinghe, *State Responsibility for Injuries to Aliens* (1967).
Assersohn, *The Biggest Deal* (1981).
Bar-Yaacov, *Dual Nationality* (1961).
Blaustein, *Constitutions of the Countries of the World* (1980–1988).
Borchard, *Diplomatic Protection of Citizens Abroad* (1915, 1928).
Bowett, *Self-defence in International Law* (1958).
Briggs, *The Law of Nations* (1952).
Briggs, *The International Law Commission* (1952).
Brownlie, *International Law and the Use of Force by States* (1963).
Brownlie, *Principles of Public International Law* (1979).
Brownlie, *System of the Law of Nations: State Responsibility* (1983).

Brownlie, *Principles of Public International Law* (1990).
De Visscher, *Theory and Reality in Public International Law* (1957).
Dicey and Morris, *Conflicts of Laws* (1980).
Donner, *The Regulation of Nationality in International Law* (1979).
Drost, *The Crime of State* (1959).
Dumbauld, *Interim Measures of Protection in International Controversies* (1932).
Dunn, *The Protection of Nationals* (1932).
Eagleton, *Responsibility of States in International Law* (1928).
Elkind, *Interim Protection: A Functional Approach* (1981).
Feller, *The Mexican Claims Commissions 1923–1934* (1935).
Fitzmaurice, *The Law and Procedure of the International Court of Justice* (1986).
Garcia-Amador, Sohn and Baxter, *Recent Codification of the Law of State Responsibility to Aliens* (1978).
Greig, *International Law* (1976).
Heikal, *The Return of the Ayatollah* (1980).
Joseph, *Nationality and Diplomatic Protection* (1969).
Joyce, *Human Rights: International Documents* (1978).
Kazemi, *Poverty and Revolution in Iran: The Migrant Poor, Urban Marginality and Politics* (1980).
Lauterpacht, *Oppenheim's International Law* (1955).
Lauterpacht, *The Development of International Law by the International Court* (1958).
Lauterpacht, Vol. 1, *International Law: Collected Papers*, ed. E. Lauterpacht (1970).
Lillich, *International Claims: Their Adjudication by National Commissions* (1965).
Lillich (ed.), *The Valuation of Nationalized Property in International Law (1972–1975)*.
Lillich (ed.), *The Iran–United States Claims Tribunal 1981–1983* (1984).
Lillich and Weston, *International Claims: Their Settlement by Lump Sum Agreements* (1975).
Mani, *International Adjudication: Procedural Aspects* (1980).
Mann, *Studies in International Law* (1973).
Miller and Stanger (ed.), *Essays on Expropriation* (1967).
O'Connell, *International Law* (1970).
Oppenheim, *International Law* (1955).
Parry (ed.), *British Digest of International Law* (1976).
Phillimore, *Commentaries upon International Law* (1879).
Roosevelt, *Countercoup* (1979).
Rosenne, *The Law and Practise of the International Court of Justice* (1965).
Salinger, *America Held Hostage: The Secret Negotiations* (1981).
Sanders (ed.), *International Arbitration: Liber Amicorum for Martin Domke* (1969).
Sandifer, *Evidence before International Tribunals* (1939, 2nd ed. 1975).
Schmitthoff (ed.), *International Commercial Arbitration* (1981).
Schwarzenberger, *International Law* (1957).
Schwebel, *International Arbitration: Three Salient Problems* (1987).
Seidl-Hohenveldern, *The Austrian–German Arbitral Tribunal* (1972).

Simpson and Fox, *International Aribtration* (1954).
Sinclair, *The International Law Commission*, (1987).
Thorpe, *International Claims* (1924).
Toope, *Mixed International Arbitration* (1990).
Vamvoukos, *Termination of Treaties in International Law* (1985).
Van den Berg, *The New York Arbitration Convention of 1958* (1981).
Westberg, *International Transactions and Claims Involving Government Parties: Case Law of the Iran–United States Claims Tribunal* (1991).
Wetter, *The International Arbitral Process* (1976).
Whiteman, *Digest of International Law* (1967).
White, *Nationalisation of Foreign Property* (1961).
White, *The Use of Experts by International Tribunals* (1965).
Woolf, *Private International Law* (1950).
Wortley, *Expropriation in Public International Law* (1959).
Zahih, *Iran Since the Revolution* (1981).

Articles

Ameli, *Book Review*, 24 Vanderbilt J. of Transnat'l L. 611 (1991).
Amerasinghe, *The Quantum of Compensation for Nationalized Property in International Law*, in Lillich (ed.), III *Valuations of Nationalized Property In International Law*, 91 (1975).
Amin, *The Settlement of Iran–United States Disputes*, J. Bus. L., May 1982.
Amin, *Iran–United States Claims Settlement*. 32 I.C.L.Q., 750 (1983).
Arias, *The Non-liability of States for Damages Suffered by Foreigners in the Course of a Riot, an Insurrection, or a Civil War*, 7 A.J.I.L., (1913).
Asken, *The Iran–United States Claims Tribunal and the UNCITRAL Arbitration Rules: An Early Comment*, The Art of Arbitration, 1982.
Belland, *The Iran–United States Claims Tribunal: Some Reflections on Trying a Claim*, 1 J. of Int. Arb. (1984).
Belland, *The Iran–United States Claims Tribunal: A Review of Developments 1983–84*, 16 Int. L.J. of Georgetown U.L.C. (1984).
Bellet, *Foreword to Symposium on the Iran–United States Claims Tribunal*, 16 Int. L.J. of Georgetown U.L.C. (1984).
Board of Editors, *The Measures taken by the Indonesian Government against Netherlands Enterprises*, 5 Netherlands Int. L.R. (1958).
Bockstiegel, *Applying the UNCITRAL Rules: The Experience of the Iran–United States Claims Tribunal*, 4 Int. Tax and Bus. Lawyer, 266 (1984).
Borchard, *The Access of Individuals to International Courts*, 24 A.J.I.L., 359 (1930).
Bowett, *State Contracts with Aliens: Contempoary Developments on Compensation for Termination or Breach*, 59 B.Y.I.L., 49 (1988).
Boyle, Chicago Daily Law Bulletin (1981).
British Branch Committee on the Enforcement of International Arbitral Awards, *Delocalised Arbitrations and the New York Convention* (1982) (Monograph).
Broches, *Arbitration in Investment Disputes*, in Schmitthoff (ed.), III *International Commercial Arbitration*, 6 (1981).

Brower, *Current Developments in the Law of Expropriation and Compensation: A Preliminary Survey of Awards of the Iran–United States Claims Tribunal*, 21 Int. Lawyer (1987).

Brownlie, *The Individual before Tribunals Exercising International Jurisdiction*, 11 I.C.L.Q., 701 (1962).

Carbonneau, *The Elaboration of Substantive Legal Norms and Arbitral Adjudication: The Case of the Iran–United States Claims Tribunal*, in Lillich (ed.), *The Iran–United States Claims Tribunal 1981–1983* (1984).

Caron, *The Nature of the Iran–United States Claims Tribunal and the Evolving Structure of International Dispute Resolution*, 84 A.J.I.L., 105 (1990).

Carlston, *Concession Agreements and Nationalization*, 55 A.J.I.L., 260 (1958).

Carlston, *Codification of International Arbitral Procedure*, 47 A.J.I.L., 226 (1953).

Carter, *The Iran–United States Claims Tribunal: Observation on the First Year*, 29 U.C.L.A. Law Review, 1093 (1982).

Christie, *What Constitutes a Taking of Property under International Law*, 38 B.Y.I.L., 307 (1962).

Claggett, *The Expropriation Issue before the Iran–United States Claim Tribunal; is "Just Compensation" Required by International Law or Not?* 16 Law and Policy in Int. Bus., 813 (1984–85), also 16 Int. L.J. of Georgetown U.L.C., (1984).

Claggett, *The Iran–United States Claims Tribunal: A Practitioner's Perspective*, in Lillich (ed.), *The Iran–United States Claims Tribunal 1981–1983* (1984).

Craig, Park and Paulsson, *French Codification of a Legal Framework for International Commercial Arbitration: The Decree of May 12, 1981*, in VII Yearbook: Commercial Arbitration, 407 (1982).

Crawford, *Decisions of the British Courts during 1985–86 Involving Questions of Public or Private International Law*, 57 B.Y.I.L., 405 (1986).

Dawson and Weston, *"Prompt, Adequate and Effective": A Universal Standard for Compensation?*, 30 Fordham L.R., 727 (1962).

de Arechaga, *International Law in the Past Third of a Century*, 159 I Recueil des Cours, 1 (1978).

de Arechaga, *State Responsibility for the Nationalization of Foreign Owned Property*, 11 N.Y.U. Int. L. and Pol., 179 (1978–79).

De Visscher, *Reflections on the Present Prospects of International Adjudication*, 50 A.J.I.L., 467 (1956).

Dietz, *Introduction: Development of the UNCITRAL Arbitration Rules*, 27 Am. J. Comp. Law, 449 (1979).

Dolzer, *New Foundations of the Law of Expropriation of Alien Property*, 75 A.J.I.L., 553 (1981).

Doman, *Postwar Nationalization of Foreign Property in Europe*, 48 Col. L.R., 1125 (1948).

Domke, *Foreign Nationalizations: Some Aspects of Contemporary International Law*, 55 A.J.I.L., 585 (1961).

El Chiati, *Protection of Investment in the Context of Petroleum Agreements*, 204 IV Recueil des Cours, 9 (1987).

Eskridge, *The Iranian Nationalization Cases: Toward a General Theory of*

Jurisdiction over Foreign States, 22 Harv. I.L.J. 525 (1981).
Feldman, *Implementation of the Iranian Claims Settlement Agreement—Status, Issues and Lessons: View from Government's Perspective*; Private Investors Abroad, 75 (1981).
Fauver, *Partnership Claims before the Iran–United States Claims Tribunal*, 27 Va. J.I.L., 307 (1987).
Francioni, *Compensation for Nationalization of Foreign Property: The Borderline between Law and Equity*, 24 I.C.L.Q., 255 (1975).
Friedmann, *The Uses of "General Principles" in the Development of International Law*, in Gross, ed., *International Law in the Twentieth Century*, Am. Soc. of I.L., 263 (1969).
Gann, *Compensation Standard for Expropriation*, 23 Col. J. Transnat'l L., 615 (1985).
Garcia-Amador, *The Proposed New International Economic Order: A New Approach to the Law Governing Nationalization and Compensation by Foreign States for the Taking of Alien Owned Property*, 13 Vanderbilt J. Transnational Law, 51 (1980).
Greenwood, *State Contracts in International Law: The Libyan Oil Arbitration*, 53 B.Y.I.L., 27 (1982).
Hakan-Berglin, *Treaty Interpretation and the Impact of Contractual Choice of Forum Cases on the Jurisdiction of International Tribunals: The Iranian Forum Clause Decisions of the Iran–United States Claims Tribunal*, 21 Tex. I.L.J., 39 (1985–86).
Hardenberg, *The Awards of the Iran–United States Claims Tribunal Seen in Connection with the Law of the Netherlands*, Int. Bus. Law, 337 (1984).
Hertz, *The Hostage Crisis and Domestic Litigation: An Overview*, in Lillich (ed.), *The Iran–United States Claims Tribunal, 1981–1982* (1984).
Higgins, *The Taking of Property by the State: Recent Developments in International Law*, 176 III Recueil des Cours, 259 (1982).
Hoffman, *The Iranian Asset Negotiations*, 17 Vanderbilt J. Transnational Law, 47 (1984).
Idelson, *The Law of Nations and the Individual*, 30 Grotius Soc., 50 (1945).
Ijalaye, *Multinational Companies in Africa*, 171 II Recueil des Cours, 9 (1981).
Jackson, *International Settlement: Agreement Concerning the Settlement of Claims, May 11, 1979, United States–Peoples Republic of China*, 20 Harv. I.L.J., 68 (1979).
Jeffery, *The American Hostages in Tehran: The I.C.J. and the Legality of Rescue Missions*, 30 I.C.L.Q., 713 (1981).
Jennings, *General Course in International Law*, 121 II Recueil des Cours, 323 (1967).
Jones, *Claims on Behalf of Nationals who are Shareholders in Foreign Companies*, 26 B.Y.I.L., 225 (1949).
Kennedy, *Enforcing International Commercial Arbitration Agreements and Awards not Subject to the New York Convention*, 23 Va. J.I.L., 75 (1982).
Kunzlik, *Public International Law—Cannot Govern a Contract, Can Authorise an Arbitration*, C.L.J., 377 (1986).

Lagergren, *Iran–United States Claims Tribunal* in Bos and Siblesz, eds, *Realism in Law-making: Essays on International Law in Honour of Willem Riphagen* (1986).
Lake and Dana, *Judicial Review of Awards of the Iran–United States Claims Tribunal: Are the Tribunal's Awards Dutch?*, 16 Law and Policy in Int. Bus., 755 (1984–85).
Lauterpacht, E., *The Iran–United States Claims Settlement Agreement: International Law Problems* (1981) (Monograph).
Lauterpacht, E., *The Iran–United States Claims Tribunal—An Assessment*, Private Investors Abroad, 213 (1981).
Leich, *The Proposed Iran Claims Act of the United States*, 77 A.J.I.L. (1983).
Leigh, *Nationality and Diplomatic Protection*, 20 I.C.L.Q., 453 (1971).
Leigh, *Judicial Decisions*, 77 A.J.I.L., 624 (1983).
Lewis, *What Goes Around Comes Around: Can Iran Enforce Awards of the Iran–U.S. Claims Tribunal in the United States?*, 26 Colum. J. Transnat'l L., 515 (1988).
Lillich, *The Rigidity of Barcelona*, 65 A.J.I.L., 522 (1970).
Lloyd-Jones, *The Iran–United States Claims Tribunal: Private Rights and State Responsibility*, in Lillich (ed.), *The Iran–United States Claims Tribunal 1981–1983* (1984), also in 24 Va. J.I.L. (1984).
Lowenfeld, *The US–Iranian Dispute Settlement Accord: An Arbitrator looks at the Prospects for Arbitration*, 36 Arbitration Journal (1981).
Lowenfeld, *The US/Iranian Hostage Settlement*, 239 Pcdgs. Am. Soc. I.L.(1981).
Lowenfeld, *The Iran–United States Claims Tribunal: An Interim Appraisal*, 38 Arb. J. (1984).
Luzzatto, *International Arbitration and the Law of States*, 157 IV Recueil des Cours, 17 (1977).
Mann, *Lex Facit Arbitrum*, in Sanders (ed.), *International Arbitration: Liber Amicorum for Martin Domke*, 157 (1967).
McCabe, *A Brief Discussion of the Algiers Declarations*, 20 Int. Lawyer, (1986).
McGarvey-Rosendahl, *A New Approach to Dual Nationality*, 8 Houston J.I.L., 305 (1986).
Messen, *Domestic Law Concepts in International Expropriation Law*, in Lillich (ed.), IV *Valuation of Nationalised Property in International Law*, 157 (1975).
Newman, *Enforcement of Judgments*, 17 Van. J. Transnational L., 77 (1984).
Norton, *A Law of the Future or a Law of the Past? Modern Tribunals and the International Law of Expropriation*, A.J.I.L., 474 (1991).
Note, *The Iranian Hostage Agreement under International Law and United States Law.* 81 Col. L.R., 822 (1981).
Note, *International Agreements: Settlement of Claims Outstanding between the United States and Iran; Algeria Declaration Concerning the Settlement of Claims by the United States and Iran (19 January, 1981)*, 22 Harv. I.L.J. 443 (1981).
Note, *Changed Circumstances and the Iranian Claims Arbitration: Application to Forum Selection Clauses and Frustration of Contract*, 16 Geo. Wash. J.I.L. and Econ., 335 (1982).
Note, *Claims of Dual Nationals in the Modern Era: The Iran–United States Claims Tribunal*, 83 Mich. L.R., 597 (1984).

Note, *Effect of Dual United States and Iranian Nationality on the Tribunal's Jurisdiction*, I.J. Int. Arb. 173 (1984).
Note, *The Standing of Dual Nationals before the Iran–United States Claims Tribunal*, 24 Va. J.I.L., 695 (1984).
Note, *Iran–United States Litigation*. Proceedings of the 77th Annual Meeting of the Am. Soc. Int. L., 3 (1983).
O'Connell, *Unjust Enrichment*, 5 Am. J. Comp. Law, 281 (1974).
Owen, *The U.S./Iran Hostage Settlement*, 75 Proceed. Am. Soc. I.L., 236 (1983).
Park, *Lex Loci Arbitri and International Commercial Arbitration: A Study in Liberal Civilian Judicial Creativity*, 55 Tulane L.R., 1 (1980).
Park, *Lex Loci Arbitri and International Commercial Arbitration*, 32 I.C.L.Q., 21 (1983).
Paulsson, *Arbitration Unbound: Award Detached from the Law of its Country of Origin*, 30 I.C.L.Q., 358 (1981).
Pechota, *The 1981 U.S.–Czechoslovak Claims Agreement: An Epilogue to Postwar Nationalization and Expropriation Disputes*, 76 A.J.I.L., 639 (1982).
Robinson, *Recent Developments at the Iran–United States Claims Tribunal*, 17 Int. Law, 661 (1983).
Rode, *Dual Nationals and the Doctrine of Dominant Nationality*, 53 A.J.I.L., 139 (1959).
Sacerdoti, *The New Arbitration Rules of I.C.C. and UNCITRAL*, 11 J.W.T.L., 248 (1977).
Sanders, *Trends in International Commercial Arbitration*, 145 II Recueil des Cours, 243 (1975).
Sanders, *Procedure and Practise under the UNCITRAL Rules*, 27 Am. J. Comp. Law, 453 (1979).
Sanders, *A Twenty Year Review of the Convention on the Recognition and Enforcement of Foreign Arbitral Awards*, 13 Int. Lawyer, 269 (1979).
Sanders, *National Reports: The Netherlands*, in VI *Yearbook: Commercial Arbitration*, 60 (1981).
Schachter, *The Right of States to Use Armed Force*, 82 Mich. L.R., 1620 (1984).
Schreuer, *Unjustified Enrichment in International Law*, 22 Am. J. Comp. Law, 281 (1974).
Schreuer, *The Implementation of International Judicial Decisions by Domestic Courts*, 24 I.C.L.Q., 153 (1975).
Schwarzenberger, *The Protection of British Property Abroad*, 5 Current Legal Problems (1952).
Selby and Stewart, *Practical Aspects of Arbitrating Claims before the Iran–United States Claims Tribunal*, 18 Int. Lawyer (1984).
Shalvarjian and Richter, *Outline of Settling Claims: The Iranian Experience*, 9 Hastings Int. and Comp. L.R. (1986).
Sinclair, *Nationality of Claims: British Practice*, 37 B.Y.I.L., 127 (1950).
Sinclair, *Some Procedural Aspects of Recent International Litigation*, 30 I.C.L.Q., 388 (1981).
Sohn, *The Iran–United States Claims Tribunal: Jurisprudential Contributions to the Development of International Law*, in Lillich (ed.), *The Iran–United States Claims Tribunal 1981–1983* (1984).

Sohn and Baxter, *Draft Convention on Responsibility of States for Injuries to the Economic Interests of Aliens*, 55 A.J.I.L., 545 (1961).
Sornarajah, *Compensation for Expropriation: The Emergence of New Standards*, 13 J.W.T.L., 108 (1979).
Sornarajah, *The Myth of International Contract Law*, 17 J.W.T.L., 187 (1981).
St Korowicz, *The Problems of the International Personality of Individuals*, 50 A.J.I.L., 535 (1956).
Stein, *Jurisprudence and Jurists' Prudence: The Iranian Forum Clause Decision of the Iran–United States Claims Tribunal*, 78 A.J.I.L., 1 (1984).
Stewart, *The Iran–United States Claims Tribunal: A Review of Developments 1983–84*, 16 Int. L.J. of Georgetown, U.L.C. (1984).
Stewart and Sherman, *Developments at the Iran–United States Claims Tribunal 1981–1983*, in Lillich (ed.), *The Iran–United States Claims Tribunal 1981–1983* (1984), also in 24 Va. J.I.L., 1 (1983).
Strauss, *Causation as an Element of State Responsibility*, 16 Int. L.J. of Georgetown, U.L.C. (1984).
Strauss, *The Practice of the Iran–U.S. Claims Tribunal in Receiving Evidence from Parties and from Experts*, 3 J. Int. Arb., 57 (1986).
Suy, *Settling U.S. Claims against Iran by Negotiation*, 29 Am. J. of Comp. Law, 523 (1981).
Swanson, *Iran–U.S. Claims Tribunal: A Policy Analysis of the Expropriation Cases*, 18 Case Western J. of I.L., 307 (1986).
Szasy, *Recognition and Enforcement of Foreign Arbitral Awards*, 14 Am. J. Comp. Law, 658 (1966).
Thompson, *The UNCITRAL Arbitration Rules*, 47 Harv. J.I.L., 141 (1976).
Troobof, *Implementation of the Iranian Claims Settlement Agreement—Status, Issues and Lessons: the Private Sector's Perspective*, Private Investors Abroad, 103 (1981).
Van den Berg, *Proposed Dutch Law on the Iran–U.S. Claims Settlement Declaration, a reaction to Mr. Hardenberg's Article*, Int. Bus. Lawyer (1984).
Van den Berg, *National Reports: The Netherlands*, XII *Yearbook: Commercial Arbitration*, 3 (1987).
Van Mehren, *The Iran–U.S. Arbitral Tribunal*, Am. J. Comp. Law., 31 (1983).
Weston, *"Constructive Takings" under International Law: A Modest Foray into the Problem of "Creeping Expropriation"*, 16 Va. J.I.L., 103 (1975–76).
Weston, *The Charter of Economic Rights and Duties of States and the Deprivation of Foreign Owned Wealth*, 75 A.J.I.L., 437 (1981).
Wetter, *Interest as an Element of Damages in the Arbitral Process*, Int. Financial L.R., 20 (1986).
Zimmet, *Standby Letters of Credit in the Iran Litigation: Two Hundred Problems in Search of a Solution*, 16 Int. L.J. of Georgetown, U.L.C. (1984).

Case notes

Note (Leigh), *Flexi-Van Leasing Inc.* v *Islamic Republic of Iran*, *General Motors Corp.* v *Islamic Republic of Iran*, 77 A.J.I.L., 642 (1983).
Note (Leigh), *Esphahanian* v *Bank Tejarat*, 77 A.J.I.L., 646 (1983).

Note (Leigh), *Grimm v Government of the Islamic Republic of Iran*, 77 A.J.I.L., 649 (1983).
Note (Leigh), *ITT Industries v Islamic Republic of Iran*, 77 A.J.I.L., 891 (1983).
Note (Leigh), *Gould Marketing Inc. v Ministry of National Defence of Iran*, 77 A.J.I.L., 893 (1983).
Note, *Case A/18*, 1 J. of Int. Arb. (1984).
Note (Leigh), *Chas T. Main International Inc. v Khuzestan Water & Power Authority*, 78 A.J.I.L., 238 (1984).
Note (Leigh), *Mark Dallal v Islamic Republic of Iran*, 78 A.J.I.L., 235 (1984).
Note (Leigh), *R.N. Pomeroy v Government of the Islamic Republic of Iran*, 78 A.J.I.L., 240 (1984).
Note (Levitin), *Nationalization: Appropriate Standard of Compensation in American International Group Inc.*, 25 Harv. J.I.L., 491 (1984).
Note (Henry and Bainbridge), *Recent Developments, Nationalizations, Standard of Compensation, American International Group Inc.*, 24 Va J.I.L., 993 (1984).
Note (Leigh), *American International Group Inc. v Islamic Republic of Iran*, 78 A.J.I.L., 454 (1984).
Note (Leigh), *Islamic Republic of Iran v United States of America A/18*, 78 A.J.I.L., 912 (1984).
Note (Leigh), *Morrison-Knudsen Pacific Ltd v Ministry of Roads and Transportation*, 79 A.J.I.L., 912 (1984).
Note (Leigh), *Gould Marketing Inc. v Ministry of Defence of Iran*, 79 A.J.I.L., 148 (1985).
Note (Leigh), *INA Corp. v Islamic Republic of Iran*, 80 A.J.I.L., 181 (1986).
Note (Leigh), *Questech Inc. v Ministry of National Defence of the Islamic Republic of Iran*, 80 A.J.I.L., 362 (1986).
Note (Leigh), *Sylvania Technical Systems Inc. v Islamic Republic of Iran*, 80 A.J.I.L., 365 (1986).
Note (Leigh), *Islamic Republic of Iran v United States of America*, 81 A.J.I.L., 428 (1987).

TABLE OF CASES

Permanent Court of International Justice and International Court of Justice

Anglo-Iranian Oil Case (*United Kingdom* v *Iran*), 42, 240, 280

Barcelona Traction Case (*Belgium* v *Spain*), 69, 89, 90, 92, 99, 101, 185, 273, 277
Brazilian Loans Case, 107, 146

Chorzow Factory Case (*Germany* v *Poland*), 164, 175, 177, 187, 196, 197, 342
Corfu Channel Case (Merits) (*United Kingdom* v *Albania*), 266

German Interests in Polish Upper Silesia (*Germany* v *Poland*), 151

Interhandel Case (*Switzerland* v *United States*), 226
Interpretation of Peace Treaties with Bulgaria, Hungary, Romania, 42

Mavrommatis Palestine Concessions Case (*Greece* v *United Kingdom*), 68, 69, 81, 263
Military and Paramilitary Activities in and around Nicaragua (*Nicaragua* v *United States*), 340

Norwegian Loans Case, 107, 117
Nottebohm Case (*Liechtenstein* v *Guatemala*), 61, 62, 63, 66, 67, 68, 70, 72, 75, 77, 80, 81

Reparation for Injuries Suffered in the Service of the United Nations, 66, 77

Serbian Loans Case, 107, 117, 118, 124, 146

Temple of Preah-vihear, 177

United States Diplomatic and Consular Staff in Tehran
(*United States* v *Iran*), 7, 134, 139, 147, 150, 219, 221, 222, 231, 280

International arbitral awards and decisions of national claims commissions

AAMCO v *Saudi Arabia*, 115, 155, 166, 169, 309, 331
Adams and Blackmore v *United Mexican States*, 65, 77
AGIP v *Congo*, 180, 193
Alsing Trading Co. v *Greece*, 307

Bermuda Asphalt Co. Case, 87
Bogovich Claim, 82
British Petroleum v *Libya*, 43, 164, 168, 171, 175, 178, 306, 307, 318
British Property in Spanish Morocco (*Britain* v *Spain*), 225
Buena Tiena Mining Co. Ltd (*Great Britain* v *Mexico*), 226

Canevaro (*Italy* v *Peru*), 65, 72, 77
China Navigation Co. Ltd (*Great Britain* v *United States*), 120
Compania Mexicana de Petroleo El Aquila S.A., 88
Cortes, Enrique & Co. Case, 87

Davis Case (*United States* v *Mexico*), 97
Delagoa Bay Railway Arbitration, 87, 164, 278
Dickson Car Wheel Co. v *Mexico*, 211
Dix Claim (*United States* v *Venezuela*), 222

Fermingo, Rafael (*Italy* v *Mexico*), 226
Flegenheimer (*United States* v *Italy*), 62, 64, 67

Gelbtrunk Claim (*United States* v *Salvador*), 223
General Finance Corp. v *Mexico*, 211
Gudmundson v *Iceland*, 154

Hein v *Hildersheimer Bank*, 65
Henry Case, 222
Hong Kong Companies Case, 87
Howard (*Great Britian* v *Mexico*), 224

Illinois Railway Co. Claim (*United States* v *Mexico*), 107, 116
Italo-Turkish War Case, 87

Janes Case (*United States* v *Mexico*), 225

Kuwait v *Aminoil*, 170, 174, 179, 190, 192, 286, 288, 290, 306, 309, 343, 345

Landreau (*United States* v *Peru*), 82, 166
Lena Goldfields Case, 43, 153, 166, 169, 178, 211, 216, 286
Liamco v *Libya*, 191, 192, 211, 343

Liberian Eastern Timber Corp. v *Liberia*, 287
Lighthouses Arbitration (*France* v *Greece*), 278
Lynch (*Great Britain* v *Mexico*), 224, 269

Mergé (*United States* v *Italy*), 66, 67, 68, 75, 77, 80, 341

Norwegian Shipowners' Claim (*Norway* v *United States*), 122, 151, 152, 164

Oldenburg, Carlos, *Re*, 65
Oldenburg Case, 77
Oskiner v *German State*, 65

Panama Sugar, Fruit and Cattle Case, 88
Parker Case, 270, 273
Pieri Dominique Case, 166
Pinson Case, 224, 273

Rann of Kutch Arbitration (*India* v *Pakistan*), 178
Revere Copper v *OPIC*, 155
Russell, William (*Great Britain* v *Mexico*), 226

Salem Case (*United States* v *Egypt*), 62, 63
Sambiaggio Case (*Italy* v *Venezuela*), 225
Santa Isabel Claims (*United States* v *Mexico*), 226
Sapphire International Petroleum Ltd v *NIOC*, 155, 166, 167, 286, 306, 307, 309, 310
Shufeldt Case (*United States* v *Guatemala*), 97, 101, 114, 164
Sporring and Lönnroth, 154
SPP v *Egypt*, 287
Standard Oil Co. (*United States* v *Reparations Commission*), 88
Stevenson Claim, 84
Straub Claim, 82

Texaco (TOPCO) v *Libya*, 43, 155, 165, 169, 175, 191, 306, 308, 318, 331
Trail Smelter Arbitration (*Canada* v *United States*), 280

Ziat, Ben Kiran Case (*Great Britain* v *Mexico*), 101

Awards and Decisions of the Iran–United States Claims Tribunal

Aeromaritime Inc. v *Iran*, 268
Aeronautic Services Inc. v *Air Force of Iran*, 254
Alcan Corp. v *Ircable Corp.*, 96, 97, 275

Table of cases

American Bell International Inc. v Iran, 136, 183
American International Group Inc. v Islamic Republic of Iran, 96, 148, 171, 182, 186, 193
AMF Overseas Corp. v Government of Iran, 37
Amoco International Finance Corp. v Iran, 35, 48, 148, 149, 172, 187, 188, 189, 195, 201, 203, 342
Amoco Iran Oil Co. v Iran, 35, 115, 174
Anaconda of Iran Inc. v Iran, 125

Bakhiari v Iran, 79
Behring International Inc. v Iranian Air Force, 5, 279
Bendix v Iran, 79
Blount Bros Corp. v Ministry of Housing and Development, 51, 119, 319
Boeing Co. v Iran, 284

Carlson v Iran and Meli Industrial Group, 49
CBS Inc. v Iran, 195
CMI International Inc. v Iran, 111, 123, 131, 143
Craig v Ministry of Energy of Iran, 51, 52, 128

Dallal v Iran, 291, 326
Dames Moore v Iran, 214, 220, 250
Daniel, Mann, Johnson and Mendenhall v Iran, 268
DIC of Delaware v Iran, 143, 112, 125
Dresser Industries Inc. v Iran, 236, 244
Drucker, George W. v Foreign Transaction Co., 236, 237, 245, 247

Ebranhimi v Iran, 79
Economy Forms v Iran, 124, 125, 143
Espahahanian v Bank Tejarat, 61, 70, 71, 73, 74, 319
E-Systems Inc. v Iran, 282, 283
Exxon Corp. v Iran, 289

Flexi-Van Leasing v Iran, 85, 96, 270, 274, 275, 276, 277
Ford Aerospace Communications Corp. v Air Force of Iran, 236, 246, 283
Futura Trading Inc. v Khuzestan Water and Power Authority, 215

General Motors Inc. v Iran, 274, 277
Gibbs & Hill Inc. v Tavanir, 236, 244, 245
Golpira v Iran, 61, 70, 73, 74
Goodrich, B. F., Co. v Kian Time Manufacturing Co., 268
Gould Marketing Inc. v Ministry of National Defence, 135, 136, 301, 314
Grimm v Iran, 84, 209, 219, 221, 227, 228, 232, 234
Gruen Assoc. Inc. v Iranian Housing Co., 319

Haji-Bagherpour v United States, 10, 219
Halliburton Co. v Doreen/IMCO, 213, 236, 241, 248, 249

Hilt v *Iran*, 128
Hoffland Honey Co. v *NIOC*, 209
Honeywell Information Services Inc. v *Information Systems Iran (Isiran)*, 94
Housing and Urban Services International Inc. v *Tehran Redevelopment Corp.*, 100
Howard, Needles, Tammen and Bergendoff (HNTB) v *Iran*, 236, 245

INA Corp. v *Iran*, 148, 172, 183, 194, 343, 345
International School Services Inc. v *National Iranian Copper Industries*, 137, 301
International Technical Product Corp. v *Iran*, 163, 279
Intrend v *Iran Air Force*, 319
Iowa State University v *Ministry of Culture*, 128
Iran v *United States (Case A/1)*, 267, 277, 296, 297, 351
Iran v *United States (Case A/2)*, 60, 217
Iran v *United States (Case A/18 Dual Nationality)*, 61, 74, 78, 109, 112, 243, 299, 341, 342
Iran v *United States (Case A/21)*, 109, 299
Isaiah v *Bank Mellat*, 83, 111, 212
ITT Industrial Inc. v *Iran*, 184

Judge Mangard, *Re*, 44–7

Kimberly-Clark Corp. v *Bank of Markazi Iran*, 130, 132

Lianosoff v *Iran*, 83
Lockheed Corp. v *Iran*, 216

McCollough & Co. Inc. v *Ministry of Post*, 288, 289
McHarg and Others v *Iran*, 284
McLaughlin Enterprises Ltd v *Iran*, 129
Main, Chas T., International Inc. v *Khuzestan Water and Power Authority*, 127
Main, Chas T., International Inc. v *Mahb Consulting Engineers Inc.*, 51, 319
Michelle Danielpour v *Iran*, 78
Mobil Oil Iran Inc. v *Iran*, 23, 133, 137, 141, 142, 147, 199, 344
Motorola Inc. v *Iran National Airlines Corp.*, 159

Nemazee v *Iran*, 79
New York State University v *Ministry of Culture*, 128

Oil Fields of Texas Inc. v *Iran*, 110, 121, 122, 163

Phelps Dodge Corp. v *Iran*, 148, 149, 161, 185, 186, 187, 188, 194, 195
Phillips Petroleum Co., Iran v *Iran and NIOC*, 48, 98, 113, 137, 143, 162, 172, 174, 175, 188, 190, 196, 199, 200, 203, 204, 205, 252, 342
Pomeroy, R. N. v *Iran*, 129, 131

Queens Office Tower Associates v *Iran Air*, 123, 136, 137, 138
Questech Inc. v *Ministry of National Defence of Iran*, 140, 142, 283

Table of cases 383

Rankin, Jack v *Iran*, 231
Raygo Wagner Equipment Co. v *Star Line Iran Co.*, 156, 319, 320
Raymond International (UK) Ltd v *Shahpur Chemical Co.*, 37
Rexnord Inc. v *Iran*, 157, 319, 320
Reynolds, R. J., Tobacco Co. v *Iran*, 119
Rockwell International Systems Inc. v *Iran*, 283

Saghi v *Iran*, 77
Schlegel Corp. v *National Iranian Copper Industries Co.*, 215
Sealand Service Inc. v *Iran*, 148, 160, 161, 214, 230
Sedco Inc. v *NIOC*, 148, 149, 158, 159, 185, 187
Short, Alfred v *Iran*, 231
Singer Company v *Iran National Airlines Corp.*, 93
Sola Tiles, 282
Starrett Housing Corp. v *Iran*, 87, 94, 98, 99, 125, 157, 161, 188, 199, 276, 279, 290
Stone & Webster Overseas Inc. v *National Petrochemical Co.*, 236, 245, 248
Sylvania Technical Systems v *Iran*, 136, 140, 288, 290

TAMS v *Iran*, 186, 189
TAMS v *TAMS-AFFA*, 160, 161, 184
TCSB Inc. v *Iran*, 214, 247, 250
Technology Enterprises Inc. v *Foreign Transaction Co.*, 254
Teichmann Inc. v *Hamadon Glass Co.*, 132

Warnecke & Assoc. v *Bank Mellat*, 51, 319
White Westinghouse International Co. v *Sepah Iran*, 268, 287
William L. Pereiera Assoc. Iran v *Iran*, 139, 142
Woodward-Clyde Consultants v *Iran*, 51, 119, 120, 319

Yeager, Kenneth, v *Iran*, 210, 231

Zokor International Inc. v *Iran*, 236

National courts

Albert Reef, 154

Banco National de Cuba v *Chase Manhattan Bank*, 24, 25, 181, 345
Banco National de Cuba v *Sabbatino*, 24, 25

Cabolent, N. V., v *NIOC*, 306
Carvalho v *Hull Blyth (Angola) Ltd*, 240

Dallal v *Bank Mellat*, 213, 268, 291, 306, 313, 315, 316, 317, 322, 326, 328, 330, 332, 334, 348
Dames & Moore v *Regan*, 216

Electronic Data Systems v *Social Security Organisation of Iran*, 5

Gotaverken v *Libya*, 312, 316, 318, 319, 332

La Abra Silver Mining Co. v *United States*, 305
Laconia, The, 327

Messina v *Petrococchino*, 327
Ministry of Defence of Iran v *Gould Inc.*, 301

Osthoff v *Hofele*, 152

Poehlmann v *Kulmbache Spinnerei A.G.*, 152

Société Europenne d'Etudes et d'Entreprises v *Socialist Federal Republic of Yugoslavia*, 314
Société Vinicole de Champagne v *Mumm Champagne & Importation Co. Inc.*, 305
Socobel v *Greek State*, 304
Steinberg et al. v *Custodians of German Property*, 305

Textron Inc. v *Iran*, 328

Zwack v *Kraus Bros & Co.*, 153

INDEX

agent, 19, 44, 46, 258, 269, 349
Algeria, 12, 14, 20
Algiers Declarations, 13–14, 21, 22,
    75, *see also* Claims Settlement
    Declaration; General
    Declaration
  supplementary agreements to, 14,
    20–1
    Escrow Agreement, 14, 20
    Technical Agreement, 14, 20, 296
    Undertaking of Iran and US, 14,
    20
appointing authority, 45, 46–50, 51,
    53, 54, 55
arbitrator
  appointment of, 43–4, 48–50, *see
    also* appointing authority
  assault of and by, 53–4
  challenge to, 44–50, 200
  impartiality, 44, 48, 49, 54
  resignation, 50–3, 54
  substitute for, 41
award
  on agreed terms, *see* settlement
  distinguished from Tribunal decision,
    24
  enforcement of, *see* enforcement and
    recognition of awards
  recognition by third states, *see under*
    enforcement and recognition of
    awards
  validity of in the absence of an
    arbitrator, 203

changed circumstances, 133–4, 139–42,
    237–43, *see also* contract, *force
    majeure*; contract, frustration
cheque, 74, 83, 213, 287, 291
choice of law clause, *see under*
    governing law of claims
claims, *see also* statement of claim
  arising out of hostage crisis, *see
    under* tort
  assignment of, 84
  contracts between Iran and US
    governments, *see under*
    jurisdiction of Tribunal
  debts and contract, *see* contract
  of less than $250,000, 19, 33, 103,
    258, 346
  nationalisation and expropriation,
    see expropriation
  nationality of, *see under* nationality
    of claim
  other claims affecting property
    rights, *see* tort; unjust
    enrichment
  presentation of, 103, 258, 261–5
  settlement of, *see* settlement
  statistics of, 6, 20, 36, 103
  time-barred, 20, 35, *see also* time
    limits
  types of claim before the Tribunal,
    24, *see also* jurisdiction of
    Tribunal
Claims Settlement Declaration, 17–20,
    21–5, 33, 39, 59, 86, 87, 91, 93

Article I, 30, 33–5
Article II, 18, 35
  Paragraph 1, 23, 24, 59, 60, 98, 100, 103, 107, 145, 218–21, 228, 235–54, 341
  Paragraph 2, 18, 60, 104
  Paragraph 3, 60, 61
Article III, 18
  Paragraph 1, 18, 43
  Paragraph 2, 18, 19, 33, 46, 257
  Paragraph 3, 33, 103, 258
Article IV, 19, 293, 294, 298, 300, 333
Article V, 19, 27, 103–13, 118, 121–7, 143–4, 146, 148, 237, 240, 289, 344
Article VI, 19
  Paragraph 1, 19, 92, 277
  Paragraph 2, 60, 61, 91–3, 97, 100–2, 267
Article VIII, 20
concurring opinions, 110, 132, 148
  Aldrich, 76, 184–5
  Holtzman, 76, 110, 183, 290
  Mosk, 111, 122, 275
  Riphagen, 76
contract, 120–43, *see also* forum selection clauses
  assignment of, 122
  breach, 115, 130–3, 162–3, 167, 169, 171, 174
  changed circumstances, *see* changed circumstances
  concessions, 141, 142, 147, 162, 187, 195, *see also* expropriation
  corporate succession to contractual liabilities, 121–2
  force majeure, 133, 135–8, 139, 142, 173, 199
  formation, 127–9
  frustration, 133, 138–9, 142
  governing law, *see* governing law
  part performance of, 112
  repudiation, 135, 169–71
  state responsibility, *see* state responsibility
  suspension, 173
  validity, 129–30
controlled entities, 156–7, 235
corporations, 92–5
  control of, *see under* nationality of claim
  evidence of ownership of, *see under* evidence of
  shareholders' right to bring claim; nationality of claim
customary international law, 8, 9, 10, 63, 65, 90, 105–7, 144–5, 164, 165, 170, 171, 176–82, 227, 234

damages, 176–206, 344–5
  compensation, 162, 171–5, 176–206
  date accrue from, 173, 178
  equitable considerations, 202
  future profits, 189–206, 211
  future prospects, 196
  interest, 285–90
  lump sums between states, *see* lump sums
  mental anguish and grief, 84
  restitution, *see* restitution
  standard of compensation, 176–91, 341, 342
    assets, 176–8, 182–7
    concessions, 172–5, 178–82, 187–91
    illegal expropriation, 177–8
    large-scale nationalisations, 178–82, 187–90
    particular property, 176–7
  support from husband, 228–30
  unjust enrichment as a measure, 210–16
  valuation, 191–206
    book value, 192
    date, 205
    discounted cash flow method, 48, 197–206, 342–4
    expert evidence, 199
    going concern, 183, 194, 198, 205–6
    oil concessions, 195–206
    social and economic conditions, 193–5, 198, 206

Index

debts, 117–20
development of international law,
    27–8, 55, 75, 80, 89, 90, 107,
    126, 145, 182, 206, 341–7
diplomatic protection, 64–5, 68–9,
    72–3, 75, 80–1, 87–97, 102,
    108–10
discounted cash flow method, *see under*
    damages, valuation
dissenting opinions in Tribunal
  Ameli, 183, 189
  Holtzman, 37, 124, 139, 183, 213,
    229–34, 239–41, 243, 274, 275,
    290
  Kashani, 158, 273, 273–4
  Khalilian, 203
  Lagergren, 236
  Mosk, 239–41, 250, 251
  Sani, 157, 320
  Shafeiei, 161
dramati personae
  Aldrich, 43, 48, 49, 76, 185, 204, 236
  Ameli, 188, 189, 205
  Ansari, 52
  Bahrami-Ahmadi, 53, 300
  Bellet, 44, 50–4, 236, 270
  Bocksteigel, 54
  Briner, 48–9, 200
  Carter, 6, 13
  Christopher, 12, 15, 253,
  Esharagh, 325
  Holtzman, 37, 43, 76, 110, 124, 139,
    183, 213, 221, 236, 239, 240,
    243, 249, 274, 290
  Kashani, 44, 53–4, 158, 273, 274,
    276, 325
  Khalilan, 48–9, 203–4, 342
  Khomeini, 5, 9
  Lagergren, 30, 44–50, 168, 172, 183,
    270, 271, 272, 277, 307
  Mangard, 30, 45–54, 236, 270
  Moons, 43–50, 53
  Morozov, 10, 11
  Mosk, 43, 52–3, 76, 111, 122, 236,
    239, 240, 241, 250, 251, 275, 320
  Mostafavi, 53, 300
  Muskie, 19
  Noori, 49–50
  Pinto, 31
  Reagan, 13
  Riphagen, 51–4, 76
  Rovine, 269
  Sani, 51, 52, 230
  Shafeiei, 45, 53–4, 161
  Tarazi, 11, 13
  Virally, 342
dual nationality, *see under* nationality

economic sanctions, 6–7, 11, 14, 16,
    21, 27
enforcement and recognition of arbitral
    awards, 19, 262, 293–335, *see
    also* governing law of the
    arbitration; satisfaction of
    awards; Security Account;
    treaties, New York Convention
  denationalised awards and the New
    York Convention, 304–11,
    313–15
  enforcement of
    awards in Iran and the US, 324
    awards in third-party states,
      305–6, 308, 311
    international claims tribunal
      awards, 306–11
    international commercial arbitral
      awards, 306–17
    Iran–US Claims Tribunal awards,
      317–35
    with states parties, 306–11
  recognition and enforcement of
    awards outside the New York
    Convention, 315–17
  recognition of
    awards in third-party states, 306,
      313
    international claims tribunal
      awards, 305–11
Escrow Agreement, *see under* Algiers
    Declarations, supplementary
    agreements to
European Court of Human Rights,
    146, 154
evidence, 265–79

admissibility, 265–6
burden of proof, 265, 273
expert, 278–9, *see also under* damages, valuation
judicial notice of US statistics, 271–4
evidence of
contract, part performance, 112
nationality, 70–4, 76, 79–80
nationality of corporation, 91, 93, 267–78
assertion of, 267–9
direct evidence of, 275–6
sworn statements of, 275–6
voting stock only, 271, 272, 275
expropriation, 3, 4, 145–206, 340, 342
contractual rights, 106–7
definition, 145–7
by interference with owner's rights, 106–7, 156–9, 171–3, 182–7
of concessions, 107, 162–3, 172–5, 178–82
governing law of, *see* governing law of claims, expropriation
legality of, 163–75

force majeure, *see* under contract
formalistic approach by Tribunal, 55
forum selection clauses, 13, 18, 235–54
'binding', 237, 238–49
exclusive Iranian jurisdiction, 237
competent courts, 240, 241, 248
Iranian arbitration, 240, 244, 248
non-contractual remedies as a basis for jurisdiction, 250–1
not established, 249
selected issues only, 244–7
'Majlis position', 235, 251–4
France, law of
administrative contract, 167
arbitration, 312, 316
freeze of Iranian assets, *see under* United States law, executive orders

General Assembly Resolutions
1803 (Permanent Sovereignty over Natural Resources, 1962), 164, 165, 169, 179, 180, 185–6, 344
3198 (1976), 42
3201 (1974), 165, 344
3281 (Charter of Economic Rights and Duties of States, 1974), 165, 169, 179, 344
General Declaration, 14–17, 94
General Principle A, 14
General Principle B, 15, 329
paragraph 1, 14
paragraph 2, 15
paragraph 3, 15
paragraph 4, 16
paragraph 5, 16
paragraph 6, 16
paragraph 7, 16, 294, 297
paragraph 8, 16
paragraph 9, 16
paragraph 10, 16
paragraph 11, 16, 17, 18, 218–28, 232–4
paragraph 14, 17
paragraph 15, 17
paragraph 16, 17, 36
paragraph 17, 17, 18, 24, 36, 294
point I, 15
points II–III, 15
point IV, 17
preamble, 14
general principles of international law, 9, 65, 68, 105–7, 124, 188, 189, 205
general principles of law, 76, 106, 110–12, 115, 118–20, 129, 130, 131, 143, 144, 146, 167, 184, 210–12, 214, 286, 303
governing law of the arbitration
under Dutch law, 320–6
international claims tribunals, 301–11
international commercial arbitration, 301–11
Iran–US Claims Tribunal, 317–20, 343

Index 389

proposed amendments to, 323–6
governing law of claims, 22, 23, 105–13, 115, 116, 122, 140, 251, 343
  choice of law clauses, 18, 27, 104, 111, 112, 121–7, 129, 144, 234–49
  contractual claims, 105–7, 112, 115, 121–7, 143–4
  expropriation claims, 104, 113, 114, 145–7
  official claims, 107–8
  private claims, 105–7
  trade usage, 18
  Tribunal's discretion to determine, 103–8, 110–13, 121–7, 143–4
  unjust enrichment claims, 211
government endorsement of hostage taking, *see* Iran, adoption of hostage-taking

interim measures, 280–5
  after judgment, 284
  power under Tribunal rules, 281
  stay of proceedings in municipal courts, 282–3
International Centre for Settlement of Investment Disputes, 180, 349
International Chamber of Commerce Court of Arbitration, 328, 329, 349
International Court of Justice, 7–10, 73–7, 117, 147, 219, 229–31, 266, 305, 309, 340
  Statute of
    Article 38, 120, 210
    Article 41, 8
    Article 59, 305
International Law Commission, 42, 43, 222, 224, 225, 227
International Monetary Fund, 326
interpretation of Algiers Declarations, *see under* jurisdiction of the Tribunal
Iran
  adoption of hostage-taking, 5–9, 222

assets seized by US, *see under* United States law, executive orders
Imperial government, 2, 9, 147
Islamic revolution, 2–3, 9, 99, 135, 147, 162, 163, 185, 205, 206, 218, 221, 228–33, *see also under* jurisdiction of the Tribunal, exclusions
'Majlis position', 12, 18, 251–4, *see also under* forum selection clauses
trade sanctions, *see under* United States law, executive orders
Iran, law of
  Civil Code
    Article 193, 129
    Article 247, 129
    Article 248, 129
  Constitution, Article 44, 4, 156
  contract, ratification by conduct, 127
  currency regulations, 326
  Law of Nationalisation of Insurance and Credit Enterprises, 189
  nationality, 73
  partnership, 100
  Protection and Development of Iranian Industries Act, Single Article Act, 99, 163, 173, 252, 253
Islam, 9, 286, 288

jurisdiction of the Tribunal, 18, 262, *see also* claims, types of claim before the Tribunal; nationality of claim
  actions of private individuals, 225–8, 232
  actions of revolutionaries, 221–4, 228–33
  compared with international arbitral tribunals, 20, 105–7
  compared with municipal courts, 22–5, 104
  forum selection clause, *see* forum selection clauses

government against government, 18, 23, 59, 103–4
government against national, 217
hostage crisis, 217–20
interpretation of the Declarations, 18, 24, 60, 103
national against government, 18, 59, 102–4
national against national, 217
popular movements, 220–33, 232
settlement, *see under* settlement

Libya, law of, 177
lump sum settlements between states, 179, 180, 185, 339, 344

'Majlis position', *see under* forum selection clause; Iran

nationalisation, *see* expropriation
nationality, *see also* diplomatic protection
  corporations, 86–102, *see also* evidence of, nationality of corporation nationality of claim, corporations
  dual nationality, 61–81
    Chamber Two awards and decisions, 70–4
    diplomatic protection, 68–9
    espousal of claims, 62–9
    nationality of natural persons, 61–9
    Tribunal awards and decisions, 69–85
  evidence, *see under* evidence of natural persons, 70, 71, 73, 76, 77–81
  partnerships, 97–101
nationality of claim, *see also under* evidence of
  continuity of ownership, 81–5
  corporations, 86–102
    control of, 86, 91, 92–9
    evidence, *see* evidence of, nationality of corporation
    death of original claimant, 83–5

partnership claims, 97–101
shareholder claims, 87, 90, 91–7
Netherlands
  courts, 306, 311, 312, 314, 317, 319, 321
  law, 306, 313, 317–23, 331–5, 247–349
  proposed bill, 317, 318, 319, 323–6, 331–5

partnership, 97–101
Permanent Court of Arbitration, Secretary General of, 45–6
Permanent Court of International Justice, 147, 187, 263, 304
Presidential Order
  No. 1, 30
  No. 8, 30
  No. 9, 30
  No. 27, 30, 53
  No. 29, 30, 53
  No. 33, 54
procedure of tribunal, 257–92, *see also* arbitrator; claims, presentation of; evidence; evidence of; interim measures; time limits; Tribunal rules and UNCITRAL rules
  finality of awards, 258, 291–2
  interlocutory awards, 260
property abandoned by US nationals, 2, 232, 233

quantum meruit, 241, 249–51
quasi contract, *see* unjust enrichment

restitution, 178, 249–51

satisfaction of awards, 295–301, *see also* Security Account
  in favour of Iran and Iranian nationals, 298–300
Security Account, 16, 21, 27, 34–5, 293–4, 296–8, 347
  maintenance of, 297–8
  payments from, 296–7
settlement

Index 391

Award on Agreed Terms, 32–5
 before arbitration, 32–4
 limited by jurisdiction of Tribunal, 34–5, 296–7
 payment of, 296–7
 small claims, 34
shareholder claims, *see under* nationality of claims
sovereign immunity, 7, 17, 220, 306, 307
sovereignty, 8, 164–6, 178
stabilisation clause, *see also* expropriation, 167, 171
state responsibility, 25, 106–9, 113, 114–16, 145–7, 205, 231
 acts of private individuals, 225–8, 231
 acts of revolutionary movements, 221–4, 226–7, 229–33
 contracts and debts, 105–7, 114–16
 expropriation, 105–7, 145–7
 torts, 207, 208–9, 210
statement of claim, 29, 35–6
 amendment, 36–7
Switzerland
 courts, 328–31
 law, 328–31

Technical Agreement, *see under* Algiers Declarations, supplementary agreements to
time limits
 amendment of claim, 36–7
 filing of claim, 35–8
 negotiations before arbitration, 32–3
tort, 207–10
 chattels and bank accounts, 209–10
 husband killed, 208–10
treaties, interpretation of
 ambiguity, 238
 contra proferentum, *see* words and phrases, *contra proferentum*
 effective interpretation, 240, 242–3
 ordinary meaning, 237, 243
 preparatory work and circumstances, 238
 term to have some meaning, 240

treaties and analogous instruments
 Bulgaria, Hungary (1950), 42
 Convention on the Prevention and Punishment of Crimes against Internationally Protected Persons (1973), 8
 European Human Rights Convention, 154
 Hague Convention on Conflict of Nationality Laws (1930), 62, 64, 67, 74, 80
  Article 1, 62
  Article 4, 64, 71, 72, 74, 80
  Article 5, 72
 New York Convention on the Recognition and Enforcement of Foreign Arbitral Awards, 300–2, 311–15, 328, 333–5, 347–9
 Optional Protocols to the Vienna Conventions, 9
 Treaty of Amity, Economic Relations and Consular Rights (Iran–US), 9, 98, 147–50, 175, 184–90, 344
  Article 4, 148, 186
 Treaty of Friendship (US–Italy), 98
 Treaty of Peace, 42
 United Nations Charter, 11
  Article 2, 11
  Article 33, 11
  Article 51, 11
 US–China, 180
 US–Czechoslovakia, 82, 91, 180
 US–Hungary (1973), 91
 US–Yugoslavia (1948), 82, 90
 Versailles, 262, 264, 295
 Vienna Convention on Consular Relations (1963), 8–9
 Vienna Convention on Diplomatic Relations (1961), 8–9
 Vienna Convention on the Law of Treaties (1969), 74
  Article 31, 74
  Article 62, 134
Tribunal, *see also* Tribunal rules
 administration, 31–3

Administrative Directive
  No. 1, 32
Annual Report
  No. 1, 30, 32
  No. 2, 30, 32
  No. 3, 32
  No. 4, 32
Chambers
  assignment of cases, 32
  Chairmen of, 30–1
  independence of, 30
  membership, 30, *see also*
    arbitrator
  special, 30–1, 54
full tribunal
  relinquishment of cases to, 30
  type of case dealt with, 30, 31
jurisdiction, *see* jurisdiction of
    Tribunal
legal precedents and methodology,
    341–7
membership, 29, 30, 39, 43, 44
President, 32
  appointment, 30, 44
  Orders, *see* Presidential Order
  powers, 30, 31, 53
procedure, *see* procedure of Tribunal
Secretariat, 31
size and structure, 30, 43, 44
suspension of proceedings, 53

Tribunal rules, 46, *see also*
    UNCITRAL rules
  Article 1, 41, 260
  Article 2, 40, 260
  Article 5, 40–1
  Article 6, 40–1, 46
  Article 7, 40–1
  Article 8, 40–1
  Article 9, 40, 46–9
  Article 10, 40–1, 46–9
  Article 11, 41, 45–9
  Article 12, 41, 46–9
  Article 13, 41
  Article 14, 41
  Article 17, 31
  Article 19, 260

  Article 20, 260
  Article 21, 260
  Article 22, 260
  Article 23, 260
  Article 24, 265–6
  Article 25, 265–6
  Article 26, 281
  Article 27, 278–9
  modifications of UNCITRAL rules,
      40–2, 260
  Section I, 259
  Section II, 259
  Section III, 259

UNCITRAL rules, 40–2, 257–61, 346,
    see also Tribunal rules
Undertaking of Iran and the US to the
    Declarations, *see under* Algiers
    Declarations, supplementary
    agreements to
United Kingdom
  arbitration law, 303, 328
  partnership law, 97
  recognition of Tribunal's awards,
      326–8
United States courts
  litigation pre-Tribunal, 4–5, 7
  pre-judgment attachment, 4–5, 7, 21
  stay of proceedings, 4, 284
  substitute forum, 4, 7, 22–5
  termination of claims, 18, 21
United States law
  arbitration, 303
  Arms Control Act, 17
  common law, 113
  contract, 128
  Constitution, 21–2
  Executive Orders
    12170 (freezing Iranian assets),
        6–7
    12205 (prohibiting transactions
        with Iran), 6
    12282 (incorporating Algiers
        Declarations into US law), 220
    12285 (compensation commission
        for hostages), 220
    12294 (stay of proceedings), 5, 283

Index

Foreign Sovereign Immunities Act, 1976, 220
International Claims Settlement Act, 1949, 90
partnership, 97
Restatement (2d), Foreign Relations of US (1965), 179
state law
  Idaho, 123
  Iowa, 124
  New York, 123
United States rescue mission (military invasion), 10–11, 219–20
unjust enrichment, 113, 172, 208, 210–16, 250–1
  relationship with contract, 212, 213, 214, 215, 216, 250
  relationship with expropriation, 211, 214, 215

words and phrases
  acta jure imperii, 306
  acta jure questionis, 306
  compromis, 280
  contra proferentum, 243
  ex aequoet bono, 105, 130
  force majeure, *see under* contract
  imprévision, 134
  in abstracto, 277
  in vacuo, 309
  lex arbitri, 301, 309, 310, 317–19
  lex fori, 303
  lex loci arbitri, 302–3, 315, 317–19
  lex mercatoria, 312
  lex specialis, 90, 148, 184
  loi procedure francaise, 312
  lucrum cessans, 177, 191, 196, 197, 205
  mutatis mutandis, 40
  pacta sunt servanda, 116, 167
  persona non grata, 9
  quantum meruit, *see quantum meruit*
  rebus sic stantibus, *see* changed circumstances
  res judicata, 305, 306, 316, 335
  restitutio in integrum, 169, 177, 187, 191